Historians on
Hamilton

Historians on *Hamilton*

How a Blockbuster Musical Is Restaging America's Past

Edited by

Renee C. Romano *and*
Claire Bond Potter

RUTGERS UNIVERSITY PRESS
NEW BRUNSWICK, NEWARK, AND CAMDEN,
NEW JERSEY, AND LONDON

Library of Congress Cataloging-in-Publication Data
Names: Romano, Renee Christine. | Potter, Claire Bond, 1958–
Title: Historians on Hamilton : how a blockbuster musical is restaging
America / edited by Renee C. Romano and Claire Bond Potter.
Description: New Brunswick : Rutgers University Press, [2018] |
Includes bibliographical references and index.
Identifiers: LCCN 2017033851| ISBN 9780813590301 (cloth : alk. paper) |
ISBN 9780813590295 (pbk. : alk. paper)
Subjects: LCSH: Miranda, Lin-Manuel, 1980- Hamilton. |
Hamilton, Alexander, 1757-1804.
Classification: LCC ML410.M67976 H57 2018 | DDC 782.1/4—dc23
LC record available at
https://lccn.loc.gov/2017033851

A British Cataloging-in-Publication record for this book is
available from the British Library.

♾ The paper used in this publication meets the requirements
of the American National Standard for Information Sciences—
Permanence of Paper for Printed Library Materials, ANSI z39.48–1992.

www.rutgersuniversitypress.org

Manufactured in the United States of America

Contents

Historians on
Hamilton

Introduction

History Is Happening in Manhattan

Renee C. Romano and
Claire Bond Potter

America has gone *Hamilton* crazy. Lin-Manuel Miranda's musical about Alexander Hamilton, "the forgotten founding father," was an unlikely subject for a Broadway hit. But it has become a widely acknowledged turning point in American theater history. Since it first opened Off-Broadway on January 20, 2015, at the Public Theater, *Hamilton: An American Musical* has been showered with recognition. Nominated for an unprecedented sixteen Tony Awards, it won eleven, as well as a Grammy, a Pulitzer, and eight Drama Desk Awards. It has become a cultural, political, and historical phenomenon with such widespread appeal that, as *Time* magazine reported in the fall of 2016, not only were children demanding *Hamilton*-themed birthday parties and Halloween costumes, but adults were also incorporating lines from the show into their wedding vows.[1]

"History is happening in Manhattan," the cast sings exuberantly in Act I, as the Schuyler sisters sneak downtown in search of the American Revolution and "a mind at work." But these words also resonate with the work taking place every night on the stage of the Richard Rodgers Theatre. *Hamilton* is making history, and its impact is being felt well beyond the rarefied haunts of Broadway. History teachers are picking up on their students' enthusiasm to spice up their courses, books about the American Revolution are flying off the shelves, heritage sites associated with Alexander Hamilton are experiencing heavy traffic, and the catchy lyrics seem almost universally

The marquee at the Richard Rodgers Theater, where *Hamilton* has been playing since it opened on Broadway in August 2015. *(EQRoy/Shutterstock.com)*

recognizable. A recent comedy video describes this last phenomenon as "Hamilaria," a newly discovered social disease characterized, a mock doctor explains, by "an uncontrollable urge to sing lyrics from the hit musical *Hamilton* when prompted by cue lines from everyday conversation." In the video fans blurt out snatches of songs in restaurants, church, school, and other public places as friends and strangers alike cringe. The symptoms associated with Hamilaria, the doctor notes, may seem "completely normal" to those affected by it, "but in the real world it can be a problem."[2]

Instead of going to the "Weehawken Institute" to manage our symptoms, as the video suggests, we decided to treat our Hamilaria by editing a volume of essays that would help students and fans dig more deeply into the show. While *Hamilton*'s popularity is ripe fodder for satire, there's no denying a critical and commercial success that is sparking a burst of popular interest in early American history, conversations among teachers about how to capitalize on *Hamilton*'s popularity with young people, and lively disagreements among scholars, curators, and history buffs about how the show represents the national past.

For those who have perhaps lived without television, radio, the Internet, or media of any kind for the past few years, the musical draws on Ron Chernow's 2005 Pulitzer Prize–winning popular biography, *Alexander Hamilton*, to bring this lesser-known founder out of the shadows. The musical begins with our hero's arrival in New York from the West Indies as a young man, traces his service in the American Revolution, his accomplishments as the first Treasury secretary under President George Washington, and his involvement in what may be the nation's first sex scandal. The musical ends with Hamilton's early death in a duel at the hands of fellow founder and vice president Aaron Burr. Both a political tale and a character study, the musical seeks to get inside the head of an ambitious and sometimes ruthless man, famously obsessed with making his mark on history, to understand his spectacular rise and fall.

But it is less the story than the means of telling it that has won *Hamilton* such attention and acclaim. The brainchild of Lin-Manuel Miranda, a New Yorker who grew up in the Inwood section of Manhattan and who spent summers with his grandparents in Vega Alta, Puerto Rico, the show is, in his words, "a story about America then, told by America now." It draws on musical traditions from hip hop, to rap, to R&B in order to convey the energy, ambition, and drive of the young founders, artistic choices that have made its score catchy, quotable, and singable. And perhaps most attention grabbing, young black, Latinx, and Asian actors portray nearly all of the historically white characters depicted in the musical, reflecting Miranda's goal to have the staging of this national founding story "look the way our country looks."[3]

As an ever more multiracial America struggles for ways to acknowledge its diversity in the twenty-first century and, simultaneously, articulate a sense of American identity, *Hamilton* literally stages that conversation. Often described as Miranda's most daring decision, the flipped casting challenges Broadway's long history of using whites to play black, Asian, and Latinx roles, offering people of color an opportunity to narrate America's origin story. While historians and other critics have been divided on how to characterize the show's racial politics, those associated with the play certainly believe that they are making an important statement. In the best-selling book that Miranda and coauthor Jeremy McCarter have released about the making of *Hamilton*, McCarter describes it as a theatrical "revolution." It is "a musical that changes the way that Broadway sounds," Miranda and McCarter write, one "that alters who gets to tell the story of our founding, that lets us glimpse the new, more diverse America rushing our way."[4] Whether truly revolutionary or not—a subject that several essays in this volume consider—*Hamilton*'s traditional political story, told through Afro-Caribbean music and by a multiracial cast, has seemed to capture the political zeitgeist of the Age of Obama.

And it's captured the cultural zeitgeist as well. From the moment it opened Off-Broadway, *Hamilton* has earned raves from critics, fans, and even some historians. Since the revised show opened on Broadway in August 2015, it has broken records of every kind: for the highest-grossing weekly box office for any show in Broadway history ($3.3 million for the performance of eight shows in November 2016), to the most Tony nominations for a single show (sixteen; *Hamilton* won eleven including Best Musical, Best Score, Best Book, and Best Director). Even as Miranda has created new companies (another long-term production has opened in Chicago, it is heading to London's West End, and producers are launching two national touring companies), tickets are still hard to come by. They are so scarce, and sold at such outlandish prices (a single seat can command several thousand dollars on the secondary market) that *Hamilton* not only spawned its own counterfeit ticket market, but also inspired new, and long overdue, federal legislation against "bots," high-speed ticket buying software run by scalpers.[5]

When they cannot get inside the theater, fans have found numerous ways to connect with the show and become part of its history. Miranda posted the original cast recording to YouTube, betting that listeners would be so taken with it they would then pay for it. He was right. Reaching #3 on the *Billboard* chart in 2015, *Hamilton* became the first cast recording to ever reach #1 on the publication's rap chart, and had gone triple platinum (selling more than three million copies) by February 2017. Fans can't get enough. They have also snatched up *The Hamilton Mixtape*, which features covers from the show sung by a range of artists, from pop crooner Kelly Clarkson to hip-hop artist Chance the Rapper. It debuted at #1 on the *Billboard* Top 200 chart. And then there is *Hamilton: The Revolution*, written by Miranda and McCarter to accompany the musical. Known informally as the "Hamiltome," it offers a behind-the-scenes tour of the show's evolution, staging, and impact, with Miranda's annotations on all of the lyrics. A hit in its own right, the first print run of 60,000 copies sold out almost immediately, it ranked #1 on the *New York Times* list of best-selling nonfiction books for seven months in a row, and it can be found just about anywhere, including the shelves of Walmart. The success of the musical has also helped Ron Chernow's biography of Hamilton find a new audience almost a decade after it was first published.[6]

Everything *Hamilton* touches seems to turn to gold: some journalists have begun to refer to the show as "Hamilton, Inc." Morphing into its own little corporate empire, it has become ripe for imitation. The musical has spawned so many parodies—from "Jeb!: An American Disappointment" (shared as a Google Doc) to "Rudiloph" about perennial misfit Rudolph the Red-Nosed Reindeer—that a July 4th blogpost in *Vice* warned Americans that just as the founders had had to throw of the yoke of their British oppressors, the nation was "once again weighed down by an oppressor: *Hamilton* parody videos."[7] Children across the country have dressed up as characters from the show for Halloween; there are *Hamilton*-themed birthday parties and bat mitzvahs complete with colonial costumes, "pin the cannonball on King George" games, and water cannon "duels."[8] *Hamilton* has, moreover, achieved two pop culture milestones of Americana that are nearly unheard of on Broadway: *Saturday Night Live* tapped Lin-Manuel Miranda to host the October 8, 2016, show, and the three actresses who originated the roles of the Schuyler sisters on Broadway were featured in the opening of the 2017 Super Bowl singing an a cappella version of "America the Beautiful." In the wake of the show's extraordinary success, the Treasury Department changed its mind about its plans to replace the "$10 founding father" on America's currency with a woman (current plans are to give Andrew Jackson on the $20 the boot). And while it is always a challenge to quantify the impact of any one piece of popular culture, both "Hamilton" and "Jefferson" have become hot baby names, probably for the first time since the nineteenth century.[9]

Hamilton has also become a popular topic for debate among professional historians, who have been blogging, tweeting, editorializing, and writing both favorable and critical reviews of the show since its opening. While elite and popular culture is frequently inspired by the past, from the seemingly constant stream of movies set during World War II to award-winning novels like Colson Whitehead's *Underground Railroad* (2016), very few of these have drawn such sustained attention and critical engagement from historians.[10] But *Hamilton* deserves—indeed, it demands—this kind of scholarly attention. With its widespread appeal, the show has the potential to shape how Americans understand the nation's early history for some time to come. And as part of a genre of fictional and nonfictional accounts of the Early Republic, which one of our contributors has dubbed "Founders Chic," *Hamilton* has created a common space for contemporary political debates about partisan politics, race, multiculturalism, and immigration. Moreover, as a show that has repeatedly been labeled as "revolutionary," *Hamilton* needs to be explored as a historical phenomenon in its own right.

Historians on Hamilton takes up the challenge that Miranda himself made to us when he was just beginning to write the show. "I want the historians to take this seriously," he told Ron Chernow the first time they met.[11] From the start, Miranda sought to create an account of the founding generation that *could* be taken seriously. He hired Chernow as a historical consultant to make sure that he wasn't straying too far from the historical record (or at least, as one of our authors points out, the record as it is represented in

Chernow's own work) as he crafted a dramatic script from Alexander Hamilton's story. Although by his own admission Miranda didn't take any college history classes, he acted like a historian as he worked on the play, doing research, reading Hamilton's writings, and traveling to sites from Hamilton's past. He read widely in early American history and consulted with experts who could help him better understand the politics and culture of the Revolutionary era, including a contributor to this collection whose book on honor shaped the portrayal of the duels in the show. Certain numbers from *Hamilton* quote directly from primary sources and founding documents, while others reference well-known published sources. "The Farmer Refuted," a rhetorical battle between pamphleteers Alexander Hamilton and Samuel Seabury over whether America should seek independence from Britain, is dramatized in *Hamilton* as a live debate in which Hamilton responds irreverently to Seabury's plodding, conservative arguments.

While clearly not a work of academic history, Lin-Manuel Miranda hoped that academic historians would want to engage with his creative foray into the past. We took on that challenge. We believe that *Hamilton* offers more for historians to consider than whether its portrayal of the American Revolution and the early national period is accurate (although we are happy to say that several of our authors do just that). But we also believe that the play is about how history unfolds, and how events are narrated across generations. It emphasizes the human side of history, and what it means to have a vision for the future. From the moment that George Washington warns Hamilton that "history has its eyes on you," the young founder frets about how he will be portrayed in a historical record that will outlast him. Once the Revolution is won, Hamilton is constantly preoccupied with promoting and protecting his legacy: how he will go down in history—described in the show as "planting flowers in a garden you never get to see"—is a central theme.

The musical also strikes at the heart of what historians do: as it makes clear, history is not simply a matter of facts, but is an interpretation of the existing archival record actively constructed by whoever is serving as the historian. The musical acknowledges that there are certain things we simply cannot know—indeed, there is a whole song about how we don't really know what went down between Hamilton, Jefferson, and Madison in the "Room Where It Happens" when Hamilton won support for his debt plan by agreeing to support a move of the nation's capital from New York City to the banks of the Potomac. But it also, the musical insists, matters "who tells your story."

So we assembled a group of experts to tell their story about *Hamilton*. Whatever Miranda's interest in having scholars engage with his work, we believe that historians need to take *Hamilton* seriously because it has already demonstrated its enormous potential to shape what Americans know and understand about both the man and this era. Although professional historians are sometimes reluctant to admit it, television, movies, fictional works, museums, and family lore often shape people's perceptions of the past more than scholarship does. As one chapter points out, a hugely popular work like *Hamilton* may well influence America's visual, aural, and narrative image of the American Revolution and its aftermath for generations.

The effect of popular culture on the public mind is a matter of keen interest for historians. *Hamilton*'s popularity deserves particular scrutiny because the musical's version of history is finding its way into people's heads through the catchy soundtrack and its memes, and perhaps most powerfully, its inclusion in school curricula at the elementary, secondary, and college levels.[12] Many social studies and history teachers see the show as a godsend since, as one chapter points out, it has given them new ways to connect to their students and promote excitement about early American history. They are pairing snippets from the soundtrack with historical documents, asking students to write their own historical rap battles, and even developing whole syllabi around the show (one of which is included in this volume). As fifth-grade teacher Addie Matteson, who developed what she calls "Hamilessons" for her class, noted: "It's a pretty great show and as a teaching tool, it's pretty darn near perfect. The story is gripping, more so because it is (mostly) true, the content is obsessively well researched and based largely on primary sources, and the language is complex and fun."[13]

The educational potential and reach of *Hamilton* has been most fully realized in what is known as the #EduHam Project, in which live performances are paired with formal learning. Funded by a grant from the Rockefeller Foundation in coordination with the Gilder Lehrman Institute of American History, the project offers deeply discounted tickets to high school juniors at schools in New York and Chicago where a high number of students are on the free or reduced lunch program. It also offers teachers a ready-made curriculum for teaching *Hamilton*, including an eleven-page guide that shows how the lesson plans align with the Common Core Standards.[14] In New York City, as many as twenty thousand students—or one in four high school juniors—were able to see *Hamilton* in the first year of the project.

New York City high school students line up for a May 2017 #EduHam matinee performance, courtesy of the Rockefeller Foundation and the Gilder Lehrman Institute of American History. *(Walter McBride/Getty Images)*

We are also been intrigued by widespread assertions that the musical is "revolutionary," or that it is unprecedented in its cultural, aesthetic, or political impact. For historians, such claims are something like catnip: it drives us to want to dig in and to explore descriptions of the *Hamilton* phenomenon that are fundamentally historical. In fact, few historians believe that there are contemporary events that have no meaningful past (#everythinghasahistory is currently a popular tag on the American Historical Association Twitter account). So we were curious: is *Hamilton* a rupture from the past or does it fit within tried-and-true literary and theatrical conventions? Is it revolutionary to use hip hop and rap to tell the story of the nation's founding, or have vernacular culture and deliberately skewed casting practices always played a role in national storytelling?

Perhaps there are other revolutions to examine in *Hamilton*: for example, the ways that the show—with Miranda as digital mastermind—has drawn on the social media world to promote itself. Or perhaps it is the diverse nature of the fan base that makes *Hamilton* unprecedented. After all, as several chapters in this volume point out, it is pretty rare to find something that former Democratic president Barack Obama and former Republican vice president Dick Cheney—*Hamilton* fans both—can agree on. All of these questions call for an historical perspective, and we are happy to say that scholars who study everything from theater and music history to U.S. political and social history have joined us to provide some answers.

Hamilton has, moreover, become a site of engagement, commentary, and debate about many political issues that have long and vexed histories in the United States. The *New Yorker*'s Adam Gopnik described the show as a metaphor for the Obama era. "At the simplest presentational level," he writes, "it shows previously marginalized people taking on the responsibility and burden of American history."[15] And yet, as some of our authors explain, despite its musical and casting choices, *Hamilton* still offers a traditional story of the founding, one that largely marginalizes and ignores the actual experiences of people of color in the nation's history. *Hamilton* raises perhaps the most fundamentally political questions in all of American history: Who belongs in this county? Who owns—and who tells—its story?

Although the show's connection to contemporary politics inspired many of this volume's writers, the chapters in this book engage with *Hamilton* on many different levels besides the political. Some explore the historical world of eighteenth-century America; others focus on the show's creative choices and its place in the history of theater and the media. Some essays place *Hamilton* in conversation with other representations of the nation's founding, and many delve more deeply into the show's racial politics, a particularly vital project in the aftermath of an election that mobilized the racial anxieties and animus of white voters.

Hamilton's resonance for our contemporary political world helps to explain why we, two historians of America's more recent past, became fascinated with this popular representation of the nation's founding years. The issues to which *Hamilton* speaks seemed ever more urgent as we planned the book in the summer of 2016, when histories of race, gender, immigration, and nationalism collided with a volatile election season. We were not alone in making these connections. Politicians have always made claims on the past, and on national origin stories. But the desire to make sense of the present may have accounted, in part, for the surging popularity of the musical, even as Miranda and the original cast said goodbye to the show in mid-summer. *Hamilton* was "about how hard it is to do politics, about how people of fundamentally clashing political views tried to work together to create a shared constitutional enterprise," political scientist Richard Bernstein told the *New York Times* in April 2016. "And right now, that's a message we really need."[16]

We began this project in the midst of a presidential campaign that was at least as contentious as any early nineteenth-century contest. In the fall of 2016, it was hard not to wonder what the characters would have thought of the volatile forces swirling around us, or the duels that might have been fought in response to today's political mudslinging. Even as New York audiences eagerly cheered Hamilton and Lafayette's high-five line at Yorktown—"Immigrants, we get the job done!"—anti-immigrant sentiment and rhetoric received standing ovations at political rallies around the country. It was often difficult to separate our immersion in this project from the historical winds blowing around us: when we opened the paper to see that both Democratic candidates in the 2016 election, one a woman and one a socialist, had attended *Hamilton*, it seemed that we were living in a time at least as exciting and changeable as the election (sometimes called the "Revolution") of 1800.

But like poor Aaron Burr, we were disappointed: once again, the world turned upside down. As we waited for essays to come in, we also waited for a new political era that seemed to pose a great many of the dangers that Hamilton, James Madison, and John Jay brought to the attention of their peers in the collection of essays now known as *The Federalist Papers*. Like many Americans, we were apprehensive about this new era, and at this writing we remain so. While the Republic is no longer as fragile as it was at its birth, the American system of governance and finance that Hamilton labored over seems vulnerable to strains, some that he anticipated, others that he did not. As mass political protests (a form of politics, we hasten to add, that Hamilton himself loathed and feared) have unfolded in response to the attacks on liberal governance, it was also sometimes difficult not to wonder why it mattered to edit a volume of essays, or why the task of history matters at all in the face of great, and seemingly unprecedented challenges to the democratic order.

What, we asked, would Alexander Hamilton do?

The answer to that question is that he would have kept writing, and we did (can we resist saying that we were not giving away our shot?). If, perhaps, we historians do not build roads, provide medical care, or pass legislation, we know a great deal about the millions of people who have over hundreds of years. Our work, if not precisely in the room where it happens, helps to constitute the public sphere outside that room, the space that sustains the integrity of everything that is at stake and that is portrayed in *Hamilton*: democracy, leadership, and sound governance. "If historians are going to join the existential fight for democracy," Paul Kramer wrote in the first weeks of 2017, "they will carry out at least some of their work in widely shared spaces. In doing so they can play a part in constituting, sustaining, and defending an open, democratic public sphere that is vulnerable to many threats."[17]

This book, and the conversation we hope it sparks about history in classrooms, homes, and everywhere that audiences of *Hamilton* gather, is one of those shared spaces. So let's raise the curtain and get on with the show.

NOTES

1. Eliza Berman, "*Hamilton* Nation," *Time*, October 10, 2016.

2. "Hamilaria," written and directed by Rob McCollum, based on a concept by Kristin McCollum, with writing assistance from Manon and Lily McCollum; published to YouTube June 8, 2016, https://www.youtube.com/watch?v=4mrN_Bx9H2Q, accessed March 29, 2017.

3. Quoted in Rob Weinert-Kendt, "Rapping a Revolution: Lin-Manuel Miranda and Others from 'Hamilton' Talk History," *New York Times*, February 5, 2015.

4. Lin-Manuel Miranda and Jeremy McCarter, *Hamilton: The Revolution* (New York: Grand Central Publishing, 2016), 10.

5. Miranda launched a public war on bots that led to the passage by Congress of the "Better Online Tickets Sales Act" in December 2016. Laura Petrecca, "'Hamilton' Fans Burned by Fake Tickets," *USA Today*, June 15, 2016; Christine Stoddard, "A New Ticket Bots Law Means You Might Finally Get Those 'Hamilton' Broadway Tickets," *Music.mic*, December 16, 2016, https://mic.com/articles/162591/a-new-ticket-bots-law-means-you-might-finally-get-those-hamilton-broadway-tickets#.iEXUz3FNX, accessed April 20, 2017.

6. Alexandra Alter, "'Hamilton: The Revolution' Races Out of Bookstores, Echoing the Musical's Success," *New York Times*, May 3, 2016; Jennifer Baker, "Lin-Manuel Miranda's 'Hamilton' Steadily Becomes an All-Around Blockbuster in All Forms of Media," *Forbes*, April 13, 2016.

7. Harry Cheadle, "It's Time to Tear Down the 'Hamilton' Parody Industrial Complex," *Vice*, July 4, 2016, https://www.vice.com/en_us/article/trump-hamilton-jokes-are-obvious.

8. Eliza Berman and Marysa Greenwalt, "See How the Broadway Hit 'Hamilton' Has Completely Taken Over America," *Time*, September 19, 2016.

9. Robert Simonson, "The Hamilton Effect: 8 Unexpected (and Strange) Effects of the Smash Musical," *Playbill*, July 4, 2016.

10. A recent example would be *Reconsidering Roots*, edited by Erica L. Ball and Kellie Carter Jackson (Athens: University of Georgia Press, 2017), about the groundbreaking TV miniseries about slavery.

11. Quoted in Jody Rosen, "The American Revolutionary," *New York Times Magazine*, July 8, 2015.

12. For more, see Valerie Strauss, "The Unusual Way Broadway's 'Hamilton' Is teaching U.S. History to Kids," *Washington Post*, June 28, 2016; Zach Schonfeld, "*Hamilton*, the Biggest Thing on Broadway, Is Being Taught in Classrooms All Over," *Newsweek*, February 19, 2016; Liz Johnson, "*Hamilton* HIGH: How the Hottest Musical on Broadway Will Teach High School Juniors American History—and Make Sure They're Having Fun Learning It," *Arrive Magazine*, March/April 2016, 45–49; Linda Flanagan, "How Teachers Are Using 'Hamilton' in the Classroom," "Mind/Shift," *KQED News*, March 14, 2016.

13. Addie Matteson, "Teaching with *Hamilton*," *School Library Journal*, May 3, 2016.

14. You can access those materials at the Gilder Lehrman Institute of American History website: https://www.gilderlehrman.org/programs-exhibitions/hamilton.

15. Adam Gopnik, "*Hamilton* and the Case for Hip-Hop Progressivism," *New Yorker*, February 5, 2016.

16. Quoted in Jennifer Schuessler, "'Hamilton' and History: Are They in Sync?" *New York Times*, April 10, 2016.

17. Paul Kramer, "History in a Time of Crisis," *Chronicle of Higher Education*, February 19, 2017.

Act I

The Script

CHAPTER I

From Ron Chernow's
Alexander Hamilton to *Hamilton: An American Musical*

WILLIAM HOGELAND

Reading a popular biography of an American founder can be an absorbing and satisfying experience. A book organized around a single, compelling figure offers a window into the politics and ideology of our national origins. We meet a fascinating person; connect emotionally with the course of that person's busy life making history; mourn our companion's passing in the final chapter; and throughout, consider lessons and legacies in a way that engages us with the past. The founding of the nation is thus brought to life, on the one hand up-close, and on the other at the slight remove that encourages a pleasing degree of escapism, an important factor for every written narrative that hopes to find an audience. Via founders' biographies, many readers who might not otherwise be drawn to exploring national origins gain a satisfying feeling for the national history that professional historians have spent entire careers researching.

Yet satisfaction and accessibility pose serious risks to historical realism. Though contemporary readers are expected to accept what are called flaws in the important founders' personalities (in fact, warts-and-all portraits may only enhance the subjects' credibility and genius), the commercial basis of the founding fathers genre involves celebrating American heritage. An a priori position, so fundamental that often it doesn't need to be stated, rules the production of this popular body of work: no matter the flaws of a particular founding father, or of the nation itself, the creation of the United

States is the most important event in world history, and, on balance, one of the most fortunate.

"I don't think we can ever know enough about them," the author David McCullough has said of the founding generation.[1] Because reader interest in American history is presumed to rest on something like that proposition (McCullough's remark, for example, appears in lieu of blurbs on the jacket of his own *John Adams*), any nonfiction trade book about political actors in American history faces a significant problem. It will, sooner or later, have to struggle with facts of American history that threaten the underlying celebration upon which the genre's commercial position is predicated. Too often, the loser in that struggle is public understanding of history.

Perhaps the most influential recent founder biography is Ron Chernow's 2004 *Alexander Hamilton*. The basis for Lin-Manuel Miranda's overwhelmingly popular and well-received musical theater event *Hamilton: An American Musical*, the book is a big hit in its own right. Before writing *Alexander Hamilton*, Chernow had written successful and popular biographies of financial and business tycoons. *The House of Morgan*, his group biography of the American banking family, won the National Book Award, while *Titan*, about the industrialist John D. Rockefeller Sr., was nominated for the National Book Critics Circle Award. Plunging into the founder-biography market with *Alexander Hamilton*, Chernow sparked a widespread revival of interest in the first secretary of the treasury. The book stayed on the *New York Times* bestseller list for three months. Reviewers loved it: the book offered "the kind of synthetic narrative history and biography that is rarely done to such high standards," said Stephen B. Presser of Northwestern University, calling the book "wondrous."[2] His assessment is typical of the praise the book received. *Alexander Hamilton* won a National Book Critics Circle Award nomination and the inaugural George Washington Book Prize. Chernow's book would have been a certified and lasting hit had it never been adapted for the stage as *Hamilton: An American Musical*.

Like many readers, Lin-Manuel Miranda was captivated by the biography, and Miranda has made clear how much he relied on

Chernow for "getting the history right" as he worked on the musical. "I reached out to Ron Chernow really early," Miranda has said. "This story is more delicious and tragic and interesting than anything I could have made up." When the hip-hop artist Nas expressed an interest in learning more about the early days of the United States, Miranda gave him a copy of Chernow's *Alexander Hamilton*.[3] The book, in turn, has benefited immensely from the success of the play. As Miranda's *Hamilton* shot unexpectedly from a startling solo performance at the White House to a sold-out event at the Public Theater in New York City to a Broadway phenomenon, and then from the hottest ticket in town to what will soon be a multicity, coast-to-coast pop-culture phenomenon, the Chernow biography has found new readers, returning to the *New York Times* bestseller list and gaining Chernow credit for making a "once-forgotten founder" popular again.[4]

Hamilton fandom is part and parcel of revived popular interest in the American Revolution, as Andrew Schocket points out in this

Lin-Manuel Miranda frequently acknowledges that Ron Chernow's biography of Alexander Hamilton inspired his musical. Here he reads Chernow's book to fans just hours before the show's opening on Broadway in August 2015. *(Todd Heisler/The New York Times/Redux)*

volume. Yet the *Hamilton* phenomenon has an energy and impact all its own, a popularity far exceeding anything else in the ongoing founding-history revival. Surely one important reason for that special impact is that the show is just that, a show—witty, theatrical, bold, original, fun—and yet its importance is by no means limited to its entertainment value. In some important circles, enthusiasm for the musical has been related explicitly to the teaching of American history. As Lesley S. Herrmann, the executive director of the Gilder Lehrman Institute for American History, said to Ron Chernow on first seeing the musical, "We have to get this in the hands of kids."[5] The Gilder Lehrman Institute has long promoted the singular importance of Alexander Hamilton as a founder and the role of Chernow's biography in supporting that vision: the institute helps fund the Washington Prize, whose inaugural award was given to Chernow's book, and the biography is the required text for the institute's online course "Alexander Hamilton's America."[6] Now, in partnership with the producers and the Rockefeller Foundation, the institute is bringing the poorest public-school students to see Miranda's musical and integrating the study of Alexander Hamilton into classroom curricula.[7] Clearly the show has importance not only as a powerful and original theatrical event but also as a means of connecting students, and the general public, to founding history and to Hamilton in particular.

In assessing what students and other viewers, listeners, and fans may be learning from *Hamilton: An American Musical*, some critics and historians have raised questions about the show's accuracy and about the cultural work it does. The writer Ishmael Reed has objected to actors of color playing the roles of slaveholders.[8] Historian Lyra D. Monteiro has criticized not only the show's reverse racial casting, but also the entire genre that the Chernow book represents. "This is a way that writers of popular history (and some academic historians) represent the founders as relatable, cool guys," Monteiro told *Slate*. "Founders Chic tends to really downplay the involvement of the Founding Fathers in slavery, and this play does that 100 percent. . . . No amount of casting people of color disguises the fact that they're erasing people of color from the actual narrative."[9] In the *New York Times*, the Jefferson scholar Annette Gordon-Reed said of Miranda's character, "It's not Hamilton. It's an idea of who we would like Hamilton to be."[10] Critics have questioned the lionizing of founding nationalism and the sentimentalizing of Hamilton as a man of the people; noted a troubling absence, in a show whose casting radically upturns racial stereotype, of characters of color; and pointed to the show's all-too-easy appeal for government and business elites across the political spectrum, a question Renee C. Romano investigates in this volume.

Yet few critical questions of that kind were raised in 2004 in response to the publication of Chernow's book. Indeed, it's unlikely that many professional, academic historians would have read the book had the show not become such a phenomenon. Because the Hamilton of the show is a brilliantly creative take on the Hamilton of Chernow's biography, it's worth examining the role the book has played, not only in forming the basis for an event of such originality that nobody could have seen it coming when Chernow published, but also in establishing Hamilton's importance in the minds of general readers of narrative American history.

The Pre-*Hamilton* Hamilton Craze

Unlike Miranda's show, Chernow's hit book didn't appear as if out of nowhere, taking the world by storm with an unfamiliar topic. It's true that before the success of the biography, Hamilton hadn't received the attention the general reading public reliably gave former presidents Jefferson, Washington, and Adams, yet even as Chernow was completing the biography, a broader cultural conversation about Hamilton was already under way; that revival played an important role in the book's enthusiastic reception. Today's surprising Hamilton craze can be traced all the way back to a 1997 *Wall Street Journal* op-ed article by David Brooks and William Kristol, both then writing for the conservative magazine *The Weekly Standard*. The article made a case for what the authors called "national-greatness conservatism," promoting Hamilton, among others, as prescient about the importance of the federal government in achieving ambitious national aims at home and abroad. Rejecting laissez-faire and libertarian extremes, Brooks and Kristol saw in Hamilton's legacy a model for a balanced conservatism that retained a high regard for government power.[11]

The *National Review*'s Richard Brookhiser agreed. Five years before Chernow's book was published, Brookhiser's *Alexander Hamilton: American*, a biography notably briefer and brisker than Chernow's, presented the rehabilitated Hamilton to general readers. Brookhiser, also a conservative intellectual, took the position that today's America is Hamiltonian: a blend of high finance, central banking, federal strength, industrialization, and global power. Brookhiser curated a major exhibit for the New-York Historical Society whose title underscored the thesis: "Alexander Hamilton: The Man Who Made Modern America." The Gilder Lehrman Institute played a major role in developing that exhibit and now manages its travel to other institutions.[12]

A new Hamilton enthusiasm—not yet a craze, but already a cult—was thus under way in certain conservative political circles, and at Gilder Lehrman, when Chernow's big book came out. The project developed in 2004, the year that both *Alexander Hamilton* and the New-York Historical Society exhibit debuted, when Brooks published a major essay in the *New York Times Magazine* calling Hamilton the author of a balanced American tradition favoring limited government activism in service of social mobility and national unity. He also favorably reviewed Chernow's biography in the *New York Times Book Review*.[13] Giving narrative life to the Brooks-Kristol-Brookhiser theme that Hamilton is, in Chernow's words, "the messenger from a future that we now inhabit," the book brought existing interest in Hamilton to a higher pitch.[14] At the swearing-in of Treasury Secretary Henry Paulson in 2006, President George W. Bush noted the importance of Hamilton's legacy, and Paulson himself remarked that his father had been "a real Alexander Hamilton fan."[15]

Liberals, and those corporate-friendly Democrats known as neoliberals, were taking up Hamilton too. In 2006, Robert Rubin and

Roger Altman launched a Brookings Institution economic policy initiative called the Hamilton Project, representing, as the project's news release said, "traditional American values of opportunity and upward mobility."[16] In 2009, Peter Orszag, formerly of the Hamilton Project, became President Barack Obama's budget director and had Hamilton's portrait brought from the National Gallery and hung in his office.[17]

Miranda's *Hamilton* thus represents the ultimate flowering, on Broadway, of a process that began in the late 1990s and has come to pervade many aspects of our political and popular culture. That process has arrived at a vision of the man and his importance most influentially realized in Chernow's *Alexander Hamilton*, on which not only Miranda, but also many other Hamilton fans have learned to rely. Miranda's musical has, then, greatly expanded the scope and reach of the representation of Chernow's *Alexander Hamilton*, with its origins in the founding father genre predicated on celebration of America's national heritage. How, we might ask, has that origin story shaped the Hamilton we encounter on the stage?

Chernow's Hamilton

In bringing the biography to the stage, Miranda followed Chernow's lead by making Alexander Hamilton the protagonist, and in that sense the "hero" ("a hero and a scholar," according to the musical) of the piece. Any play of the kind Miranda wrote must have such a character. Any popular biography of a founding father must have one, too. But the effort, as Miranda has put it, "to get the history right" via reliance on Chernow's *Alexander Hamilton*, brings to light important conflicts among drama, biography, and history. While the show may succeed as a gripping and impressive theatrical event, and undoubtedly succeeds as a fascinating cultural phenomenon, it fails to address or even acknowledge key issues in the actual history of Alexander Hamilton. Originating not with Miranda but with Chernow, that failure raises issues about the nature of accuracy and accessibility in public history as a whole and suggests purposes the musical may be serving for those, like members of the Gilder

Lehrman Institute, who insist that the show serves not only as entertainment but also as a powerful educational tool.

One aspect of Chernow's book that especially attracted Miranda is its presentation of Hamilton as the archetypal American immigrant, possessed of a relentless commitment to succeed in a new country. "I recognize that relentlessness in people I know," Miranda told *NEA Magazine*. "Not only in my father who came here [from Puerto Rico] at the age of 18 to get his education and never went back home, just like Hamilton, but also so many immigrant stories I know. . . . They know they have to work twice as hard to get half as far. That's just the deal—that's the price of admission to our country."[18] Miranda's lines "Immigrants: we get the job done," and "another immigrant coming up from the bottom," draw on Chernow's description of Hamilton as embodying "an enduring archetype: the obscure immigrant who comes to America, re-creates himself, and succeeds despite a lack of proper birth and breeding."[19]

But Alexander Hamilton was not an American immigrant, at least not in the sense intended by Chernow when he invokes the idea. Of course, all European dwellers not only in the thirteen British North American colonies, but also anywhere on the continent, came out of an experience that must be called migrant. In "A Summary View of the Rights of British America," Thomas Jefferson celebrated the supposedly free roving and settling of what he took to be Americans' Saxon ancestors. And while Jefferson viewed such migration as both a universal right and an exceptionally American accomplishment, members of the continent's indigenous nations—those whose rights were obliterated by Jefferson's theories of free-ranging white settlement—had long been moving too. From one region to another, they explored new lands, settled in new places, dominating or being dominated by new people. Such movements, populating not just North America but the entire globe, still mark human life today.

That's obviously not what Chernow means when associating Hamilton with the immigrant experience in America. He is referring to an ethos in which the culture of the United States, usually against the will of hidebound earlier arrivers, is invigorated by the contributions of outsiders. No such ethos existed, and there was no United States in which such an ethos might have thrived, in the late eighteenth century when Hamilton, a citizen of the empire, moved from one of that empire's colonies, the British West Indies, to another of its colonies, New York. If Hamilton is an American immigration archetype, then Benjamin Franklin, arriving in Pennsylvania from Massachusetts, would have to be considered in a similar light. But he isn't, because the immigration archetype Chernow invokes refers to a late nineteenth-century phenomenon, beginning well after the demise of the British imperium in America that Hamilton did so much to combat. Indeed, that later phenomenon was a result of the nationalism and industrialization that Hamilton had dedicated himself to creating. Shoehorning Hamilton's arrival into a grand, upbeat, widely revered national story about the American melting pot, and endowing his subject with supposedly special relevance, Chernow reads later history back into founding history. So complete is the redefinition of American immigration that, in "Yorktown," Miranda makes the Marquis de Lafayette an immigrant too.

This American immigration fantasy connects with another aspect of the Hamilton story that David Brooks and others have emphasized politically, Chernow developed narratively, and Miranda now dramatizes theatrically. "Hamilton came from nothing," Brooks writes, while Chernow describes his Caribbean boyhood as "squalid" and claims that "no other founder had to grapple with such shame and misery."[20] Miranda puts the issue succinctly in the opening lines of the show: Hamilton was "dropped in the middle of a forgotten / spot in the Caribbean by providence / impoverished, in squalor."[21] A uniquely disadvantaged background throws the supposed immigrant's rise to founding father status into especially exciting relief.

Hamilton did suffer deep disadvantages, but he didn't, in some qualitatively special way, come from nothing. As Chernow relates in his early chapters, Hamilton was born out of wedlock and abandoned by his father, a second son who might as well have been *trying* to fulfill the stereotype of a ne'er-do-well. Hamilton was then effectively orphaned by the death of his mother. They had not, however, been abjectly poor. She had a store and other inherited property, including enslaved Africans, and Hamilton should have had at least a modest inheritance. But the court gave it all to his mother's husband, the man she had left for Hamilton's father. In one harsh move, the court combined the stigma of out-of-wedlock birth with an abrupt loss of prospects.

So at an early age, Hamilton had to go to work. It was in working for a living that he discovered and displayed the remarkable talents that began his move up in the world. That's a background that, to the modern eye, contrasts appealingly with the aristocratic backgrounds of those who became Hamilton's political rivals, Jefferson and James Madison, squires whose families had been in Virginia, and rich, for a number of generations. But Hamilton was hardly alone among his peers in coming from disadvantage, being put to work at an early age, or being born outside North America. Chernow presents the other founding fathers as having been "reared in tidy New England villages or cossetted on baronial Virginia states."[22] But Hamilton's mentor in finance and politics was Robert Morris, by 1776 the richest man in America and the "financier of the Revolution." One of the most influential people in Hamilton's life, Morris is absent from the musical, presumably because Chernow's book mentions him only glancingly. Born in utter poverty, and in England, Morris also started at the bottom, and worked his way up in business to become perhaps more critical to American independence than anyone else except George Washington.

Similarly, Benjamin Franklin arrived in Philadelphia penniless, a fugitive printer's apprentice. He too went to work, and he became not only rich but also renowned internationally as a scientist and both locally and in England as a politician; he became, from his unpromising artisan beginnings, important to the national founding. Thomas Paine, an artisan's son born in England, served as an able seaman on a British privateer, one of the most degrading jobs a free white male could then endure; his pamphlet "Common Sense" influenced the drive for American independence. Henry Knox, the Revolutionary artillery general who became the first secretary of war, was abandoned by his father and had to leave school at twelve to support his family by clerking. George Washington, largely disinherited in favor of his elder half-brothers, had to go to work in his teens too. In portraying Hamilton's disadvantage as unique among the founders, Chernow distorts historical context, and both he and Miranda neglect the degree to which the ambitions of so many of the founders were fired by their dogged efforts to lift the burden of disadvantage.

Perhaps the most appealing aspect of this fictional Hamilton is his participation in what Chernow calls "staunch abolitionism."[23] While Miranda's score refers to abolitionism only rarely—Hamilton and his friends refer to themselves as "a bunch of revolutionary manumission abolitionists" and John Laurens sings that "we'll never be truly free / until those in bondage have the same rights as you and me"—many who have written about the show have emphasized this aspect of Hamilton's political vision. A typical example comes from the conservative magazine *The Federalist*: "Miranda makes much of Hamilton's abolitionism, coming as he did from the West Indies, where the brutality of slavery was a constant, daily tableau."[24] That tableau is also mentioned in Miranda's opening number, which describes Hamilton's hometown as a place where "every day . . . slaves were being slaughtered and carted / across the waves."

The image is drawn directly from Chernow's book. A widely received piece of Hamilton lore has long had it that the horrors of the Caribbean slave markets were so painfully seared on the boy's brain that as a man he was inspired to oppose the traffic in human souls. All of the major Hamilton biographies—along with Chernow and Brookhiser, they include Henry Cabot Lodge, John C. Miller, Broadus Mitchell, Willard Randall Sterne, and Forrest McDonald—tell some version of that story. Yet none can cite a primary source for it. Randall cites Mitchell, Miller cites Lodge, and so forth; the story has become such common knowledge that Chernow doesn't even provide a citation. He just passes it along as a given. The story's origin is unknown, and while plausible, it's just as probably fanciful,

but it adds poignancy and sympathy and Chernow repeats it without probing its veracity.[25]

Hamilton did oppose the institution of African slavery. His policies promoted an economy driven by industrially organized labor,
urban and rural. As Miranda's "Cabinet Battle #1" suggests, Hamilton's economic philosophies contrasted with the agrarian vision of
Jefferson, which lauded the white yeoman free-holding farmer even
though Jefferson's own success relied on a large-scale plantation and
the labor of enslaved black people. But that contrast is a far cry from
the abolitionism that Chernow claims for Hamilton. When Miranda
says "abolitionist manumissionists" he is following Chernow in con-
flating two different things: abolitionists, who pushed to eradicate
the institution nationally, by law; and manumissionists, those who
voluntarily freed their slaves. As a nationalist eager to get the Constitution signed, Hamilton supported, without any recorded misgivings, the three-fifths clause that wrote slavery stubbornly into the
mechanics of national government, over and against petitions by
Quakers, whom we might more accurately call the leading abolitionists of their day. Scholars' inability to determine with utter cer-
tainty whether Madison or Hamilton wrote *Federalist* 54, which
rationalizes the fateful clause, speaks volumes. In this area, the two
were one.

It's true as well that the New York Manumission Society, to
which Hamilton belonged, not only worked to get slave owners in
New York to free their slaves but also pushed for gradual abolition
of the institution in the state. Yet as Chernow points out, slave ownership was no bar to membership in the society. Many in both the
North and the South had deep concerns, no doubt often sincere,
about the vileness of the institution. Many of those same people also
held people in bondage, including Hamilton himself. Chernow,
though reluctant on this point, admits that the Hamiltons owned
"one or two household slaves" and points to letters showing Hamilton arranging slave transactions, which he hopefully, and possibly
correctly, suggests were made on behalf of in-laws. Accepting with
evident difficulty the possibility that Hamilton "*may*" (Chernow's

italics) have held slaves, the biographer segues quickly into a discussion of Jefferson's Monticello, vastly more slave-dependent than Hamilton's household. The likelihood of Hamilton's participation in the institution despite his manumissionist leanings becomes, in Chernow's rendering, an opportunity to reengage the age-old historiographical war with the Jeffersonians.[26]

By downplaying Hamilton's relationship with slavery, and by portraying Eliza Hamilton's responsibility, before her marriage, for her mother's many slaves as "terribly jarring," Chernow misses an opportunity to bring to life how not only how pervasively but also how perversely the institution of slavery functioned in early America.[27] For Chernow, Eliza's managing slaves when she opposed slavery is incongruous, but that kind of contradiction was common. Told more realistically, Alexander Hamilton's story might offer Americans a deeper understanding of how even those who saw slavery as cruel could participate in and benefit from the entrenched economic system it supported.

Instead, Chernow endows Hamilton with a progressive rectitude on slavery out of all proportion to his real thoughts and actions. What ends up staying with readers, with Lin-Manuel Miranda, and with his audiences—no doubt including those schoolchildren whom the Gilder Lehrman Institute brings to the show and develops curricula for—is the false impression that Hamilton was special among the founding fathers in part because he was a staunch abolitionist. That impression hinders, rather than promotes, understanding of slavery's significance and place in America's past.

Missing the Main Point: Hamiltonian Finance

With those themes of immigration, upward mobility, and abolitionism, Chernow characterizes Hamilton in appealing ways. Yet the Chernow character's most damaging effect on public understanding of Hamilton, and of the United States' rise as a commercial and military power of global reach, for which Hamilton's fans rightly credit their hero, involves not those false additions but the subtraction of what really does make Hamilton important: our founding high-finance man's historically decisive intertwining of American wealth with American military power in his career-long struggle against American democracy.

Miranda's Hamilton, drawn from Chernow's, emerges on stage as a kind of disruptive democratic phenomenon, a man whose irresistible upward mobility will shatter class codes, thus creating upward mobility for others, too. David Brooks is among those who have advanced the idea that Hamilton fostered a new kind of social mobility, asserting that he "spent his political career trying to create a world in which as many people as possible could replicate his amazing success."[28] A talking head in a 2006 PBS documentary on Hamilton puts it more succinctly: Hamilton believed (as many Americans do) that "if you work hard, you should rise to the top."[29]

That idea is reflected, via Chernow, in Miranda's opening, where Hamilton "got a lot farther by working a lot harder / by being a lot smarter / by being a self-starter." And that's probably the lesson the Gilder Lehrman Institute hopes will be impressed upon the underserved schoolchildren it selects to bring to the show: American society is open to your rise; like Hamilton, you can come from nothing and win the race to the top. One of the institute's units on the founding period, designed for public-school teachers in compliance with Common Core standards, puts the issue this way: "Alexander Hamilton is known as a self-starter. He was born without the social and financial advantages of many of the other people considered Founding Fathers, but was ambitious enough to successfully overcome these barriers."[30] Hamilton was able to overcome significant disadvantages posed by social and financial barriers, the lesson plan goes, because he possessed sufficient ambition and was enough of a self-starter.

Yet even a superficial engagement with the historical Hamilton would reveal that for him the essential components of American society had nothing to do with enabling others access to the heights he had scaled with such impressive speed. Certainly his vision had nothing to do with democracy, a term that in his day mainly referred to radically populist ideas about social equality, seething in the years leading up to and coming out of the Revolution, and just what

Hamilton set out to defeat. None of the famous founders, except Thomas Paine, was a democrat: for all of their mutual conflicts, almost all agreed that participation in the electoral franchise should be limited to free white men of sufficient property and that standing for office should require even more property. Popular movements hoped to defeat the property qualification, in order to sway American society toward policies encouraging economic equality: fixing prices, issuing paper currencies, taxing wealth; founding-era radicals like the Pennsylvania organizers Thomas Young and James Cannon went even farther, hoping to put a legislative cap on how much property anyone could legally own.[31] All of the famous founders feared and loathed such movements, seeing them as confiscatory and redistributive—the term was "leveling"—but Hamilton was the man who developed practical means of crushing them—by identifying national security with elite finance. That's what actually matters, to us and to Hamilton, about his career, in large part because, just as the Hamilton fans Brooks, Brookhiser, and Chernow claim, his policy did presage the industrial, imperial America that we know today. It's called Hamiltonian finance, and without a critical understanding of its premises and purposes, there can be no serious understanding either of Alexander Hamilton or of the emergence of the United States as a world power.

Miranda's funny, energetic "Cabinet Battle #1" participates in a widespread misunderstanding about Hamiltonian finance, having to do with the founding public debt of the United States, which was all-important to Hamilton's policy and thus to his historical importance and the flourishing of the nation. While it's hardly surprising that the ins and outs of government finance failed to strike Miranda as fodder for thrilling theater, it's worth noting that he didn't get much of a chance to consider the dramatic potential of the founding debt, because despite that story's centrality to Hamilton's lifelong passions and existential purposes, Chernow's biography doesn't offer him the material to do so. The actual story is quite dramatic, in part because it drove Hamilton more than once in the direction of outright criminality, but it shows Hamilton—and the early American nation—in a light unlikely to appeal to readers and theatergoers eager to celebrate the founding.[32]

Chernow's noting that in the 1780s, nationalists like Hamilton, as well as his then-partner in politics Madison, wanted to place the Confederation Congress in a position to "retire the huge war debt" will sound reasonable and familiar to many readers.[33] The phrasing suggests that federal and state debts incurred in fighting and winning the Revolutionary War had become, by war's end and thanks to chaotic management, dangerously large, and that as a thinker and actor on public finance Hamilton would be particularly concerned to get them paid off. Miranda's Hamilton can thus insult Jefferson and Madison by saying they're "in worse shape than the debt is in," because Chernow presents the debt as a major national problem that Hamilton, on becoming Treasury secretary, had to face up to and pay down.

In fact, in the 1780s Hamilton spent pretty much every moment of his political life trying to swell the war debt to massive proportions, for cogent financial, military, and national reasons, well-explored in historical scholarship.[34] The most important part of the debt took the form of interest-bearing bonds, held mainly by American high-finance insiders, a small group of rich investors in the war who expected a nice return on that investment. As the conflict neared its end, a key faction in the Confederation Congress, led by that same Robert Morris whose importance to Hamiltonian policy Chernow nearly ignores, and including the young Hamilton and Madison, engaged in a project to build American nationhood around ensuring that those bondholders would receive regular interest payments. This ingenious plan to yoke the small, wealthy, interstate investing class to a proto-national authority involved not paying off the debt but funding it, via taxation. As Treasury secretary, Hamilton's greatest accomplishment was to make that scheme a reality, and he further tied investors to the federal project via "assumption," a related Morris idea of the early 1780s that Hamilton, as Treasury secretary, brought to fruition in 1790 when he persuaded Congress to assume all of the individual states' war debts in the federal one.

A statue of Alexander Hamilton outside the U.S. Treasury Department commemorates his importance in shaping early financial policies that helped tie elite families to the national project. *(Shutterstock.com)*

Hamilton thus found ways to keep the richest families in the country connected to a national power to collect taxes, throughout the country, in support of a national debt; and to establish, as a foundation of American strength, the identification of the investing and military-officer classes with those making decisions for the new nation. The legacy lies not in paying off the Revolutionary War debt, as many readers come away from Chernow's biography with good reason to believe, but in growing and sustaining a federal debt as a fundamental element in building the kind of nation that might expand geographically and industrially and compete with other nations militarily and commercially. It is precisely those early contributions to the emerging power of the United States that drew such strong admiration, long before the advent of *Hamilton: An American Musical*, from conservative and neoliberal Hamilton fans alike. Yet even while Chernow's popular account lionizes Hamilton as a forerunner and author of modern America, it persistently elides and glosses over the realities and specifics of the economic policies and political tactics by which he brought that legacy about, which, if better understood, would raise conflicts for modern conservatives and modern liberals alike.

Elements of today's right wing, for example, who follow Hamilton closely in nationalist ambition and high regard for military strength and even military adventure, recoil from the kind of large public debt supported by aggressive federal taxation that Hamilton believed was essential to supporting national strength. And yet to the kind of conservative who admires Hamilton uncritically, that contradiction doesn't emerge: the real nature of the founding debt, and of Hamilton's relationship to it, have been magically removed from public discourse. Liberals, for their part, placing progressive hopes in federal government power, are not wrong to admire Hamilton as that power's first and most assertive author. Yet were his use of federal executive power to suppress democratic expression, subordinate federal judges, bamboozle Congress, and amplify military power more explicitly and viscerally understood, liberals reading about Hamilton would face the kind of political and ideological conflicts that can make the reading of history far from comforting.

Any realistic telling of Hamilton's rise and impact would draw readers of all political stripes into a possibly disconcerting confrontation with the overwhelming elitism of the founding generation. That elitism, well-known and taken fully for granted by professional historians, is alluded to breezily at best in most of the popular narratives, as if elitist ideology and practice can have little salience in the rise of a nation ultimately democratic. Yet an intimate and dramatic immersion in the real Alexander Hamilton's life, work, and importance to our national founding, presented not by way of heritage celebration or conservative and neoliberal apologetics, would bring the purposes and consequences of that elitism powerfully to life, raising painful questions, not easily resolved, either in the founding era or today, about American democracy, its origins, and its relative strength and fragility. Those are questions that many citizens might find useful, struggling with the bitterly divided national politics of 2017, when considering matters of race, class, equality, power, legitimacy in government, and the future of the nation.

Miranda's musical, however, inspired by and following Chernow, only gives thrilling dramatic expression to the historical denial that Chernow's biography embodies. In Chernow's character of Alexander Hamilton, as dramatized to immense cultural effect by Miranda, the glorifications and erasures on which popular historical narrative depends have taken over the public history of the American founding in a newly powerful way.

Why We Miss the Real Hamilton

Fans of the show, as well as some historians, may object that Miranda's *Hamilton* is a play, not a work of historical scholarship, and thus doesn't deserve critical analysis or censure. That would be a fairer point if the Gilder Lehrman Institute and others weren't framing the show as important precisely because of its educational value as history. Scholars and critics aren't wrong to question the show's accuracy and emphases and reflect critically on what cultural work it may be doing, for good and ill.

But the fans have a point too. These questions do come somewhat late in the game. To well-intentioned nonspecialist readers of American history, the reviewers and prize-giving organizations and other cultural certifiers long ago endorsed the play's source, Chernow's *Alexander Hamilton*. Although a few historians wrote essays critical of Brookhiser's New-York Historical Society's Hamilton exhibition, the history profession as a whole has been nearly silent on Chernow's approach in the biography. Only now, in response to the popularity of a Broadway musical, have high-profile historians begun raising questions about a story that has been strikingly popular in book form. And they're still mostly questioning the play, not the book it was drawn from.

This lack of interest in criticizing the book reflects a larger historiographical issue, reflecting on reasons that professional historians as a whole have long shown less interest in Hamilton than in Washington, Jefferson, Madison, Franklin, and Adams. Most of those men have a body of intellectual and philosophical writing, the kind of thing that historians like, but Hamilton's best-known exegetical papers are far more mundane. He wrote nothing as expansive as Jefferson's "Summary View," or the first draft of the Declaration of Independence; nothing as original and salient as Madison's "*Federalist* 10"; nothing as broad or deep as Franklin's dozens of philosophical and scientific essays; nothing as trenchant and definitive as Adams's "Thoughts on Government." Hamilton's best and most characteristic work is not to be found in efforts like his "Full Vindication of the Measures of Congress," or "The Farmer Refuted," or even, for that matter, in his *Federalist* essays. He was at least as smart as any of his contemporaries, and far more legislatively adroit than any of them, but his ideas were yoked to the pragmatic and the tactical. He didn't, like Madison, style himself a Greek philosopher.

To get to know Hamilton through his writing, you'd have to get interested in the First Report on the Public Credit, to consider certain parts of it in relation to other parts, to marvel at the tables and schedules, to rework the numbers for accuracy and let yourself be browbeaten into submission. That report and the revenue bill Hamilton wrote and attached to it for Congress's use are amazing phenomena, two chambers of the beating heart of his national vision. To know Hamilton, you would also have to know his other big reports to both the confederation and the U.S. Congress, and the correspondence with Washington after the Newburgh crisis of 1783, and the letters he wrote on behalf of the president and others in the cabinet, and his subtly manipulative interoffice cabinet memos, and the pseudonymous demagoguery in his pamphlets ginning up war fever in the eastern capitals against the whiskey rebels. Only in that way can you feel what he was trying to do.

And while many historians have of course read much of that material, it doesn't seem to excite them. Professional historians of the American founders have, as a group, been more interested in the founders' reading lists, ideology, cultural practices, and personal and political relationships, than in the kind of record of politics in support of policy that Hamilton left behind. Even those scholars who do view Hamilton through a political history lens have been drawn more to the ins and outs of his rivalries and machinations, especially in the 1800 election, the relationship with Aaron Burr and the fatal duel, and less to the motivations and technical processes by which he engineered the all-important economic policies that brought the nation into being in the 1790s.

Historians have thus largely ceded Hamilton to popular biographers who write within a publishing world where celebrating America's heritage and history sells. Chernow's book reflects both the appeal and the limitations of that approach: the author tells an entertaining and seemingly authoritative story—"delicious and tragic and interesting," as Miranda says—that whitewashes, glosses over, and gets wrong some of the most important things Hamilton did. And yet there's little else on Hamilton intended to appeal to general readers, and the givens of publishing popular history have led to a situation in which books that combine a genuinely narrative style with a genuinely critical approach are few and far between.

In that context, there's an important way in which professional, academic historians might further aid the development of public engagement with history that projects like Chernow's and Miranda's aspire to, and thus with the informed exercise of citizenship itself. The project would require historians' ceasing to by and large ignore, and in some cases to patronize, the big, popular history books. Historians should take such subjects and characters seriously, if only because they attract such wide public interest. Historians might treat founders' biographies the same way professional historians' are supposed to treat one another's work, by asking questions, making fully informed endorsements, articulating dissenting opinion, and offering competing interpretations.

Some professional historians have already made that decision. Still, the paucity of critical response by academic historians to Chernow's book, highlighted by the comparatively voluminous academic response, both enthusiastic and critical, to Miranda's musical, has had a deleterious effect on public understanding of Alexander Hamilton's overwhelming importance as a political figure, and of the American founding as a whole. The public excitement about founding history generated by *Hamilton: An American Musical* may offer an opportunity to consider new modes of engagement between the public and the profession.

NOTES

1. David McCullough, *John Adams* (New York: Simon & Schuster, 2001), dust jacket.

2. Stephen B. Presser, "Alexander Hamilton," *Journal of American History* 93, no. 1 (2006): 192–193.

3. Mark Binelli, "'Hamilton' Creator Lin-Manuel Miranda: The Rolling Stone Interview," *Rolling Stone*, June 1, 2016, http://www.rollingstone.com/music/features/hamilton-creator-lin-manuel-miranda-the-rolling-stone-interview-20160601.

4. Janice Simpson, "The Man Who First Brought Us Hamilton: Ron Chernow on Serving as Lin-Manuel Miranda's 'Right Hand Man,'" *Playbill*, January 12, 2016, http://www.playbill.com/article/the-man-who-first-brought-us-hamilton-u2014-ron-chernow-on-serving-as-lin-manuel-mirandas-right-hand-man.

5. Valerie Strauss, "The Unusual Way Broadway's 'Hamilton' Is Teaching U.S. History to Kids, *Washington Post*, June 28, 2016, https://www.washingtonpost.com/news/answer-sheet/wp/2016/06/28/the-unusual-way-broadways-hamilton-is-teaching-american-history-to-kids/?utm_term=.3ceb605c62e6.

6. "George Washington Prize," Gilder Lehrman Institute for American History, https://www.gilderlehrman.org/programs-exhibitions/george-washington-prize; "Alexander Hamilton's America," Gilder Lehrman Institute for American History, https://www.gilderlehrman.org/programs-exhibitions/alexander-hamilton%E2%80%99s-america.

7. "*Hamilton: The Musical* and the Rockefeller Foundation Announce Partnership to Provide 20,000 NYC Public School Students with Tickets to *Hamilton* on Broadway with $1.46 Million Grant," Rockefeller Foundation, October 27, 2016, https://www.rockefellerfoundation.org/about-us/news-media/hamilton-the-musical-and-the-rockefeller-foundation-announce-partnership-to-provide-20000-nyc-public-school-students-with-tickets-to-hamilton-on-broadway-with-1-46-million-grant/.

8. Ishmael Reed, "'*Hamilton: The Musical*: Black Actors Dress Up like Slave Traders . . . and It's Not Halloween," *Counterpunch*, August 21, 2015, http://www.counterpunch.org/2015/08/21/hamilton-the-musical-black-actors-dress-up-like-slave-tradersand-its-not-halloween/.

9. Quoted in Rebecca Onion, "A 'Hamilton' Skeptic on Why the Show Isn't as Revolutionary as It Seems," *Slate*, April 5, 2016, http://www.slate.com/articles/arts/culturebox/2016/04/a_hamilton_critic_on_why_the_musical_isn_t_so_revolutionary.html.

10. Quoted in Jennifer Schuessler, "Thomas Jefferson, Neither God Nor Devil," *New York Times*, April 5, 2016, https://www.nytimes.com/2016/04/06/books/thomas-jefferson-neither-god-nor-devil.html?_r=0.

11. David Brooks and William Kristol, "What Ails Conservatism," *Wall Street Journal*, September 15, 1997, https://www.wsj.com/articles/SB874276753849168000.

12. "Alexander Hamilton: The Man Who Made Modern America," Gilder Lehrman Institute for American History, https://www.gilderlehrman.org/programs-exhibitions/alexander-hamilton-man-who-made-modern-america.

13. David Brooks, "How to Reinvent the G.O.P.," *New York Times Magazine*, August 29, 2004, http://www.nytimes.com/2004/08/29/magazine/how-to-reinvent-the-gop.html; David Brooks, "Creating Capitalism," *New York Times Book Review*, April 25, 2004, http://www.nytimes.com/2004/04/25/books/creating-capitalism.html.

14. Ron Chernow, *Alexander Hamilton* (New York: Penguin, 2003), 6.

15. "Bush Speaks at the Swearing In of Treasury Secretary Paulson," *Washington Post*, July 10, 2006, http://www.washingtonpost.com/wp-dyn/content/article/2006/07/10/AR2006071000478.html.

16. "Brookings Institution Launches the Hamilton Project," *Brookings*, April 5, 2006, https://www.brookings.edu/news-releases/brookings-institution-launches-the-hamilton-project/.

17. Ryan Lizza, "Money Talks," *The New Yorker*, May 4, 2009, http://www.newyorker.com/magazine/2009/05/04/money-talks-4.

18. Quoted in Don Ball and Josephine Reed, "Lin-Manuel Miranda: Immigrant Songs," *NEA Arts Magazine*, February 2016, https://www.arts.gov/NEARTS/2016vi-telling-all-our-stories-arts-and-diversity/lin-manuel-miranda.

19. Chernow, *Hamilton*, 4.

20. Brooks, "How to Reinvent the G.O.P."; Chernow, *Hamilton*, 5.

21. Lin-Manuel Miranda, "Alexander Hamilton," *Hamilton: An American Musical*, Atlantic 551093–2, 2015, compact disc. All later quotations from the musical are from this source.

22. Chernow, *Hamilton*, 8.

23. Ibid., 6.

24. Natasha Simons, "The Real Hero of 'Hamilton' Is Aaron Burr," *The Federalist*, January 27, 2016, http://thefederalist.com/2016/01/27/the-real-hero-of-hamilton-is-aaron-burr/.

25. Chernow, *Hamilton*, 33, 210.

26. Ibid., 210–212.

27. Ibid., 210.

28. Brooks, "Creating Capitalism."

29. "Transcript," "Alexander Hamilton," *American Experience*, http://www.pbs.org/wgbh/amex/hamilton/filmmore/pt.html.

30. Julie Baergen, "Founding Fathers: Franklin, Jefferson, Hamilton, and Madison," Gilder Lehrman Institute of American History, https://www.gilderlehrman.org/history-by-era/hamilton/resources/founding-fathers-franklin-jefferson-hamilton-and-madison.

31. Many well-regarded works, by no means always in mutual agreement, have explored the ideology and impact of the founding-era popular movement's economic radicalism, as well as founding elites' reactions to it. See, for example, David Freeman Hawke's *In the Midst of a Revolution* (Philadelphia: University of Pennsylvania Press, 1961); Garry Wills's *Inventing America: Jefferson's Declaration of Independence* (reprint; New York: Mariner Books, 2002), especially the first chapter; Carl Becker's *The History of Political Parties in the Province of New York, 1760–1776* (Madison: University of Wisconsin Press, 1909); and Gary Nash's *Urban Crucible: The Northern Seaports and the Origins of the American Revolution* (Cambridge, MA: Harvard University Press, 1986).

32. For the drastic risks to the country, and to his own reputation, that Hamilton was willing to run in order to establish reliable payments to the bondholders as a basis of nationhood, see Richard Kohn's *Eagle and Sword: The Federalists and the Creation of the Military Establishment in America, 1783–1802* (New York; Free Press, 1975) and E. J. Ferguson's *The Power of the Purse: A History of American Public Finance, 1776–1790* (published for the Institute of Early

American History and Culture at Williamsburg, VA, by the University of North Carolina Press, 1961).

33. Chernow, *Hamilton*, 175.

34. See particularly E. J. Ferguson's *The Power of the Purse: Woody Holton, Unruly Americans, and the Origins of the Constitution* (New York: Hill & Wang, 2008); and Terry Bouton, *Taming Democracy: "The People," the Founders, and the Troubled Ending of the American Revolution* (Oxford: Oxford University Press, 2009).

CHAPTER 2

"Can We Get Back to Politics? Please?"

Hamilton's Missing Politics in Hamilton

JOANNE B. FREEMAN

Hamilton's Hamilton is a complex figure. Immigrant, soldier, abolitionist, secretary of the treasury, adulterer, duelist (not to mention a "bastard, orphan, son of a whore and a Scotsman"): all receive ample play.[1] Some of these claims are more accurate than others; other essays in this volume grapple with the complexities of calling Hamilton an immigrant or an abolitionist. But the play only glances at Hamilton's most important and influential role: politician.

To be sure, Hamilton the politician has his moments in *Hamilton*. We see him at the Constitutional Convention (proposing "his own form of government!").[2] We see him fretting about his plan for the national assumption of state debts, and then negotiating the bill's passage in "The Room Where It Happens." We see him in cabinet meetings talking (or rather, rapping) about national credit, the growth of industry, and relations with revolutionary France. We see him sparring with Thomas Jefferson and James Madison. We see him weighing in on the fraught presidential election of 1800. We get a vague sense that Hamilton's policies were forward-looking and modern, as opposed to the policies of *Hamilton*'s Jefferson, who represents the nation's slaveholding past.

But we don't see the passions and ideals behind Hamilton's politics. We don't see his desperate desire to strengthen the national government—to an extreme degree. We don't learn that his vision of a centralized New World government was grounded in his admiration of Old World Great Britain. We don't learn of Hamilton's impulsive habit of seeking military solutions to political problems. We don't see his deep distrust of the masses and his doubts about democracy. Until his dying day, Hamilton believed that the American republic was bound to fail. *Hamilton* doesn't dig that deep.

Nor does it need too. *Hamilton* is a musical, not a work of history, and as such, it focuses on human drama above all else, following the biographical lead of its main source, Ron Chernow's *Alexander Hamilton*.[3] This isn't to say that playwright Lin-Manuel Miranda didn't do his research. Although there are errors, and much is missing from the play, or simplified to the point of abstraction or near invisibility (for example, the impact of slavery on the new nation), it contains a remarkable amount of history for a piece of musical theater. Not many Broadway shows tackle topics like the national assumption of state debts, or set a president's Farewell Address to music as *Hamilton* does in "One Last Time." Bits of Hamilton's correspondence appear in the play virtually word for word. And there is an entire song devoted to unpacking the curious logic of dueling; "Ten Duel Commandments" describes the *code duello* and honor culture by blending my own work with the musical stylings of rapper Biggie Smalls. (Full disclosure: for Hamilton's letters and the logic of dueling, Miranda relied on my first two books, *Alexander Hamilton: Writings* and *Affairs of Honor: National Politics in the New Republic*).[4]

But historical context doesn't get center stage in *Hamilton*; indeed, sometimes it isn't even waiting in the wings. *Hamilton* is one man's story told from a Hamilton-centric point of view, tracking his rapid rise from impoverished obscurity to political power, followed by his self-destructive fall from power and death by duel at the hands of Vice President Aaron Burr. Miranda's interest in this biographical approach was apparent whenever we chatted. He was interested in Hamilton's inner motives and personality; he wanted to explore the many (many!) self-destructive aspects of Hamilton's life and career. And the play reflects Miranda's interests. Although its enormous influence and appeal understandably have put some historians on alert about its underlying message and implications, above all else, *Hamilton* is a work of historical fiction, exploring one man's personality, character, and contradictions as translated for the stage.[5]

As someone who has studied Hamilton for decades, I'm familiar with the highs and lows of his character, and they make for good storytelling. In many ways, Hamilton's greatest strengths and weaknesses were one and the same. His drive, persistence, high ambitions, intense energies, laser-like focus, and writerly flair raised him to power. But taken too far, these same gifts made him impulsive and indiscreet, a loose cannon whose personal and political liabilities brought him to ruin. It is for good reason that a play about Hamilton makes for good theater. It's hard to look away from the careening car chase of his life, including the flaming crash at its end.

But none of this drama makes sense without the fuel of Hamilton's politics. His uncompromisingly extreme political goals and no-holds-barred style of politicking propelled his rise and fall. Indeed, his ambitions for the nation and for himself were intertwined. As Hamilton explained in 1792, his twin goals as secretary of the treasury were "to do material good" and "to acquire reputation."[6] As problematic as Hamilton's personality could be, it was his politics that made him the political lightning rod of the republic's first decade.

So who was Hamilton the politician? In a word, he was divisive— a supreme irony given that centralization and a strong unified state were the driving goals behind his politics. However logical those goals may seem today, in the early national United States they were controversial. Having just broken away from a monarchy, many Americans were justifiably leery about creating a strong centralized national government led by a powerful executive officer. They believed that they were engaged in an experiment in republican government; in a world governed by monarchies, they were attempting something new. So Hamilton's centralizing ideas were justifiably frightening to many, who saw him as an elitist throwback to corrupt Old World regimes.

Thus the tensions and conflicts at the heart of Hamilton's political career. He dedicated his life and energies to promoting his radically centralized—yet profoundly conservative—vision for the new nation, a vision that seemed justifiably threatening to many Americans. There was a reason why Hamilton was denounced as a monarchist until the end of his days. Although he insisted time and again that he was committed to the nation's experiment in government, he seemed to be chipping away at its republican foundations.[7]

And in some ways, he was. Although Hamilton recognized that the new nation was a republic, he did his best to bolster it with the trappings of monarchy. His plan of government at the Constitutional Convention featured a national executive and senators who served for life during good behavior, much like a king and House of Lords. Although these ideas were rejected as too extreme, Hamilton never stopped working to empower the government. In 1789, when newly elected President George Washington asked him for advice on presidential etiquette, Hamilton's suggestions were high-toned, to say the least. He thought that Washington should have a formal European-style levee once a week at a set day and hour, during which he could chat with visitors who would be formally introduced by government officials; after thirty minutes of meeting and greeting, the president would "disappear." He should be equally off limits to the public, including the elite, Hamilton counseled. To protect the dignity of his office, the president should accept no social invitations and return no visits. And only senators—not representatives—should have individual access to him, Hamilton thought. As monarchical as Hamilton's suggestions seem, he wanted to push further, but feared that popular "notions of equality are yet in my opinion too general and too strong . . . for so high a tone as in the abstract might be desireable."[8]

Why this campaign to empower the government? Enemies attributed it to Hamilton's corrupt desire to line the pockets of his wealthy friends, and possibly his own pockets as well. But Hamilton's efforts were grounded in fear. What he feared above all else in the new republic were competing claims of power. He never fully believed that the nation's republican form of government could with-stand the destabilizing pull of strong state governments. He admit-ted as much in a memo written for his eyes only at the close of the Constitutional Convention in 1787. Noting that if Washington wasn't elected president, conflicts between the national government and state governments would probably destroy the union, he then added: "This after all seems to be the most likely result."[9] Within two weeks of the close of the convention, Hamilton already assumed that at some point in the future, the national government would collapse.

On a deeper and more instinctive level, Hamilton also feared the power of the democratic multitude. A republic was grounded on public opinion to an extreme degree. To Hamilton, this was a potentially fatal vulnerability; the instabilities of the populace were bound to lead to anarchy and ruin, a fear that became ever more powerful given the social disorder and bloodshed in revolutionary France, which intensified year by year, and—to Hamilton and his supporters—seemed likely to spread to American shores. The "real Disease" in the American republic was "DEMOCRACY," he insisted in 1804.[10]

Thus Hamilton's habit of grasping at military solutions to political problems. More than once, when told about an organized protest against the government, he advised armed resistance. Note, for exam-ple, his impulse in 1798, when the Kentucky and Virginia legisla-tures passed resolutions condemning Congress's Alien and Sedition Acts—four bills that clamped down on immigrants and noncitizens, and criminalized false criticism of the national government. Out-raged at such open resistance to acts of the central government, Hamilton yearned to march an army on Virginia and put the legis-lature "to the Test of resistance."[11] In 1794, when people in western Pennsylvania rebelled against his excise tax on whiskey, he went fur-ther. With Hamilton's encouragement, Washington and Hamilton (who was acting as secretary of war in Henry Knox's absence) led a sizable armed force to quash the rebellion, though it had fizzled by the time they reached it. Even so, a point had been made. As

Hamilton advised his friend, Secretary of War James McHenry, in 1799 during the nation's Quasi-War with France, "Whenever the Government appears in arms it ought to appear like a Hercules, and inspire respect by the display of strength."[12]

Clearly, Hamilton's distrust of democracy was heartfelt, and it never wavered—a less than admirable aspect of his politics that has no place in *Hamilton*. Even during the Revolution, as committed as he was to American independence, Hamilton fretted about the violent impulses of the "unthinking populace." Alarmed when some colonists rampaged a Loyalist printer's office, he admitted that he was "more or less alarmed at every thing which is done of mere will and pleasure, without any proper authority."[13] Distrustful of popular unrest and disorder, Hamilton was a conservative revolutionary, willing and even eager to topple British rule for the sake of colonial rights, but valuing the stability of law and order above all else.

This mix of radical impulses and conservative yearnings shaped Hamilton's actions during his peak years of power as the nation's first secretary of the treasury. The opening gambit of his tenure

George Washington reviewing troops deployed against the Whiskey Rebellion at Fort Cumberland, Maryland, 1795. *(The Metropolitan Museum of Art, New York, NY)*

was dramatic: in his First Report on the Public Credit (1790), he proposed having the national government assume responsibility for Revolutionary War debts owed by state governments. In forcing debtors to turn to the national government for repayment, he hoped to reinforce its authority and power. But his idea was so alarmingly centralizing that it nearly failed. Congress was deadlocked for weeks (with Hamilton struggling behind the scenes to "get my plan through Congress," as he explains in *Hamilton*'s "Take a Break"). In the end, Hamilton's assumption plan passed only through his negotiations with influential Virginia congressman James Madison, who promised to get votes for the plan in exchange for Hamilton's assistance in moving the national capital south to the banks of the Potomac River. As *Hamilton* suggests, Jefferson brokered this deal, arranging a dinner at his home—"the menu, the venue, the seating"—so that Hamilton and Madison could come to terms.[14]

Hamilton's plan to create a national bank (1790) was equally controversial. Not only did it increase federal power, but it also seemed to go beyond the bounds of the Constitution, which didn't give the government the power to create a bank. Although Washington expected to veto the bill, he gave Hamilton a chance to defend it. Hamilton's aggressive response not only persuaded Washington to withhold his veto, but also established an important precedent concerning the loose construction—or broad interpretation—of the Constitution, dramatically increasing the power of the national government in the process.

It's easy to see why Hamilton's policies as secretary of the treasury were so divisive, and why people distrusted his commitment to a republican form of government. Asked in 1803 to defend himself against the charge that his plan of government during the Constitutional Convention was "intended as an introduction to Monarchy," he insisted that it had been "conformable with the strict theory of a Government purely republican; the essential criteria of which are that the principal organs of the Executive and Legislative departments be elected by the people and hold their offices by a <u>responsible</u> and temporary or <u>defeasible</u> tenure." Hamilton had known that "the people of this country would endure nothing but republican government," he argued, and he had felt that it was "right and proper that the republican theory should have a fair and full trial." To ensure that trial, he had tried to give the government "all the energy and stability reconciliable with the principles of that theory."[15] For America's republican government to have a fair chance, Hamilton thought, it needed to be buttressed as much as "republican theory" would allow. Some bought this argument. Many didn't, creating a cloud of suspicion that shadowed his every political move.

Of course, Hamilton fed that distrust by praising the British government publicly and with fervor. He was never shy about advancing his views and vision—as unpopular as they might be—and always thought that he was right. He never lived down his declaration at the Constitutional Convention that the British government was "the best in the world: and that he doubted much whether any thing short of it would do in America."[16] But Hamilton didn't stop there. In private and public conversation with friends and enemies, he repeatedly pointed to Great Britain as a model of good government. In a young republic newly broken from Great Britain that seemed likely to slip back into monarchy, he seemed like a dangerous monarchical extremist.

This isn't to say that Hamilton didn't have supporters. He had many—indeed, enough for many of his plans to succeed. By and large, these were conservative moneyed men, often merchants or businessmen, although public opinion sometimes supported him. In time, these like-minded people became known as Federalists.[17] *Hamilton* doesn't depict Hamilton as a party politician; indeed, the word "Federalist" appears in the lyrics only once.[18] Instead, the political trajectory of the play focuses on the creation of the "Southern motherf*ckin' Democratic-Republicans," depicted as united mostly by their hatred of Hamilton. Vaguely southern and agrarian in orientation, *Hamilton*'s Democratic-Republicans represent the defiant resistance of the status quo. They're also a good foil for Hamilton.

But in real life, the Democratic-Republicans were more than Hamilton-haters. They had a vision for the republic that was as ambitious and heartfelt as its Federalist equivalent.[19] They envisioned an agrarian America with a limited national government, populated by vigilant self-supporting farmers. There were two core visions of the republic in this period and two sides to the period's partisan warfare, with the Federalists fighting to empower the national government and the Republicans trying to limit it.

Hamilton reduces this conflict to a battle between past and present, depicting Hamilton as a forward-looking avatar of the future who envisioned a powerful, industrialized America and did his best to push the nation toward that goal as opposed to a backward-looking agrarian, slavery-supporting Jefferson. There is some truth in this telling. Over time, the United States followed in the early modern British Empire's footsteps, becoming a world power economically, militarily, and politically, as the Federalists had hoped. And by twenty-first-century standards, Jefferson's yeoman farmer–centric vision of the United States seems decidedly premodern.

But depicting Hamilton as the future and Jefferson as the past does a grave disservice to our understanding of the founding era and its implications. Neither man's political vision was that simple. The historical Jefferson was forward-looking in important ways, particularly in his faith in the strivings and energies of the democratic multitude. Jefferson's commitment to a democratic politics was as heartfelt as Hamilton's distrust of it. Federalist leaders "say that man cannot be trusted with his own government," Jefferson scornfully repeated in 1802, glorying in the Republican triumph in the election of 1800 and its likely legacy. His "most earnest wish" was "to see the republican element of popular controul pushed to the maximum of its practicable exercise."[20]

In contrast, Hamilton's distrust of democracy was born of Old World fears and assumptions. Never shy about courting the rich and well-born in the hope of using their influence to bolster the government, Hamilton was aggressively elitist. This may seem hard to square with his obscure origins; surely the man who John Adams called the "bastard brat of a Scotch pedler" was not elite in status.[21] But although Hamilton's illegitimate birth led to a lifetime of

"T. Jefferson President of the United States of America / John Adams is no more," reads the text in what is one of the earliest examples of partisan imagery, a banner celebrating Jefferson's victory over Adams in the presidential election of 1800. *(Division of Political History, National Museum of American History, Kenneth E. Behring Center)*

sneers from his political foes, he was considered a gentleman, as his many affairs of honor attest; fighting a duel with an inferior was deemed dishonorable, and no one had that qualm about dueling with Hamilton.

Even among gentlemen, however, Hamilton was more elitist than many—though he never called the American people "a great beast," as many have claimed since Henry Adams first publicized the charge in 1889.[22] That bit of hearsay has stuck to Hamilton's reputation because it is believable given his aristocratic mindset. Of course, Hamilton didn't much trust the better sort either; he believed that all men were governed by their selfish passions, and that only a strong government could channel those passions to serve the public good.

Power was at the heart of most of Hamilton's policies; his elitism was bound up with his fundamental lack of trust in the power and stability of a republican form of government.

Clearly, neither Jefferson nor Hamilton was only modern or pre-modern, right or wrong. As tempting as it is to take sides in their battle—which frames most of *Hamilton*'s second act—they represented two sides of a broader conversation about American nation-hood and national character that went far beyond these two men, and indeed, far beyond a handful of national politicians. There was no single right answer to the period's political problems, no one path to national power and prosperity. Indeed, there was no guarantee that America's political experiment would survive at all. The American founding wasn't the start of a straight path to the present. It was a tense, trying, unstable, hopeful, fearful time of high ambitions, big risks, and even bigger stakes. People of all kinds—not only elite leaders—were aware of the potential crises at hand, and were finding their way, one step at a time.

With the benefit of hindsight, it's easy to overlook the period's crisis mentality; the word "founding" in and of itself assumes the nation's survival.[23] But listen to the thoughts of some incoming national politicians in 1789 as the national government got under way. They believed that they were guiding the ship of state without a compass. Virginia Representative James Madison felt that he was "in a wilderness without a single footstep to guide us." Maryland Senator William Maclay confessed in his diary, "The Whole World is a shell and we tread on hollow ground every step."[24] There was no telling what would happen. This sense of contingency was an enormous shaping influence on the new nation's politics.

On this count, *Hamilton* has much to offer. Although it takes great liberties with the period's history, shifting events, collapsing time, simplifying conflicts, and focusing on a small band of white leaders, it gets the underlying *spirit* of the moment right. In part, it does this through its music. With its sung-through dialogue, its unconventional rap- and hip-hop-infused score, its energy and high emotions, and its blend of past and present, *Hamilton* is an unexpected and rule-breaking piece of theater that captures the contingency and experimentation of America's founding. The music's bravado, urgency, and seeming improvisation powerfully reflect the charged dynamics of the time.

Hamilton's exceedingly human characters also capture the spirit of the moment. Multicultural, emotionally rich, and depicting America's founders as real people, the play pushes audiences past their assumptions about a staid and inevitably successful founding story. As smoothed out, simplified, and often idealized as *Hamilton*'s main characters may be, they are unquestionably, feelingly human. Caught in a historical moment and struggling to find their way, they remind audiences that nothing about America's beginnings was foreordained.

Hamilton's human side also offers insight into the logic behind the period's notoriously nasty politics. Convinced that the republic might fall, politicians in the 1790s engaged in a lot of dirty politicking, including mud slinging, name-calling, fib-telling, and street fights aplenty. The play's second act offers a glimpse of this dissension, largely through the characters of Jefferson, Madison, and Burr, who join in angry, snide opposition to Hamilton in "Washington on Your Side," and then try to destroy his political career by accusing him of speculating in government funds. "The Reynolds Pamphlet" shows Hamilton's response, detailing how he wrote a pamphlet confessing to a personal sin—adultery—to clear his public name, an act that hurt those closest to him. The Republicans' wild celebratory response to Hamilton's confession ("he's never gon' be President now") doesn't show the Republicans in a very good light; we see them glorying in a man's destruction. There is a mean, personal edge to Republican politicking as depicted in *Hamilton*—which is true to the period, but wasn't limited to the Republicans.

Hamilton's Hamilton has fewer hard edges, though the real Hamilton had many. He practiced a sharp, often nasty form of politics, suffering no fools and slashing at foes to defend his policies and character. There's a reason why Hamilton became entangled in *ten* affairs of honor over the course of his life, although all but his final duel with Burr were settled through negotiations; when it comes to involvement in honor disputes, no first-rank founder comes close. He was a fighter in every sense of the word, and he gloried in the fight, even when it backfired—as with the Reynolds pamphlet, or with his equally ill-advised pamphlet attacking John Adams, his own party's presidential candidate, in 1800—summed up by the phrase "Sit down, John, you fat mother [bleep]" in the play.[25] In some ways, Hamilton was his own worst enemy.

Clearly, when it comes to Hamilton and politics, there are big gaps in *Hamilton*. But the musical is a starting point, not an ending. Some people may walk away assuming that its central character was a hero, and go no further. But many people will want to know more. And if historians and teachers take up this challenge and offer realistic, nuanced, blunt assessments of Hamilton, his politics, and his times, people will learn that he wasn't just a founder hero. They'll see that he wasn't always right, or even wise; rather, he was part of a conversation that sometimes aimed high and sometimes aimed low, and in doing so, they'll discover the real complexity of America's founding.

They'll also see that political debates don't necessarily pit good guys against bad guys. America's founding could have followed many paths. As much as we like to divide the period into an epic battle between Hamilton and Jefferson, the new nation required them both and extended far beyond them. Given the divisiveness of today's politics, it's easy to forget that the American political system is grounded in debate and compromise. But so it is. And both Hamilton and Jefferson—and more important, the American public— contributed to the political give and take of the time. The end result was a blend of views, not a simple victory of one over another. *Hamilton* doesn't emphasize this. But it's well worth remembering.

NOTES

Title quote is from Lin-Manuel Miranda, "The Election of 1800," *Hamilton: An American Musical*, Atlantic 551093–2, 2015, compact disc.

1. Miranda, "Alexander Hamilton," ibid.

2. Miranda, "Non-Stop," ibid.

3. See also Joanne B. Freeman, "How *Hamilton* Uses History," *Slate*, November 11, 2015, http://www.slate.com/articles/arts/culturebox/2015/11/how _lin_manuel_miranda_used_real_history_in_writing_hamilton.html accessed January 10, 2017; idem, "Will the Real Alexander Hamilton Please Stand Up?," *Journal of the Early Republic* (forthcoming, 2017).

4. Joanne B. Freeman, *Alexander Hamilton: Writings* (New York: Library of America, 2001); idem., *Affairs of Honor: National Politics in the New Republic* (New Haven: Yale University Press, 2001). The title, style, and structure of "Ten Duel Commandments" pays homage to Biggie Small's "Ten Crack Commandments."

5. See for example Lyra D. Monteiro, "Race-Conscious Casting and the Erasure of the Black Past in Lin-Manuel Miranda's *Hamilton*," *The Public Historian* 38, no. 1 (February 2016): 89–98; Nancy Isenberg, "Let's Not Pretend That 'Hamilton' Is History," *Zocalo*, March 17, 2016, http://www.zocalopub licsquare.org/2016/03/17/lets-not-pretend-that-hamilton-is-history/ideas/nex us/, accessed February 19, 2017,; Annette Gordon-Reed, "*Hamilton: The Musical*: Blacks and the Founding Fathers," National Council on Public History, History@Work, April 6, 2016, http://ncph.org/history-at-work/hamilton-the -musical-blacks-and-the-founding-fathers/, accessed February 19, 2017; Jennifer Schuessler, "'Hamilton' and History: Are They in Sync?," *New York Times*, April 10, 2016; Ken Owen, "Historians and Hamilton: Founders Chic and the Cult of Personality," *The Junto*, April 21, 2016, https://earlyamericanists.com/ 2016/04/21/historians-and-hamilton-founders-chic-and-the-cult-of-personality/, accessed February 19, 2017.

6. Hamilton to Edward Carrington, May 26, 1792, in *Hamilton: Writings*, 741.

7. On Hamilton and republicanism, see especially Gerald Stourzh, *Alexander Hamilton and the Idea of Republican Government* (Stanford, CA: Stanford University, 1970); James H. Read, *Power versus Liberty: Madison Hamilton, Wilson, and Jefferson* (Charlottesville: University Press of Virginia, 2000); Michael P. Federici, *The Political Philosophy of Alexander Hamilton* (Baltimore: Johns Hopkins University Press, 2012).

8. Hamilton to Washington, May 5, 1789, in *Hamilton: Writings*, 515–517.

9. [Conjectures About the New Constitution], c. late September 1787, in ibid., 167–170.

10. Hamilton to Theodore Sedgwick, July 10, 1804, in ibid., 1022.

11. Hamilton to Theodore Sedgwick, February 2, 1799, in ibid., 913–914. The Kentucky Resolutions argued that individual states could declare federal

laws unconstitutional; the Virginia Resolutions argued that states had the right to "interpose" when faced with unconstitutional federal laws.

12. Hamilton to James McHenry, March 18, 1799, in ibid., 915.

13. Hamilton to John Jay, November 26, 1775, in ibid., 43–46.

14. "The Room Where It Happens," *Hamilton*.

15. Timothy Pickering to Hamilton, April 5, 1803, Founders Online; Hamilton to Pickering, September 16, 1803, in *Hamilton: Writings*, 1002–1003.

16. When Hamilton said this at the convention, he knew it would be controversial. He followed up the quoted passage by saying: "He hoped Gentlemen of different opinions would bear with him in this." James Madison, Notes on Hamilton's Speech in the Constitutional Convention, June 18, 1787, in ibid., 156.

17. It's worth noting that the Federalists who opposed the Anti-Federalists during the constitutional debate were not identical to the Federalist alliance that developed during Washington's presidency. When the new government went into effect, there weren't two political parties in play. National political alliances of Federalists and Republicans didn't take shape until roughly 1792, sparked by the passage of parts of Hamilton's financial plan and the French Revolution.

18. It appears in "Washington on Your Side," *Hamilton*. The word also appears in a reference to *The Federalist Papers* (which in reality was simply known as *The Federalist*) in "Non-Stop."

19. For two classic studies of Jeffersonian Republicanism, see Lance Banning, *The Jeffersonian Persuasion: Evolution of a Party Ideology* (Ithaca, NY: Cornell University Press, 1978); and Drew McCoy, *The Elusive Republic: Political Economy in Jeffersonian America* (Chapel Hill: University of North Carolina Press, 1996).

20. Jefferson to David Hall, July 6, 1802; Jefferson to Isaac H. Tiffany, August 26, 1816, Founders Online.

21. Adams to Benjamin Rush, January 25, 1806, Founders Online.

22. Adams probably found the quote in Theophilus Parsons Jr., *Memoir of Theophilus Parsons, Chief Justice of the Supreme Judicial Court of Massachusetts* (1859); supposedly, someone told someone who told Parsons, whose son recorded it in his memoir of his father. Adams then repeated it in *History of the United States of America during the First Administration of Thomas Jefferson*, 2 vols. (New York: Charles Scribner's Sons, 1889), 1:85. Stephen Knott, *Alexander Hamilton and the Persistence of Myth* (Lawrence: University Press of Kansas, 2002), 73–74, 253n18.

23. On the period's crisis mentality, see Joanne B. Freeman, "The Election of 1800: A Study in the Process of Political Change," *Yale Law Journal* 108 (June 1999): 1959–1994.

24. Madison to Jefferson, June 30, 1789, in *The Papers of James Madison*, edited by J. C. A. Stagg (Charlottesville: University of Virginia Press, 1962–): 12:268; William Maclay, diary entry, January 7, 1790, in *The Diary of William Maclay and Other Notes on Senate Debates*, edited by Kenneth R. Bowling and Helen E. Veit (Baltimore: Johns Hopkins University Press, 1988), 179.

25. "The Adams Administration," *Hamilton*. The two pamphlets were Hamilton, "Observations on Certain Documents Contained in No. V & VI of 'The History of the United States for the Year 1796,' In Which the Charge of Speculation Against Alexander Hamilton, Late Secretary of the Treasury, is Fully Refuted. Written by Himself" (Philadelphia: Printed for John Fenno, by John Bioren, 1797); idem., "Letter from Alexander Hamilton, Concerning the Public Conduct and Character of John Adams, Esq. President of the United States" (New York: Printed for John Lang, by George F. Hopkins, 1800).

CHAPTER 3

Race-Conscious Casting and the Erasure of the Black Past in *Hamilton*

Lyra D. Monteiro

The American public has long been enthralled with the mythology of the founding fathers. Though a recent (and recurring) trend within popular history writing, "Founders Chic" can also be experienced on historic house tours at places such as Mount Vernon, Monticello, and Hamilton Grange that focus on lauding while also humanizing the founders.[1] Overall, the impression these sites give of the Revolutionary era echoes the majority of American history textbooks: the only people who lived during this period—or the only ones who mattered—were wealthy (often slave-owning) white men. There are exceptions to this pattern, such as the African American programming at Colonial Williamsburg, the interpretation of the mills at Lowell, Massachusetts, and the Smithsonian's recent exhibition about the enslaved families at Monticello.[2] Such challenges to the "exclusive past" are absolutely necessary for our present, as we strive to live up to an ideal of all people being equal and create a world in which women's voices are no longer silenced and Black Lives Matter.

Currently on Broadway, MacArthur fellow Lin-Manuel Miranda's hip-hop musical *Hamilton* brings to life the founding era of the United States in an engaging show that draws heavily on Ron Chernow's 2004 biography, *Alexander Hamilton*. The play follows its main character from his childhood in the Caribbean—as the opening line of the show puts it, he was "a bastard, orphan, son of a whore and a / Scotsman"—through his meteoric rise to serve as

George Washington's assistant during the Revolutionary War, his career as the nation's first secretary of the treasury, the decline of his political career following a sex scandal, to his death in a duel with Vice President Aaron Burr. With a cast dominated by actors of color, the play is nonetheless yet another rendition of the "exclusive past," with its focus on the deeds of "great white men" and its silencing of the presence and contributions of people of color in the Revolutionary era.

The play began at New York's Public Theater, performed before sold-out crowds in an extended run. In a *New York Times* cover story, Michael Paulson hailed *Hamilton* as "a turning point for the art form and a cultural conversation piece."[3] While only time will tell if *Hamilton* represents a turning point, the musical has undeniably sparked a cultural conversation. Before opening on Broadway, the show had already sold over two hundred thousand tickets, one of the largest pre-opening sales figures in Broadway history. Since then, critics have overwhelmingly praised the production.

The play is fairly historically accurate, reflecting Chernow's work as the show's historical consultant. The inaccuracies that do remain serve an important narrative purpose—an early scene in a tavern where the Marquis de Lafayette, Aaron Burr, Hamilton, John Laurens, and Hercules Mulligan meet could never have happened, while some other events are transposed in time.[4] The play also makes impressive use of actual historical documents, many of which are set to music during the play. For example, Samuel Seabury's "Free Thoughts on the Proceedings of the Continental Congress," George Washington's Farewell Address, and the letters Burr and Hamilton sent to each other prior to their duel become songs, with the actors even singing the signatures, "A-dot-Burr" and "A-dot-Ham."

The actors consciously refer to the shaping of historical memory throughout the play, from early references to "when our children tell our story," to a beautiful, moving scene in which Hamilton's wife, Eliza, heartbroken at her husband's betrayal, sings "I'm erasing myself from the narrative" as she burns her letters. The play's final song—and final line—also drives home the importance of the creation of historical narratives: "Who Lives, Who Dies, Who Tells Your Story?"

However, on some of the most important issues of this period—race and slavery—the musical falls short. Race is, in some ways, front and center in this play, as the founding fathers are without exception played by black and Latino men. These choices, which creators and critics have dubbed "colorblind casting," are in fact far from colorblind. The racialized musical forms that each of the characters sings makes this particularly clear. For example, among the actors playing the three Schuyler sisters, the one who sings the "white" music of traditional Broadway (Philippa Soo as Hamilton's wife, Eliza), reads as white (she is actually Chinese American), while the eldest sister Angelica, who sings in the more "black" genres of R&B and rap, is black (Renée Elise Goldsberry). Similarly, King George III, who sings "white" sixties Britpop, is performed by a white actor (Jonathan Groff—who was cast to replace another white actor, Brian D'Arcy James, who left the show after its initial run at the Public Theater) while the hip-hop-spouting revolutionaries are all black and Latino. The fact that writer Lin-Manuel Miranda, a Puerto Rican, plays Hamilton, further makes clear the intentions behind the casting. His stand-in, Javier Muñoz (who performs once a week in Miranda's stead), is also Puerto Rican, marking Hamilton's Caribbean connection in contrast to the other Euro-American founders, all of whom are black.

While most critics love the casting—calling it imaginative, accessible, and thought-provoking—others take issue with the premise of casting black actors as the founding fathers. In a piece subtitled "Black Actors Dress Up Like Slave Traders . . . and It's Not Halloween," Ishmael Reed asks, "Can you imagine Jewish actors in Berlin's theaters taking roles of Goering? Goebbels? Eichmann? Hitler?"[5]

When asked directly in a *Wall Street Journal* interview about how it feels to portray a white slave-owner, Daveed Diggs, who plays Jefferson, avoided the question altogether.[6] By contrast, theater critic Hilton Als perceives "something new and unrecognizable . . .

Lin-Manuel Miranda and the multiracial cast of *Hamilton* performing onstage during the 70th Annual Tony Awards at the Beacon Theatre on June 12, 2016, in New York City. *(Theo Wargo/Getty Images for Tony Awards Productions)*

on the stage—a dramatic successor to Derek Walcott's and Jamaica Kincaid's literary explorations of the surreality of colonialism."[7]

Chernow's reaction to the play's casting is telling: "I remember . . . thinking 'Oh my goodness, they're all black and Latino! What on earth is Lin-Manuel thinking?' I sat down . . . thinking to myself '. . . I need to sit down and talk to Lin-Manuel alone. We're talking about the founding fathers of the United States.'"[8] That incongruity is precisely what makes the play special to Diggs, who plays Thomas Jefferson and the Marquis de Lafayette and says, "I walked out of the show with a sense of ownership over American history. Part of it is seeing brown bodies play these people."[9] This idea that black and brown people were not actually part of this history is reflected in a line from a radio spot advertising the show, which declares, "This is the story of America then, told by America now." Others, including Chernow, have described the cast as representing "Obama's America."[10]

The idea that this musical "looks like America looks now"[11] in contrast to "then," however, is misleading and actively erases the presence and role of black and brown people in Revolutionary America, as well as before and since. America "then" *did* look like the people in this play, if you looked outside of the halls of government. This has never been a white nation. The idea that the actors who are performing on stage represent newcomers to this country in any way is insulting. Miranda is Puerto Rican, meaning his parents and even his grandparents were born American citizens; the African American actors in the play may have ancestors that fought in the same Revolutionary War depicted on stage—and may also be the descendants of enslaved people on whose backs the founders built their fortunes and sustained their lifestyles. More pointedly, it is problematic to have black and brown actors stand in for the great white men of the early United States in a play that does not acknowledge that the ancestors of these same actors were excluded from the freedoms for which the founders fought.

This realization brings attention to a truly damning omission in the show: despite the proliferation of black and brown bodies onstage, not a single enslaved or free person of color exists as a character in this play. For the space of only a couple of bars, a chorus member assumes the role of Sally Hemings, but is recognizable as such only by those who catch Jefferson's reference to the enslaved woman with whom he had an ongoing sexual relationship. Unless one listens carefully to the lyrics—which do mention slavery a handful of times—one could easily assume that slavery did not exist in this world, and certainly that it was not an important part of the lives and livelihoods of the men who created the nation.

During the Revolutionary era, around 14 percent of New York City's inhabitants were African American, the majority of whom were enslaved.[12] In the Caribbean, the numbers were much higher. In the 1790s, a slave was present in one in five of the city's white households.[13] Thus, every scene in the play contains an opportunity for an enslaved character—from the tavern where the revolutionaries meet in Act I, to the Winter's Ball where Hamilton meets his

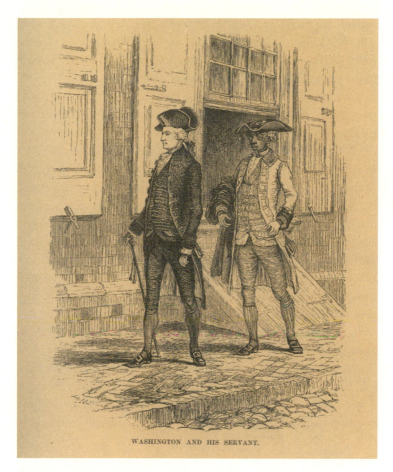

WASHINGTON AND HIS SERVANT.

In just one of the many ways in which people of color were always present in Revolutionary-era America, this 1885 image from Charles Carleton Coffin's *Building the Nation: Events in the History of the United States* shows George Washington with his "manservant." As the text relates, "When he [Washington] walked the streets, his body-servant in livery followed him at a respectful distance." *(The Library Company of Philadelphia)* future wife, Eliza. In the show-stopping tune "The Room Where It Happens," in which Aaron Burr (played by Leslie Odom Jr.) laments his exclusion from the dinner where Hamilton, Jefferson, and Madison made secret decisions, the line "No one else was in the room where it happened" completely erases the slaves who would have been in that room serving dinner.

This pattern of erasing the presence of black bodies continues throughout the play, as the role of people of color in the Revolution itself is silenced. Although abolitionist John Laurens did not succeed in raising the black battalion that the actor portraying him refers to twice in the play, thousands of people of color participated in the war—some as soldiers, but many others as groomsmen and in other service capacities, aiding white troops. Indeed, one of the first men to die in the Revolution was a man of African and Native American ancestry, Crispus Attucks, who was killed by the British in the Boston Massacre in 1772. More blatantly, the play omits the role of Hercules Mulligan's slave, Cato, who bravely assisted Mulligan's efforts to spy on the British.[14] In *Hamilton*, Mulligan sings about these accomplishments as if they were his alone.

In the script itself, slavery is unquestionably downplayed. In interviews, Miranda points to the brief lyrical references as proof that the play takes slavery seriously. He emphasizes that the third line of the play mentions slavery—but the reference is so vague that it requires historical knowledge to understand its meaning and obscures Hamilton's participation in the institution ("by fourteen, they placed him [Hamilton] in charge of a trading charter. / And every day while slaves were being slaughtered and carted / away across the waves, he struggled and kept his guard up").

On the other hand, *antislavery* receives more emphasis, represented in the first act by Laurens and later, following Hamilton's death, when Eliza sings, "I speak out against slavery. / You could have done so much more if you only had / Time." In reference to the musical, the historian David Waldstreicher notes that Miranda follows a familiar pattern: "Founders Chic historians emplot slavery when it serves to upraise the character of their heroes, i.e. Adams and

Hamilton, and diss their flawed characters, i.e. Jefferson."[15] Indeed, the only time that slavery is mentioned for more than a single phrase is in one of Hamilton's rap battles with Jefferson, where he taunts:

> Would you like to join us, or stay mellow,
> Doin' whatever the hell it is you do in Monticello? . . .
> A civics lesson from a slaver. Hey neighbor,
> Your debts are paid cuz you don't pay for labor.
> "We plant seeds in the South. We create."
> Yeah, keep ranting,
> we know who's really doing the planting.[16]

In interviews, Miranda has noted, "When I encountered Alexander Hamilton I was immediately captivated. He's an inspirational figure to me. And an aspirational one."[17] Elsewhere, it has been reported that "Hamilton reminded him of his father."[18] It is hardly surprising that someone who displays this kind of adoration of a founding father would find it difficult to truly incorporate slavery into the story of his life. Though it does not appear in the play, in interviews Miranda has stressed Hamilton's membership in the New York Manumission Society, while glossing over the fact that members of his wife's family were major slave owners. While Hamilton himself may not have owned slaves, he certainly was linked to transactions involving them, including hiring them from their owners to do work for him. In this, Miranda follows Chernow's book closely, which speaks of Hamilton's abolitionism at every opportunity while eliding his involvement with slavery. One wonders whether, had he employed a person of color as his historian, Miranda would have been able to write a play that downplays race and slavery to the extent that this one does. But there are few historians of color who work on the founding fathers, let alone on Alexander Hamilton specifically—most are driven instead by projects that chip away at the exclusive past typified by the cult of the founders. The question of slavery comes up frequently in interviews with cast members, and their answers tend to mirror Miranda's—often citing that third line or a rap battle over slavery that was cut from the show. Cast member Christopher Jackson told the *New Yorker* that the musical provided an implicit critique of slavery: "The Broadway audience doesn't like to be preached to. . . . By having a multicultural cast, it gives us, as actors of color, the chance to provide an additional context just by our presence onstage, filling these characters up."[19]

Miranda certainly is bringing back to life what *New York Times* theater critic Ben Brantley calls "a thoroughly archived past," and as such, his work bears certain responsibilities to the public. Thus, it is concerning that the play adopts the old bootstrap ideology of the "American Dream," with the second line in the play hailing how Hamilton, despite his humble origins, "got a lot farther by working a lot harder, / by being a lot smarter, / by being a self-starter." This may account for the universal acclaim Hamilton has received from conservative commentators.[20] Such a narrative is particularly problematic in this case, as it belies the ways in which structural inequalities block many people of color from achieving the American Dream today. It is also historically inappropriate, given that the play is set in a world in which, no matter how much harder they worked, the direct ancestors of the black and brown actors who populate the stage and sing these lines would never have been able to get as far as a white man like Alexander Hamilton could.

The play can thus be seen as insidiously invested in trumpeting the deeds of wealthy white men, at the expense of everyone else, despite its multiracial casting. It is unambiguously celebratory of Hamilton and Washington, and though it makes fun of Jefferson, he is nonetheless a pivotal figure. Sadly, that is where this revolutionary musical fails to push any envelopes: the history it tells is essentially the same whitewashed version of the founding era that has lost favor among many academic and public historians. Here there is only space for white heroes.

In an interview with the *Wall Street Journal*, cast member Leslie Odom Jr. said that, before being in the show, "I was a student of African-American history. I cared way more about the achievements and hard-won battles of black people in this country than I did about the founding fathers. But this show has been such a gift to me in that way because I feel that it's my history, too, for the first time ever. We all fought in the Revolutionary War. I think this show is going to hopefully make hundreds of thousands of people of color feel a part of something that we don't often feel a part of."[21] But is it necessarily a good thing to feel ownership over a celebratory, white narrative of the American past? Is it a good thing for people of color to feel connected to the story of Hamilton, Washington, Jefferson, Madison, and Burr? Or is this the historical version of the Clarks' Doll Test that was so pivotal in the *Brown v. Board of Education* decision, encouraging people of color to see the important past as limited to the deeds of white men, while further silencing the historical role of people of color?

It is also noteworthy that people of color probably do not comprise the majority of the audience—the Broadway League finds that about 80 percent of all Broadway ticket buyers are white.[22] This does not stop creators and spectators from repeatedly calling the musical "accessible," which is coded language suggesting that young people and people of color cannot understand history unless it is made "accessible" to them. Treasury Secretary John Lew said that when talking with Miranda, Chernow, and the cast, "They kept coming back to the importance of bringing history to a broader audience, and they talked about raising money to bring more students to future shows, to open it up in an accessible way to expose more people to a very important chapter of our history."[23] Embedded here is the rhetoric of access and exposure that plagues museums and historic sites that are wedded to missions of "sharing" the exclusive past with a public that wants something more.

In this case, there are also racial implications to the plan, funded by the Rockefeller Foundation and the Gilder Lehrman Institute of American History, to bring twenty thousand public school students to the show: in New York City, the overwhelming majority of schoolchildren are black and brown.[24] Whenever a historical story is shared, it has an ideological component. What ideology is being inculcated by a show like this, at the same time that it engages its audience?

The musical undoubtedly does have a special impact on this audience. Seth Andrew, the founder of Democracy Prep Public Schools, took 120 students to see the show and reported, "It was unquestionably the most profound impact I've ever seen on a student body."[25] And Miranda has noted that young people "come alive in their heads" when they're watching the show.[26] If the goal is to make them excited about theater, music, and live performance, great. But reviews of the show regularly imply that what is powerful about the show is how it brings *history* to life. So I ask again: Is this the history that we most want black and brown youth to connect with—one in which black lives so clearly do not matter?

NOTES

This essay was previously published as "Race-Conscious Casting and the Erasure of the Black Past in Lin-Manuel Miranda's *Hamilton*," in *The Public Historian* 38, no. 1 (February 2016): 89–98.

1. H. W. Brands, "Founders Chic," *Atlantic*, September 2003, http://www.theatlantic.com/magazine/archive/2003/09/founders-chic/302773/.

2. Richard Handler and Eric Gable, *The New History in an Old Museum: Creating the Past at Colonial Williamsburg* (Durham, NC: Duke University Press, 1997); Cathy Stanton, *The Lowell Experiment: Public History in a Postindustrial City* (Amherst: University of Massachusetts Press, 2006); "Slavery at Jefferson's Monticello: Paradox of Liberty," http://slavery.monticello.org/slavery-at-monticello.

3. Michael Paulson, "'Hamilton' Heads to Broadway in a Hip-Hop Retelling," *New York Times*, July 12, 2015, http://www.nytimes.com/2015/07/13/theater/hamilton-heads-to-broadway-in-a-hip-hop-retelling.html.

4. For more on Miranda's use of history, see his discussion of his ahistorical choices on Rap Genius (http://genius.com/Lin_Manuel), and Joanne B. Freeman's assessment of his use of history "How *Hamilton* Uses History," *Slate*, November 11, 2015, http://www.slate.com/articles/arts/culturebox/2015/11/how_lin_manuel_miranda_used_real_history_in_writing_hamilton.html.

5. Ishmael Reed, "'Hamilton: The Musical': Black Actors Dress Up Like Slave Traders . . . and It's Not Halloween," *CounterPunch*, August 21, 2015, http://www.counterpunch.org/2015/08/21/hamilton-the-musical-black-actors-dress-up-like-slave-tradersand-its-not-halloween.

6. Branden Janese, "'Hamilton' Roles Are This Rapper's Delight," *Wall Street Journal*, July 7, 2015, http://www.wsj.com/articles/hamilton-roles-are-this-rappers-delight-1436303922.

7. Hilton Als, "Boys in the Band," *New Yorker*, March 9, 2015, http://www.newyorker.com/magazine/2015/03/09/boys-in-the-band.

8. Quoted in Judy Rosen, "The American Revolutionary," *T Magazine*, July 8, 2015, 59.

9. Quoted in Janese, "'Hamilton' Roles Are This Rapper's Delight."

10. Jennifer Schuessler, "Starring on Broadway, Obama and Alexander Hamilton," *ArtsBeat* (blog), *New York Times*, July 18, 2015, http://artsbeat.blogs.nytimes.com/2015/07/18/starring-on-broadway-obama-and-alexander-hamilton.

11. Paulson, "'Hamilton' Heads to Broadway in a Hip-Hop Retelling."

12. Patrick Rael, "The Long Death of Slavery," in *Slavery in New York*, edited by Ira Berlin and Leslie M. Harris (New York: New Press, 2005), 114.

13. Steven Mintz, "New York and Slavery," *New-York Journal of American History* 66, no. 2 (Fall/Winter 2005): 54.

14. Paul R. Misencik, *The Original American Spies: Seven Covert Agents of the Revolutionary War* (Jefferson, NC: McFarland, 2014), 110–122.

15. Comment on Joseph A. Adelman, "Hamilton, Art, History, and Truth," *The Junto* (blog), August 31, 2015, http://earlyamericanists.com/2015/08/31/hamilton-art-history-and-truth.

16. Miranda, "Cabinet Battle #1," *Hamilton*.

17. Quoted in Rosen, "American Revolutionary."

18. Rebecca Mead, "All about the Hamiltons," *New Yorker*, February 9, 2015, http://www.newyorker.com/magazine/2015/02/09/hamiltons.

19. Quoted in ibid.

20. David Brooks, "The Hamilton Experience," *New York Times*, February 24, 2015, http://www.nytimes.com/2015/02/24/opinion/david-brooks-the-hamilton-experience.html; Peggy Noonan, "How to Stage a Revolution," *Wall Street Journal*, April 10, 2015, http://www.wsj.com/articles/how-to-stage-a-revolution-1428620603; Richard Brookhiser, "Funky Founder," *National Review*, March 21, 2015, http://www.nationalreview.com/article/415767/funky-founder-richard-brookhiser.

21. Quoted in Kathryn Lurie, "Playing the Man Who Shot Hamilton," *Wall Street Journal*, August 6, 2015, http://www.wsj.com/articles/playing-the-man-who-shot-hamilton-1438896589.

22. Michael Paulson, "New American Stories," *New York Times*, September 13, 2015, sec. AR; Broadway League, "The Demographics of the Broadway

Audience, 2013–2014," http://www.broadwayleague.com/index.php?url_identi fier1/4the-demographics-of-the-broadway-audience.

23. Annie Lowrey, "Treasury Secretary Jack Lew Loved Hamilton," *Daily Intelligencer* (blog), *New York*, August 27, 2015, http://nymag.com/daily/intelli gencer/2015/08/treasury-secretary-jack-lew-loved-hamilton.html.

24. Gordon Cox, "Broadway's 'Hamilton' Will Play to 20,000 New York City Public School Students," *Variety*, October 27, 2015, http://variety.com/2015/ legit/news/hamilton-tickets-new-york-city-public-school-students-1201627589/.

25. Quoted in Paulson, "'Hamilton' Heads to Broadway in a Hip-Hop Retelling."

26. Quoted in Simon Vozick-Levinson, "Revolution on Broadway: Inside Hip-Hop History Musical 'Hamilton,'" *Rolling Stone*, August 6, 2015, http:// www.rollingstone.com/culture/features/revolution-on-broadway-inside-hip -hop-history-musical-hamilton-20150806.

CHAPTER 4

The Greatest City in the World?

Slavery in New York in the Age of Hamilton

LESLIE M. HARRIS

Lin-Manuel Miranda's *Hamilton: An American Musical* is undoubt-edly a celebration of New York's immigrant history and its cen-trality to the nation's history. By depicting Alexander Hamilton as an immigrant who moved from rags in the Caribbean to riches in New York City amid the establishment of the new nation, and by having people of color portray the founding fathers, their wives and their sisters, Miranda has reinforced the United States' and New York's perception of themselves as a nation and a city of immigrants. "Immigrants, we get the job done!" declare Hamilton and Lafayette as they prepare for the Battle of Yorktown. In this play, the "job" is military service during the Revolutionary War, as well as the intel-lectual labor necessary to the creation of the Constitution, the fed-eral government, and our economic system.

But claiming Hamilton's migration to North America as the ultimate immigrant story obscures two elements of the nature of migration in Hamilton's era. One is that that Hamilton is traveling within the British Empire as a British citizen, and thus is not an immigrant from the Caribbean in the ways that we would imagine his status today. As I will discuss below, Hamilton is actually part of a small and elite group of migrants with significant cultural and financial capital. Secondly, Miranda has also reinscribed the invisi-bility of one group of migrants in the story of American progress: enslaved Africans. Few accounts of our immigrant past include the forced migration of African laborers, who were the majority of

immigrants (migrants *in*) to the Americas in Hamilton's era. Histories of twentieth-century U.S. immigration have only recently begun
to include African-descended peoples' migration to the United States
from Africa, Latin America, and the Caribbean as part of the history of American immigration; in these histories, the Statue of Liberty stands watch only over European migrants.[1] Surely it is difficult
to fit the history of African forced migrations into the generally
celebratory tone of traditional immigrant histories that are characterized by the desire for freedom: the vast majority of people of
African descent arrived in the Americas between the sixteenth and
late nineteenth centuries chained in the holds of stinking slave ships.
And only for a very few was movement out of slavery and into freedom and "riches" possible.

James Madison and Thomas Jefferson warn Hamilton of the
dangers of discussing slavery in "Cabinet Battle #3," a scene deleted
from the play and the only one that engages the issue of slavery. If
emancipation is included in the Constitution, "Every single slave
owner will demand compensation," and Jefferson will be slandered
with talk of his enslaved "mistresses." "Do you really wanna have
that conversation?" Madison and Jefferson ask. Hamilton replies,
"No," and George Washington makes the final decision to take
the topic off the table: "Slavery's too volatile an issue. We won't get
through it."[2] But by ignoring this shameful history, and the fact that
slavery was indeed discussed thoroughly during the Constitutional
Convention, the musical downplays one of the central moral dilemmas for the founding fathers; in addition it erases the contributions of people of African descent, particularly those enslaved in the
northern states, whose history is less well known. Enslaved people's
labor was foundational to the building of New York City and to
the economy that made not only New York but also the Americas a
place of opportunity for Europeans. Enslaved and free black people's
critique of the Revolutionary era, through their actions and their
writings and their insistent claims for more inclusive definitions of
freedom are crucial to understanding the founding years that *Hamilton* depicts. The history of African Americans in New York during

the Revolutionary era and the Early Republic creates an important counterpoint to the celebratory story of the rise of American freedom, and helps explain the more conservative elements of the Hamiltonian Revolution—not only in terms of race, but also in terms of its vision for the nation as a whole. In the end, *Hamilton* is racially mischievous but not transformative or radical theater. Like Pinkster and Governor's Day—the colonial holidays during which slaves in some of the northern colonies got to elect governors and rule for the day—the play uses racial allegory and the specter of slavery to avoid direct confrontations with either.

Slavery underpinned the economy of the Americas, and thus, the economy and financial culture of New York. Enslaved people were also a critical part of the labor force. Owning slaves was a way to attain and consolidate wealth, and served as a sign of elite status and economic savvy. Today, participation in the stock market or employment of workers as a small business owner indicates a level of status, independence, and business acumen that is highly prized, even if difficult to maintain. In the same way, in the eighteenth century, ownership of slaves, whether a few or many, represented a step beyond working for oneself. Slavery could also produce great wealth, as was true for George Washington, Thomas Jefferson, and Alexander Hamilton, all of whom married into the families made rich by slaves.

We have recently begun to better understand the importance of slave owning to our founding fathers, thanks to the work of scholars such as Annette Gordon-Reed, Henry Wiencek, and Erica Armstrong Dunbar.[3] Historians and journalists have also started to challenge the false division between the southern part of the United States as a land of slavery and the northern part as a land of freedom by revealing the centrality of slavery to all thirteen insurgent British North American colonies, to the development of capitalism, and to institutions ranging from universities to the legal system to the federal government itself. Indeed, recent controversies about the meaning of the three-fifths compromise in the Constitution have forced public questioning of the degree to which our founders could have

imagined a world without slavery. Predictably, and fruitfully, scholars are divided on this question, and yet to have the debate is to
reinforce the centrality of slavery to its rightful place in the pre–
Civil War United States.[4]

Rather than focusing on the absence of slavery from the play,
as others have, I want to raise three questions about Alexander
Hamilton's world as it related to slavery in the eighteenth century.
First, what was the importance of slavery to Alexander Hamilton
himself? Second, what was the importance of slavery to New York
City at the time of Hamilton's arrival in the city, and how did slavery in New York compare to Hamilton's experiences in St. Kitts,
Nevis, and St. Croix? Finally, what were the contours and the intentions of antislavery activism in the eighteenth century, and where
does Hamilton fit into that picture?

Asking these questions reveals the ways in which the American
Revolution retained hierarchies based on race and labor, even as
it pointed to a future much less hierarchical. While violent change
was common during this era throughout the Atlantic World—as
exemplified in the American Revolutionary War, the French and
the Haitian Revolutions, and the expulsion of Native Americans
from the new nation—many whites feared as much as anything
the possibility of slave revolts and retribution by free black people
against their former white owners. This fear made them reluctant to
arm blacks in exchange for freedom during the American Revolution. It also made white Americans very uneasy about the Haitian
Revolution: the revolt of enslaved people against French rule, if successful, might also lead to racial uprisings in the United States. The
variety of ways in which slavery ended between the late eighteenth
century and the late nineteenth century indicate how difficult it
was to undo the system of slavery—and the many ways it happened.[5] Our question, then, is not about whether it was possible
to end slavery, but whether those who worked toward ending it—
Hamilton included—were willing to make real sacrifices in order to
do so, much as they had for their own freedom from the British.

Alexander Hamilton, Slavery, and Antislavery

> Rachel assigned a little boy named Ajax as a house slave to
> Alexander. . . . This early exposure to the humanity of the slaves
> may have made a lasting impression on Hamilton, who would be
> conspicuous among the founding fathers for his fierce abolitionism.
>
> —RON CHERNOW, *Alexander Hamilton*

> A job with a slave trader [in St. Croix] rescued him from poverty.
> Donations from slave traders saved him from despair. His new life
> [in New York] began with his arrival on a slave trader's ship. . . .
> His tuition and fees were paid from the sale of barrels of rum,
> manufactured on slave plantations, that Cruger's firm sent to
> New York.
>
> —CRAIG WILDER, *Ebony and Ivy*

> . . . while slaves were being slaughtered / And carted across the
> water
>
> —LIN-MANUEL MIRANDA, "Alexander Hamilton,"
> *Hamilton: An American Musical*

Ron Chernow at length, Craig Wilder succinctly, and Miranda in a phrase all make clear that slavery was central to Alexander Hamilton's life.[6] Hamilton's success, New York City's prosperity, and indeed, the economic trajectory of the Americas were all built on slavery. Indeed, Hamilton's connection to slavery is emblematic of the many aspects of the slave trade that underpinned the colonial Atlantic economy, of which New York was a crucial part. Few Europeans at the time questioned the centrality of slave labor to the success of the American and European economies. Slavery existed throughout the Americas, in every European colony. As the historian David Eltis has detailed, enslaved Africans formed the majority of migrants to the Americas before 1820. British ships alone imported three Africans for every European they brought to the Americas—and Britain was not even the largest importer of African slaves. Slavery was legal until the late eighteenth century in most European countries. Enslaved black people were the norm, not the exception, in the creation of European economic wealth. For most Europeans in the Americas in the eighteenth century, slave labor, directly or indirectly, was crucial to their survival.[7]

Enslaved blacks outnumbered whites in the part of the world where Alexander Hamilton was born. On Nevis, the Caribbean island of Alexander Hamilton's birth, there were eight times as many enslaved blacks as whites in the population; on St. Croix, where he came into his youth, the proportion was twelve to one. Both of these islands thrived on the production of sugar produced on plantations by enslaved people. Hamilton spent most of his life in the admittedly small ports of Charlestown in St. Kitts, and Christiansted in St. Croix: his mother and father were merchants, albeit not very successful ones, in these places.[8] His mother's parents owned approximately ten slaves on a small sugar plantation on Nevis. From them, Hamilton's mother Rachel inherited at least three adult female slaves who made up part of the household retinue of five adult females and four child slaves who Hamilton knew in these early years of his life. In addition to employing enslaved labor in her business and household, Rachel also hired out her slaves for additional income.

How did growing up in a slave society shape the young Alexander? Hamilton biographer Ron Chernow argues that he may have felt more kindly toward enslaved blacks due to the fact that one of the children, a young boy named Ajax, helped take care of him. But a host of contemporaries and historians have argued that such connections between slave-owning children and enslaved people led to the opposite: a sense of elitism and entitlement to the labor of slaves as well as to the inherited wealth bondspeople often represented. As Thomas Jefferson stated in *Notes on the State of Virginia*, "The whole commerce between master and slave is a perpetual exercise of the most boisterous passions, the most unremitting despotism on the one part, and degrading submissions on the other. Our children see this, and learn to imitate it. . . . This quality is the germ of all education in him. . . . The parent storms, the child looks on, catches the lineaments of wrath, puts on the same airs in the circle of smaller slaves, gives a loose to his worst of passions, and thus nursed, educated, and daily exercised in tyranny, cannot but be stamped by it with odious peculiarities."[9] Indeed, many children of slave owners had early relationships with enslaved caretakers, but these intimate relationships rarely led them to develop an antislavery mentality. Instead, children raised by and around enslaved people more typically developed a sense of ownership over them, and came to see them as all whites did: as a central source of wealth to be passed down through families along with land, furniture, and other goods in wills and as gifts, used as collateral for loans, and sold to pay debts.

The harsh reality of slavery on sugar plantations and in port cities did drive a few European residents of the Caribbean to develop arguments against the institution. Benjamin and Sarah Lay, Quakers from Britain, lasted only two years as shopkeepers in Barbados between 1718 and 1720 before fleeing back to England for twelve years; they migrated once again to Philadelphia by 1732. According to Benjamin, the Lays tried to help the undernourished enslaved people they saw daily in Barbados by distributing food too rotten to sell to their free customers, but this action only emboldened enslaved people to steal from them repeatedly in search of the food denied them by their owners. In addition, Sarah witnessed their Quaker neighbor hang an enslaved man upside down and then whip him until his blood pooled under him. These shocking abuses led the Lays to leave Barbados and the opportunities for wealth creation the island had held for them. In both England and Philadelphia, the Lays became outspoken critics of the wrongs of slavery, refusing to use slave-produced goods—most obviously, sugar—and publicly criticizing fellow Quakers who continued to sell slaves and employ slave labor. Benjamin's actions led to his censure by the Friends in England and in Philadelphia, and his ultimate expulsion from the Philadelphia Yearly Meeting before his death in 1759, although the Quakers reclaimed him as an early antislavery activist later in the century.[10]

The extraordinary lengths to which the Lays went to separate themselves from slavery in the Caribbean and in North America stand in stark contrast to Hamilton's accommodating path during his time in the Caribbean and after his arrival in New York. To be fair, the Lays' actions represented a form of antislavery activism that was viewed as extreme by their contemporaries. Furthermore, any decision to oppose slavery that Hamilton might have desired to make during his time in the Caribbean would have been limited by his youth, and even more importantly, by his father's desertion of his family and the twin losses of his mother and the cousin who had guardianship over him following his mother's death.

The play makes much of the early death of Hamilton's mother as a way to emphasize how his move from the Caribbean to New York City was a move from rags to riches. But it bears noting that Hamilton, even with all of these difficulties, was still part of a tiny elite in the Americas. His forebears, as *free* migrants, were among the 10 percent of those aboard British ships who did not come to the Americas already beholden to labor for someone else. In other words, 90 percent of those who came to the Americas on British ships before 1800 were either African slaves or Europeans who were indentured or indebted to others.[11] Hamilton was descended from the independent 10 percent who were not. As such, he was no doubt recognized in the small European communities of which he was part as a legitimate heir to cultural capital, even though his mother's first husband had obtained a ruling against him as a legitimate heir to his mother's estate.

His father's desertion and the loss of his mother and his guardian were certainly emotionally and economically wrenching. But Hamilton's economic difficulties were temporary. Indeed, his absorption into a wealthy merchant family shortly after his guardian's death, and his clerkship with the St. Croix office of the New York firm Beekman and Cruger would quickly set him back on the path to economic security and wealth. But these experiences also reinforced for him the obvious link between wealth and slavery as an economic institution: Beekman and Cruger provisioned slave-owning planters with all they needed to be successful, and at least once a year, the firm invested in a shipment of slaves from Africa, the riskiest and yet highest investment return for one's money in the eighteenth century. Hamilton was caught in the classic moral dilemma of the late eighteenth century as freedom emerged as a central tenet of the Revolutionary era: his new life following the death of his mother and cousin provided him with more financial stability and opportunities for education and future elite status than he had ever had before. Yet, that path was paved with the bodies of enslaved people.

By the time Hamilton left the Caribbean for North America in 1773, he had been profoundly shaped by slavery—as was true of everyone else in the Americas at this time. His move to New York placed him amid the largest urban slave population in Britain's mainland American colonies.

People of African Descent in Hamilton's New York

In New York you can be a new man

> —LIN-MANUEL MIRANDA, "Alexander Hamilton,"
> *Hamilton: An American Musical*

It rather hurts an European eye to see so many negro slaves upon the streets, tho' they are said to deminish yearly here.

> —PATRICK M'ROBERT, 1774

In 1774, Scottish traveler to New York, Patrick M'Robert, complained that "It rather hurts an European eye to see so many negro slaves upon the streets,"[12] but for Alexander Hamilton, streets teeming with people of African descent would have been the norm from his childhood. Indeed, compared to the Caribbean, New York City had many *fewer* enslaved people, who formed between 14 to 16 percent of the population in the pre–Revolutionary War years. But the port city's deep reliance on slavery would have been familiar to, and perhaps even comfortable for, this ambitious young migrant. The founding of Dutch New Amsterdam and its subsequent seizure in the late seventeenth century by the British, who renamed it New York, were both rooted in the hopes that it would become the central North American slave market. By the time of Hamilton's arrival,

Rhode Island's merchants had bested New York in that department.[13] But the early goals for the slave trade, as well as the New
York colony's continued involvement in provisioning slave societies
to the south, ensured that the city contained the largest number of
urban slaves outside of the South. When Hamilton arrived in New
York in 1772, 14.3 percent of the city's population and 20 percent
of the colony's population were of African descent. As importantly,
40 percent of New York City households owned slaves—a larger
percentage than the quarter of southern households that owned
slaves in the antebellum U.S. South.[14]

Enslaved people of African descent labored throughout the city,
often working and living intimately with whites of all classes. White

This 1642 Dutch engraving shows the presence of African slaves from the
earliest days of settlement in New Amsterdam, which eventually became
New York. *(Sarin Images/Granger—All rights reserved)*

artisans who lived and worked in household workshops owned an average of one or two enslaved people. They typically performed domestic work or helped in making shoes, carpentering, iron working, and other trades, and then slept in kitchens, cellars, attics, and workshops just steps away from white families. In wealthier households, slightly larger retinues of enslaved people—five or more—were responsible for the upkeep of households as cooks, butlers, and maids, as well as performing the more intimate labor of taking care of children and assisting men and women with their toilets. Slave owners also hired out enslaved people to those who did not have their own slaves, thus creating additional ways to extract wealth from their labor. Enslaved people worked unloading ships on the port city's docks, in hotels, as assistants in shops—there was no part of the economy where enslaved laborers were excluded, although white workers regularly attempted to stem competition with them. Although Patrick M'Robert was told during his pre-Revolutionary visit to the city that slavery was on the decline, in fact the number of slaves increased after the Revolutionary War, even after New York passed its first gradual emancipation law in 1799. In short, white New Yorkers were comfortable with owning slaves and with making money from the slave trade and slave-produced goods. Into the first decade of the nineteenth century, owning an enslaved person remained a sign of wealth and status for the city's elite.[15]

Alexander Hamilton's marriage to Elizabeth Schuyler in 1780 brought him into one of the wealthiest slave-owning families in the soon-to-be state of New York. Elizabeth was descended from the Dutch Schuyler and Van Rensselaer families, both of which owned thousands of acres of farmland in upstate colonial New York. Farms in the North did not grow the labor-intensive crops that led southern plantation owners to assemble large numbers of slave laborers. But these farms did make money provisioning southern colonies with foods such as flour and butter, commodities that were not produced on farms obsessed with money-making crops. Slaves on these northern farms labored outdoors to produce provisioning goods, and they performed endless tasks in the mansions of farm owners

For Sale,
A LIKELY, HEALTHY, YOUNG
NEGRO WENCH,
BETWEEN fifteen and sixteen Years old:
She has been used to the Farming Business. Sold for want of Employ.—Enquire at
No. 81, William-street.
New-York, March 30, 1789.

Ads promoting the sale of enslaved people were
common in New York City newspapers in the late
eighteenth century. *(Schomburg Center for Research in
Black Culture, Photographs and Prints Division, The New
York Public Library, Astor, Lenox and Tilden Foundations)*

that supported the elite lifestyle of these founding New Yorkers.
Elizabeth's father Phillip Schuyler owned an estate near Albany, New
York's capital, along with up to twenty-seven slaves, which made him
one of the elite slave owners in eighteenth-century New York. The
largest was the Philipse family of Philipsburg Manor, who owned
close to fifty slaves in the lower Hudson Valley.[16] Both Elizabeth
and Alexander spent time at the Schuyler mansion: Elizabeth during the war and her first pregnancy and Alexander when engaged in
state business. Thus, both would have been well acquainted with the
various forms of slavery practiced in both rural and urban New
York. They would have seen their own future wealth, via inheritance,
tied up at least partially in slave property. And they would have
been concerned about what offering freedom to enslaved people
would have meant for the maintenance of their lives, both on a
daily basis in terms of the labor enslaved people provided, and in
terms of cash value.[17]

The Hamiltons settled in New York City in 1783, as the war ended.
In doing so, they were part of a reclamation of the city by American
forces newly suspicious of the black labor in their midst. During the
war, New York had become a center of black resistance to the Patriot
side. The British, following Lord Dunmore's Proclamation, offered

freedom to blacks who joined them in the fight against the Americans. In contrast, the Patriots offered emancipation only sparingly, with each province determining whether it would enlist blacks and offer freedom to the enslaved in return for service. In the end, neither the British nor the Patriots did particularly well by enslaved Americans during the war. Only 800 southern slaves made it to the British lines, and they were forced to serve as laborers, since British corps refused to arm and employ them as soldiers; many died of smallpox and other diseases during their service. In addition, slaves owned by Loyalists were not included in Dunmore's offer. But those who left Patriot owners and made it to New York City found greater opportunities. Between the beginning of the British occupation of the city in September 1776 and the war's end in 1783, thousands of former slaves made their way to the city. After the British surrender, from 3,000 to 5,000 Loyalist blacks left through New York's port with the former occupiers and their Tory allies, with most heading to Nova Scotia and London, although some were reenslaved in British Caribbean islands.[18] Americans would seek the return of Patriot slave property for decades to come, to no avail.

But not all enslaved people sided with the British, and the years during and after the American Revolution also include the story people of African descent struggling to expand the meaning of American freedom to include their own emancipation. Hamilton, like other New York revolutionaries, initially ignored the pleas of Marquis de Lafayette and other antislavery European allies to end slavery as part of the fulfillment of the American Revolution's ideas. In doing so, Hamilton and his fellow founders lost the opportunity to capitalize on the destabilization of slavery in both the North and South at the end of the Revolutionary War. They of course feared losing the southern colonies but also recognized the importance of slave labor to the new nation's economy. The northern states that provided for gradual emancipation during and immediately after the Revolutionary War were those that were least dependent on slave labor or that contained a relatively small number of slaves: Vermont, Pennsylvania, Connecticut, Massachusetts, and Rhode

Island. In contrast, New York and New Jersey were the last two
states to legislate gradual emancipation, in 1799 and 1804 respec-
tively, indicative of both the large number of slaves each held and
the centrality of slave labor to their economies. Indeed, although
New York finally ended slavery in the state in 1827, New Jersey's last
enslaved people only gained freedom with the passage of the Thir-
teenth Amendment after the Civil War.[19]

In New York, Hamilton was a founding member of the New
York Manumission Society, the central voice of the antislavery movement: this has been cited as crucial evidence of his abolitionist sen-
timents. Founded in New York City in 1785, the society's board
contained Quakers and others who had completely divested of their
slaves; it also contained slave owners such as John Jay and those who
had a relationship to slavery, like Hamilton. As Chernow discusses,
Hamilton did attempt to push the manumission society to more
actively end slavery. Shortly after its founding, the Ways and Means
Committee of which he was a member proposed that manumission
society members free their adult slaves: those about forty-five years
old should be freed immediately; those between ages twenty-eight
and thirty-eight should gain freedom in seven years; and those
under twenty-eight should be freed by age thirty-five. Although
this detailed timetable would have provided most slave owners
with many years of labor from their slaves, as well as released them
from caring for elderly slaves, the manumission society refused to
agree to the plan, and Hamilton's committee was dissolved. Hamilton continued his work with the manumission society, however, and
even became a legal counselor, assisting free blacks who whites ille-
gally claimed as their slaves, and trying to prevent New York's slave
owners from selling their slaves south as the possibility of gradual
emancipation loomed.[20] The New York Manumission Society did
real work to end slavery. But members of the society argued for
gradual emancipation, and most did not free their own slaves during their lifetimes. Indeed, the historian Shane White has argued
that if the members of the manumission society had emancipated

their own slaves in 1795, they would have freed 10 percent of the enslaved people in New York City.[21]

It remains unclear whether Hamilton actually owned slaves during this time period. But his in-laws certainly did and at times he supported his relatives in maintaining their business relationships to slavery, balancing his antislavery commitments and his family's commitments to slave labor in a way that was typical of elite New Yorkers of the time. He may have purchased slaves for his wife's sister Angelica and her husband John Church in 1796 and 1797. In 1799, an enslaved woman named Sarah who the Churches brought with them to New York from Maryland turned to the manumission society to gain her freedom: once in New York, enslaved people from other locales were to be freed, under the law. It may have been through Hamilton's intervention that Sarah did gain her freedom, but the Churches continued to employ other slaves as laborers in the waning days of slavery in New York. Alexander and Elizabeth also occasionally hired enslaved people to labor in their home.[22]

The gradual emancipation law that New York passed in 1799, just five years before Hamilton's death, freed no slaves. Rather, it freed the children born to enslaved mothers on and after July 4, 1799, after they had served their mothers' owners. That period of continued bondage lasted until age twenty-one if that child was female, and twenty-eight if male. The law reflected the concerns that whites had about the ability of formerly enslaved people to survive in freedom. Although some antislavery activists were concerned about the impact of racism on blacks, and the ways in which whites would exclude blacks from participating as full citizens economically and politically, more were driven by the belief that black people could not survive independent of white control without a lengthy apprenticeship to freedom. The differing ages for freeing the offspring of enslaved women also indicate a further motive behind the law: a desire to extract labor from these indentured servants as a partial repayment to slave owners for the loss of economic capital the emancipation law represented. Freeing women earlier meant that owners would not be responsible for the children women might bear while indentured; indeed, many New York City slave owners in particular had long discouraged enslaved women from bearing children by selling them if they were perceived to be too fertile.

Passed long after the end of hostilities with Britain, New York's emancipation law was not approved entirely because of revolutionary fervor, despite its July 4 start date. Indeed, many historians agree that the legislature passed the law because the growing number of European immigrants to the city made it economically possible for New York's lawmakers to imagine a workforce without slavery. Unfortunately, over the course of the nineteenth century, imagining a workforce without slavery would also lead white workers and employers to also imagine a workforce without blacks. As slavery ended, white workers began to exclude New York's black men from skilled artisan positions. Throughout the antebellum era, black workers were also excluded from the nascent union movement; after the 1840s, black and Irish workers battled for the lowest rungs on the employment ladder; eventually, the Irish won this battle for employment and equality. While New York was a land of opportunity for European immigrants, it became a land of limited freedoms and inequality for the city's first, forced migrants, people of African descent.

Finally, emancipation had dire consequences for some enslaved New Yorkers. Even with the terms of the indentures favoring slave owners as they did, some owners did try to sell enslaved people south to recoup their losses more directly, which was in violation of the law. Active members of the New York Manumission Society began to protect enslaved people from being sold south; Hamilton may have been among them. In doing so, the society began a slow pivot away from the most conservative aspects of the law they had worked to pass, toward greater cooperation with blacks themselves to preserve and expand their freedom. This was a struggle that would continue long after Hamilton's death in 1804.

Conclusion

> Do you really wanna have that conversation?
> Slavery's too volatile an issue. We won't get through it.
>
> —LIN-MANUEL MIRANDA, "Cabinet Battle #3,"
> *Hamilton Mixtape*

In the fall of 2005, a year and a half after Ron Chernow's *Alexander Hamilton* appeared, and a decade before *Hamilton: An American Musical*, the New-York Historical Society opened its path-breaking exhibition "Slavery in New York." All three works were designed to appeal to popular audiences and all were phenomenally successful. As an expert on African Americans in New York City before the Civil War, I was one of the advisers to "Slavery in New York." My goal was to bring out of the shadows the ways in which New York City, home to Alexander Hamilton for the last decades of his life, relied on slavery and enslaved people of African descent for its establishment, survival, and wealth; and how African Americans contributed to the political ideas of this nation. Yet even as Lin-Manual Miranda's phenomenally successful musical uses contemporary black art forms to bring to life an acknowledged "founding father" of the United States, to date too few studies of the founding fathers or the history of slavery have successfully interpenetrated stories like those of Alexander Hamilton.[23] While Miranda has tried to modernize the presentation of Hamilton, he does so without dealing with one of the central connections between past and present: the diverse social and racial reality within which Hamilton lived in New York City. Indeed, Chernow's book does a better job with this than does the play.

I am sympathetic to one of the strongest themes of the musical: "Immigrants: we get the job done!" *Hamilton*, like Lin-Manuel Miranda's earlier musical, *In the Heights*, celebrates the immigrant past of this nation in ways that we clearly still need to be reminded of today. But as with the vast majority of the work on U.S. immigration, the role of the forced migration of millions of enslaved people of African descent remains absent from the center of these celebratory immigration histories. Miranda portrays New York City as a land of opportunity for Hamilton; by extension, he implies, it was a land of opportunity for everyone. It is, the show's characters proudly sing, "the greatest city in the world." But this depiction of New York's immigrants as a success story is only possible by excising the forced migration of people of African descent from that story about the past. It means ignoring the complex histories of so many other immigrant groups who struggled for decades, if not centuries, to achieve the dream of equality. Indeed, many of these immigrant groups succeeded by distinguishing themselves explicitly from the fate of African Americans, enslaved and free. By buying into definitions of the nation that reified European ancestry, and then American whiteness, immigrant groups such as the Irish in the antebellum period, and European Jews and Italians in the twentieth century, helped to create a history that erased the labor, physical and intellectual, of people of African descent who had argued for a more radical definition of freedom.[24] This freedom, born in the same revolution that Hamilton promoted, included doing away with slavery; granting freedom to all who fought on behalf of the American Patriots; and asking for equal pay for equal work. This freedom would be centuries in the making, and may still be incomplete.

Rather than having those people populate *Hamilton*, and complicating the idea of revolution and of freedom, even briefly, Miranda's play calls to mind an earlier tradition of an acceptable way for African Americans to participate in the body politic: Pinkster, or Governor's Day. This holiday, possible in the Northeast in a way that was too dangerous in the South, allowed a single day annually in which black communities in rural and urban settings, enslaved and free, could elect a king or governor for the day, to adjudicate disputes among both blacks and whites. Some historians have argued that this holiday was an important way for enslaved blacks to "practice" political activism, to make their needs and desires public, if only for a day. Some have linked Pinkster and Governor's Day back to African carnival traditions, as well as European traditions of misrule, in which those on the bottom were briefly on top.[25] As in *Hamilton*, blacks got to inhabit the roles of the elites—but only for a day.

The degree to which such festivals could diminish the power of slaveholding elites was highly limited. There are no accounts that depict kings or governors granting freedom to large swathes of northern slave communities nor even of punishing abusive enslavers. Indeed, most accounts don't discuss in any detail the distinctive political expressions of African Americans. As much as Pinkster and Governor's Day holidays may have shaped leadership patterns in African American communities, it's pretty clear that these holidays did little to change the attitudes of most whites toward African American political activism.

Indeed, as blacks gained freedom in New York, New Jersey, and Massachusetts, where these holidays were celebrated, they simultaneously lost the possibility of equal participation in mainstream politics, via suffrage and office holding. Pinkster and Governor's Day gradually disappeared from the landscape as free African Americans in the North turned almost immediately to the hard, decades-long work of redefining American freedom as a status inclusive of themselves and their still-enslaved brothers and sisters in the southern states, as well as to securing full and equal citizenship. In building antislavery societies, fighting for the ballot, and seeking economic equality, they did not simply inhabit the positions of the slaveholding founding fathers; rather, they critically engaged with the limits of the white founders' humanitarian vision, and claimed their own experiences—their own intellectual and physical labor—as integral to the success of the new nation.

NOTES

I'd like to thank Renee C. Romano, Claire Bond Potter, Caitlin Fitz, and Craig Wilder for their helpful comments and encouragement.

1. The recent controversy over Dr. Ben Carson's classification of enslaved people as immigrants highlights the ways in which we continue to choose to

see immigration as only a choice made willingly, rather than understanding the movements of people as forced by many different conditions, of which slavery is no doubt the most problematic. For an account of Carson's speech, see Liam Stack, "Ben Carson Refers to Slaves as 'Immigrants' in First Remarks to HUD Staff," *New York Times*, March 6, 2017, https://www.nytimes.com/2017/03/06/us/politics/ben-carson-refers-to-slaves-as-immigrants-in-first-remarks-to-hud-staff.html?_r=0. For a critique of Carson's speech, see Tera W. Hunter, "Slaves Weren't Immigrants. They Were Property," *Washington Post*, March 9, 2017, https://www.washingtonpost.com/posteverything/wp/2017/03/09/slaves-werent-immigrants-they-were-property/?utm_term=.3392ff25d0dd.

For twentieth-century histories of immigration that go out of their way to ignore people of African descent, see David Reimers, *Still the Golden Door: The Third World Comes to America* (New York: Columbia University Press, 1987). Subsequent books by Reimers include the post-1970s migrations, but ignore earlier migrations from the Caribbean. See Irma Watkins-Owens, *Blood Relations: Caribbean Immigrants and the Harlem Community, 1900–1930* (Bloomington: Indiana University Press, 1996) and Ira Berlin, *The Making of African America: The Four Great Migrations* (New York: Viking, 2010).

2. Lin-Manuel Miranda, "Cabinet Battle #3" lyrics, on https://genius.com/Lin-manuel-miranda-cabinet-battle-3-lyrics, accessed May 13, 2017.

3. Annette Gordon-Reed, *Thomas Jefferson and Sally Hemings: An American Controversy* (Charlottesville: University Press of Virginia, 1997); and idem, *The Hemingses of Monticello: An American Family* (New York: Norton, 2008); Lucia Stanton, *"Those Who Labor for My Happiness": Slavery at Thomas Jefferson's Monticello* (Charlottesville: University Press of Virginia, 2012); Henry Wiencek, *Master of the Mountain: Thomas Jefferson and His Slaves* (New York: Farrar, Straus, and Giroux, 2012); and idem, *An Imperfect God: George Washington, His Slaves, and the Creation of America* (New York: Farrar, Straus and Giroux, 2003); Erica Armstrong Dunbar, *Never Caught: The Washingtons' Relentless Pursuit of Their Runaway Slave, Ona Judge* (New York: Atria/37 INK, 2017). Note that Wiencek's 2003 book *An Imperfect God* claims to be the first written on Washington and slavery.

4. See "The Constitution's Immoral Compromise," *New York Times*, February 26, 2013, https://www.nytimes.com/roomfordebate/2013/02/26/the-constitutions-immoral-compromise; Sean Wilentz, "Constitutionally, Slavery Is No National Institution," *New York Times*, September 16, 2015, https://www.nytimes.com/2015/09/16/opinion/constitutionally-slavery-is-no-national-institution.html?_r=0; and David Waldstreicher, "How the Constitution Was Indeed Pro-Slavery," *The Atlantic*, September 19, 2015, https://www.theatlantic.com/

politics/archive/2015/09/how-the-constitution-was-indeed-pro-slavery/406
288/, for a few examples.

5. Patrick Rael, *Eighty-eight Years: The Long Death of Slavery in the United States, 1777–1865* (Athens: University of Georgia Press, 2015); Thomas Holt, *The Problem of Freedom: Race, Labor, and Politics in Jamaica and Britain, 1832–1936* (Baltimore: Johns Hopkins University Press, 1991); Ada Ferrer, *Freedom's Mirror: Cuba and Haiti in the Age of Revolution* (New York: Cambridge University Press, 2014); Christopher L. Brown, *Moral Capital: Foundations of British Abolitionism* (Chapel Hill: University of North Carolina Press, 2006); David Brion Davis, *The Problem of Slavery in the Age of Revolution, 1770–1823* (Ithaca, NY: Cornell University Press, 1975); and idem, *The Problem of Slavery in the Age of Emancipation* (New York: Knopf, 2014), to name just a few works that explore these questions.

6. Ron Chernow, *Alexander Hamilton* (New York: Penguin, 2003), 23; Craig Wilder, *Ebony and Ivory: Race, Slavery, and the Troubled History of America's Universities* (New York: Bloomsbury Press, 2013), 48; Manuel, "Alexander Hamilton," *Hamilton.*

7. David Eltis, *The Rise of African Slavery in the Americas* (Cambridge: Cambridge University Press, 2000), 8–14.

8. Chernow, *Alexander Hamilton*, 21, location 649, digital edition.

9. Thomas Jefferson, *Notes on the State of Virginia* (1787), edited by William Peden (1954, 1982; rpt. Chapel Hill: University of North Carolina Press, 2011), 162.

10. Andreas Mielke, "'What's here to do?' An Inquiry Concerning Sarah and Benjamin Lay, Abolitionists," *Quaker History* 86, no. 1 (Spring 1997): 22–44; Wilford P. Cole, "Henry Dawkins and the Quaker Comet," *Winterthur Portfolio* 4 (1968): 34–46, on Quaker reclaiming of Benjamin Lay as an antislavery activist.

11. Eltis, *Rise of African Slavery*, 8–14.

12. Patrick M'Robert and Carl Bridenbaugh, "Patrick M'Robert's 'Tour Through Part of the Northern Provinces of North America,'" *Pennsylvania Magazine of History and Biography* 59, no. 2 (April 1935): 142.

13. Christy Clark-Pujara, *Dark Work: The Business of Slavery in Rhode Island* (New York: NYU Press, 2016), chap. 1.

14. Leslie M. Harris, *In the Shadow of Slavery: African Americans in New York City, 1626–1863* (Chicago: University of Chicago Press, 2003), 46–47; David Gellman, *Emancipating New York: The Politics of Slavery and Freedom, 1777–1827* (Baton Rouge: Louisiana State University Press, 2006), 40–41.

15. On slaves as status symbols, see Shane White, *Somewhat More Independent: The End of Slavery in New York City, 1770–1810* (Athens: University of Georgia Press, 1991), 46; on slave labor, ibid., chaps. 1 and 2; and Harris, *In the Shadow of Slavery*, 26–33.

16. Chernow, *Alexander Hamilton*, 211. Historic Hudson Valley in Tarrytown, New York, manages Philipsburg Manor as a living history museum, and has completed a large amount of research about slavery on the site, and is currently working through an extensive web-based interpretation of slavery at the site and in the colonial North, funded by the NEH. See www.hudsonvalley.org.

17. For the best overview of slave-trading families and their involvement in the New York economy and politics see, "'Bonfires of the Negros': The Bloody Journey from Slave Traders to College Trustees," chapter 2 in Wilder, *Ebony and Ivy*, esp. 47–70. For Hamilton's marriage into the Schuyler family and issues with slavery, see Chernow, *Alexander Hamilton*, 211–212.

18. Benjamin Quarles, *The Negro in the American Revolution* (1961; rpt. Chapel Hill: University of North Carolina Press, 1996), remains the most thorough account of black activism during this time. See also Gary B. Nash, *The Forgotten Fifth: African Americans in the Age of the Revolution* (Cambridge, MA: Harvard University Press, 2006); Sylvia Frey, *Water from the Rock: Black Resistance in a Revolutionary Age* (Princeton, NJ: Princeton University Press, 1993); and Cassandra Pybus, *Epic Journeys of Freedom: Runaway Slaves of the American Revolution and Their Global Quest for Liberty* (Boston: Beacon Press, 2006). On the Revolution in New York City, see Graham Hodges, *Slavery, Freedom, and Culture among Early American Workers* (Armonk, NY: M. E. Sharpe, 1998), 65–86; and "Liberty and Constraint: The Limits of Revolution," in *Slavery in New York*, edited by Ira Berlin and Leslie M. Harris (New York: New Press, 2005).

19. Arthur Zilversmit, *First Emancipation: The Abolition of Slavery in the North* (Chicago: University of Chicago Press, 1967); Rael, *Eighty-eight Years*; Harris, *In the Shadow of Slavery*; James J. Gigantino II, *The Ragged Road to Abolition: Slavery and Freedom in New Jersey, 1777–1865* (Philadelphia: University of Pennsylvania Press, 2016).

20. Chernow, *Alexander Hamilton*, 214–218, 239–240, 581–582.

21. White, *Somewhat More Independent*, 86.

22. Chernow, *Alexander Hamilton*, 211–212. Chernow argues in this section that the Hamiltons may have occasionally hired enslaved people rather than owned them in the early years of their marriage; and that by 1804, they seem not to have owned any slaves at all, according to a letter written by Angelica Schuyler, Eliza Hamilton's sister.

23. The most successful example of this kind of work, which illuminates both the character of slavery and the character of a "founding father," is the work of Annette Gordon-Reed on the relationships between Thomas Jefferson and the enslaved members of the Hemings family.

24. David Roediger, *The Wages of Whiteness: Race and the Making of the American Working Class* (New York: Verso, 1991); Thomas Guglielmo, *White on Arrival: Italians, Race, Color, and Power in Chicago, 1890–1945* (New York: Oxford University Press, 2003); Eric Goldstein, *The Price of Whiteness: Jews, Race, and American Identity* (Princeton, NJ: Princeton University Press, 2006).

25. On Pinkster, see Shane White, "Pinkster: Afro-Dutch Syncretism in New York City and the Hudson Valley," *Journal of American Folklore* 102, no. 403 (January–March 1989): 68–75; A. J. Williams-Myers, "Pinkster Carnival: Africanisms in the Hudson River Valley," *Afro-Americans in New York Life and History* 9 (1985): 7–17; Sterling Stuckey, *Going Through the Storm: The Influence of African American Art in History* (New York: Oxford University Press, 1994), 53–80; and Joseph Reidy, "'Negro Election Day' and Black Community Life in New England, 1750–1860," *Marxist Perspectives* 1 (1978): 102–117.

CHAPTER 5

"Remember . . . I'm Your Man"

Masculinity, Marriage, and Gender in Hamilton

CATHERINE ALLGOR

The best art challenges what we think we know, even as it relies upon implicit and explicit assumptions shared by the audience. One of the sheer joys of Lin-Manuel Miranda's *Hamilton* is his clever use of pop culture assumptions and references that we all understand. Sometimes the play is in the vocabulary: "You're the *worst*, Burr"; or "Immigrants: We get the job done!" which became one of the big applause lines of the show as the presidential campaign became infected with nativism. Other times, Miranda juxtaposes contemporary conventions onto an eighteenth-century landscape. We can't help but laugh when "the guys" greet "the ladies" with "Hey, Hey, Hey" at the Winter's Ball, just like twenty-first-century bros.

Moments like this encounter between randy soldiers and husband-hunting elite women signal that the assumptions Miranda depends on to drive *Hamilton* go deep, and nothing goes as deep as gender. The term "gender" has several functions, all of which are at play in this hit musical. Gender can refer to the prescriptions that every culture has about what men and women should be and do. These ideals do not necessarily reflect reality, but they do provide the standard against which people measure their lives and the limitations on how they live them. Gender also offers a language that defines "superior/subordinate," a symbolic system that has been used by cultures throughout history to understand the hierarchies of their worlds. Gender provides a way to talk about power, about who or what is above ("male") and who or what is below ("female"). One of the reasons gender has been a cultural constant in the creation of power structures is its seemingly "natural" (first religious, and later "scientific") qualities. There are basic biological differences between men and women, so the idea goes; women are weaker than men and are thus are naturally subordinate to them. A power structure tied to that seemingly obvious fact has the power of nature, and sometimes God, to sustain it.

The people of the past did not have a language to discuss the gendered dynamics of their own societies; they did not even have the words we have today. In the Revolutionary period, while men were referred to as "men," women were "the sex." Still, issues such as war, politics, economics, and even everyday activities such as eating and sexuality were all "gendered" in ways specific to that particular milieu. "Reading" gender thus offers a fruitful way to understand past worlds on their own terms. By doing this, we not only take women and "female" activities seriously, but we also reveal how gender works in the world of men and acts as a vocabulary of power. Analyzing gendered rhetoric and dynamics offers a revealing window into histories even when women themselves are not present. There are many good reasons that we study women's lives, words, and worlds and the power systems represented by gender, but perhaps the most compelling is that by paying attention to these issues we learn things about the past that we would not know if we studied only men and male activities.[1]

In many ways, *Hamilton* is a rich example of the kind of gender history that has only come to the study of the eighteenth century since the 1970s. Like the "women's history" born from the feminist struggle, it offers representations of women's lives, describes some of the prescriptions of manhood, and demonstrates, whether consciously or not, a masculinist world view. Yet these "women's history" moments in the musical also need to be scrutinized, because *Hamilton* rarely conveys the centrality of gender as a system that ordered and organized society. As a result, *Hamilton* misses one of the most important stories of the American Revolution: the failure of the Revolution to challenge "coverture," or the system of laws

Before the American Revolution, political cartoonists used gendered and racialized images to play on men's deepest fears. In this famous 1774 image, "The able Doctor, or America Swallowing the Bitter Draught," America is depicted as a Native American woman, helpless before her tormenters, British statesmen and institutions. Such imagery sought to provoke American men to support the Patriot cause. *(Library of Congress, Prints and Photographs Division)*

that defined women's subordinate legal status. Coverture is an idea and legal reality as crucial to understanding our revolutionary origins as terms such as "liberty," "independence," and "democracy." Unlike those terms, however, it is largely unknown to the American public. Exploring the treatment of male and female characters and the representations of gender in *Hamilton* leads to the hidden history of the concept of coverture more generally, and what the failure to deal with it means as we assess exactly how "revolutionary" the American Revolution was.

As a symbol of both how hidden and how central coverture was to the American Revolution, one only needs to look at the most famous words of the most famous woman of her time. Abigail Adams's plea to "Remember the Ladies" is one of the most frequently repeated quotations of the era, but what she meant by them is widely misunderstood. Abigail wasn't talking about feminism, or even the vote, when she encouraged her husband and the Continental Congress to "be more generous and favorable" to women in any new code of laws than their ancestors had been. She was asking for a diminishment of coverture. Abigail doesn't use that term in her discussion of coverture's many burdens: it was so much a part of her world that it did not need naming. "Do not put such unlimited power into the hands of the husbands," she pleaded, and John knew what she meant.[2] But today, we need to both name coverture and understand it because its legacy haunts us today. One of the best consequences of the interest and curiosity aroused by *Hamilton* would be giving coverture its name and making it part of every American's political vocabulary.

The Great Men of History

Hamilton's popularity reflects the assumptions of many Americans about what "history" is, beliefs that go right to the heart of the role that gender plays in the historical enterprise. Professional historians have been dismayed by how many *Hamilton* audiences think that they are not seeing just art, but something true about the past. Of course, theatregoers understand that having a largely minority cast peopling a story of great white men is a comment of sorts about historical truth, but they still seem to think that the play *is* history. In some ways, they are right. With its "great man" structure, war, and conventionally defined politics as its main concerns, *Hamilton* looks like, and sounds like, capital H History. As breathtakingly contemporary as *Hamilton* is, as William Hogeland points out in this volume, in many ways it is as conventional as the book on which it is based, Ron Chernow's Pulitzer Prize–winning *Alexander Hamilton*; or any other huge tome of "Founders Chic" literature that dads around the country receive as Father's Day gifts.

Among the features of conventional historical narratives is a concentration on elite, white men, masculine activities such as war, and official records of government generated by these men. The lives and words of women and other "others" are relegated to the periphery of the narrative. This pattern is literally visible in many college and high school history textbooks. The story of great men and state-building dominates the page in columns of black-and-white text. Only the occasional box set outside the text—pink for women, blue for people of color—offers a different perspective on the past. Similarly, the plot and themes of *Hamilton* center on the issue of masculinity and the activities most associated with masculinity—war and politics—with love, sex, and family providing important but secondary subplots. The play assumes that war, in this case the American Revolution, was necessary, perhaps inevitable, and ultimately good. A few voices in the play express concern about the many costs of war. Peggy Schuyler murmurs that "It's bad enough there'll be violence on our shore," while Westchester farmer Samuel Seabury warns that "Chaos and bloodshed are not a solution," making it clear that the colonists are not united in favor of war; in the end, both are dismissed. Peggy is lectured by her sisters that there are "New ideas in the air / Look around, look around." Alexander's friends shout down Seabury and urge him to use his famed rhetoric skills to "tear this dude apart."[3] There is no sense in *Hamilton* that there was a legitimate opposition to war or even an alternative political path, either in the eighteenth century or in the modern minds of historians. Nor does the play mention the often violent persecution of Tories in New York, during and after the war. One imagines a musical number on the cutting-room floor: "The Farmer was right; or, Have you ever heard of Canada?"

Miranda draws on these conventional assumptions about the inevitability of war to offer a story that, at its heart, is about the making of a man. Early in Act I, talking to Aaron Burr, Alexander follows a statement about his low status, as an orphan without friends and family in a world where connections mattered, with his conviction that war could provide a "cure" for his social problems: "God I wish there was a war! / Then we could prove that we're worth more than anyone bargained for." Miranda's Alexander needs a war, not just to make him a man, but a man who matters to other men. Having a life of meaning is expressed as not wasting one's "shot," a term with several meanings, including hard drinking and sexual release; in this case, however, as Alexander and his friends point their fingers at the audience and "fire," emphasizes their eagerness for combat.

Though it is not completely fair to hold what is a piece of modern art to historical standards, not even the men of the American Revolution assumed war was necessary for proper manhood. While war was a viable path to social and political prominence in the eighteenth century (the second sons of the English nobility were sent off to the army well into the nineteenth century), higher education and a profession could also make a man, as they did for John Adams. Inherited land, class position, and responsibility for dependents made men, as they did Thomas Jefferson. The artist Miranda unabashedly diverts the audience from his eighteenth-century world to make important points about immigration, slavery, and other contemporary issues that tie Alexander to the audience. Why then this unquestioned assumption about war? From our twenty-first-century perch, we know that wars are not inevitable, and certainly not necessarily good. As we learn more about transgender movements and gender fluidity, modern people also know that "masculinity" is not natural, but instead constructed and contested.

Yet Miranda chooses to celebrate masculinity as a central element of the Revolution, and a certain kind of masculinity that is defined by violence, sexual conquest, and ambitious social climbing. Alongside the duels, the flirtatiousness, and the manly bluff and bluster, the play also makes fun of the young revolutionaries' opponents as less than manly. In the elongated diphthongs and a vocalizing of vowels that can only be called prissy, the dissenting Seabury's feminized presentation is taken as proof of a weak political argument. The other "womanish" character is that of King George, the only character played by that traditional exemplar of American masculinity, the white man in charge. He might sing "Remember . . . I'm your man," but his mincing tones let us know that he isn't really enough of a man to hold onto his "sweet, submissive subjects." If we have any doubts about who this person is, and the extent of his right to power, the king's high-pitched, girlish giggle and prancing about the stage seal the deal.

Hamilton's Women

Thankfully, *Hamilton* is largely free of the kind of hardcore misogyny dominant in rap/hip-hop music, perhaps even signaling new possibilities for a genre that has been much criticized for the way it portrays women and female sexuality. Much has been made of the production's cross-racial casting, but *Hamilton* plays with gender too: women in the chorus appear in masculine dress, though not the other way around. Despite this, twenty-first-century assumptions about male sexual privilege bump up against both modern sensibilities and eighteenth-century realities in ways that are discomforting.

Much is made of men enjoying sexual conquests, with the underlying belief that women are fair game. But nonmarital sex was a dangerous sport for eighteenth-century women of all classes. In the reality of their lives, a sexual encounter that might lead to pregnancy was potentially far more dangerous to health and reputation than a duel. As the male characters boasted of their prowess with women, I cannot help but contrast the role of gender in assessing the nature of risk and its place in eighteenth-century society. Dueling, which was men's purview, was an invented danger that men played with, governed by elaborate and constructed rules about honor and pride. There was even a built-in out, which *Hamilton* recognizes: "Most disputes die, and no one shoots," the chorus assures us. But in an age where sexual purity was required for marriage and when there was little effective birth control, sexuality outside or within marriage was far more lethal than a duel. Fatality came from biology, not rhetoric and choice; and while death from childbirth was a common occurrence there were other horrible, social fates for women who stepped out of line sexually. A pregnancy could doom a woman to a life on the streets characterized by poverty, prostitution, and an early death. Nowhere is an example of this more clear and poignant than Alexander's own mother's life; however, in *Hamilton*, illegitimacy becomes a man's problem. Who were the women that Alexander was tomcatting around with or with whom Hercules Mulligan boasted of having "intercourse over four sets of corsets"? Were these upper-class "ladies," or are we to understand that our heroes were exploiting poor women, such as the boardinghouse keeper's daughters or prostitutes who frequented the urban public sphere or military camps? However we are supposed to understand these sexual transactions, *Hamilton* highlights cavalier attitudes that reflect a masculinist perspective.

Reflecting the genre of "great man" history on which *Hamilton* relies, women are at best peripheral to the musical's main story. This is not to say that there are no appealing female roles; many a *Hamilton* fan will protest that their favorite characters are Eliza and Angelica Schuyler and the Schuyler sisters get some of Miranda's most lyrical and stunning songs. Miranda has even asserted that Angelica is the smartest character in the play. But not unlike the reception of David McCullough's *John Adams*, where many readers felt that the "breakout star" of the book was Abigail Adams, although history sometimes turns on Alexander's relationship to women, the female characters do not derail the narrative of male power, war, and state-building. Eliza Schuyler Hamilton might be the one left to "tell the story" (much as later the historical preservation movement was founded by elite white women), but this is a position with limited power. If we cannot see (let alone challenge) the system of gender, you can throw as many women as you want into the mix and they will be prefigured in ways that still privilege masculine values and assumptions.

When late in the play Thomas Jefferson and James Madison plead "Can we get back to politics? Yo, Please?" after a lengthy detour into Alexander's private life, his affair, his concerns with children, and his marriage, they are pleading with the audience to return to the *real* story, its masculine concerns about power, and a narrow definition of politics in which women are never "in the room where it happens." But what *Hamilton* then ignores with its conventional understanding of what constitutes politics and by moving out of the private sphere is the sobering failure of the American Revolution to fulfill its radical potential for women. Miranda does acknowledge something of women's legal position in colonial America and in a dramatic song, their social realities. In our initial meeting with the Schuyler sisters, the brilliant and bold Angelica challenges the Declaration of Independence: "You want a revolution? / I want a revelation / So listen to my declaration." She, her sisters, and the female ensemble mockingly chant the famous opening lines of that founding document, with Angelica challenging its author: "And when I meet Thomas Jefferson / I'm 'a compel him to include women in the sequel." It's a stirring moment, especially the comparison of the revolution with the revelation. For women to have achieved political equality would have indeed been beyond revolution. But the moment passes and we never get that meeting.

If it is any consolation to the fictional Angelica, however, history shows that she probably would not have been satisfied by a conversation with Thomas Jefferson, a man who famously avoided confrontation and was a master of the passive-aggressive. In fact, keeping women out of politics was a primary goal for Jefferson. In 1788, in a letter to a leading American salonnière, Anne Willing Bingham, a woman who was knowledgeable about political affairs and ideas,[4] Jefferson made his position clear: "Our good ladies, I trust, have been too wise to wrinkle their foreheads with politics," he wrote. "They are contented to soothe and calm the minds of their husbands returning ruffled from political debate. They have the good sense to value domestic happiness above all." Jefferson was writing from Paris where he was disturbed by political involvement from women of all classes. In the streets and salons, he was encountering "petticoat politicians" and he did not like it. Not only is Thomas's characterization of a "good lady" insulting to the politically involved Anne but his criticism is even more cutting, given that his letter was a reply to one of hers in which she defended French women from his characterization of them as frivolous. Bingham had declared herself "bound in Gratitude to admire and revere" the women of France "for asserting our Privileges, as much as the Friends of the Liberties

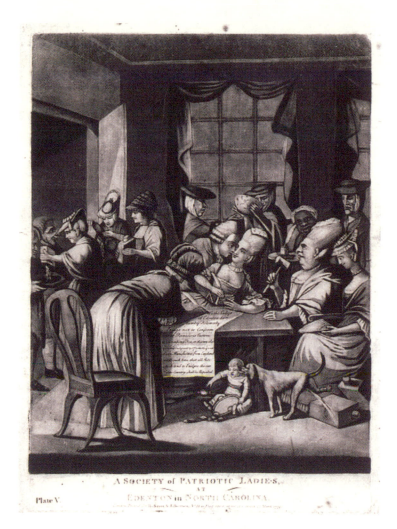

A SOCIETY of PATRIOTIC LADIES,
AT
EDENTON in NORTH CAROLINA.

Plate V.

"A Society of Patriotic Ladies, at Edenton in North Carolina." In 1774, a group of women affirmed the American cause by signing a petition promising to uphold the boycott of British goods. Their political actions shocked the Western world and inspired this engraving, which suggested that women's involvement in politics would lead to lax housekeeping and childcare, loose sexual morals, race mixing, and social disorder. Most ominously, the woman sitting in profile in the foreground suggests that if women kept politicking, they might even turn into men. *(North Carolina Office of Archives and History)* of Mankind reverence the successfull Struggles of the American Patriots." Jefferson's answer offered a rather pointed denial of Anne's equating women's political struggles for liberty with that of men's. And a critical instrument for maintaining the exclusion of women from politics was coverture, or the notion that women's political and economic interests were "covered" and represented by men.

Covered Women

Although the social realities of elite white women's lives briefly gets attention during the re-vision of Angelica and Alexander's first meeting, *Hamilton* does not fully communicate the reality of the bleak situation women found themselves in during the eighteenth century. Smart, ambitious Angelica falls in love with Alexander, but the musical makes it clear that she knows she cannot marry him, because it is her duty—as the eldest daughter in a family without sons—to marry rich in order to cement the Schuyler fortunes. The idea that marriage is Angelica's only choice to achieve economic security is pretty bleak for a modern audience. But it doesn't even come close to the reality of the period, when American women, along with their English counterparts, were legally bound to men by the institution of "coverture," which not only denied that females could have an independent legal identity, but also made marriage almost a transfer of ownership from father to husband. As a legal device, coverture had been enshrined in British law for centuries, and reified by English jurist William Blackstone when he wrote his *Commentaries* in the mid-1700s.[5] At birth, a female baby was covered by her father's identity, and then, when she married, by her husband's. The husband and wife became one—and that one was the husband. This is the origin of the practice of women taking their husband's name upon marriage. Because they did not legally exist, married women could not vote, make contracts, or be sued. They could not own or work in businesses. Married women could not own land or any other property, not even the clothes on their backs, and upon the death of her husband, a woman's legal agency would transfer to her nearest male relative.

The law of coverture was not always followed to the letter in the practice of daily life. Though women could own nothing, rich families like the Schuylers legally protected their assets from sons-in-law, ensuring transmission of money and property to grandchildren. Many women worked with their husbands, or in their stead, in businesses, dispersing goods and payments, and making informal contracts with customers and suppliers. Abigail Adams, for instance, traded stocks and bonds and speculated in western land contracts on behalf of her husband, John. Widows, single women, and even in rare cases married women could petition for a legal exception called "feme sole" that allowed them to make transactions and contracts on their own. But many women, unmarried or not, did not bother applying for this legal nicety, and instead did business with the local community by acting as monitors and enforcers. The clumsiness of coverture as a practical reality would accelerate in the eighteenth and nineteenth centuries, as the economy became more capitalistic and cash-based and women, by necessity, played a bigger role in it.

Coverture held married white women in a kind of legal slavery. Modern Americans are uneasy with the comparison of marriage to slavery, but the parallels go deeper than just the inability to own property or to vote. In the same way that white men exerted total control over black bodies—up to and sometimes including death—so they owned their wives. A man had absolute right to the "fruits" of his wife's body. He owned her labor and could even lease her to work for someone else, taking her wages. He had absolute ownership of his wife's children. If he chose, he could take custody of children after a divorce and could refuse to allow his former wife to ever see them again; and he could seize her property from other heirs upon her death, as Alexander Hamilton's mother's estranged husband actually did. A husband also had absolute right to sexual access to his wife, regardless of her wishes. Within marriage, a woman's consent was implied, so under the law, all sex-related activity, including rape, was legitimate. And of course, a husband could legally beat his wife, or ask that she be remanded to prison or to an asylum.

Hamilton's brief forays into the place of women in the Early Republic suggests that Americans do not fully understand, or have not come to terms with, the idea that our founding happened with an instrument of gender domination like coverture in place. Marriage under coverture was such an oppressive system that it can be hard for contemporary Americans to appreciate its scope and depth. While many of us are familiar with the phrase "second-class citizenship" to describe women's place in the polity, the contrast in liberties for men and those for women was so great, and eighteenth-century male control over female bodies so absolute, that women's legal status did, in fact, more closely resemble that of slaves than free citizens.

Of course, white women enjoyed some rights not available to enslaved people, women or men. While enslaved people could never legally own property, some single women and widows of means could enjoy the protection of their property by law. Wives had legal rights *in extremis*—a wife could divorce her husband or swear out a warrant against him if he committed a crime against her. Slaves could not "divorce" their masters and the law provided no refuge for them against excessive physical force. But when it came to their rights as specifically women and as wives, legally the only difference between a slave and a married woman was that a husband could not sell his wife nor could he prostitute her out, and even these distinctions were sometimes shaky. White women from England were some of the first persons sold in North America, in this case young English women brought over to be wives to male colonists. Their indentures were sold right off the boat. There was no legal treatment for enslaved people that at some times and places did not apply to white wives. Another way to understand the "slavery/marriage" dynamic is that if colonial and early national marriage was not as oppressive as the extreme form of slavery that prevailed in the United States, it certainly was as coercive as less intense forms of slavery in other parts of the world.

In the same way that a close look at the assumptions underlying the humor and references in *Hamilton* tell us something about our own culture, an examination of a piece of nineteenth-century pop culture offers intriguing historical insight into this past world. Nineteenth-century newspapers were often flimsy affairs, consisting of a few sheets, with rehashes of national and international news. But they also included little anecdotes and jokes. One joke, told over and over again, was about a man who comes into town from the hills or the backwoods, leading his wife on a halter, with a sign hanging around her neck, "For Sale." When the amused townsfolk explain that he cannot sell his wife, he is confused and confounded, which adds to the humor of the situation. By laughing at this un-educated, naïve rube, the townsfolk are able to distance themselves from such ignorance. But why wouldn't this man think he could sell a wife as one would a cow or an enslaved woman? The "slavery/marriage" comparison was too close for comfort and one way to interpret the joke is as a reflection of growing American uneasiness with the parallel. Americans understood the degraded position of wives and coped with their discomfort by focusing on the ignoramus who failed to apprehend some nuance that *they* understood, one that made a bright line between the two institutions.

There are a few moments in *Hamilton* when the brutal and complete power of men over their wives is hinted at, albeit probably inadvertently. Understanding that married women were completely dependent on husbands, and consequently completely vulnerable if a spouse did not live up to the patriarchal bargain, explains Maria Reynolds's desperation, Alexander's response, and the implications of their extramarital affair. She has been deserted by her husband, and has no access to money or property. Whether Maria means to blackmail Alexander from the start or whether she was truly desperate, she trades the only commodity she has—her body and sexuality. Coverture also makes the depth of James Reynolds's indignation understandable. Alexander did not just "cheat" with his wife but also stole from him. As the husband and wife were one, their affair was an assault on James in a way, as well as on the social order. James has earned the right not only to be angry but also to be righteous, and to extract a profit from the situation.

One of the most entertaining songs in the show offers another hint of the male power of the era, and how it offered a frame for political domination. In the number, "You'll Be Back," King George, who is stung by his colony's disloyalty, alternately woos and threatens the Americans. During an interview for the PBS *Great Performances* production *Hamilton's America*, actor Jonathan Groff calls his turn a "breakup song." But it is no mere breakup. Miranda invokes a sinister figure of the abusive spouse to characterize King George. The king wants America's "love and praise," pleading with his errant colony, "don't throw away this thing we had." Like a boyfriend-turned-stalker in a Lifetime movie, he predicts "you'll be back," playing on his colonies' softer sympathies by cajoling "you'll remember that I served you well . . . [W]hen you're gone / I'll go mad." But in the same breath, the king spells out the consequences of his subject's assertion of independence. The ultimate family destroyer, he coolly vows: "I will kill your friends and family to remind you of my love."[6]

This is the moment when the two worlds of the past and the present perfectly overlap. We know exactly what is happening from our own reference points; at the same time, the king's casting of his relationship with "my sweet, submissive subjects" echoes the rhetoric of the time, a gendered political language that stoked the resentment of American male elites. The Sons of Liberty and their leaders often invoked the metaphor of enslavement when making the case for revolution. Their use of this metaphor is jarring, especially when coming from actual slaveholders. On the Tory side, the images of the duties that wives owed to their husbands supplied the opposite rationale. One could see, however, that their roles as actual slaveholders as well as husbands gave the revolutionary male leaders a very distinct picture of what it would mean to be a slave or a wife, and they wanted neither.

A Revolution? A Revelation?

But the revolutionary moment offered possibilities to women bound in a legally subordinate status as well. When in Act I, Angelica rapturously sings: "Look around, look around at how lucky we are to be alive right now! / History is happening," she captures something true about the era for women: that there was a real hope that the Revolution would bring a transformation in the law. In the years before the American Revolution, with talk of liberty and natural rights in the air, white women were not wrong to expect that there might be some change to their degraded status. In her famous "Remember the Ladies" letter to her husband, John, Abigail Adams referenced the longstanding nature of coverture when she bade him to "be more generous and favourable to them [the present-day ladies] than your ancestors." Abigail understood the corruption of absolute power as clearly as any revolutionary theorist: "Do not put such unlimited power into the hands of the Husbands. Remember all Men would be tyrants if they could." She even obliquely referred to the shame of marital rape and physical abuse when she proposed: "Why then, not put it out of the power of the vicious and the Lawless to use us with cruelty and indignity with impunity. Men of Sense in all Ages abhor those customs which treat us only as the vassals of your Sex." Her use of the word "vicious" is key—in that era, the word was associated with sexual depravity.

But this potential was not realized. Except for a few loosened divorce laws, there was no change in the legal status of women for decades. It would take far more than a revolution, it turns out, for coverture to be meaningfully challenged. The early nineteenth century was a time of wide-ranging and wide-reaching legal reform on all levels of government but there seems to have been no discussion about coverture among the ruling men. Law and society moved on, but coverture kept women frozen in amber, with their legal status degrading over time. This is not the last time American women went backward by staying still.

The seeming silence of the founders about the issue of coverture might suggest that they cannot be held accountable for its continuation in the new American republic. In an era that spoke of issues of autonomy and about how a group of men (Parliament) had no right to virtually represent another group of men (American colonists), this inaction seems shocking. Can we say that there was an American

Revolution if nothing changed for half the white population, in addition to all African Americans and Native Americans? In the past, feminist historians have typically let the founders off the hook around the issue of women's full citizenship on the grounds that they just didn't know any better or that they simply couldn't imagine other options at the time. Historian Linda Kerber concludes that there was silence about coverture in the Revolutionary era because there was literally nothing to say. As she described it in the 1980s, "It is generally thought be both unfair and ahistorical to expect of the revolutionary generation that it initiate a radically new conception of female citizenship."[7]

That is, of course, what we used to say around the issue of the founders and slavery. But just as new research on race and slavery has complicated our sweeping assumption that "they just didn't know," we now understand that there were many moments when the framers could have allowed women of property to vote, could have let married women retain property, could have modified divorce laws, or could have set aside the rule of coverture altogether and started from scratch. They chose not to. As with the issue of slavery, it turns out that the silence around the status of women wasn't exactly a vacuum. When it came to examining the nature of women and their role in a republic based on equality, this was one of those uncomfortable silences, punctuated by odd outbursts, with all the tension that marks the difference between simply not seeing and ignoring.

In the last few years, scholars have broken that post-Revolutionary silence through a fresh look at the past. In fact, in the eighteenth century, people were thinking about what they called "the woman question," and that continued through and after the American Revolution. Kerber later reconsidered her own position when she looked at a legal situation that coverture had not anticipated. After the hostilities ceased, Kerber pointed out, state courts all across the new union had to deal with the problem of Loyalist properties. On the face of it, the rules were simple. If a Loyalist man left his home and lands in the colonies and fled to England, his property could be seized by the state as punishment for treason, depriving his heirs of any future claims. But what if, as in several prominent cases, the property in question came to the man through his wife? That is, his wife's father had entailed land to pass through his daughter to her children, circumventing the husband. It is true that in the cases that came before the court, the wives had fled the country along with their husbands, but could that be interpreted as a political statement on par with a man's desertion? After all, lawyers for plaintiffs argued, a good wife obeyed her husband and followed him. Such a woman might have been a Patriot at heart, but her own political affiliation or allegiance mattered not, as women had little or no legal or political existence. A woman's primary responsibility and allegiance was to her husband, not the state—that's the heart of coverture.

Heirs who wanted the property that would have come to them through their mothers indeed argued that the wife's desertion didn't mean anything. States who wanted to keep the confiscated property found themselves in the novel position of arguing that women could be citizens with a responsibility to the state and thus that they were fully capable of treason. In *Martin v. Massachusetts*, counsel for the state argued that when Anna Martin, the mother of the plaintiff James Martin, chose to accompany her husband back to England, that she acted in a political capacity, thus abandoning her Massachusetts property.

In the end, these cases were decided a variety of ways. James Martin got his mother's property, which is undoubtedly what she would have wanted, but he was able to do so because the justices who decided his case proceeded from a conservative interpretation of coverture. They decided that married women were not autonomous actors apart from their husbands and therefore Anna Martin's move to England did not necessarily mean she was a Loyalist. But other cases went differently, such as the Pennsylvania court's reluctance to allow Grace Galloway, wife of traitor Joseph Galloway, to will property to her son-in-law even though, unlike Anna Martin, she had stayed in the colonies. Moments like these demonstrate that the failure to ameliorate the degraded status of women was not inevitable or unimaginable, that the men who were constructing a new nation could have also envisaged new ideas of female citizenship. But they did not.

Why was there, then, such a failure of imagination when it came to women's equality? The answer brings us back to *Hamilton* and masculinity. Right after the Revolution and during the constitutional era, the framers were obsessed with an issue that was vital to the existence of the republican experiment. Historian Joseph Ellis frames this as the viability of the nation—I call it "legitimacy"— but we mean the same thing.[8] In short, no one was certain that the republican experiment would work, that the "United States" would last and the union hold. It was precisely this uncertainty that led men such as James Madison and Alexander Hamilton to create the Constitution, in order to consolidate and shore up power.

This need for legitimacy, to prove to themselves and others that the United States was a real political enterprise, caused the founders much anxiety and fear, and it may be that this anxiety of viability prevented them from addressing the glaring contradiction between the ancient rights of coverture and a government and legal system built on Enlightenment ideals. Anxiety over legitimacy made the framers and founding men sensitive to anything that would seem to diminish or challenge their authority. In an age that equated masculinity with authority, that meant anything that made them feel or seem less than men. Ceding the power over wives that coverture gave them would be emasculating, not only for them but also in the eyes of the world. One could see this time of American history as a crisis of masculinity, with masculinity equaling authority and viability. The last thing the male revolutionaries would do would be to call their masculine authority into question by freeing their wives. The presentation and primacy of masculine values, then, is one of the most historically accurate aspects of *Hamilton*.

What Happened to Coverture?

As a historian who is determined to make "coverture" a term that every American knows and understands, I was disappointed not to hear it in *Hamilton*, the most popular historically based piece of art to come along in decades, but I was not surprised. Most Americans, even lawyers and American historians, don't know the word and certainly don't understand the implications of half the white population coming into the new shiny machine of the government shackled by the ancient and creaky burden of a legal construct that denied their personhood. The ghost of coverture haunted the machine and still does. Coverture is not just a fascinating "period-accurate" issue that is ripe for artistic interpretation. What makes coverture such a compelling topic is that it was never abolished and its legacies remain with us in so many ways today. Americans who do not know this "origin story" will have a hard time understanding why women still struggle with citizenship rights even today.

Coverture has of course been severely limited since the eighteenth century. The first breaks in coverture happened with the passage of the Married Women's Property Acts in 1848, though one could argue that these rights were designed more for husbands who wished to preserve assets than any acknowledgment of women's right to own property. Through the nineteenth and twentieth centuries, various laws and acts chipped away at coverture, but they never got rid of it completely. Well into the twentieth century, native-born American women lost their citizenship if they married certain classes of foreign-born men. In many places, women were not permitted to serve on juries until the mid-twentieth century, thus encroaching on one of the most fundamental constitutional rights. "Marital rape" wasn't even recognized, let alone criminalized, until the 1970s. The idea behind coverture, that all women were wives, meant that single women occupied an ambiguous position in American law. Not too long ago, banks wouldn't lend money to single women, not even, as in a case I know, when the woman in question was actually a bank loan officer. In 2007, a husband who wanted to change his name to his wife's had to bring suit in the California courts, claiming a violation of the equal protection clause of the Fourteenth Amendment. Married women who buy property in original colony states are often asked to testify that they are operating as freely consenting persons and are not under spousal duress. These examples are all coverture.

These vestiges of coverture may just seem mildly annoying, but the fact that coverture has never been abolished makes clear that Americans have still failed to declare women equal under the law by constitutional amendment. The usefulness of such an amendment is clear; again, the comparison with the institution of slavery proves instructive. Ending slavery and granting equal rights to black men was too important a matter to be left to state law or federal decrees. It had to be enshrined into a constitutional amendment (actually three of them). That is the remedy for coverture. Perhaps we will make this change in the future. But what has it meant for Americans to have lived into an era of space travel and personal computers bearing this burden, this revolutionary promise unfulfilled?

Asking historians to weigh in on *Hamilton* can be a fraught exercise. Even as we discourage audiences from thinking a musical play is history, it seems churlish indeed to criticize such a transformative piece of theater. *Hamilton* has awakened popular appetites for stories and interpretations of the past and it surely will encourage new artists to turn to the past for inspiration. I offer this meditation on gender and *Hamilton* as a way to encourage them to build on Miranda's work by truly decentering "History."

At the beginning of this chapter, I postulated that one of the most important reasons that we study women's history is that in taking women's lives as well as gender systems seriously we find out things about the whole society that we did not know. It works in art as well. In *Rosencrantz and Guildenstern Are Dead*, Tom Stoppard reimagines Shakespeare's *Hamlet* through two minor characters in the original play. Seen with and through their eyes, the story of the mad prince and all that is rotten in Denmark looks very different. Stoppard's focus on these two characters also reveals the rich inner lives of those considered peripheral and raises fresh and often startling sets of concerns.

Women have often been seen as "minor" characters in our histories. Like an eighteenth-century gentleman, I throw down the gauntlet to any artist interested in the past as an interpretive inspiration. Follow the women and something fruitful and wonderful will happen. In a conversation about "expanding the real estate" of what hip hop can cover, Lin-Manuel Miranda states: "And I love the idea of telling the stories that you haven't heard told before and suddenly making that fair game."[9] The game is on.

NOTES

1. Joan Wallach Scott, "Gender: A Useful Category of Historical Analysis," in *Gender and the Politics of History* (New York: Columbia University Press, 1999).

2. Abigail Smith Adams to John Adams, March 31, 1776, Adams Family Papers Electronic Archive, https://www.masshist.org/digitaladams/archive/doc?id=L17760331aa&bc=%2Fdigitaladams%2Farchive%2Fbrowse%2Fletters_1774_1777.php.

3. This essay uses first names when discussing both male and female figures. Referring to biographical subjects by their last name (i.e., "Hamilton") stems from a time when most biographical subjects were male. The convention becomes problematic when women enter the story. Is Eliza "Schuyler" and then "Hamilton"? The typical compromise is to give male subjects the dignity of a surname while women are treated more familiarly with just first names. The solution of addressing everyone by first names is not perfect but if this seems excessively familiar to modern readers, at least both women and men will suffer any diminishment equally.

4. Letter exchange quoted in Rosemarie Zagarri, *Revolutionary Backlash: Women and Politics in the Early American Republic* (Philadelphia: University of Pennsylvania Press, 2008), 75–77.

5. Holly Brewer, "The Transformation of Domestic Law," in *The Cambridge History of Law in America*, vol. 1: *Early America, 1580–1815*, edited by Christopher Tomlins and Michael Grossberg (Cambridge: Cambridge University Press, 2008); Lindsay R. Moore, "Women, Property, and the Law in the Anglo-American World, 1630–1700," *in Early American Studies* (Summer 2016): 537–567.

6. Lin-Manuel Miranda, "You'll Be Back," *Hamilton*.

7. Linda K. Kerber, "The Paradox of Women's Citizenship in the Early Republic: The Case of *Martin v. Massachusetts*, 1805," *American Historical Review* 97, no. 2 (April 1992): 354.

8. Joseph J. Ellis, *Founding Brothers: The Revolutionary Generation* (New York: Vintage, 2002), 50.

9. Miranda quoted in *Hamilton's America*, *Great Performances*, PBS, October 21, 2016.

ACT II

The Stage

CHAPTER 6

"The Ten-Dollar Founding Father"

Hamilton, Money, and Federal Power

MICHAEL O'MALLEY

"But Jackson stays?" tweeted Lin-Manuel Miranda in June of 2015: "The MURDEROUS Andrew Jackson is still money?"[1] Treasury Secretary Jack Lew had just announced that the $10 bill was going to be redesigned to feature the portrait of a notable American woman, and that his department would take suggestions for an appropriate figure. Treasury has a regular schedule for updating the security features of American paper money: the $10 bill just happened to be the next one up for a redesign.[2] The cast of *Hamilton: An American Musical*, which was just on the eve of its Broadway debut, was not happy to hear the news. Miranda's show opened by promising to tell the story of the "ten-dollar founding father without a father": now the cast wondered if they would have to change the lyrics. Miranda's tweet spurred fans to voice their support for removing Jackson, not Hamilton, from a place of honor on America's money. Ron Chernow, the author of the Hamilton biography from which Miranda's musical drew, called it "really a shockingly wrongheaded decision" and insisted: "I am pro-Hamilton, not anti-women, in this controversy." Miranda himself also recognized the value of publicity. He told reporters, "I thank Jack Lew and the good people of the Treasury Department for putting Hamilton in the national news on our first day of rehearsals."[3]

Until recently, Alexander Hamilton was a hero mostly to bankers. As a historical figure he made the mistake of being more interested in practical results than in lofty and unattainable ideals. His rival Jefferson wrote eloquent lines about liberty: Hamilton wrote dense tracts on interest rates and mint ratios. Economic historians have long recognized his crucial role in stabilizing the new nation's finances, while historians of banks and banking have regretted that his ideas faced so much opposition. But for the most part only scholars specializing in the history of money and banking recognized Hamilton's particular genius. Ron Chernow's bestselling 2004 biography, which stressed Hamilton's lowly origins, outsider status, and relative enthusiasm for ending slavery, increased public notice of, and curiosity about, his life and work. *Hamilton: An American Musical* has further expanded the number and range of people celebrating the father of the national debt, changing Hamilton from a symbol of elitist management to a figure of romantic populism.

The "forgotten" founding father's new popularity has also, it seems, helped keep the face of Alexander Hamilton on our national currency. Although Lin-Manuel Miranda and fans of *Hamilton* were not alone in wanting to see Hamilton retained, it seemed especially fitting that a musical celebrating the father of the Treasury Department and his place in history should influence public debate about his image on our currency. As of this writing, Hamilton has been saved, and Andrew Jackson, who currently graces the $20 bill (and was the subject of a somewhat less popular, and less laudatory, musical), is due for demotion.

This chapter will focus on Hamilton and money—his theories of specie, banking, and value—and on how he has been depicted on U.S. currency from 1860 through the present. Hamilton's face on our money tells us a story that *Hamilton* can't: about the relationship between money, value, nationalism, and history. He did not appear on U.S. paper bills until the 1860s, and his appearance was part of a post–Civil War shift toward a centralized economy under federal control. He stood for the power of a strong, centrally managed fiscal policy, but also for the value of "nation" over state and region. But there is an even bigger story here: images we put on our coins and bills reflect our sense of what money is, where its value comes from, and why we agree to take it. Over time, that sense has changed and is changing still: Hamilton—and *Hamilton*—are both part of that evolution.

Until 1860, the country did not have anything like a uniform, standard circulating currency. Colonial Americans used a wide variety of things as money—English, French, Spanish, and Dutch coins, but also multiple forms of paper money that came and went, generating varied degrees of enthusiasm and respect. The American Revolution itself famously depended on the issue of "continental dollars" not backed by gold or silver, but simply paper notes that the law compelled you to accept. Indeed, in the musical, Alexander Hamilton complains that merchants preferred "British money" to American if they thought they could get away with it.[4] Continental dollars worked well enough to help the revolutionaries win the war, but they caused runaway inflation since the Continental Congress could not resist the temptation to simply print more money when they had bills to pay, which made each existing dollar less valuable. Hoping to make this problem worse, the British printed their own counterfeit version. By the end of the war, it took buckets full of these dollars to buy a loaf of bread, but they had done their work by the time the British surrendered. A tension between the desire for "specie" money, meaning gold or silver coin, and paper money, not backed by gold or silver, would persist for the next century.

Having seen the monetary chaos of the Revolution firsthand, Hamilton set out in 1791 to rationalize American finances. He saw banks as the key to a new commercial economy, calling them "the happiest engines that ever were invented for advancing trade."[5] But there were only four banks in total in all of the United States in 1791, two in Philadelphia, one in New York, and one in Boston. Most Americans found banks to be strange, new, and even disturbing things. The ideas in play were puzzling, and remain so: how could these institutions get away with lending more money than they actually had? Was what they loaned out—paper money—"real money"? What went on in those secret vaults? Hamilton, characteristically, was not really interested in the answers to these questions; he thought the United States should have a central bank modeled on the Bank of England, a single bank that could regulate an entire banking industry and restrain the enthusiasms of local bankers while providing abundant credit.

Hamilton's brainchild, the First United States Bank, had more than a passing similarity to the Federal Reserve system that issues our money today.[6] It would be the federal government's bank, the place where the national government deposited all its income and revenue. It would issue loans, paper money, and coins, but it would also have strict and conservative reserve requirements, meaning that it could not issue too much more paper than it had specie in its vaults. What "too much" meant was vague, and was left to the discretion of its director. These paper notes, Hamilton thought, would become the default standard money of the new United States.

Hamilton had a bastard son's keen eye for the value of appearances and the arbitrariness of social convention. Social convention, he knew, might be founded on illusion, but illusion mattered. In his 1791 report on the Establishment of a Mint (1791), he described how he thought the coinage of the new nation should work; he defined a "dollar" as 247.5 grains of gold or 3712.5 grains of silver (a "grain" is the smallest unit of measure in the English weight system, equal to 64.79891 milligrams). Though he suggested the country should have gold, silver, and copper coin in circulation, he insisted that gold was "of superior value: less liberties have been taken with it." It's not clear what these "liberties" might have been or how one would take them, and Hamilton was unsure why gold enjoyed this value or esteem, whether from "intrinsic superiority" or from "the prejudices of mankind." But he did not much care why; he cared about the making of money and the raising of capital: "There is scarcely any point, in the economy of national affairs of greater moment, than the uniform preservation of the intrinsic value of the money unit," he wrote in 1791, "on this the security and steady value of property essentially depend."

The phrase seems straightforward but in fact shows Hamilton's ambivalence about the whole idea that anything had a value that went beyond appearances. If the gold coin's value was truly intrinsic—derived entirely from the substance of the gold itself—then it would not need preserving. For example, could anyone imagine the idea of "preserving" the intrinsic value of a lump of coal? Coal might be burned or lost or smashed into smaller pieces, but no alchemy could change its intrinsic properties. Similarly, if "value" stood among gold's intrinsic properties, then it could not be taken away.

But Hamilton recognized that "intrinsic value" was a matter of perception or appearance, not natural fact, and when he argued for a strict regulation of coins' metallic content, he also stressed the importance of appearances. Silver coins, he argued, should be alloyed with copper: "The reason of this union of Silver with Copper is this—the silver counteracts the Tendency of the Copper to injure the Color or Beauty of the Coin, by giving it too much redness, or rather a Coppery hue; which a small quantity will produce; and the Copper prevents the too great whiteness, which silver alone would confer." "Too great whiteness" or "too much redness" made the silver seem inauthentic or unconvincing: oddly, silver mixed with copper might look more like silver than silver alone.

He paid similar attention to making sure that the color of gold coins was exactly right, neither too red nor too yellow nor too white, because he understood that even with gold coins, appearance mattered as much as reality. We have to assume Hamilton gained this knowledge as a young man in the mercantile trade. Orphaned at eleven, Hamilton spent several years as a clerk in an import export firm on the island of St. Croix, even taking charge of the firm for a short time at age fourteen, while the owner was at sea. Then as now, commerce depended on confidence, or the appearance of confidence. Young Alexander knew how international trade worked, and he knew how money had to cross boundaries of class, region, nation, and culture while retaining its value—a value that entirely depended on appearances.

Hamilton's own origins were "base." His father never married his mother, who was herself of uncertain character, and he made his way in the world with a combination of hard work, talent, and a fortunate marriage to Elizabeth Schuyler, a woman from a wealthy family. He knew all about alloys of the base and the pure, and about how appearance reassured. He also knew all about prejudices against people of low birth, and how they could be swayed by appearances. He wrote: "The effects of imagination and prejudice cannot safely be disregarded, in anything that relates to money."[7]

To opponents, Hamilton's proposed bank appeared to be an instrument of prejudice, a vessel of corruption and speculation, and a tool to enrich its wealthy shareholders. Hamilton hoped the First United States Bank would provide a de facto national paper money. He also hoped, because shares of bank stock were priced very high, that it would help cement the interests of wealthy investors to the fate of the new nation. That eagerness to cater to the demands of the wealthy and willingness to merge private gain with public interest outraged Jeffersonians (members of the Democratic-Republican Party), and Congress allowed the bank to lapse in 1811. By then Hamilton had met his demise in Weehawken, New Jersey, in a duel with Aaron Burr.

But in the meantime, more and more banks began appearing throughout the country, a veritable "bancomania," to use Bray Hammond's improbable phrase. Hamilton was right about banks and their relationship to commerce and economic growth. The establishment of a Second Bank of the United States, in 1816, failed to check this "bancomania," and by 1815 there were 212 banks in operation.[8] Some banks were stately and august in appearance; others reflected the rawness of the new nation.

These banks could all print their own money, and print it they did, enthusiastically. By 1850 there were approximately nine thousand different kinds of paper money circulating in the United States. These were the notes of state and local banks, not national currency. Modern readers may find this a strange idea, but in 1850 every transaction involved not just a consideration of the price of the good being bought or sold, but also of the kind of money being proffered. The official money of the United States was gold or silver coin, nicely adjusted to color as per Hamilton's prescription, but in daily life paper money notes issued by various banks lubricated exchange.

Today, it can be hard to imagine the economic phenomenon that Hamilton had hoped to control with a federal bank. Ambitious local men would pool their gold and silver assets and form a bank; they would then go to one of several printing firms and choose designs for their paper notes drawn from a range of stock images, images designed to convey enterprise, sobriety, and reliability. They would, in turn, pay the paper notes out in loans, and people—mostly people living near the bank—would take the notes. The paper notes were made, typically, from reprocessed cloth rags: indeed, opponents of paper money frequently mocked it as "rag money." With few exceptions they were simply black or green ink on white paper, sometimes with red or blue details. Ideally, people could take that paper money to the bank at any time and demand specie, which they would *probably* get, depending on the reliability of the bank at the moment. State and local banknotes generally lost value the farther they traveled from their point of issue.

These banks and their paper were regional, not national, instruments. They marked a bet people made on their own productive labor and the labor of the bank's officers. Imagine you wish to adorn your frontier town with an impressive town hall. Pool your assets, start a bank, print money in excess of said assets, and if you can convince workmen and suppliers to take it you can have your grand town hall. The town hall then brings more business, which generates more money. Local banknotes, in other words, represented local ambitions.

These bankers knew, as Hamilton had, that appearances mattered. Their money was highly decorated with images of the modern world they were willing into being: pictures of steam locomotives, looms, eagles, goddesses of liberty and of commerce, sturdy yeomen, and in the South, suspiciously cheerful slaves and bales of cotton. Because there were only a few banknote printing firms, there was a limited stock of imagery available, and you might find the same images on notes issued by banks hundreds of miles apart.[9] The standardized iconography sometimes included portraits of Washington, and the occasional local grandee paid for a specific image of himself or something dear to him, like a stamping press or a steamboat, but few famous political figures appeared. Hamilton, for all he had done to establish the basis for a national economy, was not featured on any of these pre–Civil War era bills.

Ironically, because of his association with nationalist economic policies, Hamilton had for long been, and remained, a vexed figure in 1850. American elected officials had agreed to Hamilton's First United States Bank, then abolished it, and then agreed to a Second Bank of the United States, patterned on the first, and then abolished it in turn. In the 1830s that Second Bank drew the ire of Andrew Jackson, whose supporters denounced it variously and simultaneously as an aristocratic devilment, a monster hydra of corruption, and a smothering demon mother. They claimed to support a pure "specie" money supply, gold and silver coin alone. The argument for specie was freighted with language about nature and truth. "I have ever been the enemy of banks," Thomas Jefferson wrote to John Adams in 1814, and of "the tribe of bank-mongers, who were seeking to filch from the public their swindling and barren gains."[10] John Adams believed that paper money issued in excess of actual gold reserves "represents nothing, and is therefore a cheat upon somebody."[11] In this rhetoric banks, with their issues of paper money, were deeply suspect, and so was Hamilton, the father of these scheming banks. Hamilton stood in the public imagination as the agent of wealthy elites and the author of false value, despite the fact that Americans used paper money (and banks) very extensively. A network of independent banks made credit easier to obtain and stimulated local ambitions, not national centralized goals.

Hamilton had wanted a central bank to restrain excess money-issuing, consolidate economic control, and standardize money and value: all of this worked to shore up the value of American money in an international global economy. A *privately owned* central bank would gain prestige from being the federal government's bank, and the government could use the assets on deposit in the bank as collateral for large loans. The alleged probity of bankers would prevent them from loaning the government too much money. But he also wanted American currency to serve as an emblem of *nationalism* in which commerce and the nation merged. "Base currencies," Hamilton had written in 1791, "embarrass the circulation" of money in the several states.[12]

Money has always been a symbol and instrument of state sovereignty, and this principle was at least as important. Under monarchies, coins typically bore the image of the king or queen, and marked the community of the royal domain. Money was and is an attribute of nationalism, a sign of national bonds and boundaries, and of a stable, centralized state. It was also a powerful instrument of policy: the American Revolution itself had a great deal to do with the Crown's desire to restrict and control the colonial money supply. To Hamiltonians, the thousands of local paper notes in circulation suggested an embarrassing failure of the Revolution's nationalist project. A great nation, they believed, had a consistent and uniform currency, which was not just a tool, but also an emblem of the nation's stability and authority.

The subject gets back to the value of money itself. Where does it come from? Did money derive its value from the fact that it was gold, or the fact that it bore the portrait of the queen and was backed by her military? Was paper simply a representation of gold or silver, "real" money that had tangible physical properties and intrinsic value? Or was it a sign of national authority and shared community, a representation of agreement among productive citizens? Should money be limited by nature, or was money simply a stand in for human labor and creativity? State bank notes rarely depicted national political figures like Hamilton, because the notes represented local economies, and they rarely included local people, because engraved portraits were expensive. Decorating the money with plows, steamboats, trains, and looms called attention to the productive source of wealth. Southern paper money often bore images of slaves because slave labor was the ultimate source of that paper's value, *and* because African American slavery was one of the signs of white southern community.[13] The fact that slavery was featured

Georgia bank note. *(National Numismatic Collection, National Museum of American History)*

so often on southern banknotes indicates the ways the northern and southern economies had diverged. In the south, slaves were the "specie" that backed paper money.

The Civil War ended slavery, and it also ended the practice of issuing local and state bank notes. Control of the money supply is one of the things historians point to when they talk about how the Civil War increased the power of the federal government. Ironically, during the war, both the North and the South resorted to issuing paper money, measures that forced them into a more modern, centrally regulated economy. In 1862, the federal government issued "greenback" dollars, legal tender notes, not backed by gold or silver, which the law required a creditor to take. Shortly after, the government began taxing private bank note issues to make them unprofitable. Eventually printing one's own alternative currency became a felony. The federal government thus acquired a monopoly over the production of money, and in the process both the debate about money and the appearance of the bills changed.

After 1862, American currency typically featured portraits of presidents and politicians, Hamilton prominent among them. The new money had to demonstrate the political authority of the federal government, not the busy enthusiasms of local entrepreneurs. But even then, although the symbols changed, the varieties of official U.S.

money reflected persistent themes in the political debate over money itself. From 1862 to 1913, those who wanted to use gold as the basis for paper money debated with "silverites," who wanted to use both gold and silver; and both groups fought with "greenbackers," who believed that paper money did not need to be redeemable in a precious metal. In 1880, for example, you would find "Demand Notes" from the Civil War, "Interest Bearing Notes" (also from the Civil War), "Legal Tender Notes" (the "greenbacks" of the Civil War), "National Bank Notes," "Silver Certificates," and "Gold Certificates": a decade later you would find "Treasury Notes" added to the mix, and then after 1913 "Federal Reserve Notes," which are what we use today.

Not coincidentally, Hamilton's rehabilitation as a founding father occurred during the national crisis of the Civil War: he appeared first on the "greenback" notes of 1861.[14] These were legal tender. The law compelled their acceptance, and they were not redeemable in gold; you could buy gold with them, but they were not backed by gold in vaults. They represented nothing more or less than the Union itself, and the Union's determination to prosecute the Civil War. The greenbacks needed to send a political message about a strong federal government and strong central control: Hamilton was the ideal figure to represent those qualities.

Lincoln's Treasury Department was so enthusiastic about Hamilton that they put his portrait on four different greenback notes: the $2, the $5, the $50, and then later the $20. The $2 and $50 greenbacks carry the same portrait of Hamilton in profile, dignified, though his nose seems a bit longer than one might desire in a romantic lead and there is a mildly monkeyish quality to his mouth and jaw, which extend beyond his brow line.

In the later $20 note, the profile portrait was revised: Hamilton's mouth and lower jaw were moved back and made less simian at the expense of looking more prim and schoolmasterly in the manner one expects of a banker. The $5 "greenback" notes show a three-quarter portrait of Hamilton in the lower right corner. He gazes with a combination of bold determination and mild bemusement,

1862 Greenback note featuring Alexander Hamilton. *(National Numismatic Collection, National Museum of American History)*

which seems entirely appropriate to what we can know of his character. A revised version of that portrait appeared on the $50 "Compound Interest Treasury Note" of 1864. These bills passed at face value, but were also redeemable for face value plus 6 percent interest after two or three years, compounded semi-annually. Confusingly, there were also "Interest Bearing Notes" which did not earn compound interest, but could be redeemed after two years. Hamilton appeared on both the $50 and $500 Interest Bearing Notes. In all of these three-quarter portraits he is more determined and less bemused: a man of action.

The country also issued what were called "gold certificates" (as well as "silver certificates"). These notes reflect, again, the ambiguous character of money itself. Gold certificates were printed until 1934, when Franklin Delano Roosevelt took the United States off the domestic gold standard. Hamilton appeared multiple times on these notes, in both the revised three-quarter and profile portraits. Contemporary readers may feel this bewildering array of money does not make sense, and they are right. The many different kinds of notes featuring Hamilton's image reflects conflicting ideas about money, and about the source of money's value.

Hamilton appears so often on these bills partly because he stood for the same things as the notes themselves: a mix of paper and

This $10 bill from 1933 offers a more refined profile of Alexander Hamilton. *(National Numismatic Collection, National Museum of American History)*

gold, a merger of the federal government with private business and especially with banks, and the authority of the national state. But by 1900 he had also come to represent the Revolutionary generation and their labor in founding the nation. In that sense notes with Hamilton's portrait continued to express the ambiguity of money, founded both in tangible things, actual gold, and political authority, and also in less tangible things, words and ideas and images.

In 1913, the country established the Federal Reserve system, which might be regarded as the fulfillment of Hamilton's original vision, and which continues to guide the national economy today. The Fed is a private institution that serves as the government's banker and the agent of U.S. Treasury bonds. It issues Federal Reserve Notes, which by law you must accept in payment. The fact that these notes are adorned with patriotic symbols serves to obscure the fact that they are issues of a private bank working in close cooperation with the U.S. Treasury, very much as Hamilton had imagined. Initially, in 1913, Jackson appeared on the $10 bill. In 1929, American money was redesigned and resized to its current dimensions. Jackson was promoted to the twenty and Hamilton took his place on the ten.

Hamilton's image combined the past and the present. It appeared on the front of the $10 while on the obverse was an image of the modern Treasury building. Reflecting a new industry that would drive the twentieth-century economy (and nineteenth-century images), the bill also included four, small generic motorcars. The bill is coherent in design: it shows Treasury, more or less founded by Hamilton, on a city street corner; the cars would surely earn the approval of Hamilton, who always encouraged manufactures over rural life and farming. Newspaper accounts of the new money in 1929 emphasized modernity and America's global reach. "It is crisper and stronger," wrote the *New York Times*: "it seems slimmer and more able," with "streamlines and a racing body." These bills would draw the notice of people in Cuba and Puerto Rico, England and Germany, China and Spain. Hamilton's emphasis on manufacturing and financial innovation suited the bustling mercantile world of the country in 1929.[15]

But why put Andrew Jackson, who hated banks and paper money, on the $20? Recall the importance of the Civil War to the government's control of the currency, and you can see why Jackson appears so prominently. U. S. Grant and Abraham Lincoln symbolize northern victory in the Civil War. Benjamin Franklin was a Yankee through and through. Hamilton stood for industry, commerce, and banking. Jackson, a southerner, a slaveholder, and ironically a deeply hostile opponent of banks and paper money, reflects his political faction's continued force in American life and politics. Virginia senator Carter Glass, when drafting the legislation that formed the Federal Reserve, imagined "the ghost of Andrew Jackson stalked before my face in the daytime and haunted my couch for nights."[16] Glass worried that the Federal Reserve would betray the Jacksonian tradition of gold-backed money and hostility to banks. And indeed, over the next one hundred years the United States would leave the gold standard entirely and resort to a purely paper currency, an issue that sustained William Jennings Bryan's repeated—and unsuccessful—populist campaigns for the presidency.

Although U.S. currency has changed constantly throughout the nation's history, when Treasury Secretary Jack Lew announced that the $10 bill would be redesigned to include the portrait of a then-unspecified woman and that the new ten would be released in 2020, marking the 100th anniversary of women's suffrage, the news set off an immediate controversy. "Political correctness has struck again, and this time it's coming for your cash!" warned the website "Young Conservatives," while the *Daily Caller* attributed the idea to the work of "PC thugs."[17] Others insisted it was high time a woman appeared on our paper money. Indeed, while Susan B. Anthony and Sacagawea had recently appeared on dollar coins, which almost no one used, the last woman to appear on paper money had been Martha Washington, whose portrait was on the $1 silver certificate of 1891. *Jezebel* gave a history of the many women who have appeared on the money of many nations over time, and insisted that a woman's portrait on the $10 bill would be "a distinct step forward, symbolically."[18] Ignoring critics, Treasury established a website to solicit suggestions for the appropriate woman.[19]

If the main debate focused on the choice of a woman, a second struggle focused on the choice of which bill should be transformed. A nonprofit group, Women on 20s, started a website of its own to urge that Jackson's image on the $20 bill be replaced with an as-yet-unspecified woman.[20] In April of 2015 Senator Jean Shaheen (D-NH) introduced the "Woman on the Twenty Act," which would "require the Secretary of the Treasury to convene a panel of citizens to make a recommendation to the Secretary regarding the likeness of a woman on the twenty dollar bill."[21] Historians in particular asked why Hamilton, who could easily be described as the father of the Federal Reserve System, should be removed instead of Jackson, who had been a major slaveholder (unlike Hamilton) and had presided over the Trail of Tears and other aggressive actions against Native Americans. Moreover, Jackson detested both paper money and central banking: historians and other scholars who met with Secretary Lew in September 2015 were nearly unanimous in thinking Jackson's place on the $20 bill had always been ironic at best, and that he was a much better candidate for removal than Hamilton.[22] But Jackson had military heroism and tradition on his side, and Hamilton, to his great disappointment, had never been president.

The success of Lin-Manuel Miranda's musical, opening in 2015, changed the calculation. Suddenly, Hamilton went from being the prim hero of central bankers and economists to a sinecure for ticket scalpers and the darling of preteen girls.[23] Miranda's Hamilton was a scrappy, sexy underdog possessed of genius; moreover, Miranda stressed Hamilton's immigrant status, his humble origins, and his opposition to slavery. In March 2016, Miranda borrowed from Hamilton's results-oriented pragmatism by meeting personally with Secretary Lew to urge him to keep Hamilton's portrait in place. On April 19, 2016, Lew announced that Hamilton would remain on the face of the $10, and a vignette of notable American women would appear on the back. At the same time, Lew announced that Harriet Tubman would replace Jackson on the face of the $20. Jackson, in a move that would surely have inspired one of his famous rages, would now look out from the back.[24]

The successful struggle to keep Hamilton on the $10 bill should cause us to note what is going on here: a shift, over centuries, in our sense of what money is and how that is reflected in what money looks like. Before the Civil War, Americans understood paper money's value as something connected to local character and local enterprise, and they decorated their money mostly with generic symbols—eagles, flags, goddesses of commerce, or liberty. In that world, Hamilton was a troubling symbol of elitism and centralized control. The more powerful federal government established after the Civil War shifted the iconography of money to presidents, politicians, and generals, men who served the nation and bolstered its authority. In *that* world, Hamilton was a hero who saw the necessity of centralized banking: he appeared on many different bills. That money was a symbol not of local ambition, but federal stability.

Today, we are reconsidering money again, and the presence of notable American women like Harriet Tubman on our currency points to the idea that our money derives its value not from gold, and not from the deeds of politicians alone, but from the creative labors of American citizens, woman and man. *Hamilton: An American Musical* dramatizes Hamilton's creative resourcefulness, his outsider perspective, and his capacity to make ideas into reality. These are qualities Tubman had as well. *Artistic* labor generates value and meaning: the artistic labor of putting Hamilton's portrait on money reinforced the authority of the money and the government that backed it. The artistic labor of *Hamilton* recast Alexander Hamilton as a democratic hero for multiracial America. In turn, it recast the value of both his life and work and the lives and work of its cast.

NOTES

1. https://twitter.com/Lin_Manuel/status/611310520956776448.

2. Ylan Mui, "A Woman Will Appear on the Redesigned $10 Bill in 2020," *Washington Post*, June 18, 2015.

3. Jackie Calmes, "Treasury Says a Woman's Portrait Will Join Hamilton's on the $10 Bill," *New York Times*, June 9, 2015, C2.

4. Lin-Manuel Miranda, "Stay Alive," *Hamilton*: "Local merchants deny us equipment, assistance / they only take British money / so sing a song of sixpence."

5. Alexander Hamilton to Robert Morris, April 20, 1781, at https://founders.archives.gov/documents/Hamilton/01–02–02–1167.

6. A good accessible history of the Federal Reserve can be found in William Greider, *Secrets of the Temple: How the Federal Reserve Runs the Country* (New York: Simon & Schuster, 1989). For a more recent and more scholarly account, see Allen Meltzer's *A History of the Federal Reserve*, Vol. 1, *1913–1951* (Chicago: University of Chicago Press, 2003).

7. Preceding quotations all from Alexander Hamilton, "Treasury Report on the Establishment of a Mint, January 28, 1791," in *Documentary History of Banking and Currency in the United States*, Vol. 1, edited by Herman E. Krooss (New York: Chelsea House, 1963), 95, 99, 100, 108.

8. Bray Hammond, *Banks and Politics in America from the Revolution to the Civil War* (1958; repr., Princeton, NJ: Princeton University Press, 1991), 72, 114.

9. Numismatist Richard Doty found one instance in which a printer turned an engraving of a white yeoman farmer, produced for a New York bank, into an image of a happy slave by simply darkening the figure's skin and adding a mending patch to his shirt. Richard Doty, *Pictures from a Distant Country: Images on 19th Century U.S. Currency* (Raleigh, NC: Boson Books, 2004), 58.

10. Jefferson to John Adams, January 24, 1814, in *The Writings of Thomas Jefferson*, vol. 13, edited by Andrew Adgate Lipscomb and Albert Ellery Bergh (Washington, DC, 1907), 76–77.

11. Charles Francis Adams, ed., *The Works of John Adams*, vol. 9 (Boston, 1854), 610.

12. Hamilton, "Treasury Report on the Establishment of a Mint," 100.

13. Doty, *Pictures from a Distant Country*, 58.

14. To simplify, the first issues of greenback Civil War paper money are called "Demand" notes; the second series are formally called either "United States Notes" or "Legal Tender Notes." "United States Notes" were printed until 1971. By that time they looked almost exactly like Federal Reserve Notes, except that they had a red seal and serial number.

15. Mildred Adams, "The Gigantic Task of Changing Our Money, *New York Times*, June 30, 1929, Sec. 9, 1.

16. Carter Glass, *An Adventure in Constructive Finance* (New York: Doubleday, 1927), 111.

17. John S. Roberts, "Report: A Woman May Be Featured on the $10 Bill as Soon as 2020," Young Conservatives, June 17, 2015, http://www.youngcons .com/report-a-woman-may-be-featured-on-the-10-bill-as-soon-as-2020/; http://dailycaller.com/2015/06/18/pc-thugs-wrong-to-change-ten-dollar-bill/.

18. Colette Shade, "The Un-American History of Women on Money," *Jezebel*, October 16, 2015, http://jezebel.com/the-un-american-history-of-women -on-money-1736535799.

19. By law only deceased persons may appear on American currency. The paper money must say "In God We Trust" at a location chosen by the secretary of the treasury. The secretary otherwise enjoys a great deal of authority regarding the imagery in paper money.

20. http://www.womenon20s.org/about.

21. https://www.congress.gov/bill/114th-congress/senate-bill/925; "Women on the Twenty Act," *Washington Post*, June 18, 2015.

22. The author participated in this round-table discussion with Secretary Lew and Treasurer of the United States Rosa Rios at the Smithsonian's National Museum of American History.

23. The author has observed his daughter, twelve, and her friends memorizing large chunks of *Hamilton*'s libretto and singing them with brio.

24. Michael Paulson, "Hamilton May Stay on the $10 Bill, Thanks to Broadway," *New York Times*, March 16, 2016, http://www.nytimes.com/2016/03/17/ theater/hamilton-may-stay-on-the-10-bill-thanks-to-help-from-broadway.html; Jackie Calmes, "Harriet Tubman Ousts Andrew Jackson in Change for a $20," *New York Times*, April 20, 2016, http://www.nytimes.com/2016/04/21/us/women -currency-treasury-harriet-tubman.html?_r=0.

CHAPTER 7

Hamilton as Founders Chic

A Neo-Federalist, Antislavery Usable Past?

DAVID WALDSTREICHER AND
JEFFREY L. PASLEY

In 2004 and 2005 two major exhibits funded by billionaire investors and Republican Party activists Richard Gilder and Lewis Lehrman filled the first-floor galleries at the New-York Historical Society. The first, "Alexander Hamilton: The Man Who Made Modern America," was curated by former *National Review* editor Richard Brookhiser and celebrated Hamilton as a nation-creating paragon of Wall Street and military virtues. At the peak of both the George W. Bush-era finance bubble and the post-9/11 experiment with global empire, the NYHS wrapped itself in a ten-dollar bill and decorated its lobby with life-sized statues of Hamilton and Burr firing their shots, fashioned for the occasion. The Hamilton exhibit sought to capitalize on—and reflected the popularity of—what was in 2004 an increasingly popular school of historical writing often termed "Founders Chic." The genre, which emerged in the late 1990s and came into its own with the 2001 publications of Joseph Ellis's *Founding Brothers* and David McCullough's biography of John Adams, offers individual and ensemble portraits of the founding generation aimed at the general reader.[1] Yet the exhibit was widely criticized by professional historians and venues like the *New York Times* as politically conservative hero worship, a too-naked attempt to enshrine finance capitalism and military glory as the foundation of the national story. Relatively speaking, it was a notable failure for the Founders Chic cultural trend.

A silk-screened cloth panel covers the front of the New-York Historical Society during its major 2005 Alexander Hamilton exhibit. *(Lee Snider Photo Images/Shutterstock.com)*

By contrast, the second Gilder-Lehrman–financed show at the New-York Historical Society, "Slavery in New York," was a major critical and popular success, lauded for focusing attention on the less known, but important, presence of Africans and their descendants in the city from the founding of New Amsterdam to the Civil War. Professional historians liked the second exhibit much better, tracking as it did the expanded range of people they had come to cast in the story of early American history. It also also reflected scholars' increasing emphasis on race and slavery in every place and era, not just in their traditional southern, colonial, and antebellum zones. Gilder and Lehrman had also made a major ongoing commitment to slavery-related programming with their endowment of the Gilder Lehrman Institute for the Study of Slavery, Resistance, and Abolition at Yale. One sensed greater comfort among historians with that seemingly more progressive side of their philanthropy than with the finance and warrior hagiography of the Hamilton exhibit.[2]

But as it turned out, the success of that second exhibit offered a clue as to how Alexander Hamilton would soon be rehabilitated to the top of the founder charts. Just as the exhibits were being put together, freelance journalist and popular biographer Ron Chernow, who had previously chronicled the lives of Warburgs, Rockefellers, and Morgans, turned his attention to Hamilton and hit upon a successful formula to sell the first Treasury secretary to the masses: the glamorous grit of the Big Apple, Horatio Alger with a side of Martin Scorsese, and a critic of slavery to boot. In a *New York Times* city section op-ed about his book, "Alexander Hamilton, City Boy," Chernow reported what a tonic it had been to get to know a founder who was not another stuffy, slave-owning rural grandee. Instead he found Hamilton loaded "with brash charm, bottomless energy, and worldly cunning" and "in fact the classic New Yorker and a quintessential urbanite." His book emphasized Hamilton's seeming antislavery credentials and his "immigrant" American status, whatever that might mean for an English-speaking Christian who arrived before the United States even existed.[3]

It was this version of Alexander Hamilton that Lin-Manuel Miranda encountered and become enamored with some time after finishing his first, and more modest, musical *In the Heights*, another show about immigrants struggling to make it in Manhattan. Miranda read Chernow's *Hamilton*, than languishing in movie development hell, and immediately discovered the source material for his new street founder opus. In retrospect, we can see that Miranda's *Hamilton* fused the energy and messages of the two New-York Historical Society exhibits. He valorized his chosen founder, and the nation he founded, by taking Hamilton "off the pedestal" and celebrating both, in a modern, multicultural idiom, as such idioms require, by including "all their flaws," the better to magnify their achievements.[4] At the same time, by placing black and Latino actors front and center in the story of the American founding, along with the historical concerns their presence demands, especially the problem of slavery, *Hamilton: An American Musical* seemed to push the whole subject onto new, more progressive ground.

Few commentators or historians even connected the ensuing *Hamilton* craze to the gray-haired Bush era literary fling with John Adams and George Washington. *Hamilton* seemed a departure from, if not an antidote to, the kind of popular biographies that tended toward a conservative, celebratory narrative of the nation. Ellis's *Founding Brothers* and McCullough's *Adams* were both offered to the world more or less explicitly as responses to the alleged political correctness and obscurantism of academic history writing. Published at the dawn of the George W. Bush era, it was easy to perceive a conservative valence to those books and political reasons for their popularity. In fact, both books reflected a subgenre of Founders Chic that one of us has termed "Federalist Chic," since they celebrated the American founding as seen by and through the eyes of the merchant-led elite who favored strong central government and formed what was in effect America's first ruling party of the same name.[5]

Yet the debts that Miranda's *Hamilton* owes to the Founders Chic genre that McCullough, Ellis, and others cultivated are considerable, and they rob the show of the progressive content it might be imagined to broadcast. While using hip hop to render Broadway musicals, a traditional and upscale entertainment form, cool again, and the founders to make the genre serious, *Hamilton* also sets out to rescue and renew an embarrassingly patriotic, partisan, and partial version of early American history. It makes its hero into a great white hope for the founding, spinning a neo-Federalist, anti-slavery past that is myth, not history. It drops the latest version of Founders Chic to a faster beat.

Celebrating the Founders: Framework of a Genre

What is Founders Chic? The term seems to have been coined by journalist Evan Thomas in 1999, in the wake of a wave of bestselling biographies, to refer to admiring individual portraits of major leaders of the Early Republic like Washington, Jefferson, Adams, Madison, and Hamilton. Perhaps it even more accurately describes the emergence of ensemble studies that defined the founders as a remarkable group of "brothers" or a "generation," terms used repeatedly by Joseph J. Ellis. Ellis himself, then a professor of history at Mount Holyoke College, was a kind of crossover genius who, like Chernow, simultaneously relied upon and distanced himself from contemporary academic scholarship. "Founders Chic" ironically echoed "radical chic," a phrase Tom Wolfe made famous in a 1969 magazine essay about Leonard Bernstein hosting a party for the Black Panthers.[6] The humor and irony derived from both Wolfe's mockery of the New Left's cult of personalities, and also the distance between the now-ancient deference to authentic black radicals and the new devotion to white founding revolutionaries.

Like most genres, Founders Chic has evolved since it emerged during the 1990s, and in the process has become more distinctive and easier to identify. Nearly all versions display four main characteristics that tend to reinforce one another. First, such works celebrate "the founders" or "founding fathers," seeking to give them credit for the birth of the nation and much of what is good about America, and particularly what is redemptive and enduring in the American political tradition. With little apology, they are works of literary flag-waving that seek to inspire at least a bit of national pride, in a form palatable even to reviewers and readers who would never consider waving a literal flag. Leadership and greatness are central, even overriding themes. In this sense, Founders Chic represents a revival of the Great Man theory of history that has remained relatively unchanged since Thomas Carlyle formulated it in the salad days of nineteenth-century romantic nationalism: "They were the leaders of men, these great ones; the modellers, patterns, and in a wide sense creators, of whatsoever the general mass of men contrived to do or to attain."[7] While not openly elitist, at least not usually, the Founders Chic version of Great Man history manages to convey a sunny message of flattery to power, assuring important people that they follow in important footsteps.

Second, Founders Chic writers are particularly interested in questions of character. They portray character as a pathway to understanding the personal lives of these men and relate their personalities, flaws, and relationships with each other to the course of events that shaped the nation. Personality shapes destiny and makes history. Ellis gave the focus on character as much analytical heft as anyone could in his genre-defining *Founding Brothers*: "The shape and character of the political institutions were determined by a relatively small number of leaders who knew each other, who collaborated and collided with each other in patterns that replicated at the level of personality and ideology the principle of checks and balances imbedded structurally in the Constitution."[8] By essentially equating the founding characters with the U.S. nation-state and all it represents to American readers, Founders Chic books (and *Hamilton* the musical) may even manage to outdo Carlyle, who at least understood and acknowledged that he was dealing with matters of the spirit. Our modern biographers often send similar messages about heroes embodying the nation, but in the belief that they are providing sober accounts of real politics and real life, "warts and all."

Third, in keeping with its nationalist aims, Founders Chic is avowedly establishmentarian, however much it traffics in "revolution." It favors those figures among the founding generation of political leaders who supported U.S. national institutions, as they were popularly understood at the end of the twentieth century. Proponents of the federal Constitution loom large: the rise in the use of the term "founders" as opposed to "founding fathers" came along with the bicentennial of the Constitution and the rise of "original intent" jurisprudence. It was adapted from the older, more specific term "framers," a word that denoted the actual attendees of the Constitutional Convention of 1787. Regarding the politics of the 1790s, which came to be afforded equal or greater narrative weight than the Revolution or the 1780s, Founders Chic leans heavily to the right, aligning it with the conservative nationalists of the time who ended up in the Federalist Party. They were men fearful of the French Revolution's sympathizers and of the democracy that fans of that revolution increasingly practiced in their clubs and newspapers criticizing the government. Using the major bestsellers as a guide, George Washington, John Adams, and Alexander Hamilton are the stars (if rarely the latter two between the same covers), Thomas Jefferson and Aaron Burr the foils, James Madison a puzzling side character, and many others (Tom Paine? Sam Adams?) simply absent.

Finally, and increasingly of late, Founders Chic seeks to recover what might be called a *relatable* founding, full of behavior and ideas and values modern readers can embrace as their own. Founders have been cast as the friends, fathers, spouses, or bosses we wish we had, the inspirational leaders we wish we saw on television, and, if possible, holders of views we might agree with. More and more, the most troubling aspect of the founding era, and the greatest threat to continued reader and citizen identification with its leaders, has been the failure to address slavery and racism in this new land of liberty and equality. Where the old musical *1776* used the problem of slavery as a sobering third act crisis, emphasizing the degree to which the sin fell on everyone present and threatened the new nation, the logic of Founders Chic instead seeks and highlights antislavery sentiment wherever it can be found, and looks to burnish those founding characters who qualify by association with a cause most Americans now admire.

Here there is something of a historical advantage to the Federalists, based partly on facts (such as the contrast between Jefferson's slavery problems and Adams's willingness to recognize Haiti, or Hamilton's membership in the New York Manumission Society), and partly on reader unawareness of the significant presence of slavery in the North before 1800 and the Federalists' heavy involvement in it. But New England Federalists also liked to attack the Virginia slaveocracy when it suited them, particularly to complain about the electoral disadvantages they faced because of the three-fifths clause. So the material was, and is, there, and when well plotted, Federalist antislavery becomes a reason we can still venerate the founders, or at least some of them. This is why abolition and manumission have evolved from a minor to a major key in Founders Chic.[9]

Much like Ellis's series of bestselling biographies and ensemble studies from *Founding Brothers* (2000) and *His Excellency* (2003) to *First Family* (2010) and *The Quartet: Orchestrating the Second American Revolution* (2015), *Hamilton* presents its subject and his associates (especially Washington) as "indispensable to the infant republic." Because of this, Hamilton's assassination at the hands of the unprincipled Aaron Burr becomes a tragedy of Shakespearean proportions, particularly since Hamilton's early death is foretold in the first lines of the show and the character repeatedly returns to it as a theme. This is Great Man history with a vengeance. The founding fathers in *Hamilton* fight the Revolutionary War, give us the Constitution, and create key institutions like the financial and judicial systems. They have almost magical powers, and are played by magisterial actors: in the well-written and assembled libretto-companion book *Hamilton: The Revolution*, Lin-Manuel Miranda refers to Chris Jackson, the actor who plays Washington, as "so fucking majestic." Onstage and in history, the emphasis is very much on what these men as individuals and as a small group were able to do. Ron Chernow insists that the show is "history for grownups" and doesn't deify the founders, but that is a relative rather than absolute matter, since we are constantly reminded of each character's ideals and achievements. The founders don't need to be gods so long as they can embody what we see as important national virtues. Nothing undermines their status as the "greatest generation," to use the term seized from the warriors of World War II and employed when "Founders Chic" burst on to the scene in the magazines and bestsellers during the mid-to-late 1990s. The founding fathers' humanity and their flaws, easily developed through all those letters they wrote, only makes their achievements all the more striking and worthy of reverence. In that sense, they are more than gods. Zeus and Odin make more mistakes in their respective mythologies than George Washington does in the Founders Chic canon.[10]

Updating Hamilton for a Modern Age

The portrayal of Alexander Hamilton that graces the Broadway stage eight times a week would not have been possible without the reimagining of the man undertaken by Ron Chernow. Chernow took the few known facts about Hamilton's childhood, rarely discussed by him or anyone else during his life, applied some twentieth-century storytelling conventions, and fashioned them into character-defining experiences. Our hero overcomes the trauma of a "ghastly Dickensian childhood" in the slave-haunted Caribbean islands to fight his way up the ladder of success in the mean but welcoming streets of Manhattan. "What other town would have embraced so warmly an aspiring immigrant of murky origins or tolerated the frenetic pace of his career?" Chernow asked *New York Times* readers in a 2004 article.[11] Not without some help from the many locally patriotic New Yorkers in the higher echelons of publishing, journalism, and academia, Chernow's *Hamilton* became the next big hit for Founders Chic, one that quietly that kept building even as the marketplace became more crowded. His book dealt with politics and policy as well as character and personalities, and despite his cheerleading for capitalism, worked hard to sell Hamilton to modern-day liberal admirers of urban life and government institutions. The real life Hamilton was a strikingly modern figure, climbing the meritocratic institutional ladder of higher education and the military even before they had been fashioned into meritocracies. Yet more crucial to his success were the highly traditional means of attracting elite patronage and marrying into a landed family far older and wealthier than the Jeffersons and Madisons and Washingtons.

The politics of Chernow's Hamilton are a slippery matter, far more so than the traditional forgetting of elite men's ascent to power and influence through strategic marriages. Like the Ellis and McCullough books, Chernow's shared the Federalist Chic tendency of using Thomas Jefferson's involvement with slavery—as his enemies in the Federalist Party did in the Virginian's lifetime—to cast suspicion on his advocacy for democracy, religious dissent, and other liberal ideas. Chernow used Jefferson as a foil too, but did Ellis and McCullough one better by offering Hamilton as a liberal hero. As a result, Chernow managed to create a strikingly appropriate history for the attenuated form of liberalism that became dominant in the Democratic party of Bill and Hillary Clinton, Al Gore, John Kerry, and, as it turned out, President Barack Obama. Like these contemporary figures, Chernow's Hamilton was finance friendly, allergic to radicalism, and an eager user of military, but was still interested in improving society through certain limited government programs and by expanding and protecting the individual rights of America's increasing array of what were once called "minority groups." For want of a better one, the proper term for this outlook would seem to be "neoliberal," which applies both in the academic sense of accepting and promoting a hegemonic capitalist ethos and in the more prosaic, literal one, as a label adopted in the 1980s by centrist Democrats including Gore, the Clintons, and now forgotten figures like Gary Hart.[12]

It was precisely in this neoliberal world that Lin-Manuel Miranda and his *Hamilton* were formed. Lin-Manuel's father, Luis Miranda Jr., made a career working for the centrist elements of New York's Democratic political elite, starting in the office of Mayor Ed Koch (who endorsed Gore in the 1988 primaries) and then moving on to consulting work for Senators Hillary Clinton, Charles Schumer, and a host of others. In the PBS documentary *Hamilton's America*, Lin-Manuel remarks, "I'm just playing my dad." Thus, it was no accident that the hit musical became such a touchstone for the Obama White House and hosted a 2016 Hillary Clinton campaign fundraiser at the theater itself. The tie-in libretto book *Hamilton: The Revolution* begins and ends with Obama, from Miranda debuting a song from the show at a White House event in 2009 to the president visiting the cast on stage in New York in 2015.[13]

Yet *Hamilton* does more than create a figure attuned to our neoliberal age. It updates the genre of Founders Chic through hip-hop vernacular. Boasting of all kinds is typical of hip hop, as is relating exaggerated sexual conquests. Political debates are rendered as mano-a-mano cabinet "rap battles" scripted as the dozens, and are repeated testaments to the participants' superhuman stamina. Witness one of the few lines delivered without music: Burr renders a brief account of the *Federalist* essays, informing us that Hamilton wrote a startling fifty-one, more than twice as many as the puny, Jefferson-tailing Madison and almost ten times as many as sickly John Jay. We're invited to gasp at Hamilton's boldness and sheer linguistic

Hamilton was repeatedly celebrated by President Barack Obama; here, he welcomes the cast to the White House for a performance on March 14, 2016. *(AP Photo/Jacquelyn Martyn)*

ability in giving a six-hour speech at the Constitutional Convention, although not a word is said about the content or how it was received: Hamilton famously advocated a monarchy in a speech his colleagues admired but ignored. Unlike Madison, Hamilton subsequently left Philadelphia for New York, showing little patience with being in the minority or in the give-and-take of the convention. Liberal and conservative historians alike have praised the framers of the Constitution, and especially Madison, for their reasoned argumentation and compromises; in the play, these guys rant and call names—except for Washington, who plays referee, and the ever-politic Burr. Despite its close and reciprocated embrace of the coolly rational Barack Obama, hip-hopped *Hamilton* may better express the political culture that gave us President Donald Trump: skepticism that reason matters at all in politics, last-minute manipulations of the electorate and the electoral college, and an impatience with institutional processes compared to the fast writing, the tweeting, and the shouting.[14]

This is not just Hamilton in hip hop: it is Hamilton made in the image of the play's author and leading actor. As *Hamilton: The Revolution*—the book about the musical written by Miranda and Jeremy McCarter—makes clear, Miranda deeply identifies with his subject. Like Hamilton, he himself has "a natural tendency toward diligence." We are reminded in McCarter's commentary, as well as by Miranda himself, that the play has twenty thousand words, putting it on a par, for theater, with Shakespeare (or perhaps in political literature, *The Federalist Papers*). The book version puts Miranda's manuscripts on the page, like Hamilton's letters and pamphlets, and tells us that Miranda—like the historians he consulted, Joanne Freeman and Ron Chernow—made the requisite pilgrimage to Nevis in search of nonexistent manuscript scraps. This is made most poignant on the recently released *Hamilton Mixtape*, where Miranda joins the rapper Nas in testifying that, like Hamilton, "I Wrote My Way Out," though perhaps his subject and collaborator had more formidable socioeconomic traps to escape. (Miranda, it seems, was bullied at his prestigious public magnet high school for being a nerd.) All of this is consistent with the form Miranda chose. The self-mythologizing tendency of hip-hop lyrical tropes has long been part of the genre's popular appeal—"get rich or die tryin'" is a message that speaks to upwardly mobile strivers across many boundaries of class and race. Projecting such mythologies back on Hamilton creates a perfect rapping vessel for the pride and anxieties of a top college-bound student: "Got a lot farther by working a lot harder / By being a lot smarter / By being a self-starter," advice no scoutmaster, Rotarian, or Republican politician could possibly deny.[15]

But Miranda did not see himself as imposing a form on his hero, but rather, opening up who that hero really was. For Miranda and McCarter, Alexander Hamilton himself "embodies hip hop" in his striving, in his immigrant, ostensibly traumatic origins, and his determination to "rise up." The play is peopled with hip-hop characters: immigrants who "get the job done"; slumming Schuyler sisters with attitude; spouses facing deadlines: while *Hamilton* often cleverly calls overt attention to eighteenth-century dress and mores and politics, the play also suggests that things have not changed as much as we sometimes think. Miranda's creative insights can, therefore, be a powerful wedge against nostalgia for an all-white, and idealized, founding moment, and we have to take very seriously the responses of many who say that the musical allows them to see themselves anew in the nation's founding story. Part of the delight of the show is to point out parallels between contemporary New York and that of the late eighteenth century. *Hamilton: The Revolution* (itself a runaway bestseller) is aptly titled precisely because the authors give the show the status of a movement and compare it to the American Revolution. "This is our form of protest," Chris Jackson says about the performance. According to McCarter, the show itself continues Hamilton's people-making American Revolution.[16]

Yet in its very insistence that we can all identify with selected founders, *Hamilton* depends upon Founders Chic's burnishing of the founders' reputations in the wake of late twentieth-century disillusionment, especially in the context of a renewed appreciation of the role slavery, and its reaffirmation in the Constitution, played in the nation's birth. Some historians have tried to build a more encompassing history on this approach by drawing our attention to alternative founders—black founders, and more radical or truly "revolutionary founders."[17] But with the possible exception of allowing women more time on stage than do most Founders Chic tomes, *Hamilton* does not do so. Instead it suggests that since Hamilton was a West Indian immigrant, and at least quasi-"gangsta," twentieth-century Americans can identify with him as an unproblematic outsider, regarding him with no more ambivalence than we devote to any tragic hero—and, if we are honest, just as much admiration.[18]

Similarly, the casting of *Hamilton*, in which black actors portray white statesmen to make the point of their universality (and black equality) all the more poignantly and effectively, is less disruptive to Founders Chic than it might initially appear. As Lyra Monteiro argues in this volume, there is a cost to the flipped casting, and that is the loss of the viewpoints and the visibility of slaves themselves in the history.[19] It is also a deep mistake to think of Hamilton as akin to late twentieth-century Caribbean immigrants of color who have faced North American racial discrimination. In fact, Federalists presided over the creation of the dangerous immigrant as a political category through their fear-mongering about the French and refugee radicals, a campaign that culminated in the Alien and Sedition Acts, early American history's version of McCarthyism. Hamilton was not an immigrant to North America at all in the legal sense, since Nevis was part of the British Empire. He was also of the merchant class and, regardless of his struggles, never left it; rather, he represented that class, consistently and effectively, as the voices of his political opponents in *Hamilton* convey at various points. He may have been mocked as a bastard or a creole on a few occasions, but so were other elites of questionable parentage. In other words, none of the qualities that Miranda enumerates as Hamilton's social burdens should transform the first friend and architect of Wall Street into a working-class hero, much less turn a supporter of the Alien and Sedition Acts into a poster child for multiculturalism and twenty-first-century liberalism. But all of this becomes difficult if not impossible to understand from the Federalist Chic viewpoint that Miranda has embraced.

Favoring the Federalists: The Stock Market Is Up

Identifying so resolutely with Hamilton as a nation-builder creates another problem: justifying his particularly virulent brand of partisan politics. Consistent with the Founders Chic trend more generally, *Hamilton* portrays the Early Republic with a decidedly pro-Federalist bias as well as with wishful thinking about what that meant. Paradoxically, Hamilton and the Federalists become sources of our modern democratic ideals even though they opposed them. Because we the audience are identifying with Hamilton against Jefferson, the Treasury secretary must have been right about everything—or at least, everything important to us. Relying entirely on Chernow and Joanne Freeman's *Affairs of Honor*, *Hamilton* utterly misses a generation of scholarship that pushed the origins

of American democracy back to the 1790s, following instead the
Founders Chic line about national politics as the interactions of
elites in the capital, epitomized by the ten rules of the duel.[20]

The reputations of the founders operate like a stock market
among readers: when Jefferson is down, Adams and Hamilton go
up. One can hardly sample the recent literature in this field without
noticing this, a cycle that began with Gilded Age Democrats' fasci-
nation with Jefferson, the Hamilton-worship of turn-of-the century
Republicans like Theodore Roosevelt, a Progressive and New Deal
era Jefferson revival, and a recent Hamilton comeback noticeable in
scholarship by the neoliberal 1990s.[21]

This dynamic was baked into the early years of Founders Chic.
The genre really kicked off with Joseph Ellis's *Passionate Sage* (1993),
a study of the character (sterling, the author concluded) of John
Adams; this volume was followed by two major appreciations of
Thomas Jefferson that were among the least appreciative of the whole
cycle. A blockbuster television documentary by Ken Burns on Jefferson and Joseph Ellis's follow-up bestseller, *American Sphinx* (1997),
kept a careful critical distance from its quintessentially "American"
subject, who was portrayed as capable of Reagan-like self-deception.
The emphasis on inner character made that almost impossible for a
liberal (but slaveholding) visionary like Jefferson in any case; charges
of hypocrisy were much easier to avoid for those "characters" who
defended the status quo of their time. But 1997 also proved a terrible year for Jefferson's reputation more broadly, with the publication of Annette Gordon-Reed's *Thomas Jefferson and Sally Hemings:
An American Controversy* and the nearly contemporaneous revelations that DNA testing had scientifically proven a link between some
Hemings and Jefferson descendants. Given how much of the public interest in the founders and the simultaneous celebrations of the
World War II generation (Tom Brokaw's *The Greatest Generation*
also came out in 1997, *Saving Private Ryan* the following year) was
invested in an invidious contrast with the decadent lightweights
and phonies who led America in the 1990s, it was impossible not
to connect the renewed Jefferson scandals with the sex scandals

surrounding President William Jefferson Clinton, who had theatrically identified with Jefferson as a southern populist democrat whose
election might also prove epochal. Other popular books from the
same period attacked Jefferson as a bloodthirsty fellow-traveling
Jacobin and dismissed his Declaration of Independence as an overrated pastiche of earlier, more original, declarations of rights issued
in the individual colonies.[22]

The fall of Jefferson had its consequences, as other founders filled
the literary and ideological space. By the turn of the millennium
and the ascendancy of George W. Bush, the conservative president
you would supposedly like to have a beer with, the trend was toward Benjamin Franklin, John Adams, Hamilton, and especially
George Washington, the subject of additional books by Chernow,
McCullough, Ellis, and a legion of other admirers. These were the
founders who could be portrayed as *conservative* revolutionaries—
and with some selective emphasis, as simultaneously antislavery.[23]

This synthesis solved a number of problems. It has always been
difficult for historians to avoid partisanship in writing about the
1790s, a hyperpartisan age of extremes and political creativity as
well as controversy that is really whitewashed when it is called, as
it used to be, "the Federalist Era" or "the age of Federalism."[24] At
its best, *Hamilton* delineates the problem: the importance of who
tells the story, and the waxing and waning efforts of Washington,
Hamilton, and Jefferson to rise above selfish interests for the good
of the nation. The total absence of John Adams as a character in
the musical is obviously the major change to Founders Chic in its
new, Hamiltonian phase. Although mentioned in passing, even the
song "The Adams Administration" was cut. This was partly because
of the adverse reaction of workshop audiences to the hip-hop in-
sults directed at Abigail Adams, who holds a revered place in the
annals of Founders Chic as a nascent feminist and the one true
candidate for female founder.[25] Despite this departure from genre
conventions, *Hamilton* sticks to its guns historiographically, taking
nearly all its interpretive cues from neo-Federalist—actually, what
was then known as high or anti-Adams Federalist—apologetics,

with eyes only for the development of a robust American fiscal-military state.[26]

This identification with Federalists begins with *Hamilton*'s depiction of the Revolution. The perspective of Hamilton, "the Continentalist," is also that of (some) Continental Army officers who embrace Hamilton as a friend and comrade in the second scene. The obsession with a cult of honor that is so evident in Hamilton's story was also a particularly Federalist, and most particularly a Continental Army officer, phenomenon.[27] For the Revolutionary years, of course, the identification with the Americans is more properly described as Patriot or nationalist than partisan, but it is heightened in *Hamilton* nevertheless, as it is in most celebrations of the Revolution that focus on leadership and elites. We never doubt that the Patriots were right, that they were on the side of freedom for all and self-government. The giveaway here is the uproarious presentation of King George III, in the twice-reprised "You'll Be Back" number, as a spurned lover willing to kill the founders' wives and families to remind them of his love. There is no rational British constitutional argument for sovereignty over the colonies here—it's just tyranny, and a maniacal brand of tyranny at that. As a perverse rewrite of the Declaration of Independence with its laundry list of blame for the monarch, the king's grievances in *Hamilton* are a masterpiece of historical compression (King George did go mad, although not from grief at the loss of the American colonies, and not until many years later). If only the world could have seen this George III, American independence would have been so much easier to justify, at home and abroad.

Hamilton's Hamilton is portrayed as right on every political issue, in contrast to Jefferson, who from his reintroduction to the United States in 1789 seems to doubt the need for a stronger government from a distinctly southern perspective that the real Jefferson and Madison—both nationalists by any measure throughout this period—at most might have recognized but kept under wraps. They are the sectionalists: a classic Federalist accusation that is repeatedly aimed at them even as they occasionally question the

New Yorker's Wall Street motives. The play conflates the state-building Hamilton of 1787–88 with the Hamilton that devised the financial plan—precisely the point of divergence for Jefferson and Madison. Miranda's Hamilton becomes a fighter for a "strong central democracy" even though it was the opposition that championed democracy, and Federalists, including Hamilton, who mocked them for it. Jeremy McCarter, coauthor of *Hamilton: The Revolution*, has no doubt: Hamilton is the founder who truly understood and stood for the nation and its egalitarian future. This is because Jefferson and Madison stand for the South—and slavery, which is *not* the nation—at least, not a nation anyone wishes to own. In "Cabinet Battle #1," Hamilton scoffs at receiving "a civics lesson from a slaver." Later Jefferson and Madison call themselves "southern mother-fuckin / Democratic Republicans," and in "The Election of 1800," Jeffersonian and Burrite claims that Hamilton is an "elitist" are mocked, which seems like overkill in light of Jefferson's velveteen outfit. The point is not that these partisan versions are completely wrong. The play does present some of the Federalist shibboleths about Jefferson skeptically, which seems necessary in order to ratify Hamilton's preference in 1800 for a Jefferson with "principles" over a Burr with "none." The point is that *Hamilton* subsumes the issues to the characters and their personalities, and in the process, loses sight of the struggle for democracy—a political idea that the real Hamilton, like his party, spoke of with disdain.[28]

Such a story leans Federalist in its interpretation by substituting dictates of the Founders Chic genre for historical fact. For example, from the moment of Washington's inauguration—actually, from the earliest moments of the struggle to ratify the Constitution—Federalists gushed over the greatness of their leaders and explained at length why elected officials deserved popular deference to their superior literary and political skills. This is not an arcane fact for those of us in the field: it's obvious from any period newspaper. Amid accusations of aristocracy, Federalists created a cult of Washington. Their national organ, the *Gazette of the United States*, was filled with paeans to his leadership. By the time of the election of

1796, when Federalists had made "character" itself an issue in political campaigns, Jefferson was being derided as a Francophile, irreligious ideologue, and fop. All this was the background to the original revelations about Jefferson's intimate relationship with Sally Hemings by Democratic-Republican turned Federalist journalist James Thomson Callender (that these charges were politically inspired was also a reason why Jeffersonians could effectively dismiss the story as a partisan lie for so long). This complexity is muted beyond recognition in *Hamilton*, however. In the play's depiction of the election of 1800, there are evocative intimations that Alexander Hamilton was trying to control a "paper war" that had become multiply mediated and beyond his energetic control, as readers read aloud and pages fly up in the air. In this sense, Hamilton's repeated recourse to dueling and his excessive, even obsessive pamphleteering were not just an attempt to deflect the circumstances of his birth and station, but also attempts to control a democratizing political world that would not respond to his writerly and lawyerly skills as often or completely as he would have liked.

Miranda almost gets the paradox of the young founder trapped by the older norms of his Federalist political subculture. Yet the overriding framework of honor politics and character battles—as opposed to a more modern, democratic, public opinion–oriented understanding of politics—is essentially a Federalist understanding of federalism. Its terms inevitably favor the gentlemen who tried to preserve and control it, as opposed to those who, like Jefferson and Burr, glimpsed the possibilities of a more democratic local and national politics and did so much more to advance it.

It worth noting that Miranda, and the historians he relies on, maintain a more attractive version of Hamilton and the Federalists by editing them to suit modern liberal sensibilities. We do not see the Hamilton John Adams broke with, the Hamilton who, as Treasury secretary, undermined his president, or the Hamilton who seemed to be actively seeking a war with France and wanted to attack Louisiana rather than purchase it. Nor are we privy to what happened when Federalists did try to engage in their version of democratic politics, which was to whip up the winds of nativism and politicized Christianity in a formula we now easily recognize as conservative populism. Just before his death, the not especially devout Hamilton even proposed creating an organized Christian right—in the form of network of Christian Constitutional Societies—as a way to take back American politics from Jefferson and the Democratic-Republicans. The romantic duelist has considerably more Broadway appeal than Karl Rove in knee breeches.[29]

Character and the Antislavery Plot Device

Part of what makes *Hamilton* good theater is its acknowledgment that its hero is a flawed character, taken down by his lust and his pride. That nuance is absent when it comes to the politics of slavery in Hamilton's world. Here the play follows, and even outstrips, Founders Chic tomes that present Benjamin Franklin and John Adams as abolitionists, even though their antislavery beliefs were rarely expressed publicly and were only haltingly, if that, part of their political activities toward, or at, the end of their lives. Recent biographers like Chernow have similarly taken to exaggerating Hamilton's antislavery credentials, putting what one is tempted to call a politically correct sheen on his overarching social conservatism. His role in founding the New York Manumission (not abolition) Society is taken to be a career-long "crusade," his abolitionism "fervent" and "conspicuous" despite his stance against antislavery critics of the Constitution in the New York ratifying convention.[30]

It is hard to exaggerate the centrality of slavery, or rather antislavery, in *Hamilton*. Here we dissent partially from our fellow critics, including some in this volume, who stress the absence of slaves in the play. The absence of slave voices, while telling, is not an end in itself, and it is not an absence of slavery. It is rather necessary because it preserves Hamilton himself as the voice of the oppressed. And Hamilton's antislavery becomes a sledgehammer to silence any doubt about Hamiltonian virtues. It's there at the beginning, middle, and end, and the emplotment of slavery as a theme is worthy of close attention, because it tells us something about the cultural politics of Founders Chic in the present moment—or, what makes it possible, as President Obama noted, for Dick Cheney and himself to agree on how great the play is but nothing else.[31]

When Hamilton begins to tell the story of his origins, we learn that "every day while slaves were being slaughtered and carted / Away across the waves," Hamilton was trying to get out, "hoping for something better"—suggesting that he identified with the slaves. Indeed, we learn it in *from Jefferson's first words* in the play—and who would know better? Jefferson adds that "Inside he was longing for something to be a part of, / The brother was ready to beg, steal, borrow or barter." Hamilton is a "brother" looking to join a movement. This sets up the next, remarkable, primal, and highly fictional scene in a tavern where young Alexander bonds with Lafayette, John Laurens, and Hercules Mulligan, self-described "revolutionary manumission abolitionists," a neologism that almost seems to hide the less familiar word for the less radical position that Hamilton actually held. Laurens appears three times as a "freedom-fighting abolitionist," including a ghostlike appearance as his friend's conscience in Act II. This is a strange role for a South Carolinian, although Laurens himself did have antislavery leanings, but is perhaps in keeping with the play's fanciful notion, straight out of Chernow, that a white West Indian merchant-in-training was a born abolitionist.[32] Laurens did try to get South Carolina to enlist and emancipate slaves as soldiers, and Hamilton supported the idea in a letter to his friend. Jefferson in his different capacities made arguably parallel gestures to put antislavery in the Declaration and in legislation during the 1770s and 1780s, though he complained about the British liberating his own slaves. But none of this is contextualized in terms of the British, foreign Tory, and domestic Loyalists' accusations of hypocrisy, or the views and actions of slaves themselves. It's just a matter of belief translated into politics. Laurens testifies that he and Hamilton "wrote essays against slavery" together (historians haven't found any); at Yorktown they insist, "We will never be free until we end slavery."[33]

Thus, white nationalist Federalists become martyrs and heroes in a cause that conflates the Revolution with antislavery politics, even while the imperatives of federal union silenced the actual anti-slavery forces in the Continental Congress. Though mythical, the public quality of this vocal Federalist antislavery impulse in *Hamilton* is further underlined by the repeated characterization of Burr (who was actually at least as antislavery as Hamilton) as having no principles, as someone who urges Hamilton to "talk less" and avoid controversial topics. The theme is carried into the 1790s by the cabinet battles with Jefferson and Madison, in which they alone represent the slave power. Hamilton as abolitionist is capped off in the final scene, in which Eliza Schuyler Hamilton tells us after her husband's death "I speak out against slavery," as if Hamilton had urged her to do so. It isn't enough for her to claim him as a prophet; she actually forwards an interpretation of abolitionism as the epitome of his statesmanship, stating in the line right after proclaiming her own stance: "You could have done so much more if you only had—Time."[34]

Fantasizing a Hamilton who begins by identifying with flogged slaves rather than profiting from them as a West Indies merchant could not have helped but do, and who ends as an abolitionist inspiration from the grave, *Hamilton* departs significantly from the historical record. Although he understood manumission as one solution to the problem, like most of his peers, Hamilton wasn't an antislavery activist or a "revolutionary" in that sense. It is telling that in order to celebrate and diversify the founding for our time *Hamilton* has to take such extreme liberties with its character's racial, as well as his class, politics. Call it a new log cabin myth—except that Abraham Lincoln really was of humble origins, and as he himself said, he gained a hatred of slavery by seeing the trade from his river raft on a voyage to New Orleans.[35] Hamilton never said that his Caribbean origins made him hate slavery, or that the federal government should do anything about slavery—on the contrary, he repeatedly put forward Federalist slaveholders as presidential candidates. We just wish to imagine he did, so he can be our great white hope for the founding.

Coda: When William Hamilton Gets His Shot; or,
What Have We Missed?

That's one direction for the future: a revised version of Federalist Chic that doubles down on antislavery as certain founders' legacy. But to paraphrase Miranda's Jefferson, we might also ask, *what did he miss?* We can think of one missed opportunity. In celebrating the final end of slavery in New York in 1827, the free black political leader William Hamilton (1773–1836) attacked Jefferson for his racism and hypocrisy, calling him an "ambidexter philosopher."[36] This Hamilton's turn of phrase sounds far more like Miranda's hip-hop Hamilton than anything the real Alexander Hamilton is known to have actually said.

But there may be more than coincidence at work. William Hamilton was rumored to be the illegitimate son of Alexander Hamilton. This is a possibility that no one who knows that African American testimonies about some of Thomas Jefferson's children turned out to have been true, or who has seen the play and thus knows about Hamilton's flirtations and his affair with Maria Reynolds, can blithely dismiss as "dubious," as Chernow does.[37]

No other Hamilton biographer or Founders Chic historian has found William Hamilton interesting enough to mention, much less explore, as a character in the story of the nation's founding, or the beginning of the end of slavery. The NYHS exhibit "Slavery in New York," did, however, and several historians discuss William Hamilton in the book that accompanied the exhibit. A carpenter by trade as well as the first president of the New York African Society for Mutual Relief, he was "arguably the most important public figure in antebellum black Manhattan." His activism began as early as March 1796, when he wrote a scathing letter to Governor John Jay asserting "How falsely & contradictory do the Americans speak when this land a land of Liberty & equality a Christian country when almost every part of it abounds with slavery and oppression." He displayed a number of distinctly Hamiltonian or "founding father" characteristics, including a gift for leadership, a nationalist sensibility, and a belief in writing as fighting. He delivered and published several fascinating orations for African American celebrations of abolition, and chaired the fourth annual National Negro Convention in New York in 1834. He even had his own turn with guns, fighting off anti-abolition rioters on the Fourth of July that year.[38]

The activism and the writing of William Hamilton set the stage for the actually revolutionary manumission abolitionism of the next generation. Perhaps we will not wait another generation to see him, or his movement, take center stage.

NOTES

1. Edward Rothstein, "Our Father the Modernist," *New York Times*, September 10, 2004; Mike Wallace, "Business-Class Hero," http://www.gotham center.org/uploads/4/7/4/4/47448137/wallace.business_class_hero.pdf; Mike Wallace, "That Hamilton Man," *New York Review of Books*, February 10, 2005; William Hogeland, "Inventing Alexander Hamilton," in his *Inventing American History* (Cambridge, MA: MIT Press, 2009), 1–45.

2. Ira Berlin and Leslie M. Harris, ed., *Slavery in New York* (New York: New Press, 2005); Richard Rabinowitz, *Curating America* (Chapel Hill: University of North Carolina Press, 2016), 266.

3. Ron Chernow, "CITY PEOPLE; Alexander Hamilton, City Boy," *New York Times*, April 25, 2004, http://www.nytimes.com/2004/04/25/nyregion/city-people-alexander-hamilton-city-boy.html; Ron Chernow, *Alexander Hamilton* (New York: Penguin, 2004), 6.

4. Miranda's remarks in the documentary *Hamilton's America*, *Great Performances*, PBS, October 21, 2016.

5. Jeffrey L. Pasley, "Publick Occurrences: Federalist Chic," *Common-Place* 2, no. 2 (2002), http://www.common-place-archives.org/publick/200202.shtml.

6. Jay Tolson, "Founding Rivalries," *US News and World Report*, February 26, 2001, 51–55; Evan Thomas, "Founders Chic: Live from Philadelphia," *Newsweek*, July 9, 2001, 48–49; Tom Wolfe, "Radical Chic: That Party at Lenny's," *New York Magazine*, June 8, 1970, repr. in Wolfe, *Radical Chic and Mau-Mauing the Flak-Catchers* (New York: Farrar, Straus and Giroux, 1970). For earlier analyses see Sean Wilentz, "America Made Easy: McCullough, Adams, and the Decline of Popular History," *New Republic*, July 2, 2001, 35–40; Andrew Burstein, "The Politics of Memory: Taking the Measure of the Ever More Popular Demand for Historical Greatness," *Washington Post Book World*, October 14, 2001; David Waldstreicher, "Founders Chic as Culture War," *Radical History*

Review 84 (Fall 2002): 185–194; Pasley, "Federalist Chic"; H. W. Brands, "Founders Chic, " *Atlantic Monthly*, September 2003; Barry Gewen, "Forget the Founding Fathers," *New York Times Book Review*, June 5, 2005; Andrew Schocket, *Fighting Over the Founders* (New York: NYU Press, 2014), 49–84.

7. Thomas Carlyle, *On Heroes, Hero-Worship, and the Heroic in History* (London: Chapman and Hall, 1840), 3.

8. Joseph J. Ellis, *Founding Brothers: The Revolutionary Generation* (New York: Knopf, 2000), 17.

9. The antislavery theme in Federalist political culture was first laid out in Linda K. Kerber, *Federalists in Dissent: Imagery and Ideology in Jeffersonian America* (Ithaca, NY: Cornell University Press, 1970).

10. Lin-Manuel Miranda and Jeremy McCarter, *Hamilton: The Revolution* (New York: Grand Central Publishing, 2016), 136, 58–59; Joseph J. Ellis, *Founding Brothers: The Revolutionary Generation* (New York: Knopf, 2000), 12–13; Gordon S. Wood, "The Greatest Generation," *New York Review of Books* 48, no. 5 (March 29, 2001): 17–22; Ray Raphael, *Founding Myths: Stories That Hide Our Patriotic Past* (New York: New Press, 2014), 125–141; Tom Carson, "Fables of Our Fathers," *The Baffler* 33 (2016), https://thebaffler.com/salvos/fables-of-our-fathers-carson.

11. Chernow, "Alexander Hamilton, City Boy."

12. Waldstreicher, "Founders Chic as Culture War"; Pasley, "Federalist Chic"; David Harvey, *A Brief History of Neoliberalism* (Oxford; New York: Oxford University Press, 2007); Randall Rothenberg, *The Neoliberals: Creating the New American Politics* (New York: Simon & Schuster, 1984).

13. Ken Lovett, "Now Playing: Hamilton the Political Consultant," *New York Daily News*, September 5, 2016, http://www.nydailynews.com/news/poli tics/playing-hamilton-political-consultant-article-1.2777740; "Luis A. Miranda, Jr.," *MirRam Group*, accessed February 21, 2017, http://www.mirramgroup .com/luis-miranda-jr/.

14. In this sense, *Hamilton* represents a long step backward from images of the founders that once actually made them useful role models. Think about the difference between the founders as battling rappers versus Isaac Kramnick's "The 'Great National Discussion': The Discourse of Politics in 1787," *William and Mary Quarterly* 3d ser. 45 (1988): 3–32; or John P. Roche's "The Founding Fathers: A Reform Caucus in Action," *American Political Science Review* 55 (1961): 799–816, or even the bickering Patriots bravely coming together in the earlier Broadway musical *1776*.

15. Miranda and McCarter, *Hamilton: The Revolution*, 133, 169n4; Constance Grady, "The Hamilton Mixtape's 'Wrote My Way Out' Shows Why

Hamilton's Story Is a Hip-Hop Story," *Vox*, November 18, 2016, http://www
.vox.com/culture/2016/11/18/13678548/hamilton-mixtapes-wrote-my-way-out
-nas-lin-manuel-miranda-dave-east-aloe-blacc. Compare the similar testimony
of Joanne B. Freeman in Jeff Sharlet, "I Was a Teenage Hamiltonian," *Chronicle
of Higher Education*, September 14, 2001.

16. Miranda and McCarter, *Hamilton: The Revolution*, 17, 21, 208, 284.

17. Saul Cornell, *The Other Founders: Antifederalists and the Dissenting Tra-
dition in America, 1787–1828* (Chapel Hill: University of North Carolina Press,
1999); Richard S. Newman and Roy E. Finkenbine, "Black Founders in the
New Republic: Introduction," *William and Mary Quarterly* 3rd ser. 64 (January
2007): 83–94; Newman, *Freedom's Prophet: Bishop Richard Allen, the AME
Church, and the Black Founding Fathers* (New York: NYU Press, 2008); Gary B.
Nash, Ray Raphael, and Alfred F. Young, eds., *Revolutionary Founders* (New
York: Knopf, 2011).

18. *Hamilton: The Revolution*, 157. On the desire to identify with the founders as a characteristic of conservative and "essentialist" or "fundamentalist"
approaches, see Andrew Schocket's essay in this volume and Jill Lepore, *The
Whites of Their Eyes: The Tea Party's Revolution and the Battle over American History* (Princeton, NJ: Princeton University Press, 2010). On the "fake feminism"
of the play see Nancy Isenberg, "'Make 'em Laugh': Why History Cannot Be
Reduced to Song and Dance," *Journal of the Early Republic* 37 (Summer 2017),
esp. 299–300.

19. Lyra D. Monteiro, "Race-Conscious Casting and the Erasure of the
Black Past in Lin-Manuel Miranda's *Hamilton*," *The Public Historian* 38 (February 2016): 89–98, reprinted in this volume.

20. Compare Freeman, *Affairs of Honor: National Politics in the Early
Republic* (New Haven: Yale University Press, 2001), and Ellis's books beginning
with *Founding Brothers* and through *The Quartet* (New York: Knopf, 2015),
with David Waldstreicher, *In the Midst of Perpetual Fetes: The Making of American Nationalism, 1776–1820* (Chapel Hill: University of North Carolina Press,
1997); Simon P. Newman, *Parades and the Politics of the Street: Festive Culture
in the Early American Republic* (Philadelphia: University of Pennsylvania Press,
1997); Jeffrey L. Pasley, *The Tyranny of Printers: Newspaper Politics in the Early
American Republic* (Charlottesville: University Press of Virginia, 2000); Jeffrey L. Pasley, Andrew W. Robertson, and David Waldstreicher, ed., *Beyond the
Founders: New Approaches to the Political History of the Early American Republic*
(Chapel Hill: University of North Carolina Press, 2004); Sean Wilentz, *The
Rise of American Democracy* (New York: Norton, 2005), pt. 1; Nancy Isenberg,

Fallen Founder: The Life of Aaron Burr (New York: Penguin, 2007); Jeffrey L. Pasley, *The First Presidential Contest* (Lawrence: University Press of Kansas, 2013).

21. For a thorough if pro-Hamilton account of Hamilton's changing reputation see Stephen F. Knott, *Alexander Hamilton and the Persistence of Myth* (Lawrence: University Press of Kansas, 2002). On the corresponding changes to Jefferson's reputation, Merrill D. Peterson, *The Jefferson Image in the American Mind* (New York: Oxford University Press, 1960); and Jeffrey L. Pasley, "Politics and the Misadventures of Thomas Jefferson's Modern Reputation: A Review Essay," *Journal of Southern History* 72, no. 4 (November 2006): 871–908.

22. Andrew Burstein, *Democracy's Muse: How Thomas Jefferson Became an FDR Liberal, a Reagan Republican, and a Tea Party Fanatic, All the While Being Dead* (Charlottesville: University Press of Virginia, 2015). The other two books mentioned are Pauline Maier, *American Scripture: Making the Declaration of Independence* (New York: Knopf, 1997); and Conor Cruise O'Brien, *The Long Affair: Thomas Jefferson and the French Revolution, 1785–1800* (Chicago: University of Chicago Press, 1998).

23. Pasley, "Federalist Chic."

24. John Chester Miller, *The Federalist Era, 1789–1801* (New York: Harper Torchbooks, 1960) and Stanley Elkins and Eric McKitrick, *The Age of Federalism* (New York: Oxford University Press, 1993) are still valuable, but see also, from a more Jeffersonian perspective, James Roger Sharp, *American Politics in the Early Republic* (New Haven: Yale University Press, 1993); Waldstreicher, *In the Midst of Perpetual Fetes*, ch. 3; Seth Cotlar, *Tom Paine's America: The Rise and Fall of Transatlantic Radicalism* (Charlottesville: University Press of Virginia, 2011); and Pasley, *The First Presidential Contest*.

25. Miranda and McCarter, *Hamilton: The Revolution*, 222–224. For the Abigail theme, see, among others, and in addition to the David McCullough biography of John, Edith Gelles, *Abigail and John: Portrait of a Marriage* (New York: Harper Perennial, 2010); Cokie Roberts, *Founding Mothers: The Women Who Raised Our Nation* (New York: Harper Perennial, 2005); Joseph J. Ellis, *First Family: Abigail and John Adams* (New York: Vintage, 2011); Woody Holton, *Abigail Adams: A Life* (New York: Atria Books, 2010); and Phyllis Lee Levin, *Abigail Adams: A Biography* (New York: St. Martin's Griffin, 2001).

26. This version of Hamilton, and its interpretation of events, can be followed in such scholarly works as Forrest McDonald, *Alexander Hamilton: A Biography* (New York: Norton, 1982); Karl-Friedrich Walling, *Republican Empire: Alexander Hamilton on War and Free Government* (Lawrence: University Press of Kansas, 1999); and with a less militaristic bent, Max M. Edling, *A Revolution*

DAVID WALDSTREICHER AND JEFFREY L. PASLEY

in Favor of Government: Origins of the U.S. Constitution and the Making of the American State (Oxford; New York: Oxford University Press, 2003).

27. This overlap is far from accidental considering the outsized role that Continental Army officers played on the conservative nationalist side of politics in the Early Republic. See Richard H. Kohn, *Eagle and Sword: The Beginnings of the Military Establishment in America* (New York: Free Press, 1975); Minor Myers Jr., *Liberty without Anarchy: A History of the Society of the Cincinnati* (Charlottesville: University Press of Virginia, 1983); Paul Douglas Newman, "The Federalists' Cold War: The Fries Rebellion, National Security, and the State, 1787–1800," *Pennsylvania History* 67, no. 1 (2000): 63–104.

28. Miranda and McCarter, *Hamilton: The Revolution,* 97, 153, 199–200, 258. See also Isenberg, *Fallen Founder* and Isenberg, ""Make 'em Laugh'"; contrast with the minimizing of the democracy issue in Chernow, *Alexander Hamilton,* and Freeman, *Affairs of Honor.*

29. David Waldstreicher, "Federalism, the Styles of Politics, and the Politics of Style," in *Federalists Reconsidered,* edited by Doron Ben-Atar and Barbara B. Oberg (Charlottesville: University Press of Virginia, 1999), 99–117. While over the top on some issues, a crucial work that more historians who wish to generalize about the Federalists would do well to read is David Hackett Fischer, *The Revolution of American Conservatism: The Federalist Party in the Era of Jeffersonian Democracy* (New York: Harper & Row, 1965).

30. David Waldstreicher, *Runaway America: Benjamin Franklin, Slavery, and the American Revolution* (New York: Hill and Wang, 2004); Schocket, *Fighting over the Founders,* 57–58; Chernow, *Alexander Hamilton,* 5–6, 23, 121–122, 210–116, 238–239, 580–582; David Waldstreicher, *Slavery's Constitution: From Revolution to Ratification* (New York: Hill and Wang, 2009), 146–149.

31. Miranda and McCarter, *Hamilton: The Revolution,* 284–285.

32. The most thorough account of Hamilton's limited antislavery views, written before Chernow and criticizing the exaggerations of earlier biographers John C. Miller and Forrest McDonald, is Michelle DuRoss, "Somewhere in Between: Alexander Hamilton and Slavery," *Early America Review* 15, http://www.varsitytutors.com/earlyamerica/early-america-review/volume-15/hamilton-and-slavery. DuRoss identifies a source for the notion of Hamilton as learning to be antislavery in the West Indies in a 2004 article published in the New-York Historical Society's new history magazine between the "Alexander Hamilton" and the "Slavery in New York" exhibits by distinguished historian James Oliver Horton: "Horton relies solely on secondary information. No existing documents of Hamilton's support this claim. Hamilton never mentioned anything in his correspondence about the horrors of plantation slavery

in the West Indies. Instead, Hamilton's impoverished childhood motivated him to spend his whole life trying to improve his position in society. If Hamilton hated the slave system in the West Indies, it might have been because he was not a part of it." Horton, "Alexander Hamilton: Slavery and Race in a Revolutionary Generation," *New York: The New York Journal of American History* 3 (2004): 16–17. By contrast, abolitionists were made when people who did not grow up seeing African slavery traveled to the South and the Caribbean. This began with key English-born early writers and activists Thomas Tryon, Ralph Sandiford, and Benjamin Lay: for more detail see David Waldstreicher, "The Origins of Antislavery in Pennsylvania: Early Abolitionists and Benjamin Franklin's Road Not Taken," in *Antislavery and Abolition in Philadelphia*, edited by Richard Newman and James Mueller (Baton Rouge: LSU Press, 2012), 46–59. The subsequent annals of abolitionism contain relatively few white people born in the South or the West Indies. For the later period see James L. Hutson, "The Experiential Basis of the Northern Antislavery Impulse," *Journal of Southern History* 56 (1990): 609–640.

33. Miranda and McCarter, *Hamilton: The Revolution*, 16, 97, 122.

34. Ibid., 281. Commenting on the murders at a Charleston church during the summer of 2015, just before the cast reassembled for the Broadway production, McCarter takes this to an absurd extreme in the book: "From the day Alexander Hamilton arrived in what would become the United States, he fought against everything that [Confederate] flag would come to stand for" (208).

35. Edward Pessen, *The Log Cabin Myth: Social Backgrounds of the American Presidents* (New Haven: Yale University Press, 1984).

36. William Hamilton, "An Oration Delivered in the African Zion Church, on the Fourth of July, 1827, in Commemoration of the Abolition of Domestic Slavery in this State" (New York, 1827), in *Early Negro Writing, 1760–1837*, edited by Dorothy Porter (Boston: Beacon Press, 1971), 101.

37. Chernow relegates the matter to his acknowledgments because he has no discursive footnotes and it was "too tenuous to merit inclusion in the text"—this despite the high level of rumor and speculation on slavery-related matters in his text. Chernow, *Hamilton*, 735. It should be noted that one of Alexander Hamilton's younger sons with Elizabeth Schuyler was named William. Hamilton arrived in New York in either late 1772 or early 1773, making his paternity at least possible if William Hamilton's birth date is correct.

38. Porter ed., *Early Negro Writing*, 33–41, 96–104, 391–404, 570–571; Waldstreicher, *In the Midst of Perpetual Fetes*, 343; Carla L. Peterson, "Black Life in Freedom: Creating an Elite Culture," and Manisha Sinha, "Black Abolitionism: The Assault on Slavery and the Struggle for Racial Equality," in *Slavery in*

New York, edited by Berlin and Harris, 186–187, 191, 244–245; Craig Steven Wilder, *In the Company of Black Men: The African Influence on African American Culture in New York City* (New York: NYU Press, 2001), 44, 77–78, 86–87, 91, 138–140, 148–149, quoted at 138; Leslie M. Alexander, *African or American? Black Identity and Political Activism in New York City, 1784–1861* (Urbana: University of Illinois Press, 2011), 19–22, 59–62, 88–89.

CHAPTER 8

Hamilton and the American Revolution on Stage and Screen

ANDREW M. SCHOCKET

When former Republican vice president Dick Cheney attended *Hamilton* in March 2015, his wife Lynn reported that he "loved it." Democratic president Barack Obama, who in 2009 had been treated to an early version of the show's opening song, saw *Hamilton* in New York in 2015, and he invited the cast back to the White House for a special performance. On November 18, 2016, Republican vice president-elect Mike Pence took in the show, and in a TV appearance the following weekend claimed that he, too, "enjoyed the show." In other words, as Renee C. Romano also notes in this volume, despite our current hyperpartisan culture, *Hamilton* has fans humming "My Shot" across the nation's political spectrum. That's not easy for any sort of cultural production. Conservatives and liberals tend to read different books, get their news from different cable networks, watch different TV shows, and even eat at different fast food chains (check out for yourself who's chowing down at Chick-fil-A, and who's at Chipotle).[1]

But everyone loves *Hamilton*. Sure, the tunes are catchy, the cast charismatic, the book clever, and the story compelling. But in our divided society, being good, no matter how good, often doesn't fully bridge our cultural chasms. How did this Broadway musical about the "ten dollar founding father without a father" hit the political sweet spot in American popular culture?

What makes *Hamilton* as the object of bipartisan infatuation even more striking is that the musical portrays the nation's founding, a

167

topic that historically, and especially recently, has greatly divided Americans. In my recent book, *Fighting over the Founders: How We Remember the American Revolution*, I show that while Americans almost unanimously appreciate the importance of the American Revolution, our interpretations of it serve as yet another front in our ongoing cultural and political warfare.[2] Conservatives are more likely to depict the American Revolution in what I call an "essentialist" way. They generally see it as a perfect, completed event, championed by founding father heroes, who fought for the right to personal liberty and private property. Liberals lean more toward what I call "organicism." They often view the founding as part of a darker past, a conflict as much among Americans as between Americans and the British. Unlike essentialists, organicists see the Revolution's achievements as flawed or incomplete, establishing grand principles that we as a nation still strive to meet. How Americans see the Revolution may also influence our ideological stance on everything else. When we tussle over the meanings of the American Revolution what we're really arguing about is what the nation's values are, what we think we stand for as a people, and to whom the nation belongs.

For all of its daring and originality, *Hamilton* has garnered such a wide range of fans by conforming to expectations more than first meets the ear. Americans of all ideological persuasions find *Hamilton* enjoyable because it follows an increasingly familiar set of conventions, ones that have determined how the American Revolution has been portrayed, especially on stage and screen since the turn of the millennium. Not coincidentally, film and television producers and writers have carefully calibrated and tuned these conventions precisely because they appeal to mass audiences. These narrative elements work as a feedback loop: the more we see them, the more we're familiar with them, and the easier it is to sell the next production to us as long as it is similar to what we have already seen. *Hamilton* sells, like other productions it is patterned after, because it contains elements that speak in coded and sometimes explicit ways to what each side of the ideological aisle wants to see, while carefully avoiding serious engagement with interpretations that might prove offensive to either.

The American Revolution Rebooted

Hamilton is far from the only founding story that has recently hit pay dirt. Since 2000, perhaps because the contemporary political world has been so fractious, the American public has been especially enamored with stories of, and about, the founding period. Cold War thrillers don't elicit the frisson of fear that they used to; not every television and movie villain can be from the Arab world; and super-hero and science-fiction productions, while for the most part wildly popular, cost a bionic arm and a computer-generated leg to make. American Revolution productions, then, have allure for audiences because of their familiar setting, and for Hollywood and Broadway executives because they are relatively cheap to make. No Broadway show is a sure bet, but Lin-Manuel Miranda's track record—his previous musical, *In the Heights*, was a big hit—and *Hamilton*'s success in various workshops and in its Off-Broadway run before hitting the Great White Way surely created confidence in potential investors. Just as much, though, even before a note was sung, as a genre piece *Hamilton* not only spoke to audience needs, but also catered to the requirements of the culture industry, whether in Hollywood or on Broadway, as both struggle to retain an audience in the age of customizable digital entertainment.

Almost from the moment of independence, Americans have been dramatizing the nation's founding, and it has been an intermittent subject of theater, novels, movies, and television. Mostly prompted by the bicentennial of the nation's founding, from the late 1960s through the mid-1980s a number of American Revolution–related productions graced the stage and screen. There followed, however, a fallow period. The newfound success and prevalence of founding stories since 2000 suggests that we are seeing the emergence of a new *form* of the genre, one that has some characteristics of previous productions, but nuances of its own. Like big-screen franchises such as *Star Wars* and *Star Trek*, both of which have been relaunched with updated sensibilities and state-of-the-art marketing aimed at the children and grandchildren of their first fans, the founding-era genre is getting its own makeover, which I call "American Revolution rebooted." *Hamilton* is a prime example, and—despite its originality—is also more typical of these productions than you might think. In addition, while the characteristics of *Hamilton* and its immediate predecessors demonstrate potential for finding a commercially viable sweet spot, they also further reinforce the American Revolution's status as a cultural battleground.

Among the more prominent entries in this genre reboot are movies such as *The Patriot* (2000), *Felicity: An American Girl Adventure* (2005), and *Beyond the Mask* (2015), and television offerings including *The Crossing* (2000), *Liberty's Kids* (2002–2004), *Benedict Arnold: A Question of Honor* (2003), *John Adams* (2008), *Turn: Washington's Spies* (2014–2017), *Sons of Liberty* (2015), and *The Book of Negroes* (2015). Measuring overall audiences in an age of syndication and streaming is difficult, but by at least one metric, these productions have a considerable market: as of fall 2016, they account for a combined 6.5 million DVDs sold. *Turn*, a television show about the British occupation of Long Island, New York, has had a strong, four-season run. Given the copycat nature of movie, television, and stage productions, *Hamilton*'s success ensures that more American Revolution–themed entertainment is on the way. According to author Allison Pataki, *The Traitor's Wife*, her historical novel about Peggy Shippen (who married Benedict Arnold), was optioned for a film adaptation because of "all of the excitement around *Hamilton* and the story of our nation's founding."[3] Meanwhile, movie star Channing Tatum is partnering with the creative team behind the highly popular animated show *Archer* for a Netflix production titled *America: The Motion Picture*, an animated satirical film about the nation's founding. Nothing better signals the success of a genre more than parody, which only has the chance to hit home with audiences if the conventions it makes fun of are familiar enough to spoof.

Observant viewers can easily identify the hallmarks of productions portraying the American Revolution. Some features recall productions first staged not long after the Revolution itself. Among them, the setting can be instantly visually communicated: think colonial-style houses with lots of wood and brick, plus actors in corsets, or in breeches and wigs. Chronologically, American Revolution productions generally begin in the mid-1770s or slightly after, and usually end with a definitive moment like the Declaration of Independence or the ratification of the Constitution. Their geographic setting is mostly limited to the original thirteen colonies, thus focusing on the local as opposed to the Atlantic or hemispheric context of the Revolution. We see heroes whose familiar qualities we recognize from school and popular culture: Washington is tall, forceful, and quiet; Franklin bald, sensible, and witty; Adams short, irascible, and . . . sometimes *very* irascible. Because the villains in these stories are typically British, as revealed by their snooty accents, there is little danger of public-relations blowback or loss of audience because of contemporary ethnic resentment. Meanwhile, the narrative outline of the American Revolution that most Americans believe they know is familiar in the contemporary public mind, but the details are fuzzy to all but the most knowledgeable viewers, leaving writers and directors leeway for individual story arcs to vary from broader historical trends.

These characteristics have long been features of American Revolution drama, whether on the stage or on the screen. However, new common characteristics have emerged since 2000, which, though melding with older ones, mark a significant departure from prior Revolution-themed productions. Producers and screenwriters forged these new elements in order to sell American Revolution productions to an increasingly partisan nation, giving potential viewers on either side of our ideological divide something to hang onto.

Four new narrative characteristics predominate. First is the assumption that being in favor of independence was the norm, a norm also indicated by traditionally masculine leading men. Second, Patriots in these productions are motivated by their pursuit of a loosely defined, abstract sense of "freedom." Third, Patriots solve the problems they encounter in the pursuit of that freedom by the expulsion of people who are different or don't agree with the majority. Finally, the productions appeal to modern-day racial and gender sensibilities by including more female and African American characters and by acknowledging the evils of slavery—even though these productions rarely engage with how the American Revolution resulted in the further entrenching of slavery into the new nation's society and economy. These four elements have come to shape how the general public increasingly understands the American founding, and while *Hamilton*'s casting and hip-hop delivery may be strikingly new for Broadway, its narrative fits this common mold.

Genre's Mixed Messages

These commonalities that mark the American Revolution genre reboot are important because what people see onscreen shapes their perceptions of history, and in this case, the very events that Americans look to as they think about the nation's principles. Genres are best understood as sets of structured conversations that reflect the time and culture of the people who make, read, or watch a story. Each new entry, whether on screen or stage, is created partly in response to the characteristics of previous entries, and with the knowledge that future ones will take *their* cues from it.[4] Productions can also engage with more than one genre. For example, a film like *The Patriot* is an American Revolution film. But it also follows other conventions that were popular at the time it was made, including those of the history film genre and, even more, the Hollywood blockbuster: think big-star main character, fawning love interest, explosions (the bigger the better, hopefully involving helicopters or cannons, depending on what is historically appropriate), and a happy ending.

In other words, a genre emerges from a flexible, ongoing conversation among writers, producers, marketers, and audiences, a conversation that is rejoined with each new production. Each bears similarities to the one before, and every new entry—movie, novel, musical—is both shaped by, and has the potential to reshape, the

The epic film *The Patriot* (2000) starred Mel Gibson as a South Carolina farmer drawn reluctantly into the American Revolution. *(© Columbia Pictures/AF Archive/Alamy Stock Photo)*

genre. *Hamilton*'s commonalities with, and diversions from, previous screen and stage depictions of the American Revolution indicate that its creators were more than aware of these conventions; and there is no doubt that subsequent shows for stage or screen will be made, and watched, with *Hamilton*, in mind.

Potential for certain genres to lure audiences eases the job of writers and producers by supplying them with ready-made characters and plots and also gives them a market incentive to avoid veering too far from the course mapped out by previous productions. Lin-Manuel Miranda and *Hamilton*'s financial backers could reasonably have predicted that a musical recounting of the American founding, cast with actors of color, might be a matter of considerable controversy—and if they did, they were right. That understanding may have spurred *Hamilton*'s brain trust to hew to other genre conventions that send recognizable, positive signals to partisans on either side of our cultural divide, while avoiding topics, ideas, or character traits that risked limiting its box-office returns. Musicals are expensive. *Hamilton* was widely reported to have cost $12.5 million to bring to Broadway.[5] For big-budget cultural productions, like a movie, television series, or Broadway show, the prevalence and durability of the genre reflects the need to draw big investors who can be assured that they will maximize the return on their investment. Like other American Revolution rebooted productions, *Hamilton* adheres to the four major generic conventions, allowing it to appeal broadly to organicists and essentialists while offending neither.

First, Patriotism (with a capital P) is a must for all Anglo American protagonists. As Alexander Rose, series consultant for *Turn: Washington's Spies*, and author of the book that inspired it, has noted about the difference between life's ambiguities, on the one hand, and, on the other, the necessity of communicating quickly on screen and on stage, "history is complex and drama is simple."[6] The simple convention of writing the protagonists as Patriots helps audiences to identify, almost immediately, whom to root for and against. Not surprisingly, the good guys tend to be what dominant American culture has historically coded as *good guys*: heterosexual white men. Whether New England or South Carolina farmers, Boston brewers or Philadelphia printers, our heroes, with few exceptions, are depicted as manly men, whether their weapons are quills, fisticuffs, or muskets. Bad guys, as it turns out, are not manly. Markers of Tory or British deviance in these productions—besides a style-challenged predilection for bright red jackets almost regardless of occasion— include cowardice, effeminacy, and brutality. Accordingly, *The Patriot* portrays a General Cornwallis more interested in his lodgings than the war, and a Colonel Tavington who commands his soldiers to torch a church with Americans locked inside. In the first season of *Turn: Washington's Spies*, the two most prominent British officers are the passive, ineffective Major Hewlett and the sadistically violent Lieutenant Simcoe. By interpreting the American Revolution as a fairly unambiguous, heroic struggle of good versus evil, with white manly heroes, American Revolution rebooted productions reinforce an essentialist assumption of the inherent goodness of the American project. But they also do not offend organicists who take a more critical view of the nation's founding, because the villains are Brits rather than ethnic minorities, such as African Americans or Native Americans.

Hamilton also fulfills this first convention of common expectations for founding heroes. When Hamilton first meets his friends John Laurens, the Marquis de Lafayette, and Hercules Mulligan, they are already Patriots. These Revolutionary protagonists establish their heterosexual bona fides in the song "A Winter's Ball," boasting that they are all "reliable with the / Ladies." Hamilton himself revels in the rumor that "Martha Washington named her feral tomcat" for him, and his capacity to dazzle both Eliza and Angelica Schuyler cements his qualifications as a ladies' man. Hamilton and his fellow would-be rakes, along with an imposing and sonorous George Washington, are contrasted favorably with the high-pitched and fearful Tory, Samuel Seabury, and the flamboyant dandy George III, who—in frilly costume, tone, and demeanor—calls to mind a drag queen rather than a strong king. In *Hamilton*, as with other American Revolution rebooted productions, a manly support for independence is assumed, with the opposition portrayed as scared, foppish, and violent.

As a second genre convention, American Revolution rebooted productions present the philosophical basis of the founding as a personal, abstract libertarian view of "freedom." What that freedom entails—freedom to do what? Freedom from what?—is left cloudy, beyond a vague sense that no one should be able to tell Americans what to do, and that they desire decreased government interference in their lives. In the climactic scene of the History Channel miniseries *Sons of Liberty*, for example, Samuel Adams urges the Continental Congress to declare independence in the name of "the freedom to live our lives the way we see fit, and the confidence that that freedom cannot be taken away from us." This strategy allows productions to attract a broad American audience, because after all, everyone is in favor of freedom. Such invocations of "freedom," though, constitute a special appeal to conservative viewers, who see today's federal government as overreaching through taxes and regulation, and what they perceive as the erosion of their individual rights by a predatory national government. At the same time, such productions' lack of specificity when it comes to the meanings of freedom remains inoffensive to other audience members who may define liberty differently. *Hamilton* follows this second convention explicitly. All of *Hamilton*'s friends—Burr, Laurens, Mulligan, and Lafayette—show up already in favor of independence, no explanation necessary. As if they were cribbing the script from *Sons of Liberty*'s Samuel Adams, these Patriots almost immediately "raise a glass to freedom / something they can never take away."

In the third major feature of American Revolution rebooted productions, conflict is resolved by Anglo Americans achieving unity among themselves and expelling the deviant opposition. Just as the central tension in westerns is the use of violence to establish order, in romantic comedies the surrender of individual independence to traditional monogamy, and in mobster films the tragic embrace of loyalty over law, American Revolution rebooted productions chronicle the establishment of consensus through violent exclusion. Thus *The Patriot*'s few Loyalists eventually cower under the protection of British troops, rather than continuing to live among the general population where they might enjoy the privilege of rubbing onscreen shoulders with Mel Gibson's masculine Benjamin Martin and Heath Ledger's hunky Gabriel Martin. *Liberty's Kids*' Loyalists practically disappear after independence, appearing in a couple of episodes prior to being evacuated from North America and the series. *Turn*, as befitting a show premised on divided loyalties, offers a bit more sophistication, but in its second season, Loyalist patriarch Richard Woodhull finds himself isolated as the Patriots grow bolder and take center stage.

Similarly, *Hamilton* affirms this third convention, establishing a *united* states through the removal of deviant others. Having been the sole representative of the Loyalist opposition, Seabury disappears after one token song. Poor George III is left to gloat from afar with schadenfreude expectations of American political strife once Washington leaves the presidency to John Adams. Television

and Broadway audiences could be forgiven for forgetting, or perhaps never knowing, that somewhere between a fifth and a third of
Revolutionary-era Americans preferred the Crown to independence,
and that the vast majority of those Loyalists remained in the new
nation. Sadly, such plotlines reinforce the parochialism of both conservatives and liberals in the contemporary United States, providing
a rationale for our increasing self-segregation by geography, religion,
work, and social media.

As their fourth and final characteristic, American Revolution
rebooted productions have been carefully crafted to adhere to contemporary gender and racial attitudes. They both criticize slavery
and include female and African American characters. Yet even as recent American Revolution productions pay lip service to the cause
of abolition, they fail to portray either how deeply slavery pervaded
early American society or the disruption necessary for the enslaved
to gain their liberty. Thus, viewers can feel good that they are watching a production that denounces slavery without being directly con-
fronted with anything that would too closely resemble a history of
contemporary racial inequality, much less the way that all of American society remains implicated in it. Some productions go further
than others in presenting a racially palatable Revolution. *The Patriot*'s protagonist, rather than owning other human beings, appears
to be eighteenth-century South Carolina's only equal opportunity
employer, one so loved by his African American workers that they
voluntarily rebuild his house for him. In the forty-part PBS animated children's series *Liberty's Kids*—to date, clocking in at over
twelve hours, the longest treatment of the nation's founding on
film—George Washington and Thomas Jefferson wring their hands
over the peculiar institution, but don't lift a finger to end slavery.
The animated series' only unabashed slaveholder is presented as un-
savory and unhinged. Everyone loves freedom; not to do so, in these
productions, is either evidence of mental imbalance or—heaven
forfend!—Loyalism.

As with those productions, all of *Hamilton*'s sympathetic characters either embrace abolition or remain silent about slavery. In "My

Shot," which serves as *Hamilton*'s "I want" song—what Broadway people call the piece early in a musical that reveals the main character's desire—Hamilton describes his crew as "a bunch of revolutionary manumission abolitionists." Later, during Act II's "Cabinet Battle #1," Hamilton mocks Jefferson's "civics lesson from a slaver." After the fatal duel at the end of the play, Eliza claims that Alexander "could have done so much more" to fight for abolition had he not suffered this early death, a claim that obscures Hamilton's mixed record, and lack of achievement, on ending slavery during his lifetime. Here, too, then, *Hamilton* follows the American Revolution rebooted paradigm: it offers criticism of slavery without showing its price or making it central to the plot.

American Revolution rebooted productions not only criticize slavery, but also include prominent African American characters with their own dramatic arcs. Doing so provides additional appeal to organicists, while not alienating essentialists. In *The Patriot*, Occam (Jay Arlen Jones) fights for the Patriot cause and his freedom. Moses was included in *Liberty's Kids* to provide its young viewers with an example of a free African American supporting the Patriot cause. In a slightly more complex twist, *Turn*'s Abigail (Idara Victor) and Jordan (Aldis Hodge) split their allegiances. Significantly, all of these characters either enter the action free or become free over the course of the story. They thus serve both as potential role models for African American viewers, and as a comfort to those who might find the continued enslavement of sympathetic characters too depressing. Such uncomplicated character arcs do not contest the essentialist view of a perfect American Revolution: the audience is not asked to grapple with the fact that the nation's founding, while resulting in slow abolition in the North, further entrenched slavery in the South and in the nation's political structure.

Hamilton seems to flout this particular aspect of the genre because, as Lyra D. Monteiro notes, the play doesn't include any African American characters. Still, as anyone who has seen pictures of *Hamilton*'s cast in action knows, it sure looks different from previous American Revolution productions. But that's less a violation of the American Revolution rebooted genre than it is a challenging of broader Hollywood and Broadway casting norms. Consider two recent movie westerns that feature nontraditional casting choices. Denzel Washington's star turn in *The Magnificent Seven* (2016) for the most part merely substitutes a charismatic black actor in a role previously inhabited by a charismatic white one, just as *Hamilton*'s Christopher Jackson plays George Washington and Daveed Diggs, Thomas Jefferson. By contrast, Jamie Foxx's performance in the title role of *Django Unchained* (2012) represents plot choices that rethink the western genre premised upon a leading man whose character is African American. In other words, changing the color of actors' faces can be crucial to how we view race in contemporary America, but only changes in plot and character can transform how we think about a genre, or the history it engages with.[7] With its casting choices, the *Hamilton* creative team managed again to thread the ideological needle that the rebooted American Revolution genre requires: essentialist audience members can watch or listen to the show and rally to the story of great men doing great things, while organicist fans can watch, in Miranda's words, a "story that look[s] the way our country looks."[8]

To see an American Revolution–related production analogous to *Django Unchained*, let's look to a production that was far more challenging, and, probably as a result, far less commercially successful. Joint Black Entertainment Television (BET) and Canadian Broadcasting Company's (CBC) *The Book of Negroes*, based upon the Lawrence Hill novel of the same name, follows the fictional Aminata Diallo. Born in Africa and transported to South Carolina, Diallo escapes slavery, joins black Loyalists in Nova Scotia, sails to Sierra Leone, and testifies against the slave trade in England, all while navigating the trials and tribulations faced by eighteenth-century African women thrown into the cauldron of slavery. *The Book of Negroes* portrays an ambiguous American Revolution, one in which spurning the Revolution itself and joining the British can result in freedom, and in which women might have their own history. In *Hamilton*, Eliza wonders who will tell Alexander's story, but no one even takes the time to speculate about Eliza's. As *The Book of Negroes* lead actress Aunjanue Ellis has pointed out, Aminata insists on writing her own story, an extraordinarily daring act for a woman of the time, white or black, and, for that matter, in any American Revolution rebooted production.[9]

This is not to say that *The Book of Negroes* offered a completely subversive plot: the miniseries includes a sympathetic character, "Black Sam Fraunces," who believes in the American Revolution's redemptive possibilities, and *The Book of Negroes* also emphasizes individual rather than collective liberty. Regardless, ratings and DVD sales suggest that *The Book of Negroes*' overall impact, at least quantitatively, was minimal, nor did it earn major U.S. awards or make a splash among critics. Taking a subversive approach, no matter how it might enrich conversations about the American Revolution, didn't do too much to line the pockets of the people who made it. By contrast, *Hamilton*'s far less transgressive plot and characters are the box office gift that keeps on giving to the musical's investors.

Aunjanue Ellis as Aminata Diallo in the 2015 film *The Book of Negroes*. (© *Conquering Lion Pictures/AF Archive/Alamy Stock Photo*)

Despite the qualities of *Hamilton* that may be daring, at least part of its cross-cultural and cross-political appeal lies in its ability to follow the well-trodden path of previous productions, and its capacity to navigate the potential political minefield raised by any portrayal of the American Revolution. That's not surprising because, as we know, *Hamilton* was conceived in conversation with these productions. Even more explicitly than most artists, *Hamilton*'s creator Lin-Manuel Miranda, through Twitter and through his engagement with fans on a website on which the musical's lyrics have been posted, is very much in ongoing discussion with an audience steeped in the rebooted American Revolution genre. Miranda has discussed many times how *Hamilton* is in conversation with hip hop, with history, and with Broadway musicals, but the show is also in dialogue with previous depictions of the American Revolution that his audience recognizes. It may come as no surprise to those who know the musical that Miranda's favorite scene of the HBO miniseries *John Adams* is when the title character meets King George III. As Miranda has admitted, "I'm just taking it as a given that everyone watched the *John Adams* miniseries."[10] During Act II in "The Adams Administration," Hamilton admonishes the president: "Sit down, John!" This command directly echoes the title and refrain of a song from *1776*, the 1969 Broadway musical chronicling the Continental Congress's debates over declaring independence. What might also be called a mash-up, or the conscious borrowing of material from other shows, connects *Hamilton* to previous American Revolution productions.

That doesn't mean that *Hamilton* has conjured up an eternal, bipartisan love-fest, as Americans learned following Mike Pence's visit to the show, an event that thrust the musical into the maelstrom of our current divisiveness. After the performance ended, and as Pence got up to leave the theater, Brandon Victor Dixon, who had played the role of Aaron Burr that evening, delivered a public plea from the stage to the vice president-elect, imploring him to pursue inclusive policies upon taking office. Within hours, President-elect Donald Trump tweeted an angry condemnation of the show and its

cast. Perhaps not coincidentally, soon afterward, conservative outlets also began to take a much less complimentary line on *Hamilton*
than they had before. The *National Review*, which had previous
sung the show's praises, now questioned its value.[11] Nicholas Pell's
review in *Reason* equated *Hamilton* with all that he dislikes about
liberals. He knocked the musical's treatment of history, panned its
score as unoriginal, and, even labeled its hip hop inauthentic, a
charge that might have surprised the hip-hop heavyweights who
eagerly contributed to the 2016 *Hamilton Mixtape* album.[12] Nonetheless, Pence-ilton-gate has already blown over. The eagerness with
which Americans persist in lining up to score top-dollar tickets for
the Broadway, Chicago, and the national touring versions of the
show, along with the robust sales of *Hamilton*'s cast album and its
offshoots, suggest that *Hamilton* will continue to entrance a great
many Americans regardless of their political differences.

That influence matters, because how we imagine the American
founding has been, and may always be, a reflection of what we believe the United States is all about. Which do we value more, individual independence or equality? Where should power lie, at the
federal level or with state and local governments? To what extent is
the United States a nation based upon principles, and to what
extent on shared culture? If the former, what are those principles,
and if the latter, whose culture?

One way we debate all of these questions is through our interpretations of our nation's founding, and, in this case, which interpretations we choose to consume. That's why politicians so often invoke
the founders, and why they so frequently quote familiar phrases
from the Declaration of Independence and the Constitution to draw
vague connections to contemporary policy prescriptions. That's why
lawyers, judges, and legal scholars appeal to words written well over
two hundred years ago to bolster their arguments about twenty-
first-century issues that men who rode horses and wrote with quills
could not possibly have imagined. That's why the Liberty Bell, cast
in a time of slavery, has been recruited as a symbol of social equality
for nearly two centuries, and why recent political movements have

taken to calling themselves "Minutemen" and "Tea Partiers." That's why boards of education tussle over the language of primary-school textbooks, and why just about every child in the nation has colored a picture of George Washington or participated in an American Revolution pageant.

While *The Patriot* and *John Adams* and *Liberty's Kids* and *Hamilton* are entertainment, their audiences understand them as more than that. When we watch a show, we internalize its messages. That's true even when we're advised that it is a particular interpretation, even when we're told we're watching a fictionalized account, and even when we're informed that parts of it are flat-out wrong.[13] The features that *Hamilton* shares with other American Revolution rebooted productions have consequences. Each new production that follows the formula that genre demands causes the logic of the formula to become further entrenched, creating a feedback loop hard for either the creators of such shows and movies, or their audiences, to escape.

Hamilton, for all its wonderfully clever lyrics, its innovative infusion of hip hop into the Broadway musical form, and its creative casting, deeply reinforces in its audiences a set of established lessons about the nation's founding, and, therefore, about contemporary American culture and politics. Those lessons comfort, rather than challenge, us. The depiction of great men doing great things, rather than social and political change occurring through popular movements, reassures people who, consciously or not, hew to traditional notions of power, race, and gender. The idea that independence consists of unfettered individual liberty, and that all the good guys were for it, relieves us of the responsibility for questioning the motives behind the original establishment of the country, or considering the possibility that patriotism requires both individual sacrifice *and* working together for the common good. The exclusion of opponents narrows the possibilities of what we can disagree about, absolving us of the obligation to engage with people with different views and backgrounds. Lip service to racial equality and the appearance only of free African Americans—or African Americans playing traditional roles—furthers an illusion of inclusivity. It promotes the easy but misguided belief that good intentions are necessary but also entirely sufficient to solve our deep racial differences.

Perhaps I am too pessimistic. After all, in the words of Daveed Diggs—*Hamilton*'s original Marquis de Lafayette and Thomas Jefferson—the casting of people of color as the nation's founders makes him feel less "at odds with this country." Had Diggs seen such a show as a boy, he says, "a whole lot of things I just never thought were for me would have seemed possible."[14] Surely the show's casting is having that effect on many thousands of young people of color. The use of hip hop encouraged a much broader audience to engage the history of our founding than otherwise might be inclined to give it a second thought. Already, students are going to history class compelled by *Hamilton* to study the nation's founding. Maybe, more than I realize, *Hamilton* marks a transition in how the American Revolution is portrayed, no less than the 1970 appearance on American movie screens of *M*A*S*H* and *Catch-22*, films that satirized the brutality and futility of armed conflict, helped to transform both the war movie genre and how American viewed the Vietnam war and combat in general.

History has its eyes on *Hamilton*, whose place in the narrative of how we remember the American Revolution, and therefore how we think about America itself, has yet to be fully written.

NOTES

1. Jennifer Schuessler, "'Hamilton' Puts Politics Onstage and Politicians in Attendance," *New York Times*, March 27, 2015, https://www.nytimes.com/2015/03 /28/theater/hamilton-puts-politics-onstage-and-politicians-in-attendance. html; "Pence Says No Need for Apology after 'Hamilton' Jeers, Lecture," *Fox News.com*, November 20, 2016, http://www.foxnews.com/politics/2016/11/20/ pence-says-no-need-for-apology-after-hamilton-jeers-lecture.html; Josh Katz, "'Duck Dynasty' vs. 'Modern Family': 50 Maps of the U.S. Cultural Divide," *New York Times*, December 27, 2016, https://www.nytimes.com/interactive/20 16/12/26/upshot/duck-dynasty-vs-modern-family-television-maps.html.

2. Andrew M. Schocket, *Fighting over the Founders: How We Remember the American Revolution* (New York: NYU Press, 2015).

3. Dave McNary, "'Traitor's Wife' Movie About American Revolutionary War in the Works at Radar," *Variety*, September 14, 2016, http://variety.com/2016/film/news/traitors-wife-movie-benedict-arnold-radar-1201859855/.

4. The idea of genre as a form of conversation comes from Celestino Deleyto, "Film Genres at the Crossroads: What Genres and Films Do to Each Other," in *Film Genre Reader IV*, edited by Barry Keith Grant (Austin: University of Texas Press, 2012), 218–236. For "history" as a specific genre, see Robert Brent Toplin, *Reel History: In Defense of Hollywood*, illustrated edition (Lawrence: University Press of Kansas, 2002), 8–47; Jonathan Stubbs, *Historical Film: A Critical Introduction*, Bloomsbury Film Genres Series (New York: Bloomsbury Academic, 2013), 9–35. For more readings that have affected how I think about genre, see Rick Altman, "A Semantic/Syntactic Approach to Film Genre," *Cinema Journal* 23, no. 3 (1984): 6–18; Glen Creeber, ed., *The Television Genre Book* (New York: Palgrave Macmillan, 2015); Barry Keith Grant, *Film Genre: From Iconography to Ideology* (New York: Wallflower Press, 2007); Barry Langford, *Film Genre: Hollywood and Beyond* (Edinburgh: Edinburgh University Press, 2005); Ramon Lobato and Mark David Ryan, "Rethinking Genre Studies through Distribution Analysis: Issues in International Horror Movie Circuits," *New Review of Film and Television Studies* 9, no. 2 (June 2011): 188–203; Jason Mittell, "A Cultural Approach to Television Genre Theory," *Cinema Journal* 40, no. 3 (2001): 3–24; and Jule Selbo, *Film Genre for the Screenwriter* (New York: Routledge, 2014).

5. Michael Sokolove, "The C.E.O. of 'Hamilton' Inc.," *New York Times*, April 5, 2016, https://www.nytimes.com/2016/04/10/magazine/the-ceo-of-hamilton-inc.html.

6. *Alexander Rose, Washington's Spies, and Turn*, Museum of the American Revolution: Videos, 2016, https://www.facebook.com/AmRevMuseum/videos/vb.314212505331993/1045628185523751/?type=2&theater.

7. More prominent critical evaluations include Joanne B. Freeman, "How *Hamilton* Uses History," *Slate*, November 11, 2015, http://www.slate.com/articles/arts/culturebox/2015/11/how_lin_manuel_miranda_used_real_history_in_writing_hamilton.html; Annette Gordon-Reed, "*Hamilton: The Musical*: Blacks and the Founding Fathers," *National Council on Public History*, April 6, 2016, http://ncph.org/history-at-work/hamilton-the-musical-blacks-and-the-founding-fathers/; Lyra D. Monteiro, "Review Essay: Race-Conscious Casting and the Erasure of the Black Past in Lin-Manuel Miranda's *Hamilton*," *The Public Historian* 38, no. 1 (February 1, 2016): 89–98, doi:10.1525/tph.2016.38.1.89; Rebecca Onion, "A *Hamilton* Skeptic on Why the Show Isn't as Revolutionary as It Seems," *Slate*, April 5, 2016, http://www.slate.com/articles/arts/culturebox/

2016/04/a_hamilton_critic_on_why_the_musical_isn_t_so_revolutionary.
html; Ishmael Reed, "*Hamilton* and the Negro Whisperers: Miranda's Con-
sumer Fraud," *counterpunch.org*, April 15, 2016, http://www.counterpunch.org/
2016/04/15/hamilton-and-the-negro-whisperers-mirandas-consumer-fraud/;
"Aunjanue Ellis on Aminata Diallo," *BET.com*, http://www.bet.com/video/the
-book-of-negroes/2015/exclusives/aunjanue-ellis-on-aminata-diallo.html?cid=
facebook, accessed October 3, 2016. *Book of Negroes* garnered a 0.5 Nielsen rat-
ing when first aired, and has sold 30,734 DVDs. Steve Baron, "Wednesday
Cable Ratings: College Basketball Wins Night, 'Workaholics,' 'Dual Survivor,'
'American Pickers,' 'Little Women L.A.,' & More," *TV By The Numbers by
zap2it.com*, February 19, 2015, http://tvbythenumbers.zap2it.com/2015/02/19/
wednesday-cable-ratings-college-basketball-wins-night-workaholics-dual-sur
vivor-american-pickers-little-women-l-a-more/; "Film ID," http://filmid.aca-
demicrightspress.com.ezproxy.bgsu.edu:8080/film_search/result?films[]=34
004, accessed September 21, 2016.

    8. Rob Weinert-Kendt, "Lin-Manuel Miranda and Others From 'Hamilton'
Talk History," *New York Times*, February 5, 2015, https://www.nytimes.com/
2015/02/08/theater/lin-manuel-miranda-and-others-from-hamilton-talk-history
.html.

    9. "Aunjanue Ellis on Aminata Diallo."

    10. Lin-Manuel Miranda and Jeremy McCarter, *Hamilton: The Revolution:
Being the Complete Libretto of the Broadway Musical, with a True Account of Its
Creation, and Concise Remarks on Hip-Hop, the Power of Stories, and the New
America* (New York: Grand Central Publishing, 2016), 218.

    11. Richard Brookhiser, "Funky Founder," *National Review*, April 6, 2015,
http://www.nationalreview.com/article/415767/funky-founder-richard-brook
hiser; Andrew Langer, "The Real Problem with *Hamilton*," *National Review*,
January 28, 2017, http://www.nationalreview.com/article/444363/hamilton-lin
-manuel-miranda-progressive-left-style-over-substance.

    12. Nicholas Pell, "Finally: The Case against *Hamilton*," *Reason.com*, January
14, 2017, http://reason.com/archives/2017/01/14/finally-the-case-against-hamilton.

    13. Andrew C. Butler et al., "Using Popular Films to Enhance Classroom
Learning: The Good, the Bad, and the Interesting," *Psychological Science* 20,
no. 9 (September 2009): 1161–1168; Sharda Umanath, Andrew C. Butler, and
Elizabeth J. Marsh, "Positive and Negative Effects of Monitoring Popular Films
for Historical Inaccuracies," *Applied Cognitive Psychology* 26, no. 4 (August
2012): 556–567.

    14. Quoted in Miranda and McCarter, *Hamilton: The Revolution*, 149.

CHAPTER 9

From *The Black Crook* to *Hamilton*

A Brief History of Hot Tickets on Broadway

Elizabeth L. Wollman

"Look around, look around, the revolution's happening in New York," Angelica Schuyler sings to her sisters, Eliza and Peggy, when audiences first meet them in Act I of *Hamilton*. The other characters, observing the sisters "slummin' it with the poor" in the town common, readily agree: "History is happening in Manhattan," they sing together, "and we just happen to be in the greatest city in the world!"

The history the characters in the musical are talking about is the looming American Revolution. But through 2015, *Hamilton* was so ecstatically received by critics, and so fervently embraced by audiences, that "revolutionary" quickly became the easiest go-to superlative for the show itself. Just about every critic who wrote about *Hamilton* for newspapers, magazines, trade publications, or blogs conflated the show's historic theme with its truly extraordinary reception. No mere hot ticket, *Hamilton* itself was revolutionary, according to producers at news shows like *CBS News Sunday Morning*, and journalists at publications like *Backstage*, *Playbill*, *Rolling Stone*, the *New York Times*, and the *Wall Street Journal*.[1] Of course, "revolutionary" was hardly the only superlative applied to the musical—one critic wryly noted that in lauding the show so glowingly and so frequently, the press corps had "used up all the damn words."[2] But for obvious reasons, "revolutionary" was the descriptor of choice, much to the dismay of a few dissenting voices who were very much in the minority when they argued that maybe—just maybe—*Hamilton* wasn't quite the ground-breaking, paradigm-shifting, mold-breaking production that just about everyone who saw it seemed to think it was.[3]

I loved *Hamilton* so much I saw it twice, and listened so obsessively to the cast recording when it was first released that I frequently had dreams involving its various catchy musical motifs. But as a scholar of the American musical, I've never believed that *Hamilton* is a revolutionary production, at least not in the literal sense of the world. Remarkably innovative? Absolutely. Thrillingly inventive, brilliantly packaged, expertly marketed, and extraordinarily well cast? Yup, yes, certainly, and indeed. But genuinely unprecedented, unlike anything before it, and poised to change everything that comes after it? No. Broadway just doesn't work that way.

Don't get me wrong: I understand the excitement *Hamilton* has generated, both within the industry and well beyond it. Only about 20 percent of Broadway shows even recoup their investments, so the very hottest of hot tickets are remarkably precious. But even if they are rare, some of the earlier Broadway shows that have become cultural milestones are worth exploring, since they may help us better understand how and why *Hamilton* has become so popular. Broadway's most in-demand hit productions often balance some combination of brilliant writing, casting, staging, and packaging with fortuitous timing, and in this respect *Hamilton* is no different. It arrived, after all, at a cultural moment in which various aspects of American identity were being hotly debated from a wide variety of perspectives. Through 2015, as it moved from the Public to the Richard Rodgers Theatre and rooted itself in the country's collective cultural consciousness, the American populace grew increasingly divided and divisive because of an exceptionally ugly and relentlessly cynical presidential campaign. A clear-eyed celebration of American ideals, philosophies, and a "young, scrappy, and hungry" founding generation that benefited enormously from the enthusiasm and approachability of its creator, Lin-Manuel Miranda, *Hamilton* is a masterpiece of popular culture. Steeped in the country's cherished, oft-idealized national history, Hamilton features a diverse cast of beautiful people who move to swift direction and invigorating choreography while singing an almost impossibly catchy and now incredibly popular score. It has at its helm an appealing, business-savvy author who, as Claire Bond Potter points out in her chapter, is also brilliantly adept with social media. The fact that *Hamilton* is the first Broadway musical in recent memory to become popular enough to compete with bigger, more lucrative, and easily mass-mediated entertainment forms like film and television makes it seem even more remarkable.

Nevertheless, *Hamilton* did not come out of nowhere. Nor did its creator, Lin-Manuel Miranda, who has clearly worked very hard to propel the American musical forward, in part by mining its past. *Hamilton* might be the hottest Broadway ticket of the decade—perhaps even of the century—but it's not the first Broadway musical to inspire breathless reception, introduce new theatrical innovations, or even become a cultural phenomenon. Previous hot tickets have, in some way or another, helped pave *Hamilton*'s way to Broadway, and into the musical theater canon and the web of contemporary popular culture. The story of some of these earlier Broadway phenomena can help us better understand how and why *Hamilton* has become such a success.[4]

In fact, before there could ever be a Broadway musical like *Hamilton*, there had to be such a thing as Broadway, as well as musicals that were written, staged, and performed there. For years, many scholars, critics, and historians referred to *The Black Crook*, which opened in September 1866 at Niblo's Garden on Broadway and Prince Street, as the very first Broadway musical—even though it predated the time when the American commercial theater industry had consolidated and concentrated itself in the Times Square neighborhood, or begun to proffer musical productions in which songs, dances, and characters together served a cohesive plot. A surprise hit at a time when hot tickets and long-running productions were virtually unheard of, *The Black Crook* was a frantic jumble of dance, melodrama, operetta, extravaganza, and variety that ran five-and-a-half hours and didn't make a lot of sense. It nonetheless launched a new era in America theater by sparking producers' interest in long runs, and convincing them of the allure of theatrical spectacle.

The Black Crook fell from "very first modern musical" status once scholars began pointing out that, for all its success, it was not especially groundbreaking in terms of its structure or presentational style. Many shows produced around the same time—countless extravaganzas, minstrel shows, and melodramas—combined other popular entertainment forms into one big production. Moreover, while not every *Black Crook*–era show offered songs and dances that had anything to do with one another, let alone a coherent narrative arc, a few told at least as good a story as *The Black Crook* did. Although few continue to argue that *The Black Crook* singlehandedly sparked the American musical, the production caught on with so many spectators and made so much money for its time that it is considered an important step in the development of the contemporary Broadway musical—which, after all, is not just an artistic enterprise, but a commercial one as well.

When *The Black Crook* opened, the nation's commercial theater industry was just beginning to consolidate in New York City. Longacre Square, a then-remote neighborhood that housed the carriage trade, wouldn't be developed and redubbed Times Square until the turn of the twentieth century. Most theater producers and managers made money by hiring traveling stock companies—groups of actors who together performed a series of plays in repertory for a predetermined period of time before moving on—for their theaters. *The Black Crook* was one of the first American stage productions to buck this trend: it ran for over a year in an era when the idea of keeping a show open for as long as possible to make money hadn't yet really occurred to anyone. *The Black Crook* might not have been the very first musical as we understand the genre today, but it did spark Broadway producers' continued obsession with long-running shows.

What surely inspired past historians to erroneously declare *The Black Crook* the very first Broadway musical was its accidental inception: the production was basically a stone soup that yielded surprisingly delicious results. Devised as a melodrama (a dramatic piece with stock characters and musical underscoring, designed to appeal to audiences' emotions) by the playwright Charles M. Barras, *The Black Crook* was secured by the manager at Niblo's, William Wheatley, to be performed at his theater. Meanwhile, two entrepreneurs named Henry Jarrett and Henry Palmer had booked a venue farther uptown to stage a dance spectacle for which they had purchased hundreds of costumes and tons of scenery, and hired a large group of dancers they had brought in from Europe. But when the theater they had reserved burned down, the two Henrys approached Wheatley in a panic. He agreed to combine the two productions into one extra-spectacular one, even if doing so meant delaying the opening of *The Black Crook* and making expensive alterations to Niblo's to accommodate the now-enormous cast and the many new set pieces.

Wheatley wisely decided to use these setbacks to his advantage. Much as Miranda excited interest in *Hamilton* by performing a segment at the White House and previewing others on social media, Wheatley began publicizing *The Black Crook* well before it opened. An explanation of the show's postponed opening in the *New York Times* on September 3, 1866, noted that delays were inevitable given the enormity of the alterations needed to house the production, which, readers were assured, would result in "startling transformations and elegant scenes with brilliant effects" on a stage tricked out in a way that had "never [been] seen in this country before." The show's technical requirements, Wheatley made clear, were especially complex: *The Black Crook* required many trapdoors, water tanks, mirrors, and movable panels, not to mention all the wires that would allow the large company of dancers to fly through the air. The backstage area at Niblo's, too, had to be entirely rebuilt to accommodate an enormous cast and huge, dazzling set pieces; the *Times* article went so far as to list the amount of money each alteration and production detail cost, and in some cases, how many laborers were employed to execute the changes.[5] Wheatley surely realized that emphasis on costs, renovations, gadgetry, and the resultant visual pleasures of *The Black Crook* would promote curiosity and ticket

SARONY.

A few members of the enormous cast of *The Black Crook* (1866), a spectacular, long-running Civil War–era production that took New York by storm and became one of the first hot tickets the city had ever seen. *(The Miriam and Ira D. Wallach Division of Art, Prints and Photographs, Photography Collection, The New York Public Library, Astor, Lenox and Tilden Foundations)*

sales, especially since Barras's play, a romantic melodrama, was "the least original element in the mix."[6]

The thin plot of *The Black Crook* focuses on young Rodolphe and Amina, whose love enrages the jealous Count Wolfenstein, who desires Amina for himself. Wolfenstein causes Rodolphe to fall prey to Hertzog, a hunchbacked wizard (and the title character) who gives Satan a fresh soul each year in exchange for eternal life. A fairy queen rescues Rodolphe from Hertzog and takes him to her land beneath the sea. At the conclusion of this production, which ran long into the night and included countless subplots and digressions, Wolfenstein and Hertzog are defeated, and Rodolphe and Amina live happily ever after.[7]

The Black Crook finally opened to a house "fairly packed with a mass of humanity, exceeding the crush at any time, even at that house of crushes" on September 13, 1866.[8] Most critics confirmed Wheatley's sense that Barras's play was terrible, but the production as a whole was an unparalleled triumph—"the event of this spectacular age."[9] It ran for 475 performances, taking in over a million dollars at the box office and spawning countless imitations, tours, and revivals. Wheatley continued to fuel poplar enthusiasm about the show and spin even its most negative publicity to his advantage. An op-ed piece that ran in the *New York Herald* condemning the "indecency" of the skimpy costumes and lascivious dancing only stimulated a new rush of sales at the box office, as did a series of public lectures condemning the show, delivered in fire-and-brimstone style by one Reverend Charles Smyth.[10] Whenever such free publicity waned, Wheatley added new songs, scenes, or more spectacular effects, thereby luring newcomers and encouraging those who had seen the show to return for repeated viewings.[11]

The Black Crook cemented an emphasis on spectacle that remains an important aspect of Broadway musicals. It also redirected the burgeoning theater industry's reliance on stock companies and short runs toward combination companies (casts that came together for one show and parted ways after it closed) and long runs to maximize profits.[12] Imagine how many different ways Wheatley could have sold *The Black Crook* had he, like Miranda and *Hamilton*'s producers, had access not only to the press but also the Internet, as well as an infrastructure and national population that would have supported any number of companion productions in big cities around the world.

Given its name and the fact that *The Black Crook* was a Civil War–era show, you might have initially assumed that, like *Hamilton*, it had at least something to do with race. There was plenty of commentary about race in America on the commercial stage through the second half of the nineteenth century, most infamously via blackface minstrelsy, but the burgeoning commercial theater industry catered overwhelmingly to white performers and audiences. Black performers rarely trod the boards with white ones before the early twentieth century, although after the Civil War, newly freed blacks had found a toehold in American mass entertainment by marketing themselves as the "genuine" article for minstrelsy's white audiences, and forming their own increasingly popular troupes. While theaters in New York were legally desegregated around the turn of the century, most venues nevertheless insisted on relegating black customers to the balcony, even if they desired and could afford orchestra seats.[13] In the era of *The Black Crook*, New York's theater scene, vibrant and as busy as it was, would not have known what to do with *Hamilton* had any producer or troupe of actors been brave (or foolish) enough to attempt something remotely like it in the first place.

Broadway began making halting strides toward desegregation when all-black musicals began to break through, thanks in large part to the comedy duo of (Bert) Williams and (George) Walker. Like most black American performers of their time, the duo got their start in minstrel circles, where they billed themselves as "Two Real Coons" before transitioning to vaudeville in the first years of the twentieth century. As vaudevillians, Williams and Walker were embraced by both black and white audiences. Yet despite their remarkable success as the sole black act in celebrated vaudeville houses like Koster and Bial's and Tony Pastor's Music Hall, so-called "legitimate" producers who ran the Broadway houses remained convinced that black performers would be of little interest to white audiences. Even when Williams and Walker headlined on Broadway in all-black productions like *In Dahomey* (1903) and *Bandanna Land* (1908), Broadway producers tended to dismiss their success as a fluke that was not worth attempting to repeat. It wasn't until *Shuffle Along* (1921)—an all-black show so enormously successful that it is sometimes credited as a catalyst for the Harlem Renaissance—that Broadway's industry began to introduce small if lasting innovations, both onstage and in the seats of Broadway's venues.[14]

Shuffle Along was a collaboration between four successful black vaudevillians: the comedians Flournoy Miller (1885–1971) and Aubrey Lyles (1884–1932), who together wrote and starred in the show; and the songwriting team Eubie Blake (1887–1983) and Noble Sissle (1889–1975). Despite Broadway's continued resistance to black acts, the men managed a meeting with the white producer John Cort. Cort had recently acquired an abandoned lecture hall on 63rd Street, so far north of Times Square that it was hard to justify calling it a Broadway house at all. Eager for something to put into the theater and a big fan of Miller and Lyles's act, which he had seen in Harlem, Cort agreed to produce *Shuffle Along*.[15] Yet reflecting Broadway's longstanding misgivings about black acts, Cort was unwilling to invest much in the production. Props and scenery were scant, costumes were hastily acquired from a show that had recently flopped, and the venue itself had a shallow stage poorly suited to a musical.[16] When *Shuffle Along* opened in May 1921, however, Cort suddenly had an enormous hit on his hands—and, just as suddenly, money for scenery, costumes, and hasty theater renovations.

Like most self-described musical comedies to run on Broadway at the time, *Shuffle Along* was more a series of songs, dances, and skits than a fully developed book musical. Its thin plot, which had a romance at the center, followed the antics of two dimwitted small-town grocers who decide to enter the race for town mayor, provided the winner make the loser the chief of police. The grocers, originally played by Miller and Lyles, end up competing against an honest candidate, Harry Walton, who wants to end small-town corruption and prove himself to his girlfriend's father. Regular interruptions to this narrative allowed cast members to perform vaudeville routines already well known to the audience.[17]

Shuffle Along was widely celebrated for its score, which, like *Hamilton*, drew on a range of popular and traditional genres, from blues to ragtime, barbershop, jazz, and opera. It spawned the hits "I'm Just Wild about Harry," "Love Will Find a Way" and "In Honeysuckle Time." The musical ran for 504 performances and raked in almost $8 million—over $100 million by contemporary standards, and thus about what the Broadway production of *Hamilton* grosses in a year.[18] *Shuffle Along* spawned countless imitations throughout the 1920s. It so thoroughly convinced producers that there was an audience for all-black musicals that it is sometimes mistakenly cited as the very first all-black production on Broadway. While aspects of the production reflected the virulent racism of its time, *Shuffle Along* nevertheless made some important strides. "Love Will Find a Way" became the first number to be performed genuinely and tenderly— and not just for crude comic effect—by two black characters on a Broadway stage. And many of the songs remained popular for decades: in 1948, Harry Truman would use "I'm Just Wild about Harry" as his presidential campaign song.

Yet perhaps the biggest racial impact of *Shuffle Along* was not onstage but in the house, where well-to-do black patrons mingled with white ones. At most performances, the racial mix of spectators was estimated to be approximately 90 percent white and 10 percent black. This might seem like a huge imbalance, especially for a show so celebrated by the African American public, but in fact, the black audience for *Shuffle Along* was much larger than at other Broadway shows of the time. Even today, affluent, educated, middle-aged whites purchase about 77 percent of all Broadway tickets;[19] as many critics and bloggers have pointed out, the overwhelmingly white and affluent audience of *Hamilton* stands in stark contrast to its racially diverse cast.[20] It is thus no surprise that journalists noticed black patrons in the orchestra seats at *Shuffle Along* and felt that the observation was newsworthy.[21] Even though the theater where the show played was not fully desegregated—only one-third of the orchestra seats were open to blacks—*Shuffle Along* nevertheless seems to have been the first Broadway production that seated black patrons at the same distance from the stage as whites.[22]

However, the show's popularity had consequences for black artists. As all-black Broadway shows were co-opted by white producers and creative teams eager to capitalize on the trend established by *Shuffle Along*, blacks were rapidly denied full control of subsequent 1920s Broadway productions and, as with blackface minstrelsy, their own images onstage. Still, the success of *Shuffle Along* resulted in a number of important improvements on Broadway, namely the de facto desegregation of audiences, a slow but steady move away from some of the most vile racist stereotypes, and unprecedented opportunities for an increasingly diverse talent pool in a once-impenetrably white Great White Way. All of this would lay the groundwork for a

"I'm Just Wild About Harry" was one of the most memorable numbers from the smash hit *Shuffle Along* (1921). The musical, which set off a decade-long craze on Broadway for musicals and revues with all-black casts, was celebrated for its humor, talented cast, and innovative dance numbers, but especially for its infectiously catchy, jazzy score.

(Music Division, The New York Public Library, Astor, Lenox and Tilden Foundations)

musical like *Hamilton*, which unapologetically casts actors of color in the most unstereotypical roles.

While *Shuffle Along* paved the way for more diverse Broadway shows and desegregated theaters, *Show Boat*, with music by Jerome Kern (1885–1945) and lyrics by Oscar Hammerstein II (1895–1960), pioneered the idea that a musical's content could relate directly to topical, sociocultural concerns. This musical was so unique to Broadway at the time of its premiere on December 27, 1927, that, the story goes, when the curtain fell on opening night, audiences sat in stunned silence, unsure about how exactly to respond. With *Show Boat*, Hammerstein and Kern pushed the musical forward as a genre by infusing it with believable characters, settings, and references to social issues. They also married its score and plot more closely. "To recount in any detail the plot of a musical comedy usually is a silly and banal business," Brooks Atkinson noted in his *New York Times* rave review of the production. But "the manner in which these characters . . . have been brought to life is something else again." He noted as well that if "these three contributions—book, lyrics and score—call for a string of laudatory adjectives, the production compels that they be repeated again."[23]

Show Boat reflected the influence of a number of previous productions, as well as cultural shifts that had taken place well before its 572-performance run at the Ziegfeld Theater, the glorious new venue producer Flo Ziegfeld had recently built for his shows. But absent the increased popularity of all-black musicals through the 1920s, the sociocultural impact of the Harlem Renaissance and Jazz Age, and the philosophies that Kern and Hammerstein brought to the table when they began their collaboration, there could never have been a *Show Boat*.

Like *Hamilton*, *Show Boat* was the musicalized adaptation of a best-selling book. Based on Edna Ferber's sweeping novel about three generations of performers traveling up and down the Mississippi River on a steamboat between the 1880s and 1920s, *Show Boat* includes themes of alcoholism, gambling addiction, spousal abandonment, and racism. Originally billed as "An All-American Musical

Comedy,"[24] *Show Boat* was more a drama set to music, with a relatively serious—and, thanks to Ferber's best-selling novel, familiar—story about everyday people experiencing recognizable personal and social problems. Because Kern and Hammerstein shared an interest in creating musicals in which song and dialogue contributed to plot and character development, *Show Boat* featured music and lyrics that were appropriate for the characters and settings. The score, too, borrowed widely from styles including opera, operetta, spirituals, blues, ballads, parlor songs, and jazz.

But the societal issue *Show Boat* brings most consistently to the forefront is institutionalized racism. Even the very name of the titular boat, the *Cotton Blossom*, reflects the separate, unequal lives American blacks and whites lived during the late nineteenth and early twentieth centuries, especially in the American South. Many songs, too, reflect an interest in social commentary that was rare for musicals of the time, but that Oscar Hammerstein would continue to include in his lyrics through his career.

For example, one of *Show Boat*'s most famous numbers, "Ol' Man River," is on its surface a song that grossly exaggerates "black speech patterns to ridicule the mentality of the 'coon.'" Lyrically and stylistically, the song borrows from minstrel songs and so-called "coon songs" that became popular with whites in the early twentieth century. Yet instead of mocking blacks, as these songs almost always did, "Ol' Man River" points out cultural indifference to the plight of African Americans. In the final stanza, it neatly encompasses it in a few simple lines:

> He don' plant taters
> He don' plant cotton
> An' dem dat plants 'em
> Is soon forgotten
> But ol' man river
> He jes keeps rollin' along

~

I gets weary
And sick of tryin'
I'm tired of living
And scared of dyin'
But ol' man river
He just keeps rollin' along[25]

Derived from deeply racist American song forms that had romanticized slave life on the plantation and made light of the subjugation
of black culture, bodies, and labor, "Ol' Man River" instead serves as
the emotional and philosophical anchor for the entire production.

Though its creators' aim was to elevate the musical form by giving
the show's characters, both black and white, new weight and dimension, *Show Boat* has nonetheless been read by many musical theater
historians and scholars as demeaning to its black characters, especially by contemporary standards. Unlike their white counterparts,
such criticism goes, the black characters "show no character development over the course of the three-hour musical," and serve primarily
as "background servants who help the white characters achieve all
they can in the decades-spanning work." *Show Boat* was, of course,
created by white men who, however well-meaning, reflected the
sociocultural tenor of the 1920s. In this respect, it remains very much
a musical of its time, despite countless revisions, revivals, and con-
cert and film versions. Yet just as *Hamilton* has demonstrated ways
that the Broadway musical benefits from a diversity of roles, musical styles, voices, and perspectives, *Show Boat* "raised the bar for what
the musical could be and the stories it could tell" in the late 1920s.[26]

As it developed through the first half of the twentieth century,
the Broadway musical grew from a haphazard blend of disparate
influences into a cohesive form in which plot, character, song, and
dance served a unified whole—one that, like *Hamilton*, can seem to
be about the distant past but turns out to be very much about the
present. The move toward artistic integration gained favor during
the 1930s as social realism influenced the American popular arts. By
the 1940s, theater and dance artists like Rodgers and Hammerstein,

Leonard Bernstein, Jerome Robbins, George Balanchine, José Limón, and Agnes de Mille were striving to create commercial productions that seamlessly blended dance, music, and theater. This, they reasoned, would allow Broadway musicals to incorporate weightier subject matter and "classical aesthetic principals" while simultaneously exposing audiences to various performing arts, all of which would benefit commercially and artistically in the process.[27] Both the timing and reception of *Oklahoma!*, which opened on March 31, 1943, were of great importance in setting commercial and critical standards on Broadway. The show, heralded as an exemplar of artistic integration, received superlative, almost universal praise from critics, and ran longer than any Broadway musical had to that point, finally closing in 1948 after 2,212 performances.

Like *Hamilton*, *Oklahoma!* arrived on stage at a moment when Americans hungered for positive depictions of home and country. Thus, the fact that *Oklahoma!*, which opened just over a year after the United States had entered World War II, was so steeped in Americana certainly didn't hurt its critical or commercial reception. Nor did the fact that so many of its innovations were couched in nationalistic sentiment and themes of strength in unity. Based on Lynn Riggs's 1931 play *Green Grow the Lilacs* and set in 1906 in the Oklahoma Territory, *Oklahoma!*'s love of country is constant and clear. As the lyric from the titular song reminded wartime audiences during the rousing finale, "we know we belong to the land / and the land we belong to is grand."

Oklahoma! balanced its many innovations with tradition. It features a dual plot structure that Hammerstein borrowed from operetta, one that matches a serious or even tragic romance with one that's comparatively light or comic.[28] Both plotlines follow a classic boy meets, loses, and wins back girl trajectory. Yet *Oklahoma!* departed from musical theater tradition in important ways, eschewing ingredients that had long been assumed crucial for a musical's success. It dispensed, for example, with the long-held notion that a line of chorus girls had to be present and kicking up a sequined storm at the opening curtain. Instead, *Oklahoma!* begins with a farm woman,

Aunt Eller, alone on the stage, quietly churning butter; the romantic lead, Curly, meanders in, singing the opening strains of "Oh, What a Beautiful Mornin'." Lengthy dance sequences, most notably Laurie's "dream ballet," furthered the plot or added weight and dimension to the motivations or emotions of characters.[29]

Hammerstein's lyrics were also crafted to mirror the way characters talked and behaved through the use of dialect and accent; songs were thus fully wedded to the script and used to add weight and depth to characters' actions and motivations. With *Oklahoma!* Richard Rodgers and Hammerstein proved adept at using songs to tip off audiences about characters' subconscious desires. Their frequent, celebrated use of the "conditional love song," introduced in *Oklahoma!* with "People Will Say We're in Love," helped transmit to spectators a couple's mutual attraction long before the characters themselves fully realized or acted on their feelings.

The fact that *Oklahoma!* was drenched in patriotic sentimentality made its early twentieth-century frontier setting seem remarkably contemporary.[30] Without mentioning World War II once, *Oklahoma!* moralizes throughout about American innovations, industriousness, and moral rectitude. We Americans, *Oklahoma!* reminded its wartime audiences, have long been able to tackle and resolve conflicts through hard work, dedication, integrity, and a belief in the common good. "*Oklahoma!* is not topical," the music critic Olin Downes wrote in the *New York Times*, "but there is something special of the nation and its earlier adventure in it. Under the comedic mask and the convention of spurs, revolvers and ten-gallon hats we recognize an ancestral memory, echo of an experience that went deep, a part of adventure that has made us ourselves."[31] Not unlike *Hamilton*, *Oklahoma!* offered a representation of American history that spoke to the nation's contemporary anxieties and desires.

Oklahoma! was Rodgers and Hammerstein's first collaboration in what would become a monumentally important partnership. The show's impact, and the success of the team's later works, exerted strong influence on later Broadway musicals, especially those that opened in the roughly two decades following its premiere. Yet the seismic sociocultural, political, and technological shifts that took place in the United States during the 1950s and 1960s also resulted in the decline of Tin Pan Alley and the rise of rock and roll, a widening generation gap, and new entertainment styles that put the American musical on the outs with a newly powerful population of teenagers and young adults. After years as a trendsetter and shaper of mass popular entertainment, Broadway suddenly began to strike a significant percentage of up-and-coming consumers as corny, outdated, and out of touch. Broadway's composers and lyricists scrambled to regain a foothold in American popular culture. Yet Broadway had little respect for or nuanced understanding of rock music—and it showed. It was not until 1968 that a stage musical featuring a successful blend of Broadway fare and contemporary popular music would achieve commercial and critical success on Broadway. Its success would open doors for later musicals like *Hamilton* that also used popular musical forms long foreign to Broadway to tell their stories.

Things changed in 1967 with *Hair*. Although all the shows I have described exerted influence on the aesthetic and commercial evolution of the Broadway musical, it is perhaps *Hair* that is most immediately comparable with *Hamilton*, less for its structure and presentational style than for the ecstatic way it was received, and why. Like *Hamilton*, critics and audiences celebrated *Hair* for its youthful energy, contemporary urgency, and especially its catchy, innovative score that crossed over to the pop charts. It is specifically this last aspect that caused *Hair*, which opened on Broadway in April 1968, to be hailed by some critics as nothing short of revolutionary: a musical with the potential to completely transform Broadway, its sound, its relevance, and its audience.

Some critics dismissed *Hair* as a loud, chaotic show about an obnoxious, unwashed group of dropouts, but its many supporters praised its ability to harness the theatrical mainstream to the energy and experimentation that was taking place on the theatrical fringe. At the time, the Off-Off-Broadway realm was garnering attention and praise for its artistic innovations and sociopolitical relevance, while Broadway was suffering aging audiences and a decline in cultural importance. Critics lauded *Hair* for its affectionate depiction of contemporary young people and its sensitivity to their sociopolitical concerns. Its composer, Broadway newcomer Galt MacDermot (1928–), was repeatedly cited for accomplishing what had long been deemed impossible: blending contemporary rock music with a traditional Broadway sound in a way that didn't condescend to young spectators or alienate older ones.

A topical musical that, much like *Hamilton*, gently and lovingly shed light on a much-maligned and misunderstood subculture, *Hair* had a book by actors Gerome Ragni (1935–1991) and James Rado (1932–). Built of a series of interconnected vignettes, the show follows a tribe of Greenwich Village hippies (and their New Left compatriots) as they celebrate the new sex- and drug-related freedoms of the era, dabble in mysticism and Eastern religions, protest the war in Vietnam, and struggle for civil rights at home. Ragni and Rado intended *Hair* for Broadway, but after countless rejections, they approached producer Joseph Papp (1921–1991), founder of the Off-Broadway Public Theater—not coincidentally, also the future home of *Hamilton*. A strong advocate of topical, socially relevant, risk-taking theater, Papp chose *Hair* as the inaugural production of the Public's then-new space on Lafayette Street in the East Village. But he insisted that the playwrights cut their script and find a composer to write the score. When Galt MacDermot joined the team, plans for a limited run at the Public in October 1967 commenced.

Hair was a hit at the Public when it opened on October 17, 1967. But Papp—who, like many Off- and Off-Off-Broadway denizens of the era, staunchly opposed what he saw as the crass commercialism of Broadway—let his rights to the production expire once the musical closed. Michael Butler, a savvy Chicago businessman with an interest in the counterculture, secured those rights and arranged to reopen *Hair* uptown in 1968. In its move to Broadway, the celebrated Off-Off-Broadway director Tom O'Horgan was brought in. *Hair* was partly recast, scenes were reworked, and musical numbers were added, removed, or repositioned. O'Horgan was careful to retain

Hair's experimental, Off-Broadway spirit, which he very consciously reenvisioned for Broadway's risk-averse audiences. Among *Hair*'s many Broadway innovations were a rock band that sat on the stage in lieu of a traditional orchestra ensconced in the pit, its loose "day-in-the-life" structure, its frequent disregard of the imaginary fourth wall that traditionally divides performers and audience members, its nudity, and its portrayals of sexual intercourse.

Hair was also noteworthy for tackling a number of contemporary social and political concerns. While ultimately remarkably traditional in its depiction of women, *Hair* considered, at least in passing, issues surrounding race, class, colonialism, the environment, the generation gap, the Vietnam War, and the sexual revolution. It managed to appeal not only to many traditional Broadway spectators, but also to more young people and people of color than was typical of Broadway at the time.[32] Its widespread popularity resulted in the kind of pop-culture crossover success Broadway hadn't seen since long before the rise of rock and roll. The cast recording hit #1 on the *Billboard* album charts, and songs from the show were covered by a variety of rock, pop, and R&B acts, including the 5th Dimension, Three Dog Night, the Cowsills, and Oliver.

Of course, the critics convinced that *Hair* would somehow revolutionize Broadway were wrong. Instead, the slew of rock musicals that rushed to Broadway following *Hair*'s success disappointed investors or even flopped. Even the highly anticipated *Jesus Christ Superstar*, Tom O'Horgan's 1971 stage adaptation of Andrew Lloyd Webber and Tim Rice's platinum 1970 concept album, fizzled at the box office after promising advance sales. Broadway producers quickly grew convinced that *Hair* had been more a fluke than a paradigm shift. The show would exert strong influence on rock musicals that would arrive later in the century—among them, *Rent*. But through the late 1970s and 1980s, the term "rock musical" was verboten on Broadway.

Hair did, however, exert immediate impact on the business end of Off-Broadway theater. Because Joe Papp had allowed the Public's rights to *Hair* lapse, he and his young, struggling nonprofit theater company lost out on millions of dollars that the show generated on Broadway. Furious with himself, Papp resolved never to make the same mistake again. With the Public's next major hit, *A Chorus Line*, Papp developed the business model that would play a major role in *Hamilton*'s success.

Hamilton's creators publicly recognized their debt to *A Chorus Line* while the production was still running at the Public's Newman Theater—the same house *A Chorus Line* had premiered in forty years prior. After the curtain call on *A Chorus Line*'s fortieth anniversary, *Hamilton*'s cast reenacted an indelible moment from the opening of *A Chorus Line* by lining up across the stage, holding their headshots up to hide their faces, and singing "Who am I anyway? / Am I my resumé?" before seguing into "What I Did for Love" and finally inviting the surviving members of the original *Chorus Line* cast to join them onstage.[33] Miranda credited *A Chorus Line* as one of *Hamilton*'s influences and part of "the DNA" of his show. Like *A Chorus Line*, after all, *Hamilton* is, despite its famous characters, ultimately about "regular people" who "were still able to do remarkable things."[34]

A Chorus Line perhaps most influenced *Hamilton* in its slow and steady process of development. A show about dancers auditioning for parts in the chorus line of a fictional Broadway musical, *A Chorus Line* was developed from a series of tape recordings made at several all-night rap sessions held among Broadway dancers. It was then nurtured gradually, over the course of a year, during which Papp granted Michael Bennett, the production's director and choreographer, a weekly stipend, rehearsal space, and ample time to hone the tapes into a fully realized musical. Much as *Hamilton* would be decades later, then, *A Chorus Line* benefited enormously from workshops at the Public.

Also like *Hamilton*, *A Chorus Line* cultivated its fair share of hype during the development stage. By the time it opened to near-universal raves on April 15, 1975, Clive Barnes, for the *New York Times*, immediately pronounced it part of the musical theater canon. "The conservative word for 'A Chorus Line' might be tremendous," he began, "or perhaps terrific."[35] Faced with his second enormous hit at the Public, with an unprecedented demand for tickets, and a gaggle of eager stars like Cher, Diana Ross, and Shirley MacLaine regularly popping up in the audience,[36] Papp swallowed his disdain for Broadway's commercialism and moved *A Chorus Line* uptown to the Shubert Theater three months after it opened. There, it ran for 6,137 performances over fifteen years, breaking the record for the longest-running show on Broadway and generating an estimated $30 million for the Public. With *A Chorus Line,* Papp thus established a model that would allow successful shows to provide seed money for newer artists to develop their ideas over long periods of time. *Hamilton* followed closely in *A Chorus Line*'s footsteps in 2014, going through a year's worth of workshops and development under the auspices of the Public and not insignificantly—benefiting from money *A Chorus Line* had earned decades prior.[37] Monies from the original production still help support programming and productions at the Public—as residuals from *Hamilton*, which benefited from *A Chorus Line*'s development and Broadway trajectory, surely will as well.[38]

Hamilton was, however, not purely an Off-Broadway baby. Whereas *A Chorus Line* transferred to Broadway with a million dollars in advance sales—remarkable for the time—*Hamilton* reflects a more intense commercial marketplace, and much higher stakes: it transferred to Broadway with a whopping $31 million already in the bank, and a number of other producers sharing profits with the Public.[39] *Hamilton*'s Broadway reflects influence not only from nonprofits and the Off-Broadway realm, but also from the experience of for-profit producers whose influence can be traced back to savvy businessmen like Cameron Mackintosh and Andrew Lloyd Webber, and thus to the popularization of megamusicals like *Phantom of the Opera*, *Les Misérables*, and *Cats* throughout the 1980s.

For decades, theatrical spectacle on Broadway has implied fancy costumes, dancing chorines, big casts, and enormous production numbers—aspects of *Hamilton* that enthrall audiences at present. But the approach to theatrical spectacle also changed significantly in the 1980s with the rise of new technology that allowed Broadway to more closely emulate the cinema, both aurally and visually. Throughout that decade, a number of new musicals emphasizing the technologically spectacular would eventually help transform the Broadway musical into the kind of international big business that shows like *Hamilton*, *Wicked*, and *The Lion King* benefit from today. It also, however, raised both production and ticket costs on Broadway as a whole. *Cats*, with a score by composer Andrew Lloyd Webber (1948–), would become the first in a wave of big, technologically dazzling productions that would dominate Broadway through the 1980s and early 1990s. Known for their stage effects, sung-through scores, large casts, and emphasis on universal themes, emotion, and sentimentality, these megamusicals were often savaged by critics for emphasizing spectacle and emotional treacle over artistic merit. Yet they were so consistently, enormously popular with audiences that they helped promote the phrase "critic proof."[40]

Their embrace of sentimentality, their revolving stages, and their sung-through tendencies notwithstanding, megamusicals have less of a clear stylistic influence on *Hamilton* than an advertising and marketing one. The British impresario behind many of the most commercially successful megamusicals was Cameron Mackintosh (1946–), who has long kept a shrewd eye on the potential commercial stage musicals had in the global marketplace. *Cats*, the first musical for which Lloyd Webber teamed with Mackintosh, is a case in point.

Cats opened in London's West End on May 11, 1981, and arrived, following enormous hype and a huge advance in ticket sales, at Broadway's Winter Garden Theater on October 7, 1982. Based on a cycle of poems from T. S. Eliot's *Old Possum's Book of Practical Cats*, *Cats* has the sketchiest of plots: the godlike Old Deuteronomy cat announces at the start that one cat will be selected to go to cat heaven (known as the heaviside layer). The musical ends as the down-and-out Grizabella sings the show's famous number, "Memory," before ascending heavenward on a giant, mechanized car tire. What falls in between is essentially a revue of songs and dances in styles ranging from swing to operetta to rock, performed by actors made up to resemble cats.

Many musicals fail to lure audiences due to weak plots or an overreliance on spectacle, and while critics found *Cats* to be guilty of both, its revue-like form and special effects proved to be its best assets. *Cats*'s impressive costumes, makeup, and set—a cat's-eye view of a huge garbage dump filled with oversized soda cans, old shoes, and crumpled newspapers—arguably helped sell as many tickets as the music itself. *Cats* arrived in New York in the early stages of the contemporary tourist boom, which had begun in the late 1970s with the debut of the "I Love New York" campaign. The musical connected with a newly international audience that did not need to understand much English to grasp its basic plot or appreciate its impressive visual attributes. When it closed in New York after an eighteen-year run, *Cats* had replaced *A Chorus Line* as longest-running Broadway musical. It had also become the most internationally profitable theatrical venture in history, spawning productions in cities worldwide as well as hundreds of international touring companies.[41]

Cats opened the market for Broadway as a worldwide brand, and allowed the commercial theater industry to mine the benefits of regional, touring, and international productions. Lloyd Webber's musicals might not all be remembered hundreds of years from now, but the global business model he and Mackintosh developed at the start of the so-called "British Invasion" of Broadway in the 1980s will be. It helps explain why productions of successful Broadway shows like *Hamilton* now frequently go on international tours, and open in major cities across the world.

Megamusicals fell out of fashion by the early 1990s, but the approach to Broadway musicals as a global product has only intensified through the late twentieth and early twenty-first centuries. If the new business models applied to Broadway by men like Mackintosh and Lloyd Webber help explain the seeming ease with which *Hamilton*'s producers have expanded the show beyond its geographical setting in Times Square, two very different 1990s musicals—

The Lion King and *Rent*—help explain how shows developed in or influenced by the nonprofit and for-profit realms—or in both simultaneously—can become hugely profitable tourist attractions in an increasingly commercialized and sanitized Times Square.

Discussing these two shows together might seem strange since they have so little in common, save for the fact that they opened on Broadway within a year of one another and became big hits. Indeed, structurally, stylistically, and in terms of their production histories, they couldn't be more different: *Rent* was an Off-Broadway baby with a cast of unknowns, the sparsest of sets, and an appropriately small budget, which transferred to Broadway after selling out at the tiny, nonprofit New York Theatre Workshop in the East Village. Conversely, *The Lion King* was one of the most expensive Broadway productions of its time. It featured eye-popping sets and costumes, and was produced by an entertainment conglomerate specifically for Broadway after finding enormous commercial success as an animated Disney film. Yet it is precisely these musicals' differences that demonstrate what Broadway became in the 1990s, and what it is now: a commercial center for live entertainment that has been reimagined for the newly global tourist market and increasingly replicated around the globe, and that regularly draws inspiration and financial support from both the for-profit and not-for-profit realms.

Making Times Square more accessible—and thus more taxable—had been a desire among city officials for half a century, but consensus on how to improve the area evaded numerous mayoral administrations prior to the 1990s. Under the David Dinkins administration (1990–1993), businesspeople and politicians envisioned Times Square as a cleaner, less porn- and crime-laden, more tourist-friendly version of itself. The City and State of New York, hoping to profit from the rise in tourism that the presence of international media companies could bring to the area, began to court the Walt Disney Company. By the mid-1990s, the Disney Company had become an active investor, real estate owner, and producer in Times Square. The company's arrival spurred both the removal of the neighborhood's notorious sex trade and also a sharp increase in the presence of other entertainment conglomerates. The interest entertainment conglomerates took in Broadway at the end of the twentieth century allowed the commercial theater to extend its reach globally, and to nudge its way back into the web of mass-mediated American popular culture.

Disney initially deflected such attempts at partnership. But in the early 1990s, it faced new competition from the tech explosion, and was besieged by a slew of international bad press depicting it as a company more interested in the bottom line than in quality entertainment. Thus, in 1994, the Broadway version of the Disney property *Beauty and the Beast* premiered to wary critics and enthusiastic crowds, and Disney agreed to renovate the dilapidated New Amsterdam Theater in exchange for exclusive use of the venue. The city and state agreed, as well, to lend Disney $28 million in low-interest loans in return for 2 percent of receipts from shows staged at the theater. The City of New York funded the rehabilitation of the neighborhood by courting other companies, condemning old buildings, restoring theaters, and erecting new offices, studios, entertainment centers, and retail complexes.[42] Although some locals look back fondly on the days when Times Square was home to B-movies and more mom-and-pop businesses than remain in the neighborhood at present, the area has nevertheless become one of the city's top tourist destinations, pumping billions of dollars into the city's economy every year.

Aware that it was the new kid on the block, and not a particularly welcome one at that, Disney was eager to prove itself, especially after *Beauty and the Beast*'s tepid critical reception. It thus hired esteemed Off-Broadway director Julie Taymor to direct *The Lion King*, which was scheduled as the inaugural production at the refurbished New Amsterdam Theater. Their choice marked a significant departure from *Beauty and the Beast*, a show that purposely hewed as closely to the animated film as possible. Taymor was an experienced Off- and Off-Off-Broadway director with her own distinctive style, which Disney encouraged her to apply in adapting their film for the stage. In doing so, Taymor drew on African music and culture, borrowing as well from forms including Indonesian shadow puppetry.[43] She not only directed, but also designed the costumes, puppets, headdresses, and masks the actors wear through the production.

The Lion King was not just a commercial smash: it was a critical darling that benefited as well from Disney's approach to synergy between its products. Today, *The Lion King* film not only helps sell the stage musical, but the musical, now running in a number of cities and on tour, sells Disney films. Product tie-ins, from books, to stuffed animals, to clothing, and other related merchandise, help sell both—much like the *Hamilton* cast recording and mixtape, book, and all licensed clothing, accessories, and trinkets connect in the marketplace to the production, and vice versa. Under Taymor and due in large part to her experiences in the nonprofit realm, *The Lion King* was adapted into a beautiful, moving, risk-taking production that continues to be one of Broadway's top sellers. But the power of the corporation behind it also helped make *The Lion King* the "top box office title in any medium" as of 2014, when global sales rose above $6.2 billion.[44]

When Disney first arrived in Times Square, many industry people, critics, historians, and theater aficionados voiced concern over the possibility that the power of the conglomerate would swiftly and permanently tip the delicate balance Broadway had long struck between art and commerce. Disparaging terms like "Disneyfication" and "McTheatre" were tossed around, and dire warnings about the possibility of animated film adaptations permanently destroying the market for smaller, more intimate, less moneyed Broadway productions ran rampant. For sure, Disney and the other mass entertainment businesses that followed it to Times Square did succeed in driving up production costs and making it increasingly difficult for individual producers to back shows, as impresarios like Flo Ziegfeld, David Merrick, and Cameron Mackintosh once did. But theater audiences care less about where money comes from than they do about engaging plots, strong performances, catchy scores, and carefully honed productions, which is why hit shows like *The Lion King* ran alongside hit shows like *Rent* which, like the bigger, flashier productions, exerted strong influence on a young Lin-Manuel Miranda.

A rock musical with a book, music, and lyrics by Jonathan Larson (1960–1996), *Rent* was already enjoying strong word-of-mouth before Larson died suddenly of undiagnosed Marfan Syndrome on January 25, 1996—the morning of *Rent*'s first preview at New York Theater Workshop, in the very neighborhood that the musical evokes. Based on the Puccini opera *La Bohème* and set among young artists, addicts, bohemians, and squatters in New York's then-ungentrified East Village in the waning years of the city's AIDS crisis, *Rent* was suddenly thrust into the unenviable position of benefiting from its art-imitates-life themes: living each day as if it were one's last, and celebrating love and friendship in the face of incurable disease and death. *Rent* was quickly transferred to the then-dilapidated Nederlander Theater on Broadway just in time for the very beginnings of Times Square's gentrification, and it ran until 2008.

Like *The Lion King*, *Rent* helped attract younger audiences to Broadway, and inspired a newly renovated industry to cater to them. For example, *Rent*'s producers, Kevin McCollum and Jeffrey Seller (the latter of whom is a lead producer of *Hamilton*), were some of the first to court teenagers and young adults with the promise of affordable tickets when they announced a policy that reserved $20 rush seats for the first two rows at every performance. When response to the rush policy proved overwhelming, and young, self-described "*Rent*-heads" began camping out in front of the Nederlander Theater overnight, the producers began a preshow lottery—the kind that, twenty years later, would draw crowds to "Ham4Ham" spectacles, staged prior to the matinee, in front of the Richard Rodgers Theater that *Hamilton* occupies.

Rent also renewed an interest in rock musicals, which hadn't been popular on Broadway since the early 1970s; since *Rent*, however, rock- and pop-inspired musicals have become perennial fixtures there. *Hamilton* reflects this now-widespread acceptance of contemporary rock and pop styles as part of the Broadway canon, while going a step further to also challenge Broadway audiences to embrace rap and hip-hop music as appropriate forms for the stage. Miranda, a self-described "theater geek" who was raised by musical-theater-loving, Puerto Rican parents, grew up in Washington Heights with a passion for both Broadway musicals and hip hop. He has noted that he was first inspired to try his hand at writing a musical of his own after a girlfriend took him to see *Rent* for his seventeenth birthday.[45]

Yet much as a blend of rock and Broadway fare was deemed impossible before *Hair*, a successful rap musical had long proved elusive on Broadway. Miranda would begin to change that with his first musical score, for *In the Heights*, which arrived on Broadway in 2008 after years of regional development and an Off-Broadway run at 37 Arts. Backed by *Rent* producers McCollum and Seller, as well as a team of other up-and-coming producers who joined in to shoulder the newly high costs of production, *In the Heights* featured many artists and performers who would continue to work with Miranda on *Hamilton*: actors Javier Muñoz and Christopher Jackson, choreographer Andy Blankenbuehler, musical director and orchestrator Alex Lacamoire, and director Thomas Kail. A musical that blended Broadway and Latin styles with hip hop, *In the Heights* depicted characters that are "historically underrepresented both on-stage and in Broadway audiences."[46] It benefited enormously from savvy marketing that relied heavily on traditional methods like billboards, newspaper ads, and TV and radio commercials, but that also tapped into the nascent power of online platforms like YouTube. Online, a series of funny, accessible, inviting videos were employed to reach "Latinos and younger demographic groups"; most of these clips were made by members of the production, guest celebrities, and, often, Miranda himself.[47] The formula worked. And in the years between the run of *In the Heights* and the premiere of *Hamilton*, Miranda and his team would only grow more experienced, both with the commercial theater industry and with the exponential publicity potential of the Internet.

The marketing savvy of the *In the Heights* creative team would pay off in spades, both during the run of that show and through the development of *Hamilton*. Months before the cast of *Hamilton* set foot onstage at the Public in January 2015 or wondered aloud about how a "bastard, orphan, son of a whore and a Scotsman" could have grown up to be such a big deal, the musical had sold out its entire run, a residency at the theater which was extended three times. After winning a trove of Off-Broadway awards, the show moved to Broadway in summer 2015. Over the course of the 2015–16 Broadway season, the musical and its creator won even more awards, from the Pulitzer Prize for Drama to several Tony Awards to a MacArthur "Genius" Grant to the Grammy for best Musical Theater Album. Two years into its run at the Rodgers, *Hamilton* remained one of the hottest tickets on Broadway.

While without question a well-constructed musical that appeals to a wide range of spectators, *Hamilton* is, like all hit musicals before it, simultaneously a product of its place and time, and a carefully honed product of musical theater history. It functions as accessible, exciting mass entertainment, but also as fervently patriotic and cheerfully inclusive wish fulfillment—a reassuring balm at a time of exacerbated racial tensions, unprecedented political fractiousness, and a growing sense that the American Dream is increasingly unreachable. Like *Shuffle Along*, it reflects a diversifying—if still not yet fully integrated—Broadway. Like *Hair*, it has driven the form forward with its innovative, enormously popular score. Its cast recording, which debuted at #12 on the Billboard 200, has appealed to a large and diverse swatch of the world and made colonial American history suddenly cool among the adolescent set.[48] Running on Broadway at a time when Hollywood has been heavily criticized for its lack of diversity, *Hamilton* is not only popular in its own right, but is also helping Broadway enjoy the kind of mass popularity usually reserved for its old nemeses: film, pop songs, and television.

Hamilton also takes full advantage of the most recent possibilities afforded by social media and new technologies. The availability of the album on various streaming sites is only reinforced by Miranda's knack for using sites like Twitter, which he has used to connect with and build his fan base, much in the way he and the marketers of

In the Heights used YouTube. Broadway's new global reach, too, has allowed for promotion of the musical far and wide, and has generated interest among fans—many of whom have not and may never see the show itself—on social media sites like Facebook, Instagram, and Snapchat. *Hamilton* has become a larger-than-usual Broadway hit, but again, imagine what William Wheatley could have done for *The Black Crook* back in 1866 if he had had access to Twitter.

The marketing team behind *Hamilton* cheerfully embraces the term "revolutionary," which critics and spectators have so frequently used to describe the production. Its accompanying book, the so-called "Hamiltome" is even unselfconsciously titled *Hamilton: The Revolution*. But *Hamilton* is ultimately more evolutionary than it is truly unprecedented. A student of Broadway, Miranda has applied his vast knowledge of its history to a *Hamilton* score that is layered with myriad references to past productions. *Hamilton* is postmodern entertainment in the best sense: a respectful, loving pastiche of American mass culture that allows its audience to check in at various points with mid-twentieth-century big bands, nineties girl groups, sixties Brit-pop, and composers and lyricists like Gilbert and Sullivan, Rodgers and Hammerstein, and Biggie Smalls. *Hamilton* pushes the Broadway musical forward in part by never forgetting its connections to the past.

Like the many shows that struck Broadway gold before it, *Hamilton* takes risks in some ways while remaining traditional in others. There is, for example, no departure from the classic boy meets-loses-wins-girl-back formula perfected by Rodgers and Hammerstein. There are frequent nods to the weepy, emotional expressiveness of megamusicals like *Les Misérables* and *Miss Saigon*, and plenty of reliance on the more contemporary "bromance" trend that Broadway has recently borrowed from Hollywood. As has been noted by many scholars chronicling *Hamilton*'s meteoric rise, the musical fails to challenge gendered assumptions buried deep in traditional narrative, contemporary commercial staging, and modern pop: with the occasional exception of Angelica, the men in *Hamilton* rap, while the women croon soul and R&B styles. And yet the musical has broken new ground with its score, and its insistence on casting actors of color to play characters historically understood as white. When Williams and Walker first appeared on Broadway's stages a century ago, black performers would never have dared impersonate whites on a public stage, while producers believed that white theatergoers would never support productions featuring performers of color.

That *Hamilton* has earned its place in the canon is not a matter for discussion: said canon will surely be more inclusive, more representative, and more stylistically varied than it was before *Hamilton* arrived. But each of the productions discussed here has filled gaps, strengthened the genre, and improved the way Broadway creates, markets, and performs mass entertainments for and about the people who consume them during the times in which they live. *Hamilton* has certainly done its part to push the American musical and Broadway forward, to diversify its players, to appeal to an ever-growing audience, and to innovate its sound. The production will likely inspire more hip-hop musicals and, it is hoped, more musicals about people who are not white and middle class—though whether such shows are as popular or as influential as this one surely will be is anyone's guess: Broadway is a tricky business and no one yet seems to have discovered the formula as to what makes hits like *Hamilton* happen.

But what is certain is that when *Hamilton* closes—likely to be many, many years from now, after countless tours and productions in cities all over the world—another white-hot Broadway hit will come along. Its creator might be sitting right now in a car seat, being regaled by her older brother's warbling rendition of "My Shot" as her parents drive to the store, or drifting off to sleep while his mother sings him a tender version of "Dear Theodosia." But whatever the next big hit-maker crafts for the stage will surely include *Hamilton* in its DNA. And when it opens to rave reviews, people the world over will clamor to sit for a few hours in the room where it happens.

NOTES

1. "'Hamilton': A Revolutionary Musical," *CBS News*, June 12, 2016, http:// www.cbsnews.com/news/hamilton-a-revolutionary-musical/; "Jonathan Groff on 'Hamilton,' 'Looking,' and 'Glee' Finale," *Backstage*, March 26, 2015, http:// www.backstage.com/interview/jonathan-groff-hamilton-looking-and-glee-fin ale/; Brian Hiatt, "'Hamilton': Meet the Man behind Broadway's Hip-Hop Masterpiece," *Rolling Stone*, September 29, 2015, http://www.rollingstone.com/ culture/features/hamilton-meet-the-man-behind-broadways-hip-hop-master piece-20150929; Ben Brantley, "In 'Hamilton,'" Lin-Manuel Miranda Forges Democracy through Rap," *New York Times*, February 17, 2015, https://www .nytimes.com/2015/02/18/theater/review-in-hamilton-lin-manuel-miranda-for ges-democracy-through-rap.html; Terry Teachout, "'Hamilton' Review: The Revolution Moves Uptown," *Wall Street Journal*, August 6, 2015, https://www .wsj.com/articles/hamilton-review-the-revolution-moves-uptown-1438907400 accessed February 21, 2017.

2. David Cote, "Hamilton," *Time Out New York*, August 9, 2017, https:// www.timeout.com/newyork/theater/hamilton-1, accessed February 21, 2017.

3. See for example Rebecca Onion's piece in *Slate*, "A *Hamilton* Skeptic on Why the Show Isn't as Revolutionary as It Seems," *Slate*, April 5, 2016, http:// www.slate.com/articles/arts/culturebox/2016/04/a_hamilton_critic_on_why_ the_musical_isn_t_so_revolutionary.html; James McMaster's article, "Why *Hamilton* Is Not the Revolution You Think It Is," *Howlround*, February 23, 2016, http://howlround.com/why-hamilton-is-not-the-revolution-you-think -it-is; and Lyra D. Monteiro's review essay, "Race-Conscious Casting and the Erasure of the Black Past in Lin-Manuel Miranda's *Hamilton*," *The Public Historian* 38, no. 1 (February 2016): 89–98, http://tph.ucpress.edu/content/38/1/89; all accessed February 23, 2017.

4. Material from this essay has been adapted from my book *The Critical Companion to the American Stage Musical*, forthcoming from Methuen/ Bloomsbury.

5. "Amusements," *New York Times*, September 3, 1866, 5.

6. Larry Stempel, *Showtime: A History of the Broadway Musical Theatre* (New York: Norton, 2010), 43.

7. Robert M. Lewis, *From Traveling Show to Vaudeville: Theatrical Spectacle in America, 1830–1910* (Baltimore: Johns Hopkins University Press, 2003), 200.

8. Ámusements," *New York Times*, September 13, 1866, 4.

9. Ibid.

10. Doug Reside, "Musical of the Month: *The Black Crook*," New York Public Library blog, June 2, 2011, https://www.nypl.org/blog/2011/06/02/musical-month-black-crook, accessed February 24, 2017.

11. Stempel, *Showtime*, 49.

12. Gerald Mast, *Can't Help Singin': The American Musical on Stage and Screen* (New York: Overlook Press, 1987).

13. For an overview of blackface minstrelsy, see Yuval Taylor and Jake Austen, *Darkest America: Black Minstrelsy from Slavery to Hip-Hop* (New York: Norton, 2012).

14. Anne Fliotsos, "*Shuffle Along*: New Directions in the Broadway Musical," http://web.ics.purdue.edu/~fliotsos/b/b/Shuffle_Along.html, accessed February 24, 2017.

15. Karen Sotiropoulos, *Staging Race: Black Performers in Turn of the Century America* (Cambridge, MA: Harvard University Press, 2006), 233.

16. Allen Woll, *Black Musical Theatre: From "Coontown" to "Dreamgirls"* (New York: Da Capo Press, 1989), 63.

17. Ibid., 65–69.

18. Broadway World, "Broadway Grosses—Week Ending 8/6/2017," http://www.broadwayworld.com/grosses.cfm?sortby=gross&orderby=desc, accessed March 23, 2017.

19. Contemporary demographic breakdown courtesy of the Broadway League's 2015–16 audience study: https://www.broadwayleague.com/research/research-reports/, accessed January 10, 2017.

20. See for example Gene Demby, "Watching a Brown 'Hamilton' with a White Audience," *Code Switch*, NPR, March 8, 2016, http://www.npr.org/sections/codeswitch/2016/03/08/469539715/a-brown-hamilton-a-white-audience, accessed February 24, 2017.

21. Woll, *Black Musical Theatre*, 72.

22. Sotiropoulos, *Staging Race*, 234.

23. Brooks Atkinson, "'Show Boat' Proves Fine Musical Show: Distinguished Audience Finds New Production One of Ziegfeld's Best," *New York Times*, December 28, 1927, 26.

24. Stempel, *Showtime*, 195.

25. *Paul Robeson Sings 'Ol' Man River' and Other Favorites, Recorded 1928–39*, sound recording (EMI/Angel Records, 747839, 1972).

26. Warren Hoffman, *The Great White Way: Race and the Broadway Musical* (New Brunswick, NJ: Rutgers University Press, 2014), 31–32.

27. Bruce Kirle, *Unfinished Show Business: Broadway Musicals as Works-in-Progress* (Carbondale: Southern Indiana University Press, 2005), 21–22.

28. Mast, *Can't Help Singin'*, 208–209.

29. Thomas L. Riis and Ann Sears, "The Successors of Rodgers and Hammerstein from the 1940s to the 1960s," in *The Cambridge Companion to the Musical*, edited by William A. Everett and Paul R. Laird, 2nd ed. (Cambridge: Cambridge University Press, 2008), 165.

30. Hoffman, *The Great White Way*, 63.

31. Olin Downes, "Broadway's Gift to Opera: 'Oklahoma!' Shows One of the Ways to an Integrated and Indigenous Form of American Lyric Theater," *New York Times*, June 6, 1943, X5.

32. Barbara Lee Horn, *The Age of "Hair": Evolution and Impact of Broadway's First Rock Musical* (New York: Greenwood Press, 1991), 133–134.

33. Robert Viagas, "Must Watch: *Hamilton* Sings 'What I Did for Love' to Original Cast of *A Chorus Line*," *Playbill*, April 18, 2015, http://www.playbill.com/article/must-watch-hamilton-sings-what-i-did-for-love-to-original-cast-of-a-chorus-line-com-347096.

34. Quoted in "Lin-Manuel Miranda's 'Hamilton' Generating the Same Buzz 'A Chorus Line' Did 40 Years Ago," *Fox News Entertainment*, August 5, 2015, http://www.foxnews.com/entertainment/2015/08/05/lin-manuel-miranda-hamilton-generating-same-buzz-chorus-line-did-in-140.html, accessed February 26, 2017.

35. Clive Barnes, "A Tremendous 'Chorus Line' Arrives," *New York Times*, May 22, 1975, 32.

36. "Lin-Manuel Miranda's 'Hamilton' Generating the Same Buzz."

37. Lin-Manuel Miranda, "Hamilton, a History," http://www.linmanuel.com/hamilton, accessed February 26, 2017.

38. Kenneth Turan and Joseph Papp, *Free for All: Joe Papp, the Public, and the Greatest Theater Story Ever Told* (New York: Anchor Books, 2010), 392.

39. "Lin-Manuel Miranda's 'Hamilton' Generating the Same Buzz."

40. Paul Prece and William Everett, "The Megamusical: The Creation, Internationalisation, and Impact of a Genre," in *The Cambridge Companion to the Musical*, edited by William A. Everett and Paul R. Laird, 2nd ed. (Cambridge: Cambridge University Press, 2008), 250–251.

41. Bernard Rosenberg and Ernest Harburg, *The Broadway Musical: Collaboration in Commerce and Art* (New York: NYU Press, 1992), 59.

42. Shawn G. Kennedy, "Disney and Developer Are Chosen to Build 42nd Street Hotel Complex," *New York Times*, May 12, 1995, B2.

43. Stempel, *Showtime*, 632.

44. Gordon Cox, "Broadway's 'The Lion King' Becomes Top Grossing Title of All Time," *Variety*, September 22, 2014, http://variety.com/2014/legit/

news/broadways-lion-king-box-office-top-title-1201310676/, accessed January 19, 2017.

45. John Moore, "Lin-Manuel Miranda on the Power of Theatre to Eliminate Distance," *Denver Center for the Performing Arts Newsletter*, May 20, 2015, http://www.denvercenter.org/blog-posts/news-center/2015/05/20/lin-manuel -miranda-on-the-power-of-theatre-to-eliminate-distance, accessed February 28, 2017.

46. Elizabeth Titrington Craft, "'Is This What It Takes Just to Make It to Broadway?!': Marketing *In the Heights* in the Twenty-First Century," *Studies in Musical Theatre* 5, no. 1 (2011): 50.

47. Ibid., 53.

48. Keith Caulfield, "'Hamilton's' Historic Chart Debut: By the Numbers," *Billboard*, October 7, 2015, http://www.billboard.com/articles/columns/chart -beat/6722015/hamilton-cast-album-billboard-200, accessed January 19, 2017.

CHAPTER 10

Looking at *Hamilton* from Inside the Broadway Bubble

Brian Eugenio Herrera

On October 8, 2016, Lin-Manuel Miranda hosted *Saturday Night Live*, marking the first time in the show's four-decade history that a Broadway star, without a movie or television show to promote, had appeared as host. In his opening monologue, Miranda introduced himself to the *SNL* audience: "I'm Lin-Manuel Miranda [and] I am fresh off a long run performing in my musical *Hamilton*, which is one of the biggest hits ever on Broadway." Then, he added, "So that means most of you watching at home have no idea who I am."[1]

Miranda's self-deprecating nod to the particular limits of his celebrity underscored one of the most remarkable (and stubborn) incongruities of *Hamilton*. Since its earliest performances at New York's Public Theater in early 2015, the musical's popularity has reached well beyond the walls of any theater presenting it. At the same time, *Hamilton* has not reproduced its success on the screen. It has remained a work of theater, performed a limited number of times each week by live actors, in real time on a New York City stage, for an audience of roughly 1,300 people per performance. In response to audience demand, *Hamilton* producers mounted a second standing production of the musical in Chicago in late 2016 and launched the national tour in San Francisco in early 2017. Typically, national tours do not hit the road until several years into a successful production's Broadway run, and a second full production running concurrently in a major U.S. city remains noteworthy for its rarity. The Chicago and touring productions quadrupled the number of people who could see *Hamilton* on any given night. Yet, even counting these new seats (about 1,800 in Chicago, another 2,200 or so on tour), *Hamilton*'s total nightly audience is roughly 5,300, the equivalent of one-tenth the capacity of Yankee Stadium. And unlike many events presented at Yankee Stadium, *Hamilton* is not being televised.

The stubborn limits of the live theatrical event—of time, of capacity, of geography, of cost—have proven an obstacle to many who want to experience *Hamilton* live in performance. Yet, in spite of (or perhaps because of) *Hamilton*'s obdurate theatrical limits, a broad constellation of ways to encounter the show even without being in the room where it actually happens have quickly emerged. Traditional tie-in media, such as cast recordings, companion books, and excerpted presentations on national broadcast outlets have broken sales records for a Broadway show. *Hamilton* has also spawned a host of innovative and Internet-friendly strategies for encountering the show from afar. The *Hamilton* team devised some of these "bonus features," like the hugely popular "Ham4Ham" sidewalk performances presented outside the stage door, which are also posted and widely viewed on YouTube, for the first year of the production's run.[2] Other supplemental material—like the notorious stream of online quizzes, listicles, and think pieces generated by the "*Hamilton* slack room" at Buzzfeed—came from writers and content creators not affiliated with *Hamilton*, and have populated a wide range of web outlets.[3] Still other ways to experience the musical beyond the theater, like the *Hamilton* Annotation Project at Genius.com, engaged the show's creators alongside its fans to "dig into layer upon layer of meaning" embedded in its score.[4]

This proliferation of ways to encounter *Hamilton* without ever stepping inside an actual theater has become a notable feature of its overwhelming success. Such multiple "paratheatrical" versions of *Hamilton* extend its cultural reach beyond the limits of time and place that would otherwise tether a play's impact so inexorably to the stage. As the instigator of an ongoing and dynamic cultural phenomenon, the original Broadway production of *Hamilton* is thus already part of a multimedia *Hamilton* history, an important performance within the rapidly expanding pantheon of performances available to fans before and after they actually attend *Hamilton* on Broadway, or even if they never do. Indeed, the original Broadway production now stands as just one of many variations currently circulating and having an impact in the world. It is thus understandably tempting to prioritize *Hamilton*'s significance as a multisite cultural phenomenon, and to relegate its stage-bound beginnings as one (possibly inconvenient) feature of the phenomenon's unlikely origin story.

Still, *Hamilton* remains undeniably a work of contemporary theater crafted by one of the most important American theatermakers of this century. Moreover, early interviews confirm that, from the outset, Lin-Manuel Miranda and his creative collaborators fully intended for *Hamilton* to transform what the twenty-first-century American musical (and, perhaps by extension, the American theater more broadly) might look and sound like. For historians who normally do not think about theatrical performance, such inceptive aspirations, limited as they are to the cultural niche of contemporary theater, might seem uninteresting or unimportant. After all, how significant are *Hamilton*'s theatrical origins, especially when the musical has become a multisite and multimedia phenomenon of interest to millions?

The answer is: they are very significant. While a cultural historian might see all of these phenomena as one, scholars of performance history like myself insist that any past performance—including the original Broadway version of *Hamilton* that continues to be performed today—must be taken seriously "on its own terms," not lost in the larger phenomenon of spectacular success, if its broader significance is to be fully apprehended. Within this approach, the performance historian is tasked with attending seriously to the internal logics and objectives of the past performance; discerning the aesthetic, political, or cultural conditions of possibility in which it emerged; and using these features—perhaps among others—as guiding referents for or against any scholarly pronouncement of its historical importance.

Lin-Manuel Miranda and his team clearly set out to craft *Hamilton* in ways that would have a significant impact within the cultural bubble that is Broadway, although even the show's creators may not have expected the show to have quite the influence it did. But what might *Hamilton*'s theatrical origins—a past performance defined by all the peculiar limits of time, place, geography, and cost that configure the cultural niche of contemporary theater—have to tell us about *Hamilton*'s impact beyond the Broadway bubble?

To evince how *Hamilton*'s theatrical "past" continues to guide its circulation on and beyond the stage, I want to ask three questions that foreground the show's most obvious qualities.[5] First, why did it make theatrical sense for Miranda to turn to American presidential history for content and inspiration, especially as he strategized how to follow his Latinx-themed breakthrough *In the Heights*? Next, why would Miranda "recast" that American history by having actors of color portray the nation's founding fathers? Finally, what does Lin-Manuel Miranda's being Latinx have to do with how he wrote *Hamilton*? Having explored how theatrical precedents anchor some of *Hamilton*'s most captivatingly "original" provocations, I want to revisit a notorious incident in *Hamilton*'s history—what happened when Vice President-elect Mike Pence attended the show—as one example of how a fuller understanding of what happens inside the theater can amplify our appreciation of *Hamilton*'s impact beyond it.

Barack Obama's Favorite Musical

Lin-Manuel Miranda's success with *Hamilton* is an example of how innovative artists tend to be celebrated for doing something new when they do something old, but in a different or unexpected way. As Adam Feldman noted in *Time Out New York*, "Miranda is not an adversary of the classic Broadway tradition but an heir to it. . . . For all of its innovation, *Hamilton* also is a melting pot of Broadway musicals past."[6] Because the practice of theater-making is rooted in a repertoire of long-rehearsed techniques and texts, theater audiences tend to require the comfort and familiarity of convention in order to engage, enjoy, and embrace the adventure of the new. As others in this volume have pointed out, few narratives in American life are as familiar and conventional as the story of this nation's founding.

The drama of presidential politics informed *Hamilton*'s development well before Miranda's musical was even about Alexander *Hamilton*. As Lin-Manuel Miranda tells the story, he was inspired to do a presidentially themed musical upon reading Doris Kearns Goodwin's *Team of Rivals: The Political Genius of Abraham Lincoln*.[7] "I was totally into making that [book] into a musical," Miranda recalled. However, upon learning that hit-makers Steven Spielberg and Tony Kushner were already at work on a film adaptation of the book, Miranda abandoned the notion. "I was like, I can't even touch it now."[8] However, Miranda began to scrutinize American political history for other material. Shortly thereafter, in an oft-told story, the idea for *Hamilton* popped into Miranda's head when he picked up a book by Ron Chernow while on his first vacation break from starring in *In the Heights*, the composer-performer's first Broadway success. But why would an acclaimed theatermaker riding the rising wave of success for a show about young, contemporary black and Latinx characters choose to do a musical about eighteenth-century presidential politics?

In fact, the bold, familiar outlines of the presidential narrative—whether populated by historical or imagined figures—has long been popular among dramatists and audiences, firmly establishing the presidential play as a favored subgenre within American theater history.[9] As historian Bruce E. Altschuler notes, more than forty such presidential works have been staged professionally since 1900, some earning great critical, commercial, and popular success.[10] Since the emergence of the "book musical" (or musical play in which song, dance, and dialogue are integrated into a unifying dramatic narrative) in the first decades of the twentieth century, American musicals have also depicted actual or imagined presidents with regularity. Some depict presidents or policymakers onstage, as when Franklin Delano Roosevelt joins the star of *Annie* (1977) singing "Tomorrow";

others feature presidents as off-stage characters, like those in Stephen Sondheim's *Assassins* (1990). Still other shows are built around fictional presidents.[11]

But presidential musicals have only rarely shaped presidential politics. Sometimes a musical's political impact is unexpected, as when a catchy musical number in the 1950 Ethel Merman vehicle *Call Me Madam* ("They Like Ike") introduced a turn of phrase that would become one of the most effective political slogans of the twentieth century. As the historian David Haven Blake has noted, "Long before Dwight Eisenhower had joined a political party, let alone agreed to run for office, *Call Me Madam* was advocating for an Eisenhower presidency."[12] Sometimes presidents have tried to shape musicals. Richard Nixon sought the excision of certain musical numbers such as "Cool, Cool Considerate Men" (which depicted Revolutionary War era conservatives as financially motivated warmongers) from a special White House presentation of Sherman Edwards and Peter Stone's *1776*, the meticulous restaging of the writing and signing of the Declaration of Independence that opened on Broadway in 1969 and played to great critical and commercial success before being adapted to film in 1972. The *1776* cast balked at Nixon's edits, and the command performance proceeded without the requested changes. However, when the film of *1776* was released several years later, studio head Jack Warner (an avid Nixon supporter) had "Cool, Cool Considerate Men" deleted from the film's final cut. It remains unclear whether Warner ordered the negative destroyed as a favor to Nixon or as a result of his own antipathy to the song; a copy of the number was surreptitiously preserved, however, permitting a restored version of the film to be released in 2001.[13]

However, no presidential musical before *Hamilton* has maintained as ongoing an intimacy with the actual American presidency. From the debut performance of the show's opening song at the White House in 2009 through (as proclaimed by a derisive headline on *Breitbart.com*) it becoming "Obama's favorite Broadway show,"[14] *Hamilton* has emerged as perhaps the emblematic theatrical work

John Dickinson and his fellow conservatives sing "Cool, Cool, Considerate Men" in the original Broadway production of *1776*, which ran from 1969 to 1972. *(Photofest)*

of the Obama era and, very possibly, the Obama legacy. Such a link is not unprecedented. In the weeks after her husband's assassination, Jacqueline Kennedy emphasized to journalist Theodore H. White that President John F. Kennedy was especially drawn to the 1960 musical *Camelot*, a show about the legend of King Arthur that had run successfully on Broadway during the Kennedy presidency. Noting that the First Couple often listened to the cast recording before bed, Jacqueline Kennedy paraphrased one of the musical's lyrics as she observed, "There will be great presidents again but there will never be another Camelot."[15] This framing of the JFK era as "Camelot" would soon become the stuff of presidential legend, haunting narrative reenactments of the Kennedy White House (and restagings of the musical) in the decades since. By the summer of 2016, in *Spamilton*—the parody "spoofsical" that itself became something of a runaway hit—composer Gerard Alessandrini of *Forbidden Broadway* notoriety evoked JFK/*Camelot* legend by having

Michelle and Barack Obama play their copy of the *Hamilton* cast recording as they prepared for bed.

In the many press reports on *Hamilton*'s 2015 Broadway opening, Miranda routinely quipped: "This is a story about America then, told by America now."[16] We might then view *Hamilton* as a story of the U.S. presidency's earliest days as one retold for the contemporary Obama era. *Hamilton* is not exactly a recognizable reenactment of a familiar historical narrative like *1776*, which literally stages the Declaration's signing as a tableaux vivant (or living portrait) that replicates the iconic scene depicted in *Congress Signing Independence* (1801) by Robert Edge Pine and Edward Savage. Nor is *Hamilton* a radical reinvention of the historical narrative, as in Alex Timbers and Michael Friedman's sardonic 2010 rock musical *Bloody Bloody Andrew Jackson*, which depicted the seventh president as a "restless, appetite-driven" rock star and charted his journey through "a backwoods boyhood to his fraught tenures as a land-snatching, Indian-slaughtering general and president."[17] Rather, *Hamilton* nimbly lands somewhere in between, a recognizable reinvention that fortifies the very traditions with which it breaks.

The Incoherent Tradition of Nontraditional Casting

"This is a story about America then, told by America now" would become one of the most repeated taglines for *Hamilton*, often used to describe the musical's use of contemporary musical styles to tell a historical story. But the phrase also referenced *Hamilton*'s attention-grabbing casting conceit: assigning nonwhite actors to portray the presumptively white founding fathers. Well before the show opened on Broadway, Miranda confirmed that this casting strategy was foundational not only for the original production of *Hamilton*, but for all future ones as well. "That'll be the note that goes with the school productions," Miranda affirmed, "If this show ends up looking like the actual founding fathers, you messed up."[18] Yet, as innovative as Miranda's casting concept was, it was not especially new. Indeed, *Hamilton*'s inceptive casting conceit—assigning performers of color to presumptively "white" roles—drew upon a constellation of casting practices developed primarily in the theater over much of the last century. Miranda's insistence that *Hamilton*'s casting conceit is imperative to the show's staging—even or especially beyond the Broadway bubble—anchors the musical's casting strategy within an ongoing debate over whether and how casting practices can and should address persistent "diversity" problems in contemporary entertainment.

Casting is an umbrella term used to describe not only the process through which performers are assessed for and assigned to roles, but also the meanings, effects, and implications that are activated when the selected performers enact those roles. The casting of any theatrical work must balance the artistic vision of the show's creators with the logistical demands of staging the show with actual people in real time. On the one hand, casting is a foundational creative act, crucial to the effective interpretation of a performance text before an audience. But casting is also a necessary administrative task, essential to the efficient staging of a production for its audience. Because the number of performers seeking opportunities to perform routinely outstrips the number of roles available, great power lays in the hands of those deciding who gets a part and who does not. Every act of casting is then simultaneously a creative act of interpretation and also an administrative allocation of resources (including time, money, and opportunity).

The casting of a new musical like *Hamilton* is typically determined by the production's director, who consults closely with other professionals charged with staging the show (including, but not limited to, the choreographer, musical director, and producers); and those responsible for creating it (the composer, lyricist, and librettist, among others). Roles are often cast through an audition process, wherein performers are invited (through agent submissions or open casting calls) to offer a brief demonstration of their range of relevant performance abilities as a way of introducing themselves to the production team as potential collaborators. For performers who are already well known to the production team, whether through previous collaborations or because of notable work in other productions, roles are sometimes offered without audition, with the performer's actual suitability for the role assessed in preliminary rehearsals or developmental workshop readings. For *Hamilton*, composer-lyricist-librettist Lin-Manuel Miranda worked with his longtime collaborator, director Thomas Kail, to build the show around Miranda's performance in the title role. Some principal roles were then offered to previous collaborators (like Christopher Jackson, who starred in Kail's production of Miranda's *In the Heights*, and who was part of *Hamilton*'s developmental workshop process from the beginning), and others were assigned through auditions (like Leslie Odom, who auditioned for the role of Aaron Burr not long before *Hamilton* started rehearsals for its initial run at New York's Public Theater).

Miranda's compositional strategy confronts the casting habits that would, by default, assign the roles of historically "white" characters like George Washington, Angelica Schuyler, and Thomas Jefferson to actors who would be understood as white in the contemporary moment. By scripting *Hamilton* so that "nonwhite" actors would be hired to enact these presumptively "white" figures, Miranda both drew upon and added to the constellation of casting practices that had developed in overlapping chronology over the past century within the professional American theater to address the persistent lack of quality roles available to minority and women performers.

Hamilton's casting conceit steps into the snarl of whether or not casting can address, much less solve, the persistent gaps in diversity, equity, and inclusion in contemporary theater. Over the last fifty years or so, activist actors and advocates seeking greater inclusion of actors of color on American stages have developed a range of casting interventions to enact explicit resistance to the "traditional" prominence of white, male roles in the Western theatrical repertoire.[19] Often grouped under the heading "nontraditional casting," these casting techniques typically adjust how race might inform the world of the play and can include a range of tactical approaches. "Conceptual casting" might assign minority actors to conventionally white roles as part of a broader reimagining of a familiar narrative or canonical text. Alternatively, "integrated casting" (sometimes called "societal casting") seeks to more accurately depict the ethno-racial diversity possible in the world of the play, rather than simply defaulting to white actors for ethnically nonspecific roles. "Color-blind casting" might build a theatrical world in which race has no legible meaning, while "color-conscious" casting might build a stage reality in which racial meaning might imbue, inform, and amplify the scripted drama in particular ways.

Hamilton's casting conceit draws upon all of the ostensibly distinct modes of nontraditional casting, while also remixing them in specific ways to suit the particular theatrical and storytelling needs of the show. Most obviously, the show's casting conceit is textbook conceptual casting for its assignment of minority actors to presumptively white roles in ways that reinvent, reimagine, and reinterpret a familiar narrative. Likewise, the show's deployment of color-conscious casting strategies (as in, for example, the choice to have only white actors portray the role of King George) clearly deploys racial meaning in ways that amplify the clarity and drama of the storytelling. Even as the casting of principal characters is largely thus defined by conceptual and color-conscious techniques, the casting of the chorus deploys "genderblind" and colorblind tactics in dynamic and nuanced ways, with the ensemble members fluidly stepping into and out of roles that might be gendered or racially specific (or not), and with only fleeting reliance on the performer's own racially marked or gendered body to communicate meaning. We might even argue that *Hamilton* deploys a dash of integrated or societal casting in its evocation of the multiracial tumult of eighteenth-century New York. *Hamilton* therefore offers a vivid example of how, by the turn to the twenty-first century, the disparate tactics of nontraditional casting can be used selectively, or even simultaneously, within a production.

In defying the habits of historical reenactment, and by rehearsing an alternate and nonreplicative vision of how race might play in a historical narrative, Miranda's tactical use of various of nontraditional casting techniques emphatically resists the presumptions and privileges of whiteness that have shaped American theater history.

At the same time, *Hamilton* also rehearses an additional nontraditional casting technique that we might call "compositional casting," in which the playwright scripts casting as a constitutive part of the show's composition, thereby making how the show is cast subject to copyright and other intellectual property protections. Miranda's compositional casting strategy was but one example among several similar efforts in the middle 2010s, which together suggested a tactical resistance to what had come to be called "whitewashing," or the casting of nonminority actors in roles scripted to be characters of color. As one example, in *Men in Boats*, a play that premiered in New York the same summer *Hamilton* opened on Broadway, playwright Jaclyn Backhaus offered a theatrically adventurous retelling of John Wesley Powell's nineteenth-century geological expedition into the Grand Canyon. In Backhaus's play, nearly all the characters are white men but are scripted to be portrayed onstage by a diverse ensemble of actors, none of whom are cisgender men.[20] The compositional casting strategies deployed by both Miranda and Backhaus are perhaps the most conspicuous examples of this increasingly preemptive defense by playwrights to resist the bad habits of casting convention that so persistently privilege whiteness and maleness.

Hamilton's reach will almost certainly accelerate the incorporation of compositional casting into the recognizable repertoire of nontraditional casting practices familiar to most regular U.S. theatergoers. Still, *Hamilton* does little to address an element of nontraditional casting, and many critics considered this to be its fatal flaw. As playwright August Wilson and others have long argued, nontraditional casting's tactical deployment of theatrical technique may create opportunities for actors of color within the Western theatrical tradition, but it does little to confront, let alone displace, the intransigent persistence of whiteness and maleness as the presumptively "neutral" or "universal" narrative default. Perhaps worse, nontraditional casting exploits performers of color to create the appearance of canonical transformation, while doing little to change the underlying presumptions that persist in privileging whiteness within, and outside, the theater. Despite the increasing ubiquity of such nontraditional casting techniques over the last four decades, American theater remains a tacitly "white space" in which people of color (and others marked by difference) are included only with credible justification (whether rooted in concept, integration, color-consciousness, or authorial intent) to explain the conspicuousness of their presence, especially when assuming presumptively white roles.

As I have suggested, *Hamilton*'s casting is not especially unusual within contemporary theater practice. Even so, the *Hamilton* phenomenon has brought additional scrutiny to the limits of the foundational premises underlying such "nontraditional" moves. Within theatrical circles, the intricacy of *Hamilton*'s casting strategy is routinely praised as both an artful exemplar of casting technique and also as a powerful job-generator for minority performers. Beyond the theatrical bubble, however, *Hamilton*'s complex casting strategy is either simplified as "colorblind," even by those close to the production, like historian Ron Chernow; attacked for usurping employment opportunities for white actors (as in the brief bluster surrounding the potential legality of the *Hamilton* casting notice seeking "nonwhite" performers); or critiqued for erasing or effacing the actual histories of people of color. For theatermakers, such incidents provide vivid reminders of just how unrehearsed mainstream audiences are in discerning the range of theatrical tactics and techniques potentially at play when a minority performer "takes on" a presumptively white role. At the same time, such misrecognition of *Hamilton*'s casting strategies beyond the theatrical bubble also underscores the incoherence that remains foundational to the theatrical tradition of nontraditional casting.

What Makes a Latinx Play

Hamilton is arguably the most critically acclaimed and commercially successful theatrical work authored by a Latinx artist in this century. Yet the extent to which the fact of Miranda's Latinxness should matter in critical assessments of *Hamilton* has become an open question for a range of observers, perhaps especially for Latinx theatermakers. For actor/director/choreographer Rebecca Martinez, seeing "this version of an often-repeated history voiced by people who are often ignored by history makes me want to rise up and make my narrative known."[21] This very paradox compels arts administrator Arlene Martínez-Vázquez to ask, "Is *Hamilton* acting from a place of internalized colonization?"[22] Indeed, aside from Miranda's authorial presence, how and by what measure should *Hamilton* be productively considered part of the tradition of Latinx drama?

Miranda's much-vaunted status as the composer of Broadway's first successful hip-hop musical, one that was about the Latinx Washington Heights neighborhood, rests upon his capacity to cross the border separating Broadway and Top 40 music. It has long been a truism within both the industry and the academy that the emergence of rock and roll in the 1950s and 1960s severed the musical connection between the Broadway stage and the popular playlist. Over the intervening decades, theatermakers have tried to bring Broadway and pop back together. Along the way, pastiche forms like the "rock musical" (*Hair*, 1968; *Rent*, 1996; *Spring Awakening*, 2006) or the "pop opera" (*Jesus Christ Superstar*, 1971; *Les Misérables*, 1987; *Natasha, Pierre & the Great Comet of 1812*, 2016) have earned occasional acclaim. Producers and directors have built theatrical worlds out of the song catalogues of particular music stars or eras, like *Mamma Mia* (2001) and *Jersey Boys* (2005). Pop stars like Cyndi Lauper, Sting, and U2 have also, with various levels of success, composed scores for the Broadway musical stage.

But Lin-Manuel Miranda did not import pop to Broadway, or vice versa. Instead, he straddled both in order to innovate a hybrid musical theatrical sensibility. Indeed, Miranda's capacity to build upon both popular music and music written for the stage has emerged as a signature of his style. In Miranda's breakthrough, and Pulitzer Prize–nominated, musical *In The Heights* (2008), he integrated the musical sounds, rhythmic structures, and affective thrills of a range of popular "Latin" musical styles (merengue, bachata, salsa, bolero, et cetera) into the emphatically conventional narrative, character, and emotional structures of the Broadway musical. Miranda's deft mash-up delivered a sound and sensibility resonating as simultaneously

Latin *and* Broadway, not merely Latin *on* Broadway. In *Hamilton*, Miranda forged a similarly hybrid musical apparatus, successfully melding the rigorous formal structures of the Broadway musical with those of hip hop, rap, and R&B.

Miranda's capacity to speak two musical languages simultane-ously—or his ability to "code switch"—instructs the aficionados of one musical genre in the aesthetics of the other. By doing this, he broadens the audience's understanding and appreciation of both. Miranda's musical dexterity is perhaps the most conspicuous way his Latinx heritage informs his work in *Hamilton*. In a radio inter-view, he noted that his capacity "to change depending on the room [I'm] in"—which Miranda himself termed "code-switching"—was rooted in his childhood experiences of speaking Spanish at home and translating for the nanny of his English-speaking school friends. "It's interesting to become a Latino cultural ambassador when you're seven," he commented wryly. In the same interview, Miranda also noted how his enthusiasm for disparate musical genres impelled a similarly ambassador-like desire to introduce his friends to songs and styles with which they were unfamiliar, by sharing a Broadway tune with a hip-hop fan, or vice versa, for example. In Miranda's account, his delight in using his musical fluency as a creative tactic provided the foundation for his work on the musical theater stage.[23]

Miranda's artistic inventiveness as a musical theater composer lies not so much in the making of new sounds, but in his deft capacity to integrate starkly competing musical sensibilities in ways that ex-pand audience expectations of what either pop music or Broadway can accomplish as modes of popular communication. His use of code-switching also anchors Miranda to the tradition of U.S. Latinx drama. Fluid shifts between Spanish (or Spanglish) and English have been a hallmark feature of U.S. Latinx drama since at least the 1960s. As I have argued elsewhere, the tradition of U.S. Latinx the-atermaking builds upon two parallel legacies, both of which deploy such linguistic flexibility in important and distinct ways.[24] On the one hand, the activist legacy of Luis Valdez, widely acknowledged as the pioneering leader of the activist Chicano *teatro* movement of the 1960s and 1970s, utilizes a mix of Spanish, English, and Spanglish as a primary tool in its project to make a drama that was culturally grounded, socially engaged, and politically relevant to its Latinx audience. On the other, the aesthetic legacy of Maria Irene Fornés, perhaps the most influential mentor/teacher of Latinx playwriting in the later twentieth century, embraced binguality as an experimental technique within its exploration of the ways that Latinx drama might be defined by formal innovation, linguistic precision, and experiential richness. Code-switching became an unlikely constant within the complex tradition of Latinx theatermaking, often bridging the possibly contradictory imperatives of activism and avant-gardism.

Speaking in two languages at once also emerged as one of the signal ways that Latinx theatermakers addressed Latinx audiences. The Latinx theater tradition presumes not only that Latinx audiences will be in the house, but also that Latinx audiences should matter to the theater. While activist artists within the Latinx theater tradition might privilege making plays that Latinx communities need to experience, and while more aesthetically oriented artists within the tradition might prioritize making whatever plays the Latinx theatermaker needs to make, all would likely agree on one thing: the essential importance of the Latinx theatermaker in remaking the American theater as a place where Latinx audiences are addressed with clarity, artistry, and respect.[25] Over the last half century, engaging the multilingual and multicultural fluencies of the Latinx audience has emerged as one the signal theatrical techniques within U.S. Latinx drama.

Among the code-switching techniques most favored by Latinx theatermakers is to use comedy—often an "inside joke" offered in passing—to address the Latinx members of the audience. One of *Hamilton*'s most referenced comic asides underscores how a playwright's glancing address to certain members of the audience can be discerned by Latinx audiences and non-Latinx audiences alike, in ways that also amplify *Hamilton*'s potential legibility as a Latinx work. "I still chuckle every time *Hamilton* and Lafayette crow:

On February 15, 2016, Lin-Manuel Miranda and the cast of Hamilton waved the Puerto Rican flag while accepting the 2016 Grammy Award for Best Musical Theater Album. *(Theo Wargo/Getty Images)*

'Immigrants, we get the job done,'" noted Latina journalist Monica Rohr in the *Houston Chronicle*. "It's as if Miranda is winking at me and whispering: *Tu sabes*. You know."[26] This moment's perceived nod to Latinx audiences has likewise been noted by non-Latinx observers, including those, like conservative columnist Jon Birger, who interprets "Immigrants, we get the job done!" as both "the signature line of *Hamilton*" and as affirmation of a particular political stance regarding immigration and labor law.[27]

Of course, the presence of one line that may or may not be directly addressing Latinx audiences will probably not answer the question of whether *Hamilton* is "a Latinx play" (though some would contend Miranda's authorship is answer enough). Even so, Miranda's code-switching comes out of—and enters *Hamilton* into—the U.S. Latinx theater tradition, a distinctively American genre of playmaking that uses theater as an expressive vocabulary for responding to the world, that explores dramatic form as a way to stage an experiential encounter, and that addresses Latinx peoples as valued members of the work's presumed audience. In ways both direct and indirect, Latinx drama's half-century of tradition—in which Spanish-surnamed artists routinely code-switched in politically and aesthetically adventurous ways, while always addressing Latinx audiences—created the conditions of theatrical possibility for a Latinx artist like Lin-Manuel Miranda to rewrite and restage the story of America.

Making Theatrical Sense of Pence at *Hamilton*

Few incidents underscore how differently *Hamilton* plays inside the Broadway bubble than beyond it more strikingly than what happened at the Richard Rodgers Theatre on November 18, 2016. That evening, Indiana governor Mike Pence (who had, only ten days before, been elected as Donald Trump's vice president) attended *Hamilton* with younger members of his family. Pence's mere presence in the theater occasioned a range of responses, including a spontaneous standing ovation for the line "Immigrants, we get the job done!" But it was what happened after the show that made news.

During the curtain call, the vice president-elect moved to leave the theater, ostensibly to beat the crowds (and eschewing the invitation traditionally extended to dignitaries to meet the cast backstage). A voice from the stage stopped his exit. Brandon Victor Dixon, the actor who portrayed Aaron Burr at that evening's performance, invited Pence to pause. Dixon hushed boos from the crowd as he read a prepared statement, coauthored by Lin-Manuel Miranda, director Thomas Kail, and producer Jeffrey Seller. The statement addressed Pence directly and read, in part: "We, sir, we are the diverse America who are alarmed and anxious that your new administration will not protect us, our planet, our children, our parents, or defend us and uphold our inalienable rights, sir. But we truly hope this show has inspired you to uphold our American values and to work on behalf of *all* of us. . . . We truly thank you for sharing this show—this wonderful American story told by a diverse group of men, women, of different colors, creeds, and orientations." Pence reportedly listened as Dixon spoke and then departed the theater.[28]

Accounts of the incident, some including video footage of Pence being booed as he entered the theater and recordings of Dixon's post-show speech, spread quickly on social media. By the next morning, President-elect Donald Trump had boosted the story's signal in a series of tweets excoriating the "overrated" *Hamilton* cast for their "very rude" and "terrible behavior" in disrespecting both Mike Pence ("a very good man") in the theater (which, according to Trump, "must be a safe and special place"). Over the weekend, the incident was debated both on social media and in the traditional press. Some commentators rebuked the *Hamilton* cast for breaking character to harangue the vice president-elect. Others defended Dixon for exerting his First Amendment rights. Some worried whether the tweet-storm was a deft ploy by Trump to distract from more substantial revelations about his covert business dealings, while still others fretted over what the incident augured for the treatment of the arts in the new administration.

Yet, amid the brief flurry of attention given to the incident, nearly every observer overlooked a crucial aspect of the story. Dixon's delivery of the prepared statement was not a spontaneous lecture occasioned solely by Pence's presence in the theater. Rather, it was part of an established Broadway tradition: the curtain speech on behalf of Broadway Cares/Equity Fights AIDS (BC/EFA). For nearly thirty years, the Broadway community has organized a fundraising campaign (undertaken twice annually and taking place roughly for the eight weeks before Christmas and the eight weeks prior to Easter) during which members of Broadway and other companies interrupt the curtain calls to solicit direct donations for the Phyllis Newman Women's Health Initiative and other nonprofit organizations dedicated to supporting those affected by AIDS/HIV. These donations are then collected by "Bucket Brigades" staffed by members of the cast (often still costumed) and volunteers who solicit audience members as they depart from the theater. In tandem with other benefits (like Broadway Bares), the "Bucket Brigade" campaigns have become familiar, even routine, occurrences for regular theatergoers and have evolved as a treasured tradition within the Broadway community.

This tradition also contributes sizably to BC/EFA's annual granting capacity, which exceeded $12 million dollars in 2015.[29]

Mike Pence happened to attend *Hamilton* during the winter 2016 BC/EFA fundraising campaign. Thus, Brandon Victor Dixon or another member of the *Hamilton* cast would have given a curtain speech on November 18, 2016, with or without Pence in the house. Moreover, because security requirements ensured that the production knew of Pence's presence in advance, and because the recent presidential campaign contributed to widespread awareness of Pence's failures as governor of Indiana to effectively respond to crises in HIV/AIDS and women's health,[30] the *Hamilton* team was obliged— both by the particular theatrical tradition of the BC/EFA pitch and by common courtesy—to approach that night's curtain speech with clarity of intention. Dixon's comments were thus neither spontaneous nor unscripted, but were instead guided by the established conventions of a longstanding theatrical tradition that Pence's presence shaped in important but legible ways.

The Pence episode may or may not endure as an emblematic episode of the broader *Hamilton* phenomenon. Yet, as an example of the disparity between how *Hamilton* plays within and beyond the theater, the brisk erasure of the actual theatrical context for Dixon's "Broadway Cares" speech does signal the easy elision of the varied theatrical traditions anchoring *Hamilton*'s innovations and provocations, especially when news about them moves briskly beyond the Broadway bubble. As the *Hamilton* phenomenon continues to exceed the theatrical limits of its beginnings, the musical's theatrical histories may or may not remain central to broader considerations of the musical's significance. Even so, the Pence episode underscores the enduring importance of appreciating how *Hamilton* played on the stage if we are to ever truly apprehend *Hamilton*'s import and impact beyond it.

NOTES

1. Alissa Wilkerson, "Lin-Manuel Miranda's *SNL* Remix of *Hamilton*'s 'My Shot,' Annotated," *Vox*, October 9, 2016, http://www.vox.com/2016/10/

9/13216248/lin-manuel-miranda-hamilton-donald-trump-hillary-clinton-satur day-night-live-my-shot.

2. Trevor Boffone, "Ham4Ham: Taking *Hamilton* to the Streets," *Howl-Round.com*, March 18, 2016, http://howlround.com/ham4ham-taking-hamilton-to-the-streets; Howard Sherman, "The Generous Audience Engagement of Lin-Manuel Miranda," HESherman.com, August 5, 2015, http://www.hesherman.com/2015/08/05/the-generous-audience-engagement-of-lin-manuelmiranda/.

3. Alex Nichols, "You Should Be Terrified That People Who Like 'Hamilton' Run Our Country," *Current Affairs*, July 29, 2016, https://www.currentaffairs.org/2016/07/you-should-be-terrified-that-people-who-like-hamiltonrun-our-country.

4. Alex Beggs, "Read Lin-Manuel Miranda's Genius Annotations for *Hamilton*," *Vanity Fair*, November 2, 2015.

5. In this essay, I build upon arguments and language I have developed in other works on Lin-Manuel Miranda and Latinx drama. See especially "Miranda's Manifesto," *Theater* 47, no. 2 (2017): 23–33; "But Do We Have the Actors for That?: Principles of Practice for Staging Latinx Plays in a University Theatre Context," *Theatre Topics* 27, no. 1 (March 2017); and "What Makes a Latino Play," *McCarter.org*, September 2016, http://www.mccarter.org/bathinginmoonlight/.

6. Adam Feldman, "Why 'Hamilton' Is the Musical to See Now," *Time Out New York*, July 9, 2015, https://www.timeout.com/newyork/theater/why -hamilton-is-the-broadway-musical-to-see-now.

7. Mark Binelli, "'Hamilton' Creator Lin-Manuel Miranda: The Rolling Stone Interview," *Rolling Stone*, June 1, 2016, http://www.rollingstone.com/music/features/hamilton-creator-lin-manuel-miranda-the-rolling-stone-inter view-20160601.

8. Quoted in Rob Weinert-Kendt, "Rapping a Revolution: Lin-Manuel Miranda and Others from 'Hamilton' Talk History," *New York Times*, February 5, 2015.

9. Jonathan Mandell, "Presidents on Broadway," BroadwayDirect.com, February 17, 2015, http://broadwaydirect.com/feature/presidents-on-broadway.

10. Bruce E. Altschuler, *Acting Presidents: 100 Years of Plays about the Presidents* (New York: Palgrave Macmillan, 2010), xi. Most stage depictions of American presidential politics have appeared in nonmusical (or "straight") plays. Some notable presidential plays—like Robert Sherwood's *Abe Lincoln in Illinois* (1938), which tells the story of Lincoln's early years, and Dory Schary's *Sunrise at Campobello* (1957), which depicts Franklin Delano Roosevelt's diagnosis

with polio—offer intimate, prepresidential portraits of those who would hold the office. Others—like David Hare's *Stuff Happens* (2004), which stages the political dialogue among George W. Bush and others that led to the 2003 U.S. military invasion of Iraq, and Peter Morgan's *Frost/Nixon* (2006), which depicted a series of 1977 television interviews between British journalist David Frost and Richard Nixon—use a mix of historical transcripts and fictionalized dialogue to theatricalize public events involving presidents during and after their administrations. Still others—like Richard Schenkkan's *All the Way* (2014), which depicts the first year of Lyndon B. Johnson's presidency—enact a combination of public and private scenes to craft a stage version of political biography.

11. The first notable presidential musical to feature an actual president as a principal character was Moss Hart and George S. Kaufman's *I'd Rather Be Right* (1937), which lightheartedly spoofed then-president Franklin Delano Roosevelt. Leonard Bernstein's *1600 Pennsylvania Avenue* (1976) was much more serious and examined the evolution of American race relations through a loose collection of songs and scenes as performed by various presidents, First Ladies, and the White House servants. Others were more sardonic, like Alex Timbers and Michael Friedman's rock musical *Bloody Bloody Andrew Jackson* (2010), which depicted the seventh president as a "restless, appetite-driven" rock star. The most iconic presidential musical to precede *Hamilton* was Sherman Edwards and Peter Stone's *1776*, a meticulous and emotionally intricate reenactment of the writing and signing of the Declaration of Independence that opened on Broadway in 1969. Musicals about fictional presidents include *Of Thee I Sing* (1931), *As the Girls Go* (1948), and *Mr. President* (1962).

12. David Haven Blake, "The Broadway Song That Nominated a President," *OUPblog*, June 23, 2016, http://blog.oup.com/2016/06/broadway-eis enhower-presidential-nomination/. See also David Haven Blake, *Liking Ike: Eisenhower, Advertising, and the Rise of Celebrity Politics* (New York: Oxford University Press, 2016), esp. 57–63.

13. Ferdinand Lewis, "Heated Debate About 'Cool' Cut," *Los Angeles Times*, September 7, 2001.

14. Jerome Hudson, "Obama's Favorite Broadway Show 'Hamilton' Seeks 'Non-White' Actors, Possibly Violating New York Law," *Breitbart.com*, March 30, 2016, http://www.breitbart.com/big-hollywood/2016/03/30/obamas-favor ite-broadway-show-hamilton-seeks-non-white-actors-possibly-violating-new -york-law/.

15. Theodore H. White, "For President Kennedy: An Epilogue," *Life*, December 6, 1963.

16. Edward Delman, "How Lin-Manuel Miranda Shapes History," *Atlantic .com*, September 29, 2015, http://www.theatlantic.com/entertainment/archive/ 2015/09/lin-manuel-miranda-hamilton/408019/.

17. Ben Brantley, "Old Hickory, Rock Star President," *New York Times*, April 6, 2010.

18. Quoted in Weinert-Kendt, "Rapping a Revolution."

19. Though the history of diversity initiatives I offer here is based largely on my work in process toward my forthcoming book, "Casting: A History," a number of performance studies scholars have provided foundational context for my discussion here and elsewhere. See especially Daniel Banks, "The Welcome Table: Casting for an Integrated Society," *Theatre Topics* 23, no. 1 (2013): 1–18; Faedra Chatard Carpenter, *Coloring Whiteness: Acts of Critique in Black Performance* (Ann Arbor: University of Michigan Press, 2014); Brandi Wilkins Catenese, *The Problem of the Color[blind]: Racial Transgression and the Politics of Black Performance* (Ann Arbor: University of Michigan Press, 2011); Christine Mok, "East West Players and After: Acting and Activism," *Theatre Survey* 57, no. 2 (2016): 253–263; Angela Chia-yi Pao, *No Safe Spaces: Re-casting Race, Ethnicity, and Nationality in American Theater* (Ann Arbor: University of Michigan Press, 2010).

20. Diep Tran, "Hey Playwrights: Make American History as Diverse as America," *tdf.org*, August 26, 2015, https://www.tdf.org/stages/article/1272/hey -playwrights-make-american-history-as-diverse-as-america.

21. Rebecca Martinez, "*Mi tierra*, My Testimony: A #HamilTestimonio," *Howlround.com*, May 1, 2016, http://howlround.com/mi-tierra-my-testimony -a-hamiltestimonio.

22. Arlene Martínez-Vázquez, "Vietgone, *Hamilton*, and the Decolonization of American Theatre," *Howlround.com*, March 15, 2017, http://howlround.com/ vietgone-hamilton-and-the-decolonization-of-american-theatre.

23. "Lin-Manuel Miranda on Disney, Mixtapes, and Why He Won't Try to Top 'Hamilton,'" *npr.org*, January 3, 2017, http://www.npr.org/2017/01/03/50747 0975/lin-manuel-miranda-on-disney-mixtapes-and-why-he-wont-try-to-top -hamilton.

24. Here, I build especially on my "What Makes a Latino Play."

25. Apt summary histories of Latinx drama can be found in Anne García-Romero, *The Fornes Frame Contemporary Latina Playwrights and the Legacy of Maria Irene Fornes* (Tucson: University of Arizona Press, 2016) and Jon D. Rossini, *Contemporary Latina/o Theater: Wrighting Ethnicity* (Carbondale: Southern Illinois University Press, 2008).

26. Monica Rohr, "'Hamilton': It's a Latino Thing," *Houston Chronicle*, May 13, 2016, http://www.houstonchronicle.com/local/gray-matters/article/Hamilton-It-s-a-Latino-thing-7467557.php.

27. Jon Birger, "'Hamilton' Cast Lectures VP-Elect While Barring Immigrant Actors from Broadway Roles," *Washington Observer*, November 25, 2016, http://observer.com/2016/11/hamilton-cast-lectures-vp-elect-while-barring-immigrant-actors-from-broadway-roles/.

28. Christopher Mele and Patrick Healy, "Hamilton' Had Some Unscripted Lines for Pence. Trump Wasn't Happy," *New York Times*, November 19, 2016.

29. General information about Broadway Cares/Equity Fights AIDS, including reports on annual granting amounts, can be found at the organization's website: https://broadwaycares.org/. For more on history and fundraising methods of Broadway Cares/Equity Fights AIDS, see Virginia Anderson, "Choreographing a Cause: Broadway Bares as Philanthroproduction and Embodied Index to Changing Attitudes toward HIV/AIDS," in *The Oxford Handbook of Dance and Theatre*, edited by Nadine George-Craves (New York: Oxford University Press, 2015), 922–947.

30. Megan Twohey, "Mike Pence's Response to H.I.V. Outbreak: Prayer, Then a Change of Heart," *New York Times*, August 7, 2016; Susan Rinkunas, "The 5 Worst Decisions Mike Pence Has Made About Women's Health," *NYMag.com*, July 15, 2016,http://nymag.com/thecut/2016/07/mike-pence-abortion-womens-health-record.html.

Act III

The Audience

CHAPTER 11

Mind the Gap

Teaching Hamilton

JIM CULLEN

"Helpless"—and the evocatively named Dachelle Washington—
prompted me to act.

I'd first become aware of *Hamilton* in the spring of 2015, when
I had a serendipitous opportunity to see the musical at the Public
Theater, a few months before its Broadway opening. I'd been enrap-
tured by *Bloody Bloody Andrew Jackson* five years earlier, and wasn't
expecting much from a show rooted in a hip-hop genre that I, a
child of rock and roll, respected more than I liked. So I was unpre-
pared for the force of the musical. Good as it was, though, I largely
forgot about the show until the cast album was released six months
later. I bought it on compact disk, the antiquated format to which
I pledge my allegiance. And was besotted all over again.

So much so that I tried it out on the students in my advisory at
the Ethical Culture Fieldston School in New York, where I teach history. Fieldston is an elite, private, progressive institution that prides
itself on its cutting-edge pedagogy, social activism, and commitment
to socioeconomic diversity. (The school held a daylong symposium
on intersectionality while I was revising this essay.) But at the end of
the day—or, more accurately, at the start of the day, which is where
this story begins—the place is an enclave of teenagers, and advisory
(what most schools would call homeroom) is an oasis of banter
and socializing. So I try to have packages of Oreos on hand and
encourage students to use the Smart Board to show music videos
while attending to library fines or kids missing gym credits. On this

particular crisp October day, however, I couldn't resist indulging my Hamilmania by commandeering the computer and cueing up "Helpless," curious to see how my charges would react. What I didn't expect is that they would know the song even better than I did, and that a clutch of girls, led by the thespian Dachelle, would begin singing a song whose lyrics they had already memorized. Huh, I thought. There's something happening here. And so it is that I developed "*Hamilton*: A Musical Inquiry," an elective I launched in the fall of 2016—with Ms. Washington by my side.

As a member of the baby boom, I'm very aware of the generation gap—not the one between parents and children in the 1960s, but rather the one between teachers and students in the 2010s. In many respects, attitudes toward issues such as sexuality, drug use, and race relations are not now as markedly divided between young and old as they were a half-century ago. Conversely, generational friction has long been the engine of social conflict in many societies,

In the room where it happens: the author's history classroom at Ethical Culture Fieldston School in New York City. (*Courtesy of Jim Cullen*)

among them the United States (where, it should be noted, the founding fathers were relatively young men—or, in the case of Benjamin Franklin, young at heart). But whatever their relative width, generation gaps always have distinctive contours. A big part of my job involves trying to bridge this one—which means trying to understand my charges as a prelude to engaging them.

In certain respects, this isn't particularly hard to do. A clear generational vector has animated recent social movements like Black Lives Matter or the presidential candidacy of Bernie Sanders, even if they've been broader and more complex than simply an upheaval by the young. Americans in their teens and twenties tend to be (even) more skeptical about organized religion than their predecessors: the percentage of so-called "nones," or Americans professing no religious affiliation, has risen sharply in this decade.[1] Such demographic tendencies aren't things I presume about my students, though they may affect the way I approach a subject or pitch a question ("Jonquil, a lot of people of your age tend to think X about topic Y; where do you come down?").

In a more fundamental sense, however, all teachers have to deal with a gap that's less a matter of perspective than information: a knowledge gap. By definition, to be young is to be inexperienced, which is to say uninformed. We all know, and sometimes even admire, young people who are ignorant and smart. But teachers are hired to address the former condition, in large measure because (unlike the famously elusive concept of intelligence) it *can* be addressed. Part of the joy of being a teacher is that in a way, it's so easy: the vastness of an adolescent's informational blank slate is such that you can have substantial leeway to shape their learning experience, even if curricular or administrative constraints impose external limitations—and even if students, who in other respects are *not* blank slates, draw conclusions that may not be what you intend, much less know.

This information deficit is not simply a matter of providing the details of the Treaty of Paris (take your pick as to which one). It's also contextual: I'm now working with students who were born after 9/11. These are people who typically have the dimmest idea at best of what their parents do for a living and who have never paid a cent in taxes. To put it another way, it's easier to convey the frustrations of the hopelessly indebted post–Revolutionary War insurrectionist Daniel Shays if you have a $5,700 credit card balance (the national average in mid-2016) than if you've never had a credit card in your name.[2]

Under such circumstances, a history class is never simply a matter of the stated topic at hand. It's also a meta-class with a historical artifact at the front of the room known as the teacher. Teachers are "old" even if they've only got a few years on their charges, and even if those charges sometimes exploit a teacher's own youth or inexperience in the contest of wills that's always part of a classroom experience. And, to paraphrase the old adage, as a teacher you keep getting older while your students keep getting younger. Generation gap indeed. As a white man with relatively conventional opinions for someone of my age and class—liberal to most of the outside world, conservative in the world in academia, where I have published a series of books on subjects that include Bruce Springsteen and the American Dream—I see myself as the product of a vanishing worldview that nevertheless has utility.[3] After all, you can't deconstruct narratives you never knew or understood in the first place, much less appreciate the value of new ones.

In my experience, there's no better way to close these gaps—generation gaps, knowledge gaps, identity gaps—than popular culture, which bridges constituencies, however imperfectly, more effectively than any other mediating force in our national life. That's why my pedagogic antennae went up sharply when Dachelle started singing "Helpless": it was clear, however imprecisely, that *Hamilton* was bridging the divide that separated me from my students, and that I might be able to exploit this reality pedagogically.

But how? It's one thing to note that the musical is a great teaching tool; it's another to actually translate this potential into an educational experience—which for me means structuring environments where multiple realities can be authentically engaged in a discussion format. In this regard, I enjoyed a series of advantages. The first is that I teach at a school where developing electives has long been routine and encouraged. The second is a set of unusually accessible source materials—beginning, alas, not with live performance, but with the cast album, which remains a treasure trove in its own right. Beyond that, somewhat counterintuitively, is Ron Chernow's *Hamilton* biography. Yes, it's massive, but by textbook standards the paperback is relatively cheap (about $20), since it's published by Penguin, a trade publishing house.[4] It's also worth noting the subtly appealing architecture of this and all Chernow biographies, which are segmented into manageable chapters (a strategy I suspect aided Lin-Manuel Miranda as he conceptualized his musical). So it is, for example, that there are separate ones on topics like Hamilton's family life, antagonists like Thomas Jefferson (in a Voltaire-evoking chapter "Dr. Pangloss"), and so on. This fact made it possible not only to assign the book in bite-sized chunks, but also to pair particular episodes in the book with particular songs from the cast album, such as Chernow's account of the Battle of Yorktown ("Glory") with "The World Turned Upside Down" from the musical.[5] (See the appendix to this book for a sample course syllabus.)

A third asset in teaching a Hamilton course is Hamilton himself: his writings are about as accessible as any eighteenth-century prose can be. They're widely available online, but I adopted the Library of America edition edited by Joanne Freeman, notable for judicious selections that range from *The Federalist Papers* to personal letters, like that to his childhood chum Edward Stevens or his correspondence with George Washington (I sprinkle primary source excerpts of his, Jefferson's, and James Madison's in the mix as well). Freeman's volume is a bit pricey at $40, though typically cheaper through online retailers like Amazon.com; my hope is that the Library of America will issue a paperback edition, the way it has with Abraham Lincoln's writings, for example.[6]

But the most important asset in using *Hamilton* as a teaching tool—and closing the generation gap in ways that foster genuine exchange—is what might be termed the very nature of the show: its ineluctable, almost incorrigible, instinct for bridging communities. This elasticity is far more than a matter of analogizing Alexander Hamilton to a prior-day Biggie Smalls or Thomas Jefferson invoking the message of Grandmaster Flash. The musical literally dramatizes its hybrid essence—and that of the American experience generally.

I'm not going to clutter this piece with musical exegesis likely to be better performed by others for decades to come, but to illustrate the point I'll briefly return to the discussion of "Helpless," a song one critic has described as "equal parts Cole Porter and Ja Rule."[7] The song occurs at the moment in the show when young Alexander Hamilton meets his future bride, Eliza Schuyler, both of whom express the emotions of a storybook romance. Given my own demographic orientation, what I first hear is classic girl-group Motown-era pop: Eliza (Phillipa Soo) singing lead and backed by a team of female vocalists. But when I looked into Miranda's own reference to Ja Rule—whose singing he describes as "a bear roaring at the bottom of a well"[8]—I was led back to a series of songs the rapper performed with female R&B singers, notably his 2003 hit "Mesmerize" with Ashanti. (The two would team up to perform "Helpless" on *The Hamilton Mixtape*, released in late 2016.) The video of the "Mesmerize" song, in turn, visually samples the climax of the 1978 hit movie *Grease*—both feature men and women who mimic their partners' gender performance strategies in the name of true love (to the chagrin of their homosocial partners). The film version of *Grease*, of course, was based on the 1971 musical notable at the time for its use of rock and roll in a Broadway setting, just as *Hamilton* was notable for its use of hip hop in such a setting. You can see how many directions the discourse pings here, stretching from Tin Pan Alley to gangsta rap—and the threads that connect them, among them a youthful penchant for engaging sexuality in implicit as well as explicit ways, a hallmark of adolescent experience across many generations. Perhaps more importantly, the interracial cultural appropriation, which runs in multiple ways, is not simply a means to an end, but a statement in its own right about the essentially hybrid character of American culture, whatever its particular emphasis or coloring at any given time or place.

The most obvious demonstration of this integrationist sensibility is the well-publicized multiracial casting of *Hamilton*, a fixture of the first, and thus far subsequent, productions. As some critics have noted, the musical would be experienced very differently, and much more critically, if its multicultural musical idiom had been paired with a traditionally all-white cast.[9] The foregrounding of black artists—and the fact that the original cast featured Latinx as well as Asian performers—speaks to Miranda's evident desire to assert the stake minority communities have in the nation's founding, which established an ideological framework that would provide the language, criteria, and means, if not always the reality, of emancipation. As Miranda's collaborator Jeremy McCarter noted in the "Hamiltome" companion to the musical, strategies such as these are "another way of saying that American history can be told, claimed and reclaimed, by people who don't look like George Washington and Betsy Ross."[10]

Perhaps more importantly, the musical captures important elements of the human experience—the love of children expressed in "Dear Theodosia" (tellingly, expressed by rivals who sing in harmony); the fraternal bonding of ambitious young men in "The Story of Tonight"; the marital struggles of pain, grief, and forgiveness in "It's Quiet Uptown"—that transcend both specific historical moments as well as particularistic demographic categories. As Aaron Burr tells us in "Wait for It":

Love [later verse: death] doesn't discriminate
Between the sinners and the saints
It takes and it takes and it takes
And we keep loving [living] anyway

As with so much associated with Aaron Burr, this is not entirely true: there *is* discrimination in the way things like love and death play out in American life. But a complicating residue of truth lingers.

As its detractors have noted, *Hamilton* is not a perfect musical. The dearth of black characters, as opposed to black actors, is a reasonable objection, though it should be said that there's a danger of tokenism in trying to address it.[11] No story is universal, and this one certainly isn't, either: one should not turn to this play for a nuanced treatment of race relations at the dawn of the American republic. Unlike earlier moments in U.S. history, however, it can't really be said that racial conflict has been ignored in U.S. classrooms or anywhere else in this generation. The summer reading at my school in the year *Hamilton*'s Broadway run began was Chimimanda Ngozie Adichie's 2013 novel *Americanah*. The novels of Toni Morrison (I myself am partial to her 2008 book *A Mercy* for teaching the colonial era) are staples of history and English courses across the nation. I taught the 2013 film *Twelve Years a Slave*, based on Solomon Northup's 1855 slave narrative, in the summer of 2016. Admittedly, I don't work at a typical high school. But books like Frederick Douglass's slave narrative and Ta-Nehisi Coates's *Between the World and Me*, which has sold millions of copies,[12] are now standard fare at many schools (Coates's publisher, Penguin Random House, has published a Teacher's Guide tailored to Common Core standards).[13] Facebook walls of the 2010s have been replete with news about Michael Brown, Sandra Bland, and Philando Castile.

Does this mean that students leave my or anyone else's classes with a sophisticated understanding of racism? Of course not. Progressive-minded teachers are often eager to inculcate an understanding of the workings of power in American society. But the primary power dynamic as far as many students are concerned is that between themselves and their teacher: they never forget who's doing the grading, and are often more attuned to what the grader wants than what they think (something even the smartest of them are reluctant to articulate). This is a reality one ignores at one's peril; trying too hard to prescribe outcomes is likely to backfire if the goal is fostering critical faculties.

Other objections to *Hamilton* are more broadly historiographic, rooted in the fact that Miranda's version of Hamilton rests heavily on Chernow's biography, which, like all biographies, makes arguable interpretations that reflect both a particular historical moment as well as an ideological position within it (for more on such issues, see William Hogeland's contribution to this volume). I plead guilty on this count, since so much of my course rests on Chernow, to a great extent because as high school teacher I don't have the luxury of assigning as much reading as I would if I was teaching an undergraduate or graduate seminar. In my defense, I will say that I myself have tried to keep up with recent literature on the period for a wider perspective that helped me challenge my students and pivot off the homework (which of course often went unread).[14] But here again, my job requires me to think in terms of forests, not trees: fostering an understanding that historical actors are three-dimensional people; that they could disagree, emphatically, on things that were important to them; that many of the things important to *us* will *also* become quaint, if not repellent: these are the lessons of *Hamilton* that matter most to me, because I think they're the ones most likely to matter to my students in their lives beyond the classroom.

I'll end as I began: as a baby boomer. The towering figure in my moral imagination is Dr. Martin Luther King Jr. The heart of King's vision—the vision of a Baptist minister, a fact which I believe is too often overlooked by secular academics—was integration, one I evangelize in my teaching in a variety of ways, among them civic, as I see it as my job to foster the social cohesion that can sustain the American experiment for another generation. If I, and others, have reason to suspect my motives in my embrace of that vision, I take comfort in knowing that it's much larger than I am, extending back through Frederick Douglass and Phillis Wheatley. Perhaps paradoxically, I also take comfort in knowing that there's an honorable counter-tradition that includes David Walker, Martin Delany, and Malcolm X: I'd like to believe my choices and loyalties are consequential. I stand before my students as an artifact. I hope my work with them—what I represent to them—will sustain an ongoing conversation, planting seeds in a garden I'll never get to see.

NOTES

1. See for, example, the widely cited Pew Research report of 2015: http://www.pewresearch.org/fact-tank/2015/11/11/religious-nones-are-not-only-growing-theyre-becoming-more-secular/, accessed November 15, 2016. Robert Putnam and David Campbell note the trend on their superb study *American Grace: How Religion Divides and Unites Us* (New York: Simon & Schuster, 2010), 90–102.

2. "Average Credit Card Debt in America: 2016 Facts & Figures," Value Penguin, Inc., http://www.valuepenguin.com/average-credit-card-debt, accessed November 15, 2016.

3. Without getting too bogged down in the taxonomic weeds, my generally leftist orientation reflects that of the middle third of the twentieth century—i.e., from the presidencies of Franklin Roosevelt to Lyndon Johnson—in contrast to the Progressive/progressive currents on either side of it. By which I mean that I have less confidence in the concept of progress per se (I think of politics more in terms of power rather than improvement), and think more in terms of social amelioration than social orchestration. The fact that I'm Roman Catholic has something to do with this.

4. Ron Chernow, *Alexander Hamilton* (New York: Penguin, 2004).

5. Ibid., 144–166.

6. Joanne B. Freeman, ed., *Alexander Hamilton: Writings* (New York: Library of America, 2001). The Library of America edition of Lincoln's writings, edited by Gore Vidal, was published in hardcover in 1989 and issued in paperback in 2009.

7. Elizabeth Logan, "I Have an Opinion on Every Song in *Hamilton*," *Huffington Post* blog, October 1, 2015, http://www.huffingtonpost.com/elizabeth-logan/i-have-an-opinion-on-ever_b_8223496.html, accessed August 26, 2016.

8. Lin-Manuel Miranda and Jeremy McCarter, *Hamilton: The Revolution* (New York: Grand Central Publishing, 2016), 69.

9. Rebecca Onion, "A *Hamilton* Critic on Why the Musical Isn't So Revolutionary," *Slate*, April 5, 2016, http://www.slate.com/articles/arts/culturebox/2016/04/a_hamilton_critic_on_why_the_musical_isn_t_so_revolutionary.html, accessed August 25, 2016. The skeptic in question, interviewed in the piece, is Lyra D. Monteiro of Rutgers University. See her early, and widely cited, critique of the musical, "Race-Conscious Casting and the Erasure of the Black Past in Lin-Manuel Miranda's *Hamilton*," *The Public Historian* 38, no. 1 (February 2016), reprinted in this volume. The esteemed critic and novelist Ishmael Reed makes a different objection to the nonwhite cast by asking rhetorically how a Berlin audience might react to Jewish actors playing the roles of Adolf

Hitler or Hermann Goering (see "Black Actors Dress Up as Slave Traders . . . And It's Not Even Halloween," *Counterpunch*, August 21, 2015, http://www.counterpunch.org/2015/08/21/hamilton-the-musical-black-actors-dress-up-like-slave-tradersand-its-not-halloween/, accessed August 25, 2016. But of course something of the kind was done with Mel Brooks's *The Producers*, a well-received movie (1968) and musical (2001) in which Jewish characters portrayed Nazis. The very plot premise of that show was that such an idea was indeed grotesque—and unexpectedly liberating.

10. Miranda and McCarter, *Hamilton: The Revolution*, 95.

11. This point is made, in a tone of exasperation, by John McWhorter in "The Exhausting and Useless Accusations of Racism against *Hamilton*," *Daily Beast*, April 16, 2016, http://www.thedailybeast.com/articles/2016/04/16/the-exhausting-and-useless-accusations-of-racism-against-hamilton.html, accessed August 25, 2016. "If *Hamilton* included a single slave character or two gliding around with everyone else, or had a song where a slave came out and rapped about his misery, or had a couple of the female chorus members shown doing one of the Schuyler sisters' hair before the party scene, let's face it, it would just occasion more contesting," he notes. "The slaves would be too marginal to the action, would not look miserable enough, not depicted as full human beings, etc." McWhorter, himself African American, asserts that Hamilton's critics expect too much from the play: "This country is too vast and protean a mess for the idea to hold up that any single factor, even as massive and tragic as the racial one, constitutes the key to the whole business. Yes, there is race. But there is a humongous deal more, and there always has been."

12. Joceylyn McClurg, "Ta-Nehisi Coates Writes a Bestseller," *USA Today*, July 22, 2015, http://www.usatoday.com/story/life/books/2015/07/22/ta-nehisi-coates-between-world-and-me-harper-lee-el-james-usa-today-best-selling-books/30471757/, accessed December 22, 2016.

13. See the publisher's website: http://www.penguinrandomhouseaudio.com/teachers-guide/220290/between-the-world-and-me/, accessed December 22, 2016.

14. Books I read while preparing and teaching this course include Annette Gordon-Reed and Peter Onuf, *Most Blessed of the Patriarchs: Thomas Jefferson and the Empire of the Imagination* (New York: Liveright, 2016); David O. Stewart, *Madison's Gift: Five Partnerships That Made America* (New York: Simon & Schuster, 2015); and Joseph J. Ellis, *The Quartet: Orchestrating the Second American Revolution, 1783–1789* (New York: Knopf, 2015). I also read Chernow's *Washington: A Life* (New York: Penguin, 2010).

CHAPTER 12

Reckoning with America's Racial Past, Present, and Future in *Hamilton*

Patricia Herrera

When I saw *Hamilton* for the first time Off-Broadway at the Public Theater in March 2015 and then again in August 2016 at the Richard Rodgers Theatre, I cheered and marveled at the largely black and Latinx cast. Verbally and musically dexterous, these multiracial founding fathers narrated the birth of America in a hip-hop aesthetic. I was deeply moved by the sight of a cast that reflected a contemporary America. Watching actors of color playing the roles of Alexander Hamilton, George Washington, Aaron Burr, Thomas Jefferson, James Madison, and the Schuyler sisters allowed me, a Latinx woman, to see a sliver of myself in the nation's origin story. *I'm part of America too*, I felt, a radical difference from what I typically experience when I see and hear mainstream media. People of color are often on the other side of the judicial and social story in America—behind bars as prisoners, drug dealers, gangsters, or enslaved people—but in *Hamilton*, Lin-Manuel Miranda places us at the center. We make revolution, history, law, and finance.

As someone who studies hip hop, Latinx music, and theater, I also heard myself in an acoustic environment shaped by Afro-Caribbean and Afro-American musical, oral, visual, and dance forms and practices. The music, lyrics, and sounds of jazz, R&B, salsa, reggaeton, and hip hop were interwoven with Euro-American musical tradition. This cultural mix, rarely recognized on Broadway, had my head bopping and my feet tapping. Hip-hop artists like Big Pun, Mobb Deep, Tupac, and The Notorious B.I.G were in conversation with

Broadway musicals like *Sweeney Todd*, *Merrily We Roll Along*, *South Pacific*, and *West Side Story*. In *Hamilton*, Miranda seems to mirror the inclusive democracy that America claims to be. For a few hours, at least, I was living in a cultural utopia.

My positive feelings about *Hamilton* only intensified the following year when, during an epic cross-country car trip to visit many of America's national parks, my three children became obsessed with the soundtrack of *Hamilton*. How gratifying it was to watch them hear themselves in *Hamilton* and put their own defiant flavor to "My Shot"—"Hey you, I'm just like my country, / I'm young, scrappy and hungry, / And I'm not throwing away my shot!" With anti-immigrant sentiment on the rise in our country today, hearing my children sing along with Miranda, "immigrants / We get the job done!" affirmed not only America's immigrant origins, but also my family's part in that story. For me, a first-generation American born of Ecuadorian parents who brought home pieces of garments to sew for ten cents apiece, Miranda affirmed that people like us are the backbone of America. Watching and listening to *Hamilton* while we sat at campsites, awed by America's spectacular vistas, felt like we were living the American Dream.

But as we are setting up the tent at one of the parks my euphoric feelings came to a screeching halt. My ten-year old daughter told me that, like many little girls this year, she wanted to dress up as Angelica Schuyler for Halloween. As she told me how she loved the way that Angelica raps, sings, and speaks her mind, I asked myself, "How could my beautiful brown-bodied Latina daughter want to be Angelica Schuyler, a slave owner?" It was then that I began to contemplate a new ambivalence about not only *Hamilton*, but also the image of America and the American Dream encapsulated in the national parks. The tranquil serenity of the parks and the democratic inclusivity evoked in *Hamilton* suddenly seemed to be illusions that shattered once I began to dig deeper into their respective soundscapes and landscapes. I realized I had been caught up in a utopian vision of America as a model of diversity, equality, and democracy and that it was time for me to wake up from this dream. It wasn't true.

Born during the Obama era, *Hamilton* came to us at a moment when it was possible to imagine people of color as founding fathers because of our first African American president. But by saturating our audition and vision with fantasies about a diverse political world, *Hamilton* may also make it difficult for my daughter, and perhaps other youth, to differentiate Angelica Schuyler, the historical figure and a slave owner, from Renée Elise Goldsberry, the African American actress personifying Angelica. In blurring these historical realities, *Hamilton* glosses over the fact that, as Elizabeth Wollman points out, black actors have rarely been allowed to perform on the Broadway stage for much of America's history. Most of the people on the *Hamilton* stage would have been enslaved, not making policy, if they had been alive during the eighteenth century. What, then, is the social significance of using a contemporary medium like hip hop, which is racially fraught, to narrate a founding story that doesn't, in fact, fully grapple with the legacies of slavery and racism? Does the hip-hop soundscape of *Hamilton* effectively drown the violence and trauma—and sounds—of slavery that people who looked like the actors in the play might have actually experienced at the time of the nation's birth?

America's national parks also conceal a historical reality. Sitting in the midst of this utopian federal preserve, I recalled that it is carved out of land formerly occupied by Native Americans. The late nineteenth-century initiative to preserve the wilderness for American families came at the expense of removing Native Americans and African Americans from their homes and lands. *Hamilton*, like the national parks, proclaims an inclusive narrative of American identity that obscures the histories of racism that are at the base of so much of the American experience.

Given how *Hamilton* has spilled over into everyday life and become part of a new national imaginary for people like my children, it is vital to reflect on the uncritical ways it is possible to relate and engage with Miranda's racial utopia. Coloring the stage with black and brown bodies singing and dancing to an Afro-diasporic soundscape models the practice and even tolerance of diversity, but it does

Renée Elise Goldsberry, the actress who originated the role of Angelica Schuyler on Broadway, has become a role model for many young women. Here she is shown accepting the Tony Award for Best Performance by an Actress in a Featured Role in a Musical on June 12, 2016. (Reuters/Lucas Jackson)

not equate to an inclusive narration of American history. *Hamilton* may stage the nation that at least some aspire to, but this vision does not reflect contemporary reality. My daughter's desire to be Angelica Schuyler shines a light on how I must strive for a more challenging and inclusive conversation, one that explores why the voices of enslaved people are missing, who they are, and why they seem to not matter in the story about the founding fathers of this nation.

The Politics of Hip Hop and Hip-Hop Theater on the Broadway Stage

When Miranda was invited to perform at the White House Evening of Poetry, Music, and the Spoken Word, few could have guessed that the rap he would perform about Alexander Hamilton would go viral, drawing more than five million views within ten hours.[1] The resulting musical has been a Broadway game changer and a box-office powerhouse, with a broad appeal that is unprecedented in recent theatrical history. Moreover, it has triumphed in the music and literary world. Its original cast album became the first musical to reach #1 on *Billboard*'s rap chart, and the book, *Hamilton: The Revolution*, which describes the creative journey from Miranda's first idea to its development into a blockbuster hit, has gone into its third printing, for a total of over 210,000 copies.[2]

For those who have not seen *Hamilton*, like my daughter, the soundscape becomes the medium with which to experience the story it tells about the nation's founding generation. Just as landscapes express geographic features of an area, soundscapes help to evoke a sense of place.[3] The hip-hop rhythms, beats, and sounds produced by Lin-Manuel Miranda, as the composer and lyricist, and Alex Lacamoire, as the orchestrator and music director, along with other sound designers and engineers, created an acoustic environment that immediately resonated with my family and me. This is why, probably as for many American families, their music became the soundscape for our cross-country summer road trip.

Hip hop is actually dystopian in its origins. Born at the end of the civil rights era, hip hop—an Afro-diasporic musical, oral, visual, and dance form—emerged from the politics of racial oppression in America. The hip-hop generation faced post-industrial decline, the advent of Reaganomics, urban blight, an exploding prison population, and the epidemics of crack, guns, and AIDS.[4] New York City's polycultural youth community of immigrants and migrants—including, but not limited to, Puerto Ricans, Dominicans, Jamaicans, and working-class whites—created a range of hip-hop art forms that voiced the experiences of growing up in New York City during harsh economic times and conditions of poverty in the late 1970s and early 1980s. Emceein' (rhymin'/rappin'), deejayin', taggin' (graffiti art), and b-boyin'/b-girlin' (later identified by the media as breakdancing), the four foundational elements of hip hop, revealed the experiences of urban life and publicly brought awareness of racial marginalization.[5] That is, while hip hop is a form of entertainment, it originated as a form of resistance and protest amplifying the struggle of urban realities and acknowledging the value of Blacks, Latinxs, and other disenfranchised communities.

Today hip hop extends far beyond rap and music, reaching into the realms of literature, visual art, photography, fashion, and theater. *Hamilton*'s use of a hip-hop soundscape to narrate the creation of the American nation through the life of Alexander Hamilton undoubtedly expands the boundaries of history and theater. However, although *Hamilton* has garnered much attention, it is important to note that the integration of hip hop in the theater world is not a new phenomenon. The term "hip-hop theater" was first coined by journalist Holly Bass in her *American Theatre* essay "Blowing Up the Set: What Happens When the Pulse of Hip-Hop Shakes Up the Traditional Stage?" (1999) to call attention to a new style of theater-making that explored issues faced by the hip-hop generation and that experimented with one or more the genre's cultural corner-stones since the 1990s.[6]

Hip-hop dancers, however, pushed the conventions of the theater long before the term "hip-hop theater" was coined. In 1991, the Rhythm Technicians, which included original members from the b-boy group Rock Steady Crew, created the hip-hop musical

So! What Happens Now?, which they presented at PS 122. Four years later, GhettOriginal Productions brought together Rock Steady Crew, Magnificent Force, and Rhythm Technicians to create *Jam on the Groove* (1995), which was presented Off-Broadway at the Minetta Lane Theatre. The Public Theater's *Bring in 'da Noise, Bring in 'da Funk* by poet Reg E. Gaines became the first hip-hop musical to make it to Broadway in in 1996. These performances drew on hip-hop elements to dramatize the experiences of urban youth and the realities of life for disenfranchised communities.

In 2000, Danny Hoch, Kamilah Forbes, and Clyde Valentin established the New York City Hip Hop Theater Festival (HHTF), now known as Hi-Arts, to showcase the potential of hip-hop theater. Since 2000, the festival has showcased both solo and ensemble performances that explore various hip-hop forms, and curated panels that focus on hip hop's history, evolution, and future. It seeks to promote, produce, and cultivate a kind of theater "by, about, and for the hip-hop generation, participants in hip-hop culture, or both."[7] Just as the festival began gaining in popularity, hip-hop mogul Russell Simmons (already a major promoter of the form through his recording label, Def Jam Records; his clothing empire, Phat Farm; and his television series, *Russell Simmons' Def Comedy Jam* on HBO), decided to try out theater, producing *Def Poetry Jam on Broadway* in 2002. The production harnessed the energy of slam poetry and showcased the skills of nine wordsmiths and thespians of many different races. Simulating a club setting inside the theater, a DJ surrounded by crates created a lively music vibe that mixed old-school funk and hip hop. Hip-hop language, music, fashion, and energy established itself on the Broadway stage.

Despite *Hamilton*'s success, hip hop is not necessarily an uncomplicated fit for Broadway: it is often perceived to promote violence, misogyny, and hypersexuality. By placing hip hop center stage, artists like Miranda amplify how this art form and its practitioners have shaped America's culture and history. This is precisely what Miranda achieved with his first musical *In the Heights*, which won the 2008 Tony Award for Best Musical, Best Original Score, Best

Choreography, and Best Orchestrations. Blending hip hop, rap, jazz, and pop with a salsa and merengue flair as well as incorporating hip-hop elements, such as breakdancing, graffiti writing, and rapping, *In the Heights* gained vast popularity for its representation of two days in the life of Washington Heights, a vibrant immigrant neighborhood at the tip of Manhattan.[8] Yet some theatergoers were ambivalent about attending a production that featured hip-hop, salsa, and merengue music. As Jeffrey Seller, the producer of *In the Heights* and then *Hamilton*, explained, "There was a certain degree of racism and a certain degree of fear of hip-hop that made people not wanna go see it."[9] He felt that "the label of hip-hop and Latino" limited the reach and success of *In The Heights*, since theatergoers were suspicious of "anything that hinted of rap or hip-hop."[10] So even as Miranda has been lauded for widening the appeal of hip-hop theater, the soundscape he created in *In the Heights* also raised anxiety among some traditional Broadway theatergoers.

Given his experience marketing *In the Heights*, Seller did not want *Hamilton* advertisements to categorize it as a hip-hop or rap musical, even though it was.[11] Seller even convinced Miranda to do away with the original title *Hamilton Mixtape*, which served to distance the musical from hip hop's early tradition of circulating audio cassettes with mixes of recorded music.[12] In explicitly not using the term hip-hop theater at all or making any references to hip-hop culture in the marketing plan, the publicity for *Hamilton* catered to the white theatregoers who purchase more than 77 percent of Broadway tickets.[13] In order for *Hamilton*, a musical driven by an Afro-diasporic soundscape, to fit into Broadway's Great White Way, Seller had to resort to a strategy that dates back to the "race records" marketed without images of the black artists who recorded them on the album jackets. He had to tame the representation of hip hop and race in the publicity and marketing materials just enough to make the conventional Broadway theatergoer comfortable.

Ironically, even as Seller and the *Hamilton* team launched a marketing plan that made both hip hop and race invisible, *Hamilton* was praised for moving the musical theater genre forward by

incorporating a hip-hop soundscape. Critics recognized that Miranda
had synthesized the cocky spirit of self-determination during the
American Revolutionary War era masterfully, using the hip-hop
rhythms that had formed the soundtrack of his early adult years.
But the steps producers took to ensure that their audiences would
feel comfortable consuming hip hop suggests some of the limits
of that audience's willingness to deal with friction, dissonance, and
other uncomfortable aspects of race relations the medium expressed,
rather than a more Pollyanna-ish and uncomplicated diversity.

Listening to *Hamilton* in the National Parks

But let's return to the national parks. During our epic, cross-country,
Hamilton-fueled trip, we met a park ranger at sunset for an evening
talk at Carlsbad Caverns. She presented information about bats prior
to our seeing the utterly amazing scenario of hundreds of thousands
of them exiting the cave for their nightly meal. In the guided tour
at the Grand Canyon, other park rangers pointed out the mysteri-
ous cliff dwellings of Mesa Verde, breathtaking scenery, and thriving
wildlife. Like any performance, the National Park Service mediates
nature by scripting, rehearsing, and staging its beauties so that visitors can consume and enjoy the environment with ease and pleasure. The information text panels at the national parks are also part
of the process of scripting these quintessential expressions of American democracy. Yet the narrative my family and I encountered at
the national parks gave little acknowledgment of the native people
who once inhabited these spaces, or the forced removal of native
populations from their sacred tribal lands so that white men could
hike, hunt, camp, and fish at their leisure. In fact, there were specific policies of Indian removal developed at Yosemite, Yellowstone,
and Glacier National Parks from the 1970s to the 1930s in order to
preserve nature.[14] In other words, the racial and cultural superiority
that accompanied America's westward expansion was absent in the
narrative of the national parks.

    At the center of the conservationist movement that helped to
create the parks in the 1900s was Madison Grant, the author of

Despite the fact that six tribes of indigenous Americans—Hualapal, Hopi, Zuni, Paiute, Navajo, and Havasupi people—live in the Grand Canyon, National Parks Service posters have portrayed these lands as empty and ready to be filled with tourists. *(WPA Posters Collection, Library of Congress)*

The Passing of the Great Race; or, The Racial Basis of European History (1916), in which he argued a white supremacist theory of the "Nordic" people.[15] His book helped to fuel new laws in the 1920s that restricted immigration from eastern and southern Europe and Africa, and banned migrants from the Middle East and Asia. Gifford Pinchot, head of the Forest Service under President Theodore Roosevelt, also linked the preservation of America's natural wonders to the preservation of white supremacy. According to Grant and other conservationists of the time, eugenics (or "racial hygiene") needed to be part of a public program to create a better world for future generations of white citizens. As Grant stated, "If our nation cares to make any provision for its grandchildren and its grandchildren's grandchildren, this provision must include conservation in all its branches—but above all, the conservation of the racial stock itself."[16]

Similar to the birth of America narrated in *Hamilton*, the establishment of the national parks was rooted in a history of racist violence and exclusion. Yet this history of racism is largely invisible at the national parks, where knowledgeable rangers instead frame nature as a spectacular performance of natural beauty. The actual history behind these beautiful wide-open spaces is reflected in the fact that even today, 78 percent of the visitors to the parks are white.[17] Blacks and Latinx people are vastly underrepresented as visitors. In fact, my family had decided to visit the parks because of a new White House initiative to increase their use by historically underrepresented groups. The program incentivized fourth graders and their families to experience the many federal public lands and waters of our country for free in celebration of the National Park Service's 100th anniversary.

Listening to *Hamilton* while visiting the parks made clear to me how each participates in a similar project of nation making. The national parks and the *Hamilton* script rehearse, and stage, a utopian expression of American democracy—that the future also belongs to people of color just as profoundly as anyone else—through hip hop, racially conscious casting, or initiatives that diversify the demographics of the visitors. Just as *Hamilton* creates a mirage of equity and inclusivity with its reverse casting and hip-hop soundtrack, the national parks give the illusion of timeless serenity and tranquility. However, these nation-making productions evade the racist ideologies that that were essential to the founding of America and to the creation of the parks that have come to symbolize the nation.

Reckoning with America's Racist Past

The confluence between the popular music we hear on the airwaves or in clubs and the sounds that we hear on the American musical stage has brought *Hamilton* a great deal of attention, and opened the ears of theater aficionados to the rich intricacies and complexities of hip hop. In staging an alternative, colorful America and making audible the African-diasporic soundscape that might have accompanied founders of color, Miranda gives us permission to imagine the possibilities of multicultural and racial diversity that might have existed in a nation that truly embraced freedom at its birth.

But that nation doesn't exist. Furthermore, there is a stark difference between the racial performances offered on the stage and the actual cultural experiences of artists that have been historically underrepresented in a mass culture industry dominated by whites. Black music, as the journalist, author, and former producer at New York City's WBAI radio Norman Kelley argues, operates within a "structure of stealing" that dates back to the antebellum period. This structure serves as the foundation for contemporary economic relationships between black musicians and the music industry. "The history of black music," as Kelley explains, "has been a continuous replay of the uncontested and lucrative expropriation of [B]lack cultural forms by whites."[18] Some might argue that *Hamilton* does not represent this form of appropriation since a person of color with great creative control created it, and because the original cast worked out a very lucrative profit-sharing agreement. But there is a different kind of theft happening in *Hamilton* that goes beyond monetary value: that of the voices of enslaved people. *In the Heights* similarly reflected a racially and culturally diverse America, but it did so to tell the actual stories of Latinx and other disenfranchised peoples. *Hamilton*'s cast of color instead produces the white found-ing fathers through the expressive language of hip hop. Though the show mentions slavery, it does not tell the story of dispossessed or marginalized peoples. Thus, when racial bodies take on a history that disavows race, the voices of enslaved people remain audibly silent.

The diversity *Hamilton* embodies comes at the expense of erasing enslaved people, as well as erasing the ways in which the founding fathers were directly implicated in the profit-making enterprise of slavery. The America *Hamilton* engenders celebrates bootstrap suc-cess and national patriotism, while rendering racism invisible and thus absolving our founding fathers, and other whites, from the hor-rific violence they inflicted on black people.[19] These historical era-sures in *Hamilton* put into question how we can practice diversity without actually being inclusive. Would this production be as cele-brated if the cast of color had embodied and given voice to enslaved people? It remains to be seen whether the success of *Hamilton* "will create more opportunities for hip-hop generation stories" or whether it will, instead, serve as a model for other "classic histories" to co-opt hip hop's cultural elements without, as Danny Hoch of the Hip Hop Theater Festival suggests, providing "any cultural reparations."[20]

Although we can praise *Hamilton* as a game changer for amplify-ing opportunities for actors of color and pushing back at Broadway's exclusions, we cannot be seduced by the racial progressiveness of the model of diversity it offers. *Hamilton* does not, after all, move us toward cultural reparation because it does not acknowledge the dam-age that was done in the first place. It does not hold the founding fathers responsible for wronging blacks and it does not honor those who have been wronged by slavery. An inclusive national origin story would acknowledge the practice of slavery in America, hold the founding fathers accountable, and name the long-term damage, both physical and psychological, that slavery has done to blacks. It would acknowledge that the legacy of slavery lived on through Jim Crow, segregation, and racist housing policies. It would give body and voice to enslaved people. It would commit to a future in which the master–slave relationship or racism is not repeated in modern form.

The context of the Obama era made it possible to imagine bodies of color as founding fathers, but now in the era of Trump, it seems more challenging than ever to imagine the world that *Hamilton* conjures. President Donald Trump's executive actions to limit travel from seven Muslim countries, freeze the U.S. refugee program, and vilify immigrants who live and work in the United States, goes against the rights and liberties of our diverse community and the rule of law upon which freedom and equality rest. The hateful and discriminatory language and threats, directed against Muslims, Jews, women, Latinx people, African Americans, people with disabilities, LGBTQ people, and others is nothing like the world of *Hamilton*. The number of police killings and racial profiling incidents against people of color continue to skyrocket. Despite the distance of time, the continuous history of racial injustice is all too relevant. Today's protests and demonstrations poignantly resonate with the strength and determination of the ongoing freedom struggle. There is a fierce urgency for black lives to matter now. How does *Hamilton* move that project forward?

Hamilton cannot tell us whether we will ever see America through the lens of my daughter's story, or when Americans will be ready to listen to an origin story from the perspective of enslaved, dispossessed, discriminated, and alienated bodies. Perhaps more than exemplifying diversity, *Hamilton* teaches us that we must go beyond what we visually and sonically denote as diversity if we ever hope to achieve racial equity and inclusivity. My daughter cannot easily see the historical connections between the past and present because the production, like the national parks, make the actual history of slavery and racism in America invisible. And this erasure can be damaging. We cannot build a better future without frankly acknowledging that the bodies of color on the Broadway stage today were raped, whipped, lynched, and exploited for their labor. My daughter's desire to assume the role of Angelica Schuyler is a reminder that the legacy of slavery still haunts our contemporary worldview. She unconsciously disavows the black body that brings the white body back to life. It is in hearing the haunting racist ideologies and the audible silence of black people that I begin to understand the irreconcilable ambivalence and contradiction of my own spectatorship and fandom.

So in the serenity and tranquility of the national park, as we are collapsing our tent, I say, "No, 'mija, you can't be Angelica Schuyler. The person you hear and who performs the character of Angelica Schuyler is the talented African American woman Renée Elise Goldsberry and what you love about her is the Destiny's Childesque R&B soul that she brings to that character. Aspire to be Dolores Huerta, Angela Davis, and Malala Yousafza—liberators not oppressors. Because, 'mija, you are American. I am American. We are Americans. And that's not a fantasy. That is a history that we need to reckon with."

So, I invite you to yes, imagine, dream the American Dream and then take that dream one step further and push it into reality because we've come some place but we still have not gone where we need to go. *Hamilton* is a reminder that the sonic and visual harmony of diversity is not the destination, but it is the beginning of a journey toward seeing and listening to the racial dissonance. We must dare to reckon with America's racist past in order to manifest an equitable and inclusive present and future.

NOTES

I first presented this essay as part of the panel "*Hamilton*: The Development, Casting, and Performance of a New Musical" with Trevor Boffone, Brian Herrera, Donatella Galella, and Marci McMahon at the Association of Theatre in Higher Education, Chicago, Illinois, August 2016. The paper was then further developed as part of the working session "Future in the Present: The Transtemporalities of Minoritarian Performance" convened by Soyica Colbert-Diggs, Douglas Jones, and Shane Vogel at the American Society for Theatre Research, Minneapolis, Minnesota, November 2016. I would like to thank all the panelists. The insightful conversation and feedback in and outside of the conference has greatly shaped this paper. In the early stage of writing this paper I was invited to do a TEDxRVA Women (October 2016) talk, which allowed me to work through the troubling ambivalence I experience as a Latinx mother. The TEDx team was instrumental in my thinking process, especially Risa Gomes, Tiffany Green, Leah Fremouw, Tawnya Pettiford-Wates, and Todd Waldo. Finally, a big shout-out to my daughter, sons, and husband for listening in detail.

1. Jenny Stars, "*Hamilton* Star Lin-Manuel Miranda returns to the White House and Freestyles with an Assist from Obama," *Washington Post*, March 15, 2016, https://www.washingtonpost.com/news/morning-mix/wp/2016/03/15/hamilton-star-lin-manuel-miranda-returns-to-the-white-house-and-freestyles-with-an-assist-from-obama/, accessed October 6, 2016.

2. Jesse Lawrence, "'Hamilton Is Broadway's Most Expensive Show—Ever," *Daily Beast*, May 2, 2016, http://www.thedailybeast.com/articles/2016/05/03/hamilton-is-broadway-s-most-expensive-show-ever.html, accessed October 13, 2016.

3. R. Murray Schafer, *The Soundscape: Our Sonic Environment and the Tuning of the World* (Rochester, VT: Destiny Books, 1993).

4. Tricia Rose, *Black Noise: Rap Music and Black Culture in Contemporary America* (Hanover, NH: University Press of New England, 1994), 21.

5. Jeff Chang, *Total Chaos: The Art and Aesthetics of Hip-Hop* (New York: Basic Books, 2006).

6. Holly Bass, "Blowing Up the Set: What Happens When the Pulse of Hip-Hop Shakes Up the Traditional Stage?" *American Theater* (November 1999), http://www.tcg.org/am_theatre/at_articles/AT_Volume_16/Nov99/at_web1199_blowin_up.htm.

7. Danny Hoch, "Towards a Hip Hop Aesthetic: A Manifesto for the Hip Hop Arts Movement," in *Total Chaos: The Art and Aesthetic of Hip Hop*, edited by Jeff Chang (New York: BasicCivitas, 2006), 356.

8. Ernio Hernandez, "New York–Set, Hip-Hop-Salsa-Merengue Musical *In the Heights* Starts at O'Neil Center," *Playbill*, July 23, 2005, http://www.playbill.com/article/new-york-set-hip-hop-salsa-merengue-musical-in-the-heights-starts-at-oneill-center-july-23-com-127114, accessed February 22, 2017.

9. Kara Swisher, "*Hamilton* Producer Jeffrey Seller: Tech Can't Beat Live Theater," *Recode Decode*, July 28, 2016, http://www.recode.net/2016/7/28/12318458/jeffrey-seller-hamilton-musical-broadway-podcast-transcript, accessed February 21, 2017.

10. Quoted in Thomas Geier, "'Hamilton' Makes a $500K Profit Each Week, and 9 More Jaw-Dropping Facts About Broadway Hit," *The Wrap*, April 5, 2016, http://www.thewrap.com/hamilton-broadway-profit-500k-lin-manuel-miranda/, accessed August 10, 2016.

11. Swisher, "*Hamilton* Producer Jeffrey Seller."

12. Michael Sokolove, "The C.E.O. of 'Hamilton' Inc.," *New York Times Magazine*, April 5, 2016, http://www.nytimes.com/2016/04/10/magazine/the-ceo-of-hamilton-inc.html, accessed August 1, 2016.

13. Broadway League, *The Demographics of the Broadway Audience 2015–2016*, November 2016, https://www.broadwayleague.com/research/research-reports/, accessed February 22, 2017.

14. For an in-depth discussion on the removal of Native Americans from the national parks see Philip Burnham, *Indian Country, God's Country: Native Americans and the National Parks* (Washington, DC: Island Press, 2000); Robert H. Keller and Michael F. Turek, *American Indians and National Parks* (Tucson: University of Arizona Press, 1998); and Mark David Spence, *Dispossessing the Wilderness: Indian Removal and the Making of the National Parks* (New York: Oxford University Press, 1999).

15. Jedediah Purdy, "Environmentalism's Racist History," *The New Yorker*, "News Desk," August 3, 2015, http://www.newyorker.com/news/news-desk/environmentalisms-racist-history, accessed February 20, 2016.

16. Quoted in Charles Wohlforth, "Conservation and Eugenics: The Environmental Movement's Dirty Secret," *Orion Magazine*, June 18, 2010, https://orionmagazine.org/article/conservation-and-eugenics/, accessed February 20, 2017.

17. Tik Root, "Changing the Face of National Parks," *National Geographic*, February 1, 2017, http://news.nationalgeographic.com/2017/02/diversity-in-national-parks/, accessed April 9, 2017.

18. Norman Kelley, ed., *Rhythm and Business: The Political Economy of Black Music* (New York: Akashic Books, 2005), 12.

19. Donatella Galella, "Racializing the American Revolution Review of the Broadway Musical *Hamilton*," *Advocate*, February 26, 2015, http://gcadvocate.com/2015/11/16/racializing-the-american-revolution-review-of-the-broadway-musical-hamilton/, accessed February 20, 2017.

20. Danny Hoch, "Sure, 'Hamilton' Is a Game-Changer, But Whose Game?" *American Theatre*, April 23, 2015, http://www.americantheatre.org/2015/04/23/sure-hamilton-is-a-game-changer-but-whose-game/, accessed February 20, 2017.

CHAPTER 13

Who Tells Your Story?

Hamilton *as a People's History*

JOSEPH M. ADELMAN

As with many people, my relationship with *Hamilton* began with the YouTube clip of Lin-Manuel Miranda rapping in the East Room of the White House in 2009. Since then, I have played the clip in my classroom whenever I teach a unit on the politics of the 1790s. Just as the assembled crowd in the White House did, students giggle as they watch Miranda introduce what was then a brand-new work about "the life of someone I think embodies hip hop—Treasury Secretary Alexander Hamilton."[1] Before 2015, my students would then look at me with disbelief when I would mention at the end of the clip that Miranda was actually working on a full musical about the founding father. Teaching at a regional public university in Massachusetts, the only thing I found harder to convince my students of—most of whom grew up within an hour's drive of campus—was that New York (my home town) was "the greatest city in the world."

Seven years and eleven Tony Awards later, Miranda is among the most famous popularizers of the American past in U.S. history. A Broadway show with an inherently limited live audience has become the cultural talk of the nation. Miranda, already well-known in Broadway circles for his Tony-winning first musical *In the Heights*, has gained recognition well beyond the Great White Way, making *Time* magazine's list of the 100 most influential people in 2016, being featured on *60 Minutes*, and even becoming the first Broadway composer/performer to host *Saturday Night Live*. He and many other members of the company have launched successful projects based on their *Hamilton*-earned fame. And perhaps most remarkable of all, the musical has made Alexander Hamilton popular again.

Hamilton operates at the intersection of a remarkably diverse set of fan subcultures: fans of hip hop, theater, and early American history. It offers a version of history that has appealed to Americans of all backgrounds and ages. The past comes alive in new and fresh ways in the bodies and sounds of the present. The show works for younger people, including many of my students, for whom history resonates better with rhymes and a sick beat. It also works for a somewhat older generation who understand the cultural references, which include not only classic 1980s rap and contemporary hip hop, but also the Beatles, Rodgers and Hammerstein, and Gilbert and Sullivan. People leave wanting to know more about Alexander Hamilton, his wife Eliza, sister-in-law Angelica, the battles between Jefferson and Hamilton in the 1790s, the role of slavery in the Early Republic, and (of course) Aaron Burr.

This should be a moment of triumph for historians. We can't buy publicity like this—and some of us have tried. But many of the professional historians who have jumped into the public square to make a case about the show have found it lacking as a work of history. Critics, including several contributors to this volume, have challenged not only some of the interpretations that Miranda offers, but also the musical's historical errors and omissions. Popular discussions about *Hamilton* have also picked up on this line of reasoning. In December 2015, the website *The Toast* published a satirical "Report on Alexander Hamilton Written by a Kid Who Has Only Listened to the Musical," in which the imagined student claimed that Hamilton "was America's first Secretary of the Treasury, founded the *New York Post*, and together with his friend and rival Aaron Burr invented rap in 1776."[2] And having seen the show, who could fault the student for thinking that? Certainly there are historical inaccuracies, and a few interpretive decisions that may be misguided. But do these criticisms—and many are valid—perhaps miss the broader significance?

Hamilton is art, a musical theater production, and we need to approach the show with sensitivity to the opportunities and limitations presented by that genre. When we view the show from that perspective, we can see that *Hamilton* is part of a tradition as old as the United States of "people's histories," or retellings of the past that come from among the American people rather than from professional historians. And it turns out that *Hamilton* is a model example of a people's history, one that despite its differences from professional scholarship reflects a deep understanding and respect for the historical process. The production offers many similarities to historical scholarship in its attentiveness to primary sources from the era and its sophisticated understanding of how historical narratives are constructed. Miranda clearly immersed himself in the work of scholars in order to present a comprehensive portrait, and unlike many of his cultural forebears, he has been extraordinarily transparent about the process he undertook to understand the Revolution and Early Republic, and to embed that process into the show's book.

Unlike professional historians, Miranda and his cocreators seek to understand the past not on its own terms but on those of the contemporary moment in the 2010s. Yet *Hamilton* nevertheless offers audiences a perspective on history itself, in particular because at key moments it emphasizes that we cannot fully know the past or even create a single narrative about it. It therefore presents a fascinating case study for understanding the complexity and contingency of the past, for seeing the essence of the historical narrative in new ways, and for learning about how to connect past and present through both form and content. It also makes *Hamilton* particularly useful for discussions about the distinctions between professional and popular interpretations about the American past.

The Truths Americans Desire

It's important to stress that *Hamilton* makes absolutely no claim to being a work of scholarly history. For one thing, it is simply not possible for any depiction of the past in the form of a theater production, TV show, or film to convey the same level of narrative complexity that historians have developed in writing about the Early American Republic. Instead, the show is probably more accurately described as historical fiction. Annette Gordon-Reed, among the best-known Jefferson scholars and also an ardent fan of *Hamilton*, offered precisely that assessment in a post at *Vox* in December 2015. As she noted, "creators operating in that genre have the license to make things up in order to fulfill their artistic vision. It can only go 'wrong' when the license taken with facts strains credulity, and prevents the narrative from ringing true."[3] *Hamilton* certainly fits that basic description of historical fiction. The founders, of course, were all white, rather than black and brown as the cast is, and probably lacked the metrical and rhythmic speaking talents that Miranda ascribes to them.[4] *Hamilton* does not strictly follow the historical chronology of the period it covers, nor is Miranda always consistent with even consensus arguments by historians about the period. And yet, the historical narrative the musical offers still rings true to many Americans. Why?

Some historians may quibble, but *Hamilton* and Lin-Manuel Miranda are part of a tradition of artistic and fictional depictions of the American past that stretches back to the founding era. Almost as soon as the Revolutionary War ended in 1783, Americans began to discuss, hypothesize, and conjecture about what the new nation would be, in part by arguing over how it was born. The first histories of the Revolution appeared rapidly after the end of the war, including one by South Carolinian David Ramsay, whose two-volume *History of the American Revolution* was published in 1789. In this era, most saw history as a form of literature, so Americans saw nonfiction accounts of the Revolution in a continuum with fictional accounts of the Revolution. The Revolution provided a dramatic backdrop for popular novels such as *Charlotte Temple* (1791), the plot of which hinged on an English soldier who abandoned his lover to join the British Army in New York City. For Miranda and *Hamilton*, however, the clearest ancestor in early U.S. historical literature is Mason Locke Weems. An itinerant book peddler and minister better known as Parson Weems, he published the most popular early biography of George Washington in 1800, just months after the first president's death. Like Miranda, Weems had a larger contemporary purpose for memorializing his subject, other than simply to remember the man. Influenced by evangelical Christianity, Weems sought to cast Washington as a larger-than-life saint who could serve as a moral model for nineteenth-century Americans. It worked: the biography was enormously popular, going through several dozen editions in the early decades of the nineteenth century. In so doing, Weems cemented an image of Washington that shapes popular interpretations of him to this day.

The parable that has survived most persistently from Weems's popular history is the story of young George felling his father's cherry tree. In the tale—which Weems only added to the narrative beginning with the fifth edition of the biography—Augustin Washington discovers that his favorite cherry tree has been chopped down. Irate, he demands to know who committed the crime, at which point the six-year-old George admits to the offense and declaims that he "cannot tell a lie," disarming his father. It was the story of a boy whose moral code was so strong that he could not countenance a lie even in the interest of self-preservation. It was also a complete fabrication. But the tale continues to resonate because it portrays an image of Washington as a morally centered American citizen.[5] The story about Washington persists, not because it is true, but because it tells a truth that Americans desire. Schoolchildren still hear about the cherry tree today, and rarely do they get the caveat that the story is allegorical rather than factual. Its staying power relies on its legibility to readers across generations who recognize a universally resonant encounter between a parent and child.

The public is clearly interested in watching fictional depictions of the founding era, whether historians approve of them or not. *1776* debuted on Broadway in 1969 to positive reviews, eventually winning five Tony Awards, including Best Musical, before being adapted into a 1972 film. One of my favorite little-known films, *Sweet Liberty* (1986) depicts a historian, played by Alan Alda, beside himself as his book on the Revolutionary War in the South is turned into a farce, starring Michael Caine as an actor playing Banastre Tarleton, a British cavalry commander accused of atrocities. I groan at the thought of invoking it, but Mel Gibson did make *The Patriot* (2000); and history went for a fantasy adventure in the *National Treasure* films (2004 and 2007), the first of which is so bad it's good. And in just the past decade, HBO created a six-part miniseries about the life of John Adams based on David McCullough's incredibly popular biography; AMC has produced *Turn*, loosely based on the Culper Spy Ring (which provided intelligence on the British to George Washington); and the History Channel has produced a three-part miniseries called *Sons of Liberty*.[6]

Many historians write clearly and openly for a general audience, and even more aspire to do so. Perhaps the best example of this phenomenon is Howard Zinn, the self-proclaimed radical, whose *A People's History of the United States* attempted to upend deeply held assumptions about the American past. Though now discredited among many in the historical profession for his research practices, Zinn nonetheless made history accessible to millions of Americans and encouraged thousands to pursue further study. Other touchstones of American culture have also portrayed American history for a broad audience. Walt Disney World in Florida, for instance, welcomes visitors to the park at the nostalgia-saturated "Main Street USA" and offers animatronic depictions of American presidents and innovators (the latter a nod to the nation-building role of great American corporations). In a famous essay on the park, historian Mike Wallace derided Disney's approach as "Mickey Mouse history," but also admitted that Disney had probably taught more history than any scholar.[7] Zinn and Disney represent two poles of historical interpretation that show the breadth of this genre. For Zinn, America could do nearly no right; but for Disney and its corporate partners, nearly no wrong. In each case, critics have pointed to a broader ideological agenda that may have clouded the interpretations each offers.

Historians should absolutely critique *Hamilton* and other works of art for the ways in which artists make choices about the past that are not consistent with facts. Art is not immune from criticism emanating from the fields into which it ventures, as some defenders of *Hamilton* have suggested.[8] Given how much the show relies on history, it was no surprise that in April 2016 the *New York Times* asked a number of historians to weigh in on the question, "Does *Hamilton* really get Hamilton right?"[9] Admittedly, whether that question even matters depends in large measure on one's perspective on the musical. For professional historians, both the details and the broad interpretation have an impact in terms of how the public interacts with, and thinks about, the history of the American Revolution. But it is very easy to collapse into the kind of criticism that others see as professional gatekeeping. To give a hypothetical example, one could spend a great deal of time assessing "The Farmer Refuted," an early number, in light of scholarship on revolutionary New York City, in particular the fraught and contested relationship between Patriots and Loyalists.[10] But to what end?

When historians critique *Hamilton* for its shortcomings, it can sound like sour grapes. To the average person, historical fact-checking can seem like nitpicking, especially when the target is incredibly popular. Appearing to miss the forest for the trees also leads to the risk of being read as a scold. Although it is reasonable and necessary for historians to assess and correct errors in public representations of history, a more useful question than how a given artistic work measures up to scholarly history is whether that artistic work is, to the extent that it can be, actively engaged with scholarship. The artist has a different set of obligations from the professional historian. Where a professional historian should as a matter of practice sacrifice the story in the name of factual accuracy, the artist has the reverse obligation to tell the most compelling possible story, even if it means sacrificing or rearranging a few facts.

As a writer of people's history, Miranda had to find ways to make the story personal for his audience. As he noted in an interview taped for a meeting of Early Republic historians in the summer of 2016, "My job is to chase the thing I'm passionate about and make it sing. . . . There's no blood in it if it's not a personal thing."[11] The underlying story, in other words, matters to him more than the literal, line-by-line chronology, or whether the cast of characters is complete. Miranda's line at the White House that Hamilton "embodies hip hop" was far more than a joke to introduce a song—it's a clear view of how Miranda interacts with the past. It's also why the show departs from the historical narrative at several points. Miranda was very conscious of taking artistic license with some of the history, but has argued that it was necessary to tell the story. For example, in the show the men who confront Hamilton about his affair with Maria Reynolds are Jefferson, Madison, and Burr. In reality, the three accusers were congressmen: James Monroe (the future president), Frederick Muhlenberg, and Abraham Venable. To a historian, this is a factual error, and a not insignificant one. For us, it matters a great deal to confirm who was *really* "in the room where it happened."

To an artist such as Miranda, the history is important, but it is secondary to the storytelling problem: three more characters that need to be introduced at a key moment late in the plot. Miranda could go with the historical facts and introduce these new characters. Or he could save himself a few minutes of exposition while trying to preserve what he saw as the essence of the story, which is the confrontation between Hamilton and his political enemies about the allegations of corruption. For a historian in a written piece, there is no question. We would all go with the first option with a quick digression or footnote. In our least restrained moments, we would rarely consider introducing historical figures into a space they didn't inhabit. But for Miranda and other artists, the calculation is different. As Jeremy McCarter explains in *Hamilton: The Revolution*, "Acts of dramatic license make it easier for the audience to grasp the bewildering truth about America's first sex scandal: Hamilton made a conscious decision to write something that blew up his life."[12] In a show that already pushes three hours, one can't simply toss in a few extra players. For Miranda, therefore, it's not that Monroe, Muhlenberg, and Venable don't matter, but that retaining the drama of the confrontation and moving the story forward matters more.

But these dramatic licenses should not blind historians to the important ways in which *Hamilton* reflects a quite sophisticated understanding of, and respect for historical methods and historical thinking. In fact, Miranda is remarkable for the ways in which he approaches the past. *Hamilton* is based on extensive historical research and builds its case using historical evidence. It offers both a metanarrative about the uncertainty of fully knowing the past and an astute perspective on how historical narratives differ depending on a teller's perspective. And it creatively uses music and theatrical forms to try to help audiences understand the social world of the past and the motivations of historical actors. Rather than focusing on factual errors, historians might better consider the many elements of *Hamilton* that they should admire.

In fact, Miranda's research for *Hamilton* far exceeded that of most artistic works of historical fiction. He began that process on a now-legendary vacation to the Caribbean in 2008, where he read Ron Chernow's biography of Alexander Hamilton. That he started with a popular biography written by an author with journalistic training rather than a work by a trained historian probably set the stage for other errors, as William Hogeland points out in this volume, but Chernow's book also inspired Miranda to immerse himself in Hamilton's world. The PBS *Great Performances* documentary, *Hamilton's America*, shows Miranda writing at The Grange, Hamilton's home in northern Manhattan, now a National Historic Site operated by the National Park Service. Miranda read through much of Hamilton's correspondence, visited the New-York Historical Society, consulted with Joanne Freeman, one of the authors in this volume, and otherwise did the kind of work that historians with professional training do. It shows in the musical.

Performing Primary Sources

There are some places where Miranda's fealty to the historical record is easy to see: a key section of "One Last Time" involves Hamilton and Washington reading verbatim the latter's famous Farewell Address as president in 1796. But anyone can do that, as the document is published and widely accessible. Other primary research is more difficult for a general audience to discern. As Miranda himself notes in *Hamilton: The Revolution*, much of the text for other numbers, including *The Reynolds Pamphlet*, comes directly from the writing of Hamilton and other characters in the show. The rap battles about economic policy and potential neutrality in the war between Britain and France derive from Hamilton's First Report on Public Credit and other accounts of that political struggle in correspondence and newspapers.

Miranda's research pays off most fruitfully when the show reaches its climax at the event most Americans connect to Hamilton: his duel with Aaron Burr. Here the challenge for Miranda is to explain a familiar tale of emotionally charged conflict with an outcome that seems inexplicable, even though it is the third duel depicted in the show. To many audience members, it seems unfathomable that two leading politicians, men of standing in their communities, would conceive of settling a dispute with gunfire. Here, Miranda draws on the scholarship of Joanne Freeman about the culture of honor that enveloped the era's politics and draws out the psychological and emotional process that led to the dueling ground.[13]

But he also returned to primary sources that described the simmering conflict between the two men. Our knowledge of the duel—which took place in Weehawken, New Jersey, just across the Hudson River from New York City on July 11, 1804—comes from several places. We have the series of letters that Burr and Hamilton wrote to one another in the early summer of 1804, an argument that escalated from a perceived slight against Burr uttered by Hamilton at a dinner in Albany, to the fatal encounter. Some of the dispute spilled onto the pages of New York and Albany newspapers. Not surprisingly, in the aftermath of Hamilton's death, conflicting accounts of the event emerged from the men's respective seconds.[14]

In *Hamilton*, Miranda uses the tools of the theater to help audiences better understand the mindset and culture of a world where dueling was a way of settling disputes. Early in the show, Burr begins to note that Hamilton mysteriously succeeds at moments when he

An 1870s engraved illustration of the famous 1804 duel between
Alexander Hamilton and Aaron Burr in Weehawken, New Jersey.
(Artokoloro Quint Lox Limited/Alamy Stock Photo)

appears to be falling short. In Act II, after losing his shot at the
presidency in 1800 (Burr then lost the New York governorship in
1804, which is not depicted), he decides that Hamilton must be the
source of his stalled career. The show picks up the narrative just
after the alleged dinner party insult as the two men correspond for
weeks on end, escalating the quarrel. Miranda dramatizes this exchange in the climactic number of the second act, "Your Obedient
Servant." In the number, set as a rapped war of words to a waltz
rhythm, Burr and Hamilton pour out decades of rivalry at each
other, setting the stage (literally, at the theater) for the duel. To punc-
tuate each verse, Miranda shifts the musical tone from a dark,
minor key into a bright motif highlighted by a harpsichord as each
signs off, "your obedient servant," and signs his name—with ironic,
and snarky, good cheer. The orchestration captures the absurdity
at the core of eighteenth-century correspondence, masculinity, and

dueling. Held captive by the customs of the letter-writing genre, the two men rip each other to shreds for pages on end . . . but they must, even as one threatens the other with death, observe the polite conventions of the era.

With the duel set and the men facing each other, "The World Was Wide Enough" captures the ambiguity of the conflicting accounts of the duel, and the snap judgments that men had to make when a conflict had come to a head. Miranda's attention to detail here is such that he notes in *Hamilton: The Revolution* that the title of the song comes from a quotation from the novel *Tristram Shandy*, a novel Burr read later in his life, which he used to describe his relationship with Hamilton.[15] Burr, who has served as the narrator throughout, then reprises "The Ten Duel Commandments" from Act I with details of the encounter from his perspective. Early in the number, however, he notes pointedly, "I wish I could tell you what was happ'ning in his brain." There is no omniscient narrator, only men, facing one another on stage. At the moment of the shot the music stops, and Hamilton offers what the audience knows will be his final soliloquy. Miranda has him recount episodes from his life, but mostly he frames the speech around questions:

> Burr, my first friend, my enemy,
> May be the last face I ever see?
> If I throw away my shot, is this how you remember me?
> What if this bullet is my legacy?

By this point the bullet is slowly but inexorably making its way across the stage in the fingers of an ensemble member. Hamilton and the audience see that he is about to die. Yet Miranda refuses to collapse the historical record into a neat account that answers all questions.

The sequence, beginning with the insult and ending with Hamilton's death, reveals deep research, an understanding of the complexities of evidence, a respect for the historical narrative, and a modern eye that brings fresh vision to the story in a way that most historians would shy away from. Many of the lines, though adjusted metrically, come directly from the correspondence between Hamilton and Burr in the spring and summer of 1804, and the song traces the back-and-forth that ensued as each man refuses to yield. As an artist, Miranda then layers on top the vision that jumped from the pages when he first read the letters in an archive: a dance. Historians try to paint vivid pictures with language, but recasting the correspondence between the two men as a dance captures an essence about the exchanges that is otherwise difficult to describe, except, as it turns out, in a rapped waltz.

Throughout the musical, Miranda draws on both historical research and the power afforded by the visual, verbal, and musical forms of the theater to construct and communicate sophisticated interpretations of Alexander Hamilton's character, his role in American political culture, and the social world in which he lived. First, Miranda suggests that we should look at Hamilton's life through the power of writing, making that link by using a vivid form of contemporary writing, hip hop. Consider again what Miranda said at the White House in 2009: Hamilton's life "embodies hip hop" and "the word's ability to make a difference."[16] For Miranda, that's not simply an idle comment—the entire musical makes the case that Hamilton's rise and eventual fall are intimately linked to his writing, both explicitly and implicitly. In no fewer than eleven numbers spanning the entire length of the show, we witness Hamilton either writing or talking about writing. The very last thing he does before heading to Weehawken for his encounter with Burr is to write a letter to his wife, the "best of wives and best of women," a line taken directly from Hamilton's actual final letter to Eliza.[17] For Miranda, this argument largely focuses inward as a way to understand Hamilton and his character, to explain how he saw the world and made his way through it.

Along with establishing how the written word shaped Hamilton's mind, Miranda also examines his political role in founding the

United States. Here Miranda contends that Hamilton's influence was outsized in his own time and underappreciated in our collective contemporary understanding of American history. The topic comes up regularly in the show. In the opening number, for example, the company sings that they are "waiting in the wings for" him and that "the world will never be the same;" one verse later, Aaron Burr sings that "his enemies destroyed his rep / America forgot him." In the show's version of his life, Hamilton plays a central role at the Battle of Yorktown, and his *Federalist* essays, by Miranda's telling, prove crucial to securing the Constitution's ratification. By Act II, Hamilton claims that he "wrote financial systems into existence," and in the closing number James Madison rues that Hamilton "doesn't get enough credit for all the credit he gave us." For Miranda, these two lines of argument—about Hamilton's writing and his reputation—are closely connected. They are also, as Miranda has occasionally noted in interviews, as much autobiographical as they are biographical. Like the depiction of Hamilton, Miranda rose to fame as the son of migrant parents largely on the strength of his writing, albeit of a different sort than Hamilton's.

The general public and historians will inevitably part ways in how to assess these arguments as American history. History is often most compelling as a story, and in particular when it revolves around a character who embodies many aspirational qualities. This phenomenon has driven much of what historians have derided as "Founders Chic" in the past fifteen years, as they have watched largely celebratory biographies of founding fathers achieve widespread popular and commercial success.[18] Despite this sustained popular interest, most professional historians of the Revolutionary era have shied away from grand political narratives and more generally away from a focus on great men as the driving force of history. They are loath to see anyone as "the indispensable man" of the Revolution. Historians of the Revolution and Early Republic also have serious questions about how to assess Hamilton's role in the creation of the United States. Miranda portrays Hamilton's contributions as vital, central, and positive—and historians now struggle with the idea that all three of those propositions can be embodied in a single individual.

Yet focusing too much on the play as a typical "great man" representation of history does not do justice to the sophisticated ways in which Miranda embeds his portrayal of Hamilton in an argument about the contingency of the past, or the ways in which moments in the past could have multiple possible outcomes. Miranda emphasizes the impossibility of knowing the complete story at several points in the show. That tension comes through particularly strongly in the pairing of "Helpless" and "Satisfied" at the midpoint of Act I. These are the numbers that jointly introduce Hamilton to Angelica and Eliza Schuyler, the sisters who entrance him romantically in the show (as they did in real life). As a student of history, Miranda carefully weaves the two numbers to show the uncertainty each of the three experienced at that moment, and to introduce the importance of understanding each narrator's distinct perspective. In "Helpless," we hear from Eliza Schuyler, who finds herself smitten at first glance with the young and brash Continental Army officer. Abetted by an introduction from her sister Angelica, the two begin a four-minute courtship in which Eliza repeatedly proclaims that Hamilton has left her "down for the count," and he reciprocates by declaring that "as long as I'm alive, Eliza, swear to God, you'll never feel so helpless." By the end of the number, we watch the newly married couple share a kiss.

The song feels like a brief prologue to what happens in the next scene, as we hear another version of the same events. It opens on the wedding reception, as the rowdy soldiers turn the proceedings over to Angelica Schuyler so that she can offer a toast. As she proclaims her hope that the new couple will "always be satisfied" the chorus begins singing "rewind," the stage's turntable begins to turn, and the scene literally rewinds back to that first meeting. As the creators note in *Hamilton: The Revolution*, "as staged by Tommy and the choreographer Andy Blankenbuehler, time itself seems to wind backwards, giving the show another chance to suggest that history looks very different depending on who's telling it."[19] Now we see the story unfold again, this time from the perspective of Angelica. Instead of an earnest song about Eliza falling in love, we watch her sister agonize over love just out of reach. When we return to the wedding scene, Angelica has made clear that she "will never be satisfied." By presenting the two perspectives back to back, with the same setup and much of the same dialogue, Miranda makes clear that the story looks different depending on your perspective. In a world where many people believe there is one true story and a plethora of "biased" accounts, placing two descriptions of the same event on equal footing is not only educational, but also a bit subversive.

Miranda is not writing history in the ways professional historians understand the task: he is offering an interpretive perspective about how not just to understand the past, but also how to engage with it. For him, "history" is about possible pathways, choices, and contingency. It is also, crucially, about interpreting the past through the lens of the present, which reverses the interest of most historians to understand the past on its own terms. The show ends on a question—first raised by George Washington in Act I—sung by the company as they slowly converge from a rich chord structure to a unison: "Who lives, who dies, who tells your story?" This emphasizes that the past is not completely knowable, that we must extrapolate from what we know, that we can remake the world of the past in our own image, represented by two dozen actors of color in costume as the founding fathers, and that we must be attentive to who is constructing historical narratives and for what ends.

Miranda wants to reclaim American history from the white men who created it on behalf of a multicultural generation whom he seeks to represent. His efforts to create new historical representations that reflect the perspective of a diverse contemporary America explains his drive to tell the story of the founding in hip hop, his decision to have a racially diverse cast, and the agreement that the show's producers made with the Gilder Lehrman Institute to bring New York City schoolchildren to the Richard Rodgers Theatre for steeply reduced admission.

Visual artist Grant Wood, most famous for his *American Gothic* painting, made a similar interpretive move in 1939 when he painted *Parson Weems' Fable*, a satirical take on a nineteenth-century painting by Charles Willson Peale showing Peale pulling the curtain back on his museum in Philadelphia. In Wood's reimagining, Weems pulls back the curtain on the famous cherry tree scene. There is Augustin Washington, holding his fatally injured tree. The boy George stands with axe in hand, admitting the crime. It seems a perfectly reasonable re-creation until you notice one detail that you can never un-see: the six-year-old George has the adult head of Washington from the famous Gilbert Stuart painting, which today provides the image used on the one-dollar bill. As literary scholar Steven Biel noted in the journal *Common-Place* in 2006, Wood thereby "fostered

In a homage to Charles Willson Peale's 1822 self-portrait, *The Artist in His Museum*, Grant Wood's 1939 oil painting *Parson Weems' Fable* reveals the story of Washington cutting down the cherry tree as a myth.
(Grant Wood [1891–1942], Parson Weems' Fable, *1939, oil on canvas, Amon Carter Museum of American Art, Fort Worth, Texas. 1970.43)*

patriotism by taking the national 'trait' of mythmaking as its subject."[20] Miranda's project is similar.

Historians don't get to dictate what stories artists choose to tell, nor the manner in which they choose to depict them. Even setting aside the competing impulses of professional norms, historians and artists frequently find different aspects of a given event captivating. That's not a bad thing. Most importantly, those professional impulses matter both in how they shape an individual's approach to a topic and to the outcomes they expect. The form or genre matters as well. One cannot do the same things with the past in a 300-page heavily footnoted book as one can in a film, television show, or Broadway production. But historians might well think about what they can learn from *Hamilton* about the choices we make in portraying the past, whether there might be historical truths better represented with the freedom that comes with art, and whether there are ways to make the issues and stories important to them resonate more deeply with the American public.

NOTES

1. The White House, *Lin-Manuel Miranda Performs at the White House Poetry Jam (8 of 8)*, 2009, https://www.youtube.com/watch?v=WNFf7nMIGn E&feature=youtu.be.

2. Jaya Saxena, "A Report on Alexander Hamilton Written by a Kid Who Has Only Listened to the Musical," *The Toast*, December 17, 2015, http://the -toast.net/2015/12/17/report-on-alexander-hamilton-written-by-a-kid-who -has-only-listened-to-the-musical/.

3. Annette Gordon-Reed, "The Intense Debates Surrounding *Hamilton* Don't Diminish the Musical—They Enrich It," *Vox*, September 13, 2016, http:// www.vox.com/the-big-idea/2016/9/13/12894934/hamilton-debates-history-race -politics-literature.

4. This may be another reason why John Adams was cut as a character. Even in Miranda's reimagined universe, it's not plausible he could speak in rhyme.

5. Mason Locke Weems, *The Life of George Washington; with Curious Anecdotes, Equally Honourable to Himself and Exemplary to His Young Countrymen.*, 9th ed., Shaw Shoemaker 19195 (Philadelphia: Printed for Mathew Carey, 1809),

14–15; Andrew M. Schocket, *Fighting Over the Founders: How We Remember the American Revolution* (New York: NYU Press, 2015), 59.

6. Schocket, *Fighting Over the Founders*, chap. 4.

7. Mike Wallace, "Mickey Mouse History: Portraying the Past at Disney World," in *Mickey Mouse History and Other Essays on American Memory*, Critical Perspectives on the Past (Philadelphia: Temple University Press, 1996), 133–157.

8. Aja Romano, "Hamilton Is Fanfic, and Its Historical Critics Are Totally Missing the Point," *Vox*, April 14, 2016, http://www.vox.com/2016/4/14/11418672/hamilton-is-fanfic-not-historically-inaccurate.

9. Jennifer Schuessler, "'Hamilton' and History: Are They in Sync?," *New York Times*, April 10, 2016, http://www.nytimes.com/2016/04/11/theater/hamilton-and-history-are-they-in-sync.html.

10. If a reader happens to be interested in that literature, three books to start with are: Joseph S. Tiedemann, *Reluctant Revolutionaries: New York City and the Road to Independence, 1763–1776* (Ithaca, NY: Cornell University Press, 1997); Judith L. Van Buskirk, *Generous Enemies: Patriots and Loyalists in Revolutionary New York*, Early American Studies (Philadelphia: University of Pennsylvania Press, 2002); Ruma Chopra, *Unnatural Rebellion: Loyalists in New York City during the Revolution*, Jeffersonian America (Charlottesville: University of Virginia Press, 2011).

11. Quoted in Melanie Kiechle, Twitter post, July 21, 2016, 3:32 pm, https://twitter.com/MelanieKiechle, https://twitter.com/MelanieKiechle/status/756255659562266624.

12. Lin-Manuel Miranda and Jeremy McCarter, *Hamilton: The Revolution. Being the Complete Libretto of the Broadway Musical, with a True Account of Its Creation, and Concise Remarks on Hip-Hop, the Power of Stories, and the New America* (New York: Grand Central Publishing, 2016), 225.

13. Joanne B. Freeman, *Affairs of Honor: National Politics in the New Republic* (New Haven: Yale University Press, 2001).

14. Joanne B. Freeman, "Dueling as Politics: Reinterpreting the Burr–Hamilton Duel," *William and Mary Quarterly*, 3rd ser., 53, no. 2 (1996): 289–318, doi:10.2307/2947402.

15. Miranda and McCarter, *Hamilton: The Revolution*, 272.

16. The White House, *Lin-Manuel Miranda Performs at the White House Poetry Jam (8 of 8)*; Joseph M. Adelman, "Hamilton, Art, History, and Truth," *The Junto*, August 31, 2015, https://earlyamericanists.com/2015/08/31/hamilton-art-history-and-truth/.

17. "From Alexander Hamilton to Elizabeth Hamilton, [4 July 1804]," *Founders Online*, National Archives, last modified December 6, 2016, http://founders.archives.gov/documents/Hamilton/01-26-02-0001-0248.

18. David Waldstreicher, "Founders Chic as Culture War," *Radical History Review*, no. 84 (Fall 2002): 185–194.

19. Miranda and McCarter, *Hamilton: The Revolution*, 78.

20. Steven Biel, "Parson Weems Fights Fascists," *Common-Place* 6, no. 4 (July 2006), http://common-place.org/book/parson-weems-fights-fascists/.

CHAPTER 14

Hamilton

A New American Civic Myth

RENEE C. ROMANO

In November 2016, cast members of *Hamilton* earned the censure of President-elect Donald Trump when they directly addressed his running mate, Mike Pence, at a performance. "We welcome you here," the actor playing Aaron Burr told Pence, asking that he listen to those "diverse Americans" who feared that the new administration would not protect them. They hoped that Pence would be inspired to "uphold American values" by a "wonderful, American story, told by a diverse group of men and women of different colors, creeds, and orientations." Trump immediately responded with a tweet describing the cast's action as "harassment" and calling on them to apologize. After an election where Trump had attacked immigration, called Mexicans "rapists," pushed for a national registry of Muslims, and given power and access to white nationalists, it's no surprise that he also attacked a musical that offers a radically different vision of America from the one he has both tacitly and openly promoted. Far more surprising is how few other Republicans have been critical of the show or its politics. Even Mike Pence insisted that the show was "incredible" and a "real joy." *Hamilton* has, in fact, actually bridged traditional political divides between Americans.

Consider the following. On March 9, 2016, Utah State Senator Jim Dabakis, an openly gay Democrat and founder of an advocacy group called Utah Progressives, and Utah State Representative Ken Ivory, a conservative Republican best known for urging state officials to seize federal land, donned eighteenth-century costumes to extol the virtues of *Hamilton* to their fellow lawmakers. With Dabakis dressed as King George III and Ivory as Hamilton, they urged their peers to pass a resolution honoring Lin-Manuel Miranda and his historically inspired musical. Despite their many political disagreements, these legislators' love of *Hamilton* had brought them together. Their resolution praised the musical for capturing "the human drama, intrigue, passion, perplexity, and promise of America's founding in a way that resonates with a modern and ethnically diverse America" and for captivating audiences "regardless of economic circumstances or political stances."[1] The resolution easily passed in both the House and Senate, and was quickly signed into law by Utah's Republican governor Gary Herbert.

Utah isn't the only place where *Hamilton* has had widespread appeal across party lines. President Barack Obama calls *Hamilton* "the only thing" on which he and former Republican vice president Dick Cheney agree. Conservative media mogul Rupert Murdoch

Politicians Ken Ivory (R) as Alexander Hamilton and Jim Dabakis (D) as King George urge their colleagues in the Utah State Senate to pass a resolution honoring *Hamilton* in March 2016. *(AP Photo/Rick Bowmer)*

tweeted that *Hamilton* was a "Fabulous show!" after seeing it in March 2015, while First Lady Michelle Obama has called it "the best piece of art in any form that I have ever seen in my life." Democrat Hillary Clinton, among the lucky few to have seen the show more than once, calls *Hamilton* a "great, great musical" that makes her cry every time she sees it. The show has also earned the praise of Clinton critic Bill O'Reilly, a conservative talk show host at *Fox*, who said on his program that he had heard *Hamilton* was "unbelievably good" and was happy that this historically minded musical was "so big a hit." The show has earned rave reviews not only from David Brooks, one of the *New York Times*'s conservative columnists, who called it "a jewel" that "asks you to think afresh about your country and your life," but also from liberal MSNBC host Chris Hayes, who urged anyone who is "a hip-hop head, a history buff . . . or just loves things that are awesome" to see it. *Hamilton* has been praised on the pages of both *The Nation* and the *National Review*, two magazines that are at polar ends of the political spectrum.[2]

What exactly is going on? *Hamilton* has brought Americans together across party lines, and even more remarkably, has done so with a story about America's history, a subject that in recent years has inspired heated conflict over museum exhibits, textbooks, and school curricula. Since at least the mid-1990s, debates about how American history should be represented and taught have become so contested that battlefield metaphors seem the most appropriate way to describe them. On one side of the so-called "history wars" stand political conservatives who insist that historical narratives should cultivate pride in America's past and highlight the nation's exceptionalism and continual progress toward greatness. On the other side stand people on the left who believe that celebratory, patriotic versions of U.S. history ignore the reality of racism and oppression in America's past and fail to encourage critical thinking and active citizenship.

The genius—and much of the appeal—of *Hamilton* lies in its ability to transcend what have long seemed to be these irreconcilable political positions. In *Hamilton*, Lin-Manuel Miranda has crafted a

hopeful and inclusive origin story for the nation—a civic myth—
that not only stands in direct opposition to the claims put forth by
Trump and his white nationalist supporters, but also resonates with
many people on both the left and the right. That's an extraordinary
achievement. And to understand its magnitude, we need to start by
exploring why U.S. history is such a political minefield.

The Political Stakes of America's Past

Academic historians describe their discipline as a critical engagement
with the past that focuses on evidence and encourages complex
interpretations from multiple perspectives. But, in truth, U.S. history as taught in America's public schools, as represented in national
museums, and as debated by politicians, often reflects not the academic discipline of history but the much more sacred terrain of civic
myths. Civic myths play a vital role for a nation. They represent
the shared narrative that serves as the basis for a sense of national
identity. They both reflect and aim to impart cultural and political
values. And they help define who belongs to, and who is excluded
from, the nation.[3]

   All nations have their own civic myths, but these foundational
stories have been particularly important to the United States, whose
diverse population includes people from many different ethnic,
national, religious, and racial backgrounds. Traditional American
civic myths promote patriotism and conceal the violence of continental and global expansion by portraying the United States as
an exceptional nation built on ideals of liberty and equality. They
teach that all Americans have an equal opportunity for life, liberty,
and the pursuit of happiness and that success depends only on hard
work and individual merit. These traditional narratives by necessity
downplay elements of America's history that do not fit neatly within
a story of freedom, liberty, and individual opportunity. They mini-
mize and even ignore the significance of slavery, racial violence, the
dispossession of Native American land, gendered exclusions, and
class conflict in America's past.

American history has become a political minefield whenever representations of the past that undermine this celebratory account
move beyond the limited sphere of academia. When the work of
Progressive-era historians who saw class conflict as the driving force
in American history filtered into America's schools, proponents of
patriotic history organized in opposition. The Wisconsin legislature
responded to Charles Beard's argument that the founding fathers
had crafted the Constitution to protect their personal financial interests by passing a 1923 law that forbade public schools from using
any textbooks that defamed the founders "or misrepresent[ed] the
ideals and causes for which they struggled and sacrificed." In the late
1930s and 1940s, members of the National Association of Manu-
facturers and the American Legion teamed up to get popular textbooks by educator Harold Rugg out of the New York public schools.
His books—which focused on class conflict in American politics,
analyzed poverty as a structural flaw of the American economy, and
endorsed the welfare state created by Franklin Roosevelt—did not
sufficiently portray America as a golden land of opportunity.[4]

These battles became even more heated in the 1960s and 1970s
as protest movements highlighted the inequalities in American society and professional historians began recovering and centering the
histories of those ignored in America's historical origin stories, including formerly enslaved people, Latinxs, American Indians, and
women. Conservatives accused this new social history of unfairly
harping on the nation's failings and charged that focusing on the
experience of marginalized groups would fracture the nation and
undermine the foundational myths that tied Americans together. As
new historical narratives that explored the distance between America's vaunted ideals and its reality began to reach schools and textbooks, traditionalists bristled. Reflecting this backlash against civil
rights, feminism, and gay rights in the 1980s, Ronald Reagan's secretary of education William Bennett insisted that American history
school curricula needed to impart "social and political values" that
would encourage patriotism and devotion to country. Republican

senator Robert Dole agreed, insisting that the purpose of historical education should be to teach "American greatness."[5]

In the last thirty years, conservative proponents have continued the fight to discredit versions of the past that they see as promoting a sense of shame, as unfairly stressing negative histories of racism and dispossession, and as pitting groups of Americans against each other rather than encouraging a shared sense of identity based on American exceptionalism. When a group of scholars and educators commissioned by the National Endowment for the Humanities (NEH) released a set of proposed new standards for the teaching of U.S. history in 1994, conservatives—including Lynne Cheney, the head of the NEH—charged that the standards left out "traditional history," failed to offer a "tone of affirmation," and ignored the positive stories of great individual Americans in favor of divisive stories of "group interests." Far-right radio talk show host Rush Limbaugh predicted that if the standards were adopted, they would lead to a crime wave among a generation of embittered young Americans who had been taught that "America is a rotten place."[6]

These battles over how to teach U.S. history have become even more heated in recent years. In Tennessee and Texas, state bodies have made bold efforts to control school history curricula in order to promote a mythic origin story. In 2010, conservatives on the State Board of Education in Texas approved a social studies curriculum that refers to the "Atlantic triangular trade" rather than the "trans-Atlantic slave trade," that portrays slavery as only a secondary cause of the Civil War, and that minimizes the violence of the Jim Crow era. More recently, members of a conservative Tea Party faction in Tennessee have lobbied for a bill that would forbid texts from even mentioning that many of the founding fathers owned slaves. "No portrayal of minority experience in the history *which actually occurred* [emphasis added] shall obscure the experience or contributions of the Founding Fathers or the majority of citizens, including those who reached positions of leadership," the bill mandates. And in 2014, proposed changes to the Advanced Placement (AP) U.S. History curriculum again prompted criticism from conservatives,

A March 16, 2010, cartoon by John Cole of the *Scranton Times-Tribune* satirizes the Texas legislature's efforts to require that state history textbooks celebrate free enterprise and downplay the importance of slavery. *(© 2010 John Cole—All rights reserved)*

who charged that the new framework overemphasized slavery and ignored the contributions of the founders. The changes, the Republican National Committee charged, were "radically revisionist."[7]

Labeling histories that critically engage with negative aspects of America's past "revisionist" highlights just how politicized the issue has become. In the 1930s and 1940s, proponents of teaching mythic versions of history in the schools unabashedly admitted that they were promoting a biased version of the past. Children needed histories that "taught my country right or wrong," a secretary of the Daughters of Colonial Wars argued during the campaign against Harold Rugg's textbooks. "We can't afford to teach them to be unbiased and let them make up their own minds." But as America has become more diverse and U.S. history more inclusive since the 1990s, defenders of patriotic history have taken to describing histories that focus on people of color or class conflict as biased and politically motivated. Defenders of celebratory history, meanwhile, portray the traditional narrative of great white founders as unbiased, apolitical, and true. Rush Limbaugh defends his children's book series, which he launched in 2013 to counter the "corrupted and politicized" multicultural version of America's past, as "real history without any political bias of any kind about this country."[8]

The stakes here are high. Those fighting for the traditional civic myth insist that nations need histories that promote pride, not shame. They see historical narratives that emphasize American exceptionalism, portray the United States as committed to ideals of liberty and equality, and valorize the founders and the Constitution as vital to cultivating a proud civic identity and patriotic respect among America's heterogeneous population. Without these civic myths offering a coherent national narrative, they charge, Americans will fragment into competing interest groups and the nation will fracture.

Critics of such celebratory narratives fear not only that they fail to represent the complexity of America's actual past, but also that they impoverish the capacity of Americans to be engaged, critical citizens. Perhaps the best-known proponent of a different kind of historical thinking is Howard Zinn, the late author of *A People's History of the United States*. Zinn insisted that history should focus on the lives of ordinary people who are often left out of the story—American Indians, people of color, workers, women—and show how their individual and collective actions shaped American society. The Zinn Education Project today continues his work of encouraging historical education that empowers marginalized and disadvantaged people to understand their potential to change the country. Other critics on the left contend that America's traditional civic myths serve to enable and uphold an unjust and racist political order. The Equal Justice Initiative (EJI), an organization dedicated to challenging racism in the criminal justice system, has recently shifted much of its energy to historical projects. Americans' inability or unwillingness to confront the reality of racial violence and oppression in their history, EJI founder Bryan Stevenson argues, has made it impossible to challenge racism effectively in the present. We Americans do pride very well, says Stevenson, but we have "a difficult time dealing with our shame." Traditional celebratory histories undermine "our ability to build a nation where racial justice can be achieved."[9]

Yet even amid these very politicized debates over historical education, *Hamilton* is quickly becoming an uncontroversial staple in classrooms across the country. Teachers at every level, from fifth grade to AP U.S. History and even college, have seized on the musical's incredible popularity with young people to draw their students into the history of the nation's founding. Major institutions are on the bandwagon too. The Rockefeller Foundation is spending $1.46 million to enable twenty thousand New York City eleventh graders who attend schools with high concentrations of impoverished students to go to the show, and in June 2016 it pledged an additional $6 million to expand the #EduHam Project to help one hundred thousand public school students in cities across the country see the touring version. Both Democrats and Republicans seem to agree that the musical should be used as a teaching tool. The Utah state resolution honoring *Hamilton* urged the state's teachers, "when possible and age-appropriate, to utilize the *Hamilton* soundtrack to inspire a love of American history in today's students." "This musical has to be in schools," says Greg Hughes, Utah's far-right Speaker of the House, a position that former president Obama, endorses.[10]

Hamilton might just represent the one thing both sides in the history wars can agree on. When the students in one Ohio AP U.S. History class made their own version of the iconic *Hamilton* Broadway poster, it showed Hamilton standing on a star holding aloft a copy of their classroom textbook, Howard Zinn's *A People's History of the United States*, the text perhaps most despised by political conservatives. Students in this eleventh grade U.S. History class in Shaker Heights, Ohio, had no reservations about connecting *Hamilton* to the approach taken in their Zinn textbook.[11] That same Howard Zinn book drove Lynne Cheney, the woman who had led the charge against the National History Standards in 1994 and was highly critical of proposed changes to the AP U.S. History curriculum in 2015, to launch her own children's book series emphasizing the accomplishments of great Americans. Her works sought to counter Zinn's "very dark and dire picture" of an America that had made "no progress" since its founding. Yet Cheney is also a big *Hamilton* fan, calling it a "great" show with "terrific music" whose "fact-line of the story was right on."[12] It was not, as she saw it, a version of the dreaded "revisionist" history she has spent a portion of her life fighting.

In other words, *Hamilton* appears to be open to multiple, even conflicting readings, by people with quite different political perspectives.

Hamilton's Political Miracle

So how exactly has this representation of the nation's founding—the topic that is perhaps the hottest of the potatoes in the history wars—managed to appeal to Americans across the political divide? The support among conservatives is particularly surprising given that Lin-Manuel Miranda has made no secret of his own progressive political orientation. The son of politically engaged parents (his father is a longtime Democratic political consultant and his mother a clinical psychologist who is on the board of Planned Parenthood), Miranda is an avid Democrat who has used his musical talents to support Democratic candidates like New York governor Eliot Spitzer. During the 2016 presidential election, the cast performed special matinee fundraisers for both the Democratic National Committee and Hillary Clinton. The show has garnered much praise and love from the Obama family, including President Barack and Michelle Obama's unprecedented video introduction of it on the 2016 Tony Awards. And Miranda and the cast have been outspoken in their criticism of Republican Donald Trump.

But the story that Miranda has created in *Hamilton*—and importantly, the way he tells that story in the musical—serves in many respects to fuse progressive and conservative visions of history. *Hamilton* offers a story of the nation's founding that can appeal to those who are invested in a narrative of American exceptionalism that emphasizes the nation's positive virtues and "great man" versions of history. But in focusing on a founding father who opposed slavery (or at least favored gradual emancipation), by telling his and the nation's story through contemporary Afro-Latin musical forms, and by casting blacks and Latinx actors in the roles of the founders, *Hamilton* simultaneously broadens the traditional American narrative to welcome and even center people of color who have been marginalized in America's civic myths. The genius of *Hamilton* lies in its ability to offer both those who have long owned the narrative and those who have been excluded from it a place in America's foundational story.

Take *Hamilton's* focus on the founding fathers and the nation's origins. That's a subject typically more popular with conservatives than progressives, but Miranda saw in Hamilton's story the chance to challenge traditional patriotic and civic myths that portray the founders as sacred figures who are beyond criticism. Americans have so deified the founders that "they're on rocks in South Dakota," Miranda argues. Instead, he wanted to present them as complex people with foibles and human flaws, a fact the show highlights with its portrayal of Hamilton's philandering, pride, and ambition; Aaron Burr's envy and duplicity; George Washington's self-doubt; and Thomas Jefferson's strutting hypocrisy. Even the decision about where to put the intermission reflected Miranda's quest to make these men seem like real people; he decided not to end Act I with victory in the American Revolution for fear that it would reinforce celebratory narratives that made the founders seem infallible.[13]

Yet conservatives have still found much to praise about Miranda's portrayal of the founding fathers. The musical has, much to their delight, made early American history and classic texts like *The Federalist Papers* hip again. One self-identified conservative who responded to an online question about *Hamilton* liked the show because "any discussion of history, especially of the Founding Fathers, is always positive," while another was pleased that a play about such an "important and influential founding father" was so popular. *Hamilton*, a writer in the conservative magazine *Commentary* argued, should be celebrated for sending "Americans back to their roots at a time when many are quick to tear them up and cast them aside." *Hamilton*'s portrayal of Hamilton, Jefferson, and other early American figures as complex and morally flawed also pleased conservative commentators because it served, as they saw it, to mitigate against knee-jerk criticism of them as "dead white men" who should be dismissed as hypocrites. A writer for the *National Review* hoped that *Hamilton* would help "people who were reared on a public-school revisionist history . . . come to understand why many still believe this Dead White Man is worthy of veneration." At a time when many conservatives have complained that America's first leaders, as Rush Limbaugh put it in 2014, have been wrongfully caricatured as "homophobes and bigots and racists and sexist," conservative commentators viewed the portrayal in *Hamilton* of vibrant, energetic, and human founders as "entirely earnest and deeply sympathetic."[14]

Conservative praise for *Hamilton* helping people understand why "dead white men" are worthy of veneration is particularly ironic given Miranda's insistence on having nearly all the characters in the show played by actors of color. *Hamilton* does not in fact encourage its audience to "venerate" the founding fathers. It rather seeks to "eliminate the distance" many contemporary people feel from the nation's early history—especially people of color whose own histories are ignored or elided in celebratory national origin stories—by offering a "story about America then, told by America now."[15] Miranda's America is one where rap and hip hop best express the founding zeitgeist, where people of color are portrayed as owners and shapers of the country from its very beginning.

But here again, *Hamilton* has found a way to convey America's racial history that has the potential to unite people on both sides of the political divide—or at the very least, to bring them together in conversation. On the one hand, *Hamilton*'s music and casting choices have the effect of delinking whiteness and the story of the nation's founding. Traditional national origin stories have focused on the experiences and perspectives of elite white men who are celebrated for promoting ideals of liberty and equality they did not follow in practice. People of color, whose histories these myths ignore, have been offered only the option of celebrating a history that encourages, and even demands, an innocence or amnesia about the nation's history of racial and gender exclusions. But by having actors of color play all of the founding fathers and by telling the national story through musical genres associated with black and Latinx culture, *Hamilton* boldly puts people of color on par with whites as owners and creators of the nation and its heritage.

Nor does the musical shy away from the racial and gender exclusions that mark the nation's history in spite of its vaunted rhetoric of liberty and equality. By focusing on Alexander Hamilton and emphasizing—indeed overemphasizing—his opposition to slavery, Miranda suggests that leaders who challenged "America's original sin" are more worthy of our veneration than those who defended it. While abolitionism is not a central theme of the musical, as several chapters in this volume make clear, *Hamilton* nevertheless reminds Americans that some of the men who fought the American Revolution and framed the Constitution were abolitionists, while marginalizing and even caricaturing slave owners like Thomas Jefferson and James Madison. Another slaveowner, George Washington, bows his head at the musical's conclusion in symbolic repentance for not having done more to challenge slavery during his lifetime.[16]

The show repeatedly emphasizes the hypocrisy of slavery and the exclusion of women from the polity at a time when there was so much talk about freedom, equality, and liberty. Early in Act I, the women in *Hamilton* note the limitations of the founding ideal that "all men are created equal" and argue that Thomas Jefferson needs to "include women in the sequel." And while *Hamilton* does not feature any actual black characters except for a fleeting depiction of Jefferson's enslaved mistress Sally Hemings, slavery is part of the story from the show's opening. The very first song describes the Caribbean as a place where slaves were daily "being slaughtered and carted away." Subsequent references highlight the contradiction between American freedom and liberty and the practice of slavery.

In the rap "Cabinet Battle #1," Hamilton ridicules Jefferson's invocation of the founding ideals of life, liberty, and the pursuit of happiness as "civics lesson from a slaver'" whose "debts are paid cuz you don't pay for labor."

Admittedly, slavery is not a central concern of the show, which helps explain how it is that conservatives have found much to praise about the racial message of *Hamilton*. Miranda chose to cut some of the show's original material on slavery—including a third rap battle where Hamilton and Jefferson debate a Quaker resolution to abolish slavery—because he felt that it didn't add anything new to the story. "There's only so much time you can spend on it [slavery] when there's no result to it," he explained. That perspective appeals to conservatives who insist that it's neither fair nor useful to allow the negative aspects of American history to overwhelm the positive. Conservatives recognized that *Hamilton* did not discount the accomplishments of those who fought the American Revolution and wrote the Constitution because they failed to end slavery. As law professor Tara Helfman wrote in *Commentary*, *Hamilton* "forces the audience to view the founding generation as neither heroes nor villains, but as individuals faced with formidable choices in transformative times." Nor did the show, one conservative reviewer explained, commit the cardinal sin of criticizing America's early leaders for not living up today's racial standards or "the modern codes of identity politics." The telling and teaching of early American history, he insisted, "must be more than an exercise in knocking rich, white dudes down a peg."[17] Conservatives praised *Hamilton* for portraying the founding fathers as vital figures *despite* their failure to address slavery.

Conservative commentators have also accepted and even embraced the color-conscious casting. Rather than viewing it as a threat to mythic narratives, some saw the black and Latinx cast as evidence of the power of the ideals of liberty, freedom, and individual rights that animated the American Revolution and the framers wrote into the Constitution. For Richard Brookhiser, having black and Latinx actors play the founding fathers served as a reminder that the Revolution had inspired new energy toward freedom, re-flected in an "upsurge in manumissions," as well as the language of equality in America's founding documents. For Helfman, the color-conscious casting underscored the brilliance of the American exper-iment, for it made apparent the durability of the "founding ideals" of liberty and equality.[18] In this reading, Miranda's casting choices were symbolic of just how much progress the country has made toward achieving the ideals laid out by its creators.

The show's take on immigration has also managed to please peo-ple on both sides of the political divide. Focusing on the Caribbean-born Hamilton (a man whose enemies spread rumors that he was mixed race) allows Lin-Manuel Miranda to make a progressive political argument about immigration and the importance of immi-grants in America's past and present. And by having a Latino actor play the character of Alexander Hamilton, Miranda subtly con-veys that today's nonwhite immigrants offer as much to the country as older generations of immigrants of European descent who were grandfathered in as native-born citizens of the new nation. When Hamilton and French Revolutionary war hero the Marquis de Lafayette proclaim prior to the Battle of Yorktown, "Immigrants, we get the job done," it is not only one of the biggest applause lines in the play, but it is also a succinct expression of one of the musical's key historical arguments: that immigrants, in Miranda's words, are the "renewable life-blood of our country" who "often work twice as hard and make our country better." This take on immigration reflects a point of view voiced by far more Democrats than Repub-licans. In a recent poll, 78 percent of Democrats agreed that im-migrants "strengthen our country because of their hard work and talents," compared to only 35 percent of Republicans, whose party has endorsed building a wall to keep out immigrants from Mexico.[19] *Hamilton* offered those on the left a powerful argument about the positive role immigrants have played in both historic and contem-porary America.

Conservative commentators, however, could see a confirmation of their colorblind belief in equal opportunity for all in the United

States in the musical's approach to immigration. Conservatives view the play as less about the value of today's immigrants than the narrative of American exceptionalism and the uniquely transformative power of the United States for those willing to work hard and sacrifice. "In what other land, in Hamilton's era," asked the reviewer for the *American Conservative*, "could a man have risen so far on the basis of hard work, ostentatious bravery, and genuine genius? Nowhere." For him, the casting underscored this message of social mobility and transformation, that in New York, you really could "be a new man," reinforcing a common conservative narrative that race and ethnicity are no bar to success for those willing to work hard. "Talent outweighs everything else" was the key take-away message from the show for another conservative viewer. *Hamilton* offered to conservatives the story of a self-made man who proved that America was a land of opportunity, a favorite Republican message about the importance of individual merit and effort in determining one's success. Indeed Greg Hughes, the Republican Speaker of the House in Utah, went so far as to question how any Democrats could like the show, since there were, as he put it, no "freebies" in this musical.[20]

Conservatives who have balked at the leveling influence of social history, which since the 1970s has led historians to focus on everyday people, the study of groups, and inevitably the way that systemic or structural forces affect patterns of opportunity, have also approved of the way the musical tells America's story through the biography of an exceptional individual and a self-made man. This biographical approach, "true to the experience of historical individuals," helps us better understand someone like Hamilton, Celina Durgin argued in an April 14, 2016, *National Review* article. She would take a good biography over "government-approved textbooks" any day. Lynne Cheney, who had long wanted history education to include more stories of exceptional individuals, saw in *Hamilton* the story of "human beings who achieved greatly."[21] For Cheney and others, *Hamilton* fits well within their favored "great man" version of history.

Again, viewing *Hamilton* as a "great man" version of history is ironic, given how much Miranda sought to invite Americans of all backgrounds to see themselves and place themselves in this story. The casting offers the most straightforward invitation to audiences who do not share that mythic white past, as well as audiences who may wish to. By having actors of color play all of the founding fathers, *Hamilton* boldly claims the American tradition as belonging to people of all races, especially to those originally brought here as slaves or conquered in war. The musical variety—from rap to traditional show tunes to British pop—communicates that invitation too. As Jeremy McCarter explains in the massive record of the show, *Hamilton: The Revolution*, the diversity of musical references serves as "another way of saying that American history can be told and retold, claimed, and reclaimed, even by people who didn't look like George Washington and Betsy Ross." Using the vernacular styles of young black and Latinx Americans to tell the founding story offers a similar invitation. Lin-Manuel Miranda, suggests Oskar Eustis, the artistic director who helped develop the show at the Public Theater, has achieved something similar to the work of Shakespeare in that he takes "the language of the people and heightens it by making it verse," effectively ennobling "both the language and the people saying the language." By using this heightened language of the people to tell the nation's foundational myths, Miranda "makes the country the possession of everyone," Eustis suggests.[22] *Hamilton* thus insists that America and its history rightfully belongs as much to people or color who were brought to this country as slaves or to recent immigrants as its does to descendants of the Mayflower Pilgrims. This is a powerful democratic vision even if Hamilton the man was himself an elitist. Miranda again has done the seemingly impossible: crafted a vision of history that can incorporate the perspectives of both the left and the right.

Hamilton as a New American Civic Myth

For nearly all of America's history, the national origin story has celebrated a form of American exceptionalism that encourages, and even demands, an innocence or amnesia about the nation's history of racial and gender exclusions. For how can you offer a mythic and inspiring version of American history while truthfully acknowledging slavery, settler colonialism, and the nation's long history of white supremacy? These traditional civic myths, not surprisingly, have far more appeal to whites than to people of color. But stories that emphasize America's history of racism, discrimination, and oppression hold little appeal for many white Americans and offer scant material for building a positive sense of national identity.

In *Hamilton* Lin-Manuel Miranda has found a way to rewrite America's foundational civic myths to allow people of all different backgrounds to claim full belonging in the nation no matter their race, ethnicity, or immigration status. While the musical keeps many elements of America's origin story, it spreads ownership of that story beyond the exclusive property of whites. *Hamilton* allows people of color to see themselves in the country's history, not (as several essays in this volume rightfully point out) by featuring the actual stories of people of color—all of the actors of color in the show play white characters, after all—but by making the stories of the founders more universal and inclusive. Every night, it gives ownership of America's narrative over to blacks and Latinxs, peoples who have long been marginalized, persecuted, and denied full inclusion in the United States. It thus offers a civic myth for Americans that does not require allegiance to a white version of the past. *Hamilton* lets people take part in the cult of sacred history without the usual birthright credentials and ritual obeisances," argues religious historian Peter Manseau. Constitutional legal scholar Richard Primus concurs in a June 4, 2016, article in *The Atlantic*. *Hamilton*, he argues, offers blacks and Latinos "access to the cultural power of the Founding" without having to deny their own histories or to affirm a celebratory narrative that ignores America's sins.[23]

Although some critics, including authors in this volume, argue that the musical does ask people of color to "deny their own histories," there's at least some evidence of blacks and Latinxs around the country hearing and being moved by the invitation offered by

Hamilton to feel more of a sense of ownership of, and belonging in, the nation. Members of the cast and crew have described how *Hamilton* has made them feel more part of the American tradition. Daveed Diggs, the actor who originated the role of Thomas Jefferson, felt that if he had seen black men playing the founding fathers when he was a kid, "a whole lot of things I just never thought were for me would have seemed possible."[24] Students who have seen the show as part of the Rockefeller Foundation initiative have also felt its invitation to take a sense of ownership over the American project. *Hamilton*, one black student told his principal, "made me realize that this is our country too," while an administrator at the Public Theater described students who were moved to tears by the show because "they felt like they were Americans for the first time." A teacher at a Los Angeles school with nearly all Latinx students described how the soundtrack was helping her students relate to American history like they never could before. Because of *Hamilton*, "they finally have a chance to see themselves in our country's history for the first time."[25]

Yet even as *Hamilton* puts people of color at the table in the "room where it happens," it still promotes elements of traditional American origin myths that many conservatives view as crucial to a positive national identity. In the show, America is an exceptional nation full of exceptional people, even if its genius arises from its diverse and spirited population instead of from a few former Englishmen. Miranda describes his own view of the United States as a story of progress, a place that has never been perfect, but that is always working toward being better. It's comforting, he has said, to know that all of the political battles that have been part of the nation's history since its founding are "just a part of the more perfect union we're always working towards, or try to work towards, and that we're always working on them." Conservative Tara Helfman made the same point in slightly different words: "If there is a single unifying theme in American history, it is this nation's ongoing struggle to live up to its founding ideals," a dynamic struggle that *Hamilton* embodied for her.[26]

Thus, even as *Hamilton* has offered people of diverse backgrounds a new connection to the country, it hasn't sought to make white conservatives feel that they, or their version of history, have been excluded. *Hamilton* allows people of all kinds—including those who might see themselves as most like the oft-lambasted dead white men of the past—to feel pride in America's history. Kids across the country, from wealthy suburbs to rural areas, are excited about *Hamilton*. Little white girls across the country have thrown *Hamilton*-themed birthday parties, and bat mitzvahs.[27] The show's broad reach was what excited Utah Republican state congressmen Ken Ivory, who waxed poetic about seeing young Boy Scouts sing the musical and knowing that those boys saw themselves as part of American history. "You look at those kids and they're right in the middle of it," he exulted. In its resolution honoring *Hamilton*, the Utah legislature and governor too noted the show's capacity to make people of all different backgrounds feel connected to the country's story. They expressed gratitude to Miranda for "placing [us all] in the narrative of our rich American history."[28] The musical has united rather than divided; expanded the circle of who can claim foundational American myths rather than changing who is in and who is out.

Hamilton's insistence that all Americans should feel a sense of belonging and ownership in the nation and its ability to appeal across racial, political, and class divides makes it revolutionary. But it is also what makes the story it tells quite traditional. Like the conservative cultural fighters in the history wars, *Hamilton* too has a nationalist mission of promoting a unified nation. Indeed, Jeremy McCarter concludes the huge ode to all things *Hamilton* that is the book *Hamilton: The Revolution* by focusing not on the play's revolutionary aspects, but its traditional ones. *Hamilton*, he writes, doesn't reinvent the American character. It renews it. It reminds us of the idea that Hamilton spent his life fighting for: "the necessity of *Union* to the respectability and happiness of the country."[29]

As with any representation that seeks to unify, *Hamilton* asks for concessions from both sides. It demands that whites who have long held ownership over the American narrative accept that people of color have as much a right to the nation as they do. More importantly, it asks white conservatives to let go of their tenacious hold over the nation's origin story. The resurgence of overt white supremacy that has resulted from the election of Donald Trump makes clear that this is no small compromise. Trump's victory has reinvigorated the ultimate anti-*Hamilton* position, that—in the words of alt-right leader Richard Spencer at a post-election victory gathering—"America was, until this past generation, a white country designed for ourselves and our posterity. It is our creation, it is our inheritance, and it belongs to us." Rush Limbaugh, who had almost nothing to say about *Hamilton* before the Mike Pence episode, has since begun attacking the cast as "leftists telling everybody how to live" and as "arrogant, preaching, condescending jerks warning everybody about the oncoming fascism, the danger to the planet, the danger to our country, the danger to people of color." Limbaugh characterizes Americans who view Trump as a dangerous racist, including the cast of *Hamilton*, as mentally ill.[30]

At the same time, *Hamilton* asks those on the left to accept a version of America's past that in many ways minimizes the nation's long history of racist exclusions in favor of an imperfect story about progress and freedom. That history—and the continued power of racism in the present day—makes many scholars, including me, question any narrative that portrays the story of the United States as primarily one of progress. *Hamilton*, regardless of its imaginative casting, does not in any way address the reality and experiences of people of color in the United States at the time of the founding. For some critics (including some writers whose views appear in this volume), the imaginative casting actively erases the *actual* presence and history of people of color in early America. *Hamilton*, Lyra Monteiro charges in her chapter, asks people of color to feel connected to a narrative that still is at heart a "celebratory, white narrative of the American past." Novelist Ishmael Reed is even more critical. *Hamilton*, he argues, has scrubbed the founding fathers and Alexander Hamilton "with a kind of historical Ajax" by overstating Hamilton's opposition to slavery, ignoring the slave trafficking and sexual violence committed by founders, and not even acknowledging the destruction of Native Americans as a result of settler colonialism. Reed compares having black and Latinx actors play the founders to "Jewish actors in Berlin's theaters" taking on the roles of Goering, Goebbels, Eichmann, or Hitler. The fact that *Hamilton* is being used as a teaching tool particularly enrages Reed, who calls for more Afro-centric and Hispanic schools to balance the Eurocentric curriculum he believes *Hamilton* promotes.[31] The spirited defense of the musical against these charges by conservative writers, who insist that critics like Monteiro are engaging in a pessimistic identity politics that is unhealthily fixated on "racial grievances," suggests that *Hamilton*'s compromise has perhaps been easier for conservatives to swallow than it has for those on the left.[32]

It is fair to question whether national belonging can really be achieved by art that imagines the founders as nonwhites rather than an in-depth engagement with the history of white supremacy in the United States. But *Hamilton*'s phenomenal success suggests that many Americans are willing, even eager, to embrace a more inclusive origin story. Even in the wake of the recent election that many have read as a reassertion of white ownership over the nation, the musical remains extraordinarily popular; it earned more money than any Broadway show in history in the week after the Pence episode. The Trump supporter who disrupted a *Hamilton* performance yelling, "We won! You lost! Get over it!" may—perhaps—be declaring victory prematurely.[33] Just like Alexander Hamilton was, as he famously sings, "young, scrappy, and hungry," many twenty-first-century Americans too seem hungry for an civic myth that includes Americans of all races, that celebrates the nation's diversity as part of its genius, and that recognizes, but does not become trapped by, the nation's flaws. This is a hopeful sign in our bitterly divided country.

Eight months after *Hamilton* opened on Broadway, an article in *Playbill*, the magazine aimed at theatergoers, expressed bemusement about the show's broad appeal, and the possibilities that it held out for our divided political present. Could *Hamilton*, the article teasingly asked, end congressional gridlock in Washington? If then-president Obama nominated Lin-Manuel Miranda for the Supreme Court, would Republicans actually agree to hold hearings? Could this play, it asked, "be that thing that all Americans agree on?" The Republican Speaker of the House in Utah had even higher ambitions for the musical than *Playbill* had imagined. He was "pretty much convinced," he told his colleagues, that *Hamilton* was "going to save this country."[34] That is, of course, too much to ask of any work of art or popular culture, but *Hamilton* at least offers a hopeful alternative vision that will only become more important as supporters of much more exclusionary civic myths assert their power and prominence in Trump's America.

NOTES

1. Lee Davidson, "Utah's Far Left and Far Right Join to Honor Rap Musical 'Hamilton,'" *Salt Lake Tribune*, March 9, 2016, http://www.sltrib.com/home/ 3640406–155/utahs-far-right-and-far-left; "H.C.R. 12: Concurrent Resolution Honoring Lin-Manuel Miranda, Composer of the Musical *Hamilton*," 2016 General Session, State of Utah, Chief Sponsor: Ken Ivory, Senate Sponsor: Jim Dabakis, http://le.utah.gov/~2016/bills/static/HCR012.html.

2. Jeremy McCarter and Lin-Manuel Miranda, *Hamilton: The Revolution* (New York: Grand Central Publishing, 2016), 284; Erik Piepenberg, "Why *Hamilton* Has Heat," *New York Times*, June 12, 2016; *Dailymail.com*, July 14, 2016, http://www.dailymail.co.uk/news/article-3691058/Hillary-boasts-s-seen-Hamilton-THREE-times-Virginia-rally-road-tested-potential-running-mate-Tim-Kaine.html#i-fee1a7d682bf5987; David Brooks, "The *Hamilton* Experience," *New York Times*, February 24, 2015; *All In with Chris Hayes*, transcript, March 9, 2015.

3. Rogers M. Smith, *Civic Ideals: Conflicting Visions of Citizenship in U.S. History* (New Haven: Yale University Press, 1997), 33. See also Brook Thomas, *Civic Myths: A Law and Literature Approach to Citizenship* (Chapel Hill: University of North Carolina Press, 2007).

4. The Wisconsin legislature was targeting Charles Beard's 1913 text, *An Economic Interpretation of the Constitution of the United States*. Lawrence R. Samuel, *Remembering America: How We Have Told Our Past* (Lincoln: University of Nebraska Press, 2015), 9; Joseph Moreau, *Schoolbook Nation: Conflicts Over American History Textbooks from the Civil War to the Present* (Ann Arbor: University of Michigan Press, 2003), 242–243.

5. Samuel, *Remembering America*, 95, 126.

6. Conservatives won this battle. In 1995, the Senate passed a resolution that urged the standards not be certified by the federal government and argued that any future standards should illustrate "respect for the contributions of western civilization and U.S. history, ideas, and institutions, to the increase of freedom and prosperity around the world." Democrats argued against the resolution, but agreed to support it once it was made nonbinding. Lynne Cheney, "The End of History," *Wall Street Journal*, October 20, 1994; Gary Nash, Charlotte Antoine Crabtree, and Ross Dunn, *History on Trial: Culture Wars and the Teaching of the Past* (New York: Vintage Books, 2000), 5; Mike Wallace, "Culture War, History Front," in *History Wars*, edited by Edward Linenthal and Tom Engelhardt (New York: Metropolitan Books, 1996), 185.

7. Trymaine Lee, "Tea Party Groups in Tennessee Demand Textbooks Overlook U.S. Founder's Slave-Owning History," *Huffington Post*, January 23, 2012; Chris McGreal, "Texas School Board Rewrites US History with Lessons Promoting God and Guns," *The Guardian,* May 16, 2010; Catherine Gewrtz, "Republican National Committee Condemns New AP History Frameworks," *Education's Week's Blogs*, August 11, 2014.

8. Nash, Crabtree, and Dunn, *History on Trial*, 45; Michael Kammen, "The American Past Politicized: Uses and Misuses of History," *Annals of the American Academy of Political and Social Science* (May 2008): 42–57; Simon & Schuster Interview with Rush Limbaugh, December 30, 2013, http://www .rushlimbaugh.com/daily/2013/10/30/simon_schuster_interview_with_rush.

9. Bryan Stevenson, Carnegie Medal Acceptance Speech, American Library Association Conference, June 27, 2015, http://speakola.com/ideas/ bryan-stevenson-carnegie-medal-2015; Equal Justice Initiative, *Lynching in America: Confronting the Legacy of Racial Terror* (Montgomery, AL: Equal Justice Initiative, 2015), 4.

10. Valerie Strauss, "The Unusual Way Broadway's *Hamilton* Is Teaching U.S. History to Kids," *Washington Post*, June 28, 2016; "The Rockefeller Foundation Announces $6 Million in Additional Funding for 100,000 Inner City Students Nationwide to See *Hamilton*," Rockefeller Foundation News and Media, June 23, 2016, https://www.rockefellerfoundation.org/about-us/news -media/rockefeller-foundation-announces-6-million-additional-funding-100 000-inner-city-students-nationwide-see-hamilton/; H.C.R. 12; Hughes quote from "Utah Politicos *Hamilton* Carpool Karoake," YouTube video, https://you tu.be/-87PH8uCq1c.

11. Andrea Simakis, "The Gift of 'Hamilton': Shaker High Students Make Their History Teacher's Broadway Dream Come Alive," *Cleveland Plain Dealer*, July 9, 2016.

12. Conversation between Allen Weinstein and Lynne Cheney, the National Archives, November 30, 2005, https://www.archives.gov/files/about/archivist/conversations/cheney-transcript.pdf; Jennifer Schuessler, "*Hamilton* Puts Politics Onstage and Politicians in Attendance," *New York Times*, March 28, 2015, C3.

13. Robert Weintert-Kendt, "Rapping a Revolution: Lin-Manuel Miranda and Others from 'Hamilton' Talk History," *New York Times*, February 5, 2015; Schuessler, "*Hamilton* Puts Politics Onstage and Politicians in Attendance"; McCarter and Miranda, *Hamilton: The Revolution*, 124.

14. Colin Jensen and Brady Postma quoted on *Quora*, May 8 and June 30, 2016, https://www.quora.com/what-do-conservatives-think-of-the-musical-Hamilton; Tara Helfman, "Why *Hamilton* Matters," *Commentary*, January 15, 2016; Celina Durgin, "*Hamilton* Reminds Us Why His Face Is on Our Money," *National Review*, April 14, 2016; *Rush Limbaugh Show*, transcript, April 2, 2014; Richard Brookhiser, "Funky Founder," *National Review*, March 21, 2015.

15. Quoted in Weintert-Kendt, "Rapping a Revolution."

16. Washington was, however, the only founder to manumit his slaves in his will. His will stipulated that his slaves be freed upon the death of his wife, Martha.

17. Miranda quoted in Weintert-Kendt, "Rapping a Revolution"; Helfman, "Why *Hamilton* Matters"; David Marcus, "'Hamilton' Haters Are Why We Can't Have Nice Things," *The Federalist*, April 7, 2016, htpp://thefederalist.com/2016/04/07/hamilton-haters-are-why-we-can't-have-nice-things.

18. Brookhiser, "Funky Founder"; Helfman, "Why *Hamilton* Matters."

19. Lucia I. Suarez Sang, "Lin-Manuel Miranda: Most Rewarding Part of 'Hamilton' Success Is Inspiring Students to Dream," *Fox News Latino*, April 26, 2016; Bradley Jones, "Americans' Views of Immigrants Marked by Widening Partisan, Generational Divides," *Pew Research Center*, April 15, 2016, http://www.pewresearch.org/fact-tank/2016/04/15/americans-views-of-immigrants-marked-by-widening-partisan-generational-divides/.

20. Kevin R. C. Gutzman, "Hamilton Takes Broadway," *American Conservative*, October 22, 2015, http://www.theamericanconservative.com/articles/hamilton-takes-broadway/; Dan Dunaway, "What Do Conservatives Think of the Musical *Hamilton*," *Quora*, June 6, 2016, https://www.quora.com/what-do-conservatives-think-of-the-musical-Hamilton; Hughes quote from "Utah Politicos Hamilton Carpool Karaoke."

21. Durgin, "*Hamilton* Reminds Us Why His Face Is on Our Money"; Schuessler, "*Hamilton* Puts Politics Onstage and Politicians in Attendance." For more on the conservative critique of social history, see Joyce Appelby,

A Restless Past: History and the American Public (Lanham, MD: Rowman and Littlefield, 2005), 103.

22. Quoted in McCarter and Miranda, *Hamilton: The Revolution*, 95, 103.

23. Peter Manseau, "Father Worship; Hamilton's New World Scripture," *The Baffler*, #32, 2016, http://thebaffler.com/salvos/father-worship; Richard Primus, "Will Lin-Manuel Miranda Transform the Supreme Court?" *The Atlantic*, June 4, 2016.

24. Quoted in McCarter and Miranda, *Hamilton: The Revolution*, 116, 149.

25. Zach Schonfeld, "*Hamilton*, the Biggest Thing on Broadway, Is Being Taught in Classrooms All Over," *Newsweek*, February 19, 2016; Liz Johnson, "*Hamilton* HIGH: How the Hottest Musical on Broadway Will Teach High School Juniors American History—and Make Sure They're Having Fun Learning It," *Arrive Magazine*, March/April 2016, 49.

26. Edward Delman interview with Lin-Manuel Miranda, "How Lin-Manuel Miranda Shapes History," *The Atlantic*, September 29, 2015; Helfman, "Why *Hamilton* Matters."

27. Eliza Berman, "See How the Broadway Hit *Hamilton* Has Completely Taken Over America," *Time*, September 19, 2016. Just among my own circle, I know of one *Hamilton*-themed bat mitzvah and many *Hamilton*-inspired Halloween costumes.

28. Ivory quote from "Utah Politicos Hamilton Carpool Karoake"; H.C.R. 12.

29. McCarter and Miranda, *Hamilton: The Revolution*, 284.

30. "Alt-Right Gathering Exults in Trump Election with Nazi-Era Salute," *New York Times*, November 20, 2016; Transcript, *Rush Limbaugh Show*, November 22, 2016.

31. Ishmael Reed, "'Hamilton: the Musical': Black Actors Dress Up Like Slave Traders . . . and It's Not Halloween," *Counterpunch*, August 21, 2015.

32. For David Marcus, author of the pithily titled, "*Hamilton* Haters Are Why We Can't Have Nice Things," on the conservative website, *The Federalist*, those who criticize the musical's race politics can only see art "through the prism of oppression." They want, he charges, to turn the play into "just another festival of grievance." Black conservative John McWhorter similarly accuses Monteiro and other critics of believing that "race and racism are the very essence of what America is." Marcus, "'Hamilton' Haters Are Why We Can't Have Nice Things," *The Federalist*, April 7, 2016, http://thefederalist.com/2016/04/07/hamilton-haters-are-why-we-cant-have-nice-things/; John McWhorter, "The Exhausting and Useless Accusations of Racism against 'Hamilton," *Daily*

Beast, April 16, 2016, http://www.thedailybeast.com/articles/2016/04/16/the-exhausting-and-useless-accusations-of-racism-against-hamilton.html.

33. "*Hamilton* Hits a New High," *New York Times*, November 28, 2016; Ken Meyer, "You Lost! Get Over It! Trump Supporter Disrupts *Hamilton* Performance in Chicago," *Mediaite*, November 20, 2016, http://www.mediaite.com/online/you-lost-get-over-it-trump-supporter-disrupts-hamilton-performance-in-chicago/nd.

34. Robert Viagas, "Democrats and Republicans Find Something to Agree On: A Broadway Musical," *Playbill*, March 20, 2016; Hughes, "Utah Politicos *Hamilton* Carpool Karoake."

CHAPTER 15

"Safe in the Nation We've Made"

Staging Hamilton *on Social Media*

CLAIRE BOND POTTER

On the morning of July 9, 2016, the *Hamilton* Family, or #HamFam as they like to call themselves, was holding its collective breath until the moment when Lin-Manuel Miranda would take his final bow as Alexander Hamilton at New York's Richard Rogers Theatre. From his Washington Heights apartment, a space that Miranda's social media followers know well (he broadcast from there during the renovation and move-in, and occasionally checks in over morning coffee before beginning work), the star tapped out a tweet that suggested the day was giving him a few unaccustomed jitters. "Good morning!" he wrote. "Have your wits about you, it promises to be a bit of a day. Carry extra wits in case you lose 'em, that's what I do."[1] At 8:34, Miranda hit the baby-blue send button at the bottom of the message window.

In less than a minute, the #HamFam (also known as "Hamilton Trash," or #HamilTrash) was tweeting back its gratitude for Miranda's work on the show. "I've never met you, and I haven't had the honor of seeing Hamilton yet, but I'm still quite sad this is your last day," responded a female fan, whose profile described her as "young, scrappy, and hungry." A policy director for a Washington think tank equated Hamilton with a hit musical from the 1960s that had come to symbolize a utopian moment in American liberal politics. "Don't let it be forgot that once there was a spot, for one brief shining moment that was known as #Hamilot," he freestyled.

324

"Thanks for everything." Seconds later, @riseupramsay pleaded with Miranda to broadcast the final curtain call on the live streaming app Periscope. In fact, for a decade Miranda has used YouTube, Facebook Live, Periscope, and a (now defunct) video app called Vine to share and archive his thoughts, creative meanderings, #Ham4Ham stage door performances, his family life, and backstage horseplay between cast members. Prior to his exit from the show, two other performances had been filmed for posterity. But although there are plenty of extras and outtakes available to fans, Miranda never posts anything from the live performances that his Broadway audience has waited for months, and paid dearly, to see. That evening would be no exception.

As Miranda headed off to prepare for his final show, the #Ham-Fam was left to talk among themselves, trade reminiscences, and discuss some of their favorite Miranda moments. In a common language learned from the libretto and from each other, fans with Twitter handles like @A(dot)Ham, @SUNRISELAURENS, @pamilton, and @ham4fan shared memories, reposted favorite videos, and generally did their part to sustain the nation of *Hamilton* fans that they—and Miranda—had made. Some fans had followed Miranda since his first great Broadway success, *In the Heights*, nine years earlier; others were newly minted #HamilTrash eager to impress veterans with their knowledge of the show, *Hamilton* gossip, tidbits of information about its cast, and nicknames for its stars.

Although fan communities are hardly new, and are common on the Internet, Miranda participates in online fan activities to an extraordinary extent. His skillful use of social media and devotion to digital community helps to explain why *Hamilton* has become such a ubiquitous cultural phenomenon, and why the show's popularity has spread so rapidly beyond Broadway. But how fans participate in the excitement of a show most have never seen also helps us think about how the Internet, and specifically social media, made history accessible and fun long before Miranda set Alexander Hamilton's life to music.

Hamilton's Digital Backstage

Perhaps the quintessential millennial performer in his ability to cross cultural, musical, and artistic categories, Miranda is also widely acknowledged as a social media genius. It is a sign of *Hamilton*'s enduring cultural impact that the #HamFam, which evolved from a fan community cultivated during the six years that Miranda developed the show, has continued to thrive and prosper in the many months since the star and original Broadway cast members Phillipa Soo, Daveed Diggs, Jonathon Groff, and Christopher Jackson have left the cast. One reason for this continued loyalty is Miranda's highly personal and daily communication with his 1.4 million Twitter and almost 900,000 Facebook followers, posts that often include other cast members. Miranda signals his commitment to fans by beginning every day with an inspirational, ritual good-morning tweet, and by firing off multiple tweets during the day. When he was starring in *Hamilton*, Miranda was sometimes still answering questions and joking with cast members on a live backstage video feed minutes before the opening bars of the show's first number.

In return for this backstage access, the #HamFam provides a robust and free publicity network, one that rebroadcasts the star's utterances and news about the show through numerous, unofficial, *Hamilton*-themed social media accounts. In their spare time, fans generate their own content: memes, mash-ups, images, parodies, and tribute videos that they also share on these platforms. In addition to being a site for pleasure and play, the #HamFam functions as an American Revolution–themed grassroots constituency for the multimillion-dollar *Hamilton* franchise (which includes *Hamilton* merchandise, a cast album, a cover album, and a book) as Miranda creates new companies across the United States and Europe. While Miranda's original fans from *In the Heights* form the nucleus of the #HamFam, the even larger social media network that has developed during *Hamilton*'s initial two-year run is fueling an expanded fan base for the star's new, and very different, post-Broadway projects. Some of those projects, like the children's animated feature film *Moana* (2017), the first release in a multimovie deal with the

Walt Disney Company, were in development even while Miranda was performing in *Hamilton*; *Moana*'s release within months of Miranda's exit from the play has burnished his reputation as a creative dynamo.

Like every cultural product, *Hamilton* has well-regulated, corporate, social media accounts that release official news about the show. But Miranda's own accounts are distinctly anticorporate, and his direct, authentic connection to fans recognizes and acknowledges their investment in his creativity. When the cast album came out, "it democratized everything," Miranda told *Rolling Stone*'s Mark Binelli. "It was just a week of answering questions on Twitter, watching people decode it" and seeing the show's success "amplify online."[2] Miranda's digital utterances and performances reflect a spirit of impish creativity that is sometimes crowd-sourced from the #HamFam: a live-streamed birthday kiss for Groff, an out gay man, was specifically requested by fans, who then demanded that Groff return the kiss on Miranda's birthday (he did). As a consequence, female fans in particular often seem to view the thirty-seven-year-old Miranda as an adorable, clever, and unpredictable child. Alongside this lighthearted sensibility, however, is a committed digital work ethic that has propelled Miranda's rise to theater and social media superstardom. Like many millennials, he is constantly online. He writes his own posts; records short videos of himself, his family, and friends; replies to and retweets fans; compliments fellow artists and members of the cast; and posts scraps of text that could be random thoughts, bits of conversation he has heard on the street, songs in the making—or all of these things.

These social media techniques create a spontaneous "backstage" connection to the fan base, a technique that some artists use to distinguish themselves from the thousands of other celebrities competing for attention in today's oversaturated, and highly groomed, multimedia environment.[3] To be perceived as truly authentic, the social media celebrity has to enjoy, and feed off of, the connection to fans, and Miranda clearly does. His tweets and video posts are remarkable for their playfulness, intentionality, humor, and sweetness. His friendship with Groff performs an antihomophobic sensibility, and seems to be one aspect of his feminism: it is worth noting that Miranda never engages in any sexualized horseplay that might be seen as inappropriate or harassing with the women in the cast. He supports liberal causes, like Planned Parenthood, and raised money for Hillary Clinton in 2016. At the same time, he has also worked to avoid the vitriol that infects online political speech. "I try to stay as up-to-date on what's going on in the world as possible and yet provide an oasis of positivity on Twitter," he told one interviewer, even as social media—and the streets—were exploding following Donald Trump's unexpected victory in the 2016 presidential election. "I can't control the world, but I can control what I put into the world, so I try to have my timeline be a pretty bright spot for folks who may be fighting great fights elsewhere."[4]

Miranda is producing a backstage digital archive that documents key aspects of *Hamilton*'s history, but the show's larger cultural history belongs to the #HamFam. Individual fans operate numerous Twitter, tumblr, Reddit, and Instagram accounts. The closed "*Hamilton* Memes and Things" Facebook group boasts over 50,000 members in the United States, Asia, and Europe; and the public "*Hamilton* the Musical Fans" Facebook clocks in at over 45,000 members. Fan interactions become particularly intense when the #HamFam marks significant turning points in the history of the show such as Groff's several departures and returns to the cast as George III; Miranda and the original cast's exit from the play in July 2016; Bernie Sanders's and Hillary Clinton's attendance just before the 2016 New York presidential primary; and the October 21, 2016, premiere of *Hamilton's America* (otherwise known as #Hamildoc) on PBS's *Great Performances*. Fans commemorate these moments by riffing on anthems drawn from the show. On the day of Miranda's final performance, users exchanged lines from "One Last Time," a song from Act II in which Hamilton and Washington teach Americans "how to say goodbye" to their first president, reassuring their countrymen and women that, as Miranda and Chris Jackson sing in duet, "They'll be safe in the nation we've made."

The #HamFam is, in fact, a nation within a nation, one that exists solely to celebrate, not only American history (as the #EduHam project and the resurgent sales of Ron Chernow's biography of Alexander Hamilton suggest), but Miranda and the fictionalized musical history he has conjured for them. Like prior fan communities— *Star Wars*, *Lord of the Rings*, and *Dr. Who* have devotees that long predate the Internet—*Hamilton* fans signal their dedication to the star, and to the nation he's made, by writing about their passion for the show, and making efforts to integrate *Hamilton* into their offline lives. This sometimes means visiting heritage sites and researching the American Revolution. But for many fans, learning "history" is a secondary interest to amplifying the world of the show by writing fan-fiction; posting memes and fictional text messages between *Hamilton*'s characters; bonding happily over how their obsession with *Hamilton* annoys friends and family members; debating the historical accuracy of its portrayals; and trading advice about how to weave the *Hamilton* fan experience into life's most important moments. "Do any of the people in this group have any *Hamilton*-related potential Prom proposals that I could do?" asked one teenage fan. "I tried thinking of something, but other than 'I won't throw away my shot to go to Prom with you,' I can't really think of others." Thirteen other fans of various ages responded with advice. In subsequent posts, teens displayed handmade invitations that urged a prospective date to "take a break" and go to prom; that going to prom "would be enough"; and that prom would "tell the story of tonight." One young woman promised her boyfriend to "stop singing *Hamilton* if you go with me. Prom?"[5]

Social media practitioners, or the "people formerly known as the audience," have become self-conscious cocreators of the *Hamilton* phenomenon.[6] Furthermore, the activities of the *Hamilton* fan community remind us that history—commonly perceived as an intellectual practice made up of facts, analysis, political lessons, and uniform standards that must be met by schoolchildren—can be a potent space for play and feeling, as well as for education and profit. A visit to the #HamFam's digital world should also provoke academic historians to consider how the profession may keep, or lose, its audience based on our capacity to entertain, as well as to spark serious conversations that enhance our knowledge and understanding of the past. "History texts are often snoozers because they require students to learn the vocabulary of a different era," complains executive Ted Devine in a marketing trade publication. He urges his own peers to scrutinize and learn from the popular enthusiasm Miranda has generated for "a boring industry" like U.S. history.[7] Do we also need to learn to rap? Perhaps.

This is, of course, the kind of talk that can give my fellow scholars hives. But it shouldn't, since we also know that historical scholarship often makes a significant impact beyond the campus when presented as fictionalized entertainment, live performance, memoir, game, or fantasy. Narrative formats designed to entertain create opportunities to escape the complexities of contemporary life, fantasize about the past, and even imagine a more satisfying future. As public historian Mike Wallace has noted, "Walt Disney has taught people more history, in a more memorable way, than they ever learned in school."[8] Is it any accident that the corporation that dominates popular history has recruited Miranda? No.

The *Hamilton* phenomenon—powered by massive amounts of content distributed for free on social media—may, in the end, far exceed the success of Disney's historical entertainments, all of which cost money and sometimes require the additional expense of travel to theme parks. Powered by the creative possibilities of easy to use apps, tools, and platforms, the #HamFam views the early American world Miranda has conjured as their own, customized, *Hamilton*-themed experience. In the virtual nation they've made, they fact-check and do close readings of the show; confess their feelings about events that occurred in America's founding moments; imagine how the characters would react to twenty-first-century dilemmas; crowd-source school projects about the period; post primary documents and interpretations of *The Federalist Papers*; and document their pilgrimages to heritage sites like The Grange, Alexander Hamilton's grave at Trinity Church, and the Weehawken dueling ground.[9]

The #HamFam is, therefore, an important factor, not just in a revival of interest in early American history, but in *Hamilton*'s contemporary history as a Broadway mega-hit. Arguably, the fan community's collective creative output is as or more important than the play itself, because far more people are participating in it than will ever see the show. In the future, the #HamFam archive will also be crucial to understanding the impact of the play on how "history" has been distributed and consumed as both elite and popular entertainment in the early years of the digital twenty-first century.

By their very nature, modern Broadway productions are socially and economically exclusive, and destined to become more so as the cost of producing them rises. Unlike television, the Internet, subsidized heritage sites and museums that welcome the public at a nominal cost, or presidential biographies that can be purchased at heavy discounts, Broadway's math is all wrong as a distribution model for popular history. A live, hit show can never be reproduced fast enough or cheaply enough for a mass audience. *Hamilton* may, in fact, have accelerated the inaccessibility of quality theater by reminding audiences how exciting a live performance can be. In 2014 the average cost of a ticket surpassed $100 for the first time in history; box office prices for the best seats at *Hamilton* would exceed $1,000 by May 2016.[10] The market for tickets to see the touring companies, driven in part by a frenzied national fan community, supports higher than normal regional prices as well. In spring 2017, a colleague in San Francisco noted miserably on Facebook that, despite going to the ticket site twenty minutes after tickets went on sale, "I was immediately told that I was approximately 60,000th in line and if I kept my browser open I would remain on the queue. A few hours later, now about 50,000th in line, I received a message that the advance tickets were sold out."[11] It is not exactly true that one cannot get tickets to the show: being willing and able to pay an exorbitant price on the secondary market will get anyone in the door. Tickets are available for hundreds, or even thousands, of dollars at StubHub.com and other ticket sites for almost any night a prospective audience member might want to attend.

Carrying bedrolls, pillows, and take-out food containers, many *Hamilton* fans wait outside the theater for days to get tickets offered to the public once they are declined by members of the cast and crew. *(June 21, 2016, Spencer Platt/Getty Images)*

In contrast, historical writings, art, and heritage sites that reflect Alexander Hamilton's world are normally available for free or at minimal cost. Encouraging the *Hamilton* fan community to steer their passion for the show toward more traditional "histories" signals Miranda's genuine desire to have *Hamilton* be not just be an engine for enormous profits, but also an incitement to civic education. His efforts to make the show accessible to those without means by distributing extra content across multiple platforms, holding a day-of-show ticket lottery, posting the cast album to a PBS platform and then to YouTube, forging a collaboration with the Gilder Lehrman and Rockefeller Foundations that brings schoolchildren to the play as part of a curriculum initiative, and refraining from filing desist orders on copyright infringements by fans exhibit Miranda's intellectual generosity.

These efforts also emphasize the actual play's inaccessibility to a mass audience. In order for *Hamilton* to make a major cultural impact, as well as the profits that would sustain its creative project and fuel a resurgent Broadway economy, Miranda had to be generous with the show, and also acknowledge its limits. He had to cultivate and expand the audience of people who love history and historical entertainments, a project that ensured that most of his fans would probably never have the chance to see Miranda, or anyone else, perform the role of Alexander Hamilton on stage.

Making History on the Internet

History has been a staple social media genre since blogging became popularized in the 1990s. By 2005, people like myself had discovered that the free platforms provided by Word Press and Blogger provided unfettered space to write history and historical commentary for each other and for a general audience. Together, historians who blogged blurred the boundaries between work and fun, extending the audience for our endeavors well beyond academia.[12] Since then, social media has organized every corner of many historians' lives. We have professional debates about issues that used to be the stuff of department gossip on Facebook. Currently, nearly every history department, historical association, conference, and museum has its own Facebook, Twitter, and Instagram accounts. Many formerly independent history bloggers now blog and podcast on major media platforms; and in 2017 the *Washington Post* launched a history blog. Professional historians who tweet have acquired an identity and a nickname: #twitterstorians.

Inevitably, digital technology is changing how history is written and taught, making it more accessible to so-called amateurs. In addition to traditional libraries that are putting collections on line, the Internet Archive is a goldmine of primary sources, blogs, and live performances. Activist groups like Chicago Women's Liberation, ACT UP, and #OccupyWallStreet are storing their own records, manifestos, oral histories, and images on open-access websites. While difficult to search, Facebook accounts can be downloaded and preserved, and tweets can be converted into a historical narrative through an app called Storify. In 2010, the Library of Congress inked a deal with Twitter to preserve the vast output of its users. Amateur and professional historians are also experimenting with new narrative forms distributed primarily on Twitter, Instagram, and Snapchat. Twitter accounts like BBC World War 1 (@bbcww1), World War II Today (@WWIIToday), and Hideki Tojo (@Japanese_Chief) report historical events as if they were happening in real time. Dead Presidents talk to each other through ghost accounts. "Way to make the rest of us look bad," President William H. Taft (@bathtublegacy) recently tweeted to Franklin D. Roosevelt. "Nice work with, well, everything. Though four terms seems a little bit like showing off." @PresFDR liked and retweeted it.[13]

Professionally produced history has now been available on the Internet for almost thirty years in one form or another. Today, historical media includes podcasts; channels that universities maintain on YouTube where an entire semester of history lectures originally given in an Ivy League lecture hall can be consumed at leisure; online classes produced by the History Channel; and Massive Open Online Courses (MOOCs). These historical materials respond to a range of desires: lifelong learning, home schooling, entertainment, and satisfying the anxieties of those who need to feel their time is well used on the treadmill or in the car. Though some academic historians see any or all of these materials as a potential threat to bricks-and-mortar education, and none seem to be particularly profitable, universities and individual scholars often view the free distribution of their work as good publicity, a form of public service, and a method for making the American classroom a more accessible, global, and cosmopolitan space. Education journalist Anya Kamenetz, a proponent of digital learning, goes further. School, she argues, is an increasingly scarce and expensive resource. We must "fundamentally change the way higher education is delivered or resign ourselves to never having enough of it."[14]

Another way of encountering the past on the Internet is through commercial, or "people's history," a genre written or performed in the language of ordinary folk that is (as several chapters in this book illustrate) closely related to Miranda's vision for *Hamilton*. This ranges from serious crowd-sourced endeavors like *Wikipedia* (which boasts over 30 million English-language users, and 141,000 unpaid active editors and writers generating around 800 new articles a day), to digital humanities projects, multiplayer gaming, hobby websites, school projects, and videos produced by students, artists, actors, and singers.[15] Some of these, like *Hamilton*, narrate the distant past in contemporary terms. Comedy writer Brad Neely began his career with a crudely drawn historical cartoon narrated by mouth-breathing white rappers who told George Washington's story in two minutes and twenty-three seconds. "Washington, Washington, six foot eight, weighs a fucking ton," it begins. "Opponents beware, opponents beware. He's coming, he's coming, he's coming." Since it was posted in 2009, it has had over 4.3 million views. A YouTube series launched in 2015 by the Comedy Channel called *Drunk History* features celebrities relating key moments in history like Watergate, the Astor Place Riot, and the Burr–Hamilton duel, as they become progressively more inebriated. In "Harriet Tubman Leads an Army of Bad Bitches" (2.2 million views since September 2015), comedian Crissle West relates Tubman's offer to spy for the Union and a colonel's reply: "'Yeah, obviously *my* white ass can't go down there. Absolutely you can be a spy. You go down there and do what the (bleep) you do.' So she was like, 'Okay, let me put on my field hand clothes.'"[16]

The vast majority of *Hamilton* fans under the age of forty will also have been exposed to digital archives, public history sites, Ancestry .com, or a digital supplement to a textbook for education and entertainment. In the last two decades of the twentieth century, the ability to make documents and "facts" generated by marginalized groups universally available has helped social history reshape high school curricula to reflect a more class and racially diverse past, even as conservatives have fought to retain traditional top-down narratives. In 1989, the American Social History Project/Center for Media and Learning at the City University of New York made primary documents available in a multimedia digital disc format as a supplement to the first volume of their social history textbook *Who Built America? Working People and the Nation's History*. Ten years later, ASHP/

CML built a web platform to contain an even larger collection of videos, documents, and visual resources, paving the way for a transformation in the history textbook industry toward multimedia formats that inspired critical thinking and research.[17]

For these reasons, creative storytelling and digital research, as well as entertainment, were early selling points for personal computers. Video games, sometimes framed as educational, allowed players to immerse themselves in historical dramas, and research libraries began to put selected documents on the web for patrons to access remotely. A computer industry video produced in the mid-1990s emphasized that these two innovations were linked: if the successful completion of homework depended on access to the Internet, children would become confident of their digital skills through gaming. White suburban parents featured in the video note their children's "improved grades" since the computer arrived; to demonstrate this, their son clicks to sites he visited for a research paper on the Wright brothers.[18] Research was an extension of, and indistinguishable from, an online game. The Internet and personal computing, the video suggests, had achieved the unimaginable: making writing a high school history paper fun.

Professional historians sometimes worry that ease of access will make the past, as it exists in books, archives, and museums, seem dull and lifeless by comparison to the Internet's offerings. However, *Hamilton* fans' willingness to abandon their screens and explore the tangible artifacts of the Republic's founding moments, as Miranda did when he was writing the show, suggests otherwise. Public historians know that the past can be at its most exciting when a book, a website, or a performance is in conversation with places and material objects that can be touched, toured, observed, and inhaled. A virtual history site can serve as an enticement to a first visit, or a reflective return, to historical objects, art, a public history exhibit, or a heritage site. Although public historians, archivists, and curators "initially viewed the Internet with suspicion," as Tim Grove of the National Air and Space Museum recalled in 2009, they soon learned that a digital presence enticed more visitors than ever before.[19] A tombstone, a grass-covered slope where Confederate troops dug in as they covered the retreat from Atlanta, the smoky odor of an historic eighteenth-century home, the terrifying sight of slave manacles, a child's doll, or a chair "where George Washington sat" (this is a frequent feature of historic homes like Strawberry Mansion in Philadelphia, where I grew up) can send both historian and history fan tumbling back in time.

Much has been made of Lin-Manuel Miranda's archival and secondary research into Alexander Hamilton's life and times, and his visits to heritage sites, while he adapted Ron Chernow's *Alexander Hamilton* for the stage.[20] Far less attention has been paid to the fact that his fans do these things too, in part because Miranda has alerted them to history in plain sight: *The Federalist Papers*, The Grange, Trinity Church, and the Weehawken dueling ground. Miranda's social media activity and sense of fun encourages a dynamic interplay between fans' fantasies about the past and historical facts, a genuine *Hamilton* experience that fans can have without ever having to enter the theater. Best of all, they have already inhabited Alexander Hamilton's world through the music and lyrics of the show. "Diehard fans" know, *Huffington Post* columnist Katherine Brooks wrote, that you don't need to see *Hamilton* "to love it. . . . But wait! Don't despair. Because you can listen to the Grammy-winning album. In fact, a lot of devoted fans haven't even caught the show on Broadway. But the album is so. So. Great."[21] Critical to generating mass excitement about the show, therefore, was—as public historians learned about their own collections—putting the sound track into a public domain first on the PBS web site and then on YouTube, where *Hamilton* could mesh seamlessly with the digital historical materials that had paved the way for its success.

It Must Be Nice to Have the Internet on Your Side

In the second act of *Hamilton*, Jefferson and Madison, temporarily thwarted by the president's predilection for his Revolutionary War comrade Hamilton, sing irritably that "It must be nice to have / Washington on your side." Similarly, although musical theater giants like Andrew Lloyd Webber have established long-running franchises, Lin-Manuel Miranda's career as a Broadway hit-maker has coincided neatly with the maturity of the Internet and with the rise of free social media as a daily form of communication and publicity for any successful product, literary career, social justice movement, educational institution, political campaign, or news organization. In 2008, when Miranda's first hit, *In the Heights*, moved to Broadway following its success at the Public Theater, 34 percent of American adults had a home Internet connection, and 25 percent of all American adults had at least one social media account. By 2015, when *Hamilton* spent less than five months Off-Broadway before moving to the Richard Rodgers Theatre, 65 percent of adults (most of whom were now accessing social media though mobile apps) and 76 percent of adults with a home Internet connection were using multiple social media platforms that included text images, feeds, and live video. Teenagers were even better prepared to tweet, post, and create mash-up videos about *Hamilton*. In 2015, 92 percent of teens reported that they were online every day, and a whopping 24 percent admitted that they were "online 'almost constantly.'"[22]

But being a member of the #HamFam is about more than connectivity: it's about the unexpected thrill of having access to Miranda. Walking down 17th Street in Manhattan one morning, I hear Periscope's distinctive two-note chirp. Perhaps because my iPhone is stuffed in my back pocket, the app activates automatically and I hear a familiar tone: it's Lin! There are few voices I know better nowadays. When we signed the contract for this book, I began listening to *Hamilton* everywhere I went, nearly every day, making a spectacle of myself by muttering rhymes committed to memory under my breath and responding to friends with lyrics well known to all of us. I whip out my iPhone, and there is Lin-Manuel Miranda: both he and I are plugged in with white Apple ear buds, as if we are Facetiming. Except, of course, we aren't alone: there are thousands of other fans logged on, asking questions that Miranda is answering as fast as he can.

I look at the screen: Periscope's updraft of hearts is bubbling up, as fans approve Miranda's whimsical flights of fancy and patient, often funny, responses to their questions. Although he had left the show weeks earlier, like Alexander Hamilton, he was still fully in charge, updating fans on permanent companies opening in Chicago and New York, and hinting at projects in the works. Urging us to donate money so that more schoolchildren could see *Hamilton*, he reported that 20,000 students had already attended in New York and 5,000 were scheduled to attend in Chicago. He updated us on the producers' ongoing efforts to fight ticket counterfeiters and scalpers; and, spinning his device slowly around the room, gave us a video tour of his home office—"the room where it happens," as one might say. The camera's lens paused briefly on a drawing by Miranda's two-year-old son Sebastian, and even more briefly on a pile of notebooks and papers: "Oops! You can't see any of that," Miranda grinned at us. "It's top secret." Hearts gushed upward.

The story of Hamilton fandom is not complete without an account of Miranda's skillful adoption of live-streaming apps and the live-streaming features added to well-established social media like Twitter and Facebook. They have allowed him to establish relationships with fans by broadcasting informal moments, his creative process, videos of his domestic life, spontaneous goofing around with friends and cast members, and live "backstage" antics. One evening I watched Chris Jackson put on his Washington costume, in a kind of reverse strip tease, as he answered questions from fans. Simultaneously, Miranda was bellowing songs from Beyoncé's hit album *Lemonade* outside the dressing room, and demanding to be let in. Gender switching is another favorite gag: in a #Ham4Ham stage door performance, three of the "kings"—Groff, Brian d'Arcy James, and Andrew Rannells (also an openly gay actor), sashay onto the street to screams of delight, wearing their crowns and lip synching and camping to the Schuyler sisters' anthem from Act I, while Renée Elise Goldsberry, who originated the role of Angelica, emcees and plays the role of Aaron Burr.[23] These videos can then be relived endlessly as part of the show's official YouTube archive. On any given evening these live broadcasts are, ever so briefly, exclusive to the #HamFam. People lucky enough to be sitting in the audience of *Hamilton* cannot, by definition, see them in real time, although once bitten by the *Hamilton* bug they may subsequently seek out the archive and add to it.

Cultivating social media spaces where fans can play is a long-standing practice for sports, film, and television celebrities, but it is relatively new for the theater. After *In the Heights* closed, and while Miranda was researching, writing, and workshopping *Hamilton*, he cultivated fan investment in the new project by dropping hints about what he was doing. An early, and now iconic, tweet from 2008 showed him swinging in a beach hammock reading the Chernow biography. In addition to the passionate, raw "Hamilton Mixtape" premiere at the November 2009 White House poetry event, Miranda constantly "leaked" evidence about his creative process, snippets of songs in their early stages, and musings about the historical figures in the show. New York City itself is Miranda's primary muse: many of his videos and images feature him composing and dancing in public places around Manhattan and the Bronx, and on the subway. One of my favorites is a short Vine of the artist lying in the grass at a city park, wearing ear buds. With his dog looking on, Miranda "performs" a creative block. Staring at the sky, he chants: "C'mon brain! Think of things! C'mon brain! Think of things! C'mon brain! Be so smart!" Fans enthused about how comforting they found it that their artist and hero struggled just as they did to realize his ambitions. "This was in my head the whole time I was doing my history exam," KawaiiBro responded in the comments section. "We were learning about the American Revolution."[24]

Miranda worked to call a *Hamilton* fan community into being long before the show opened: literary agents call this developing a platform. The #HamFam, while not an entirely digital phenomenon, reflects a baked-in tendency of the early Internet toward community building. Enthusiasts bond through fantasy, intellectual debate, play and other common interests communicated through

shared language and symbols. This has also gone in the other direction: *The Lord of the Rings* had so many fans among coders and the
tech community that some of Tolkien's language and symbolism
migrated into their work.

When it comes to history, this kind of community building
experience can play out as factual, fictional, or some mix of the two.
Lovers of history can be consumed by an obsession with a treasured,
perhaps romanticized—even a completely skewed—story about the
past. Scholarship can correct such obsessions, or feed them. Drew
Gilpin Faust has pointed to the "seductions" and pleasures of written
military history, a scholarly field that has always sold briskly with
general audiences and that may, she warns, give so much pleasure that
it deludes its fans about war's human costs and inoculates them to the
violence of military conflicts. Although Faust never explicitly uses
the word "fan," Tony Horwitz does so repeatedly in his descriptions
of the researcher-performers who make up the contemporary Civil
War reenactor community. Every American conflict prior to the
Korean War has an established and diverse fan community: hobby-
ists, reenactors, tourists, and amateur researchers thrived alongside
scholars long before they moved onto YouTube, Facebook, Instagram, and Twitter. History-of-war media entertainments range from
television and film to scholarly and popular literature; role-playing
games like SEGA's *Napoleon: Total War*; and the vast "edutainment"
industry of heritage sites, monuments, museums, and parks devoted
to memorializing war.[25]

A fictional television show or movie franchise offers endless
details, and remembering these details is the essence of being a good
fan. Produced in set narratives with defined characters that fans can
embrace, successful fandom is defined by inhabiting these characters
accurately (for example, some diehard *Lord of the Rings* fans have
taken to surgically reshaping their ears to better resemble elves).[26]
History offers other possibilities: tantalizing gaps, unexplored evidence, and unknown motivations that are just as exciting to the
reenactor as they are to the scholar. This creates openings for history fans to speculate about how they might have responded to a

historical crisis, inhabited a past world, or what might have been different if Alexander Hamilton had said no to Maria Reynolds. But the #HamFam also draws on established fan traditions. As interest in *Hamilton* surged in its first year on Broadway, a whole industry bloomed on the Internet to support historical fantasies based on the play. Continental Army uniforms, Schuyler sisters dresses, and generic "founders' costumes" bloomed on eBay, Etsy, and the websites of big-box stores. Fans began to costume themselves, record themselves singing covers of the songs, and post videos of reimagined encounters from the nation's founding moments.

As Miranda moves on to new projects, these fans are playing a critical role in ushering *Hamilton* into its new, mature phase as a corporate Broadway institution by creating Internet spaces where the #HamFam can welcome new members. Creating spaces for play, they are also producing battalions of future customers who will fuel a probable multidecade run for the show on the scale of hits like *Cats*, *The Phantom of the Opera*, *Chicago*, and *The Lion King*. *Hamilton* is on track to do much better, much earlier, than any of these

Hamilton fans in costume attend BroadwayCon 2016 at New York's Hilton Midtown on January 22, 2016. *(John Lamparski/WireImage)*

productions. A musical that cost $12.5 million to mount was grossing over $1.9 million a week in ticket sales alone by June 2016, and was on track to make unprecedented profits for its author, original cast, and investors. "Even if *Hamilton* isn't playing in Bangkok decades after its debut (as was the case with *Phantom of the Opera*)," wrote Michael Paulson and David Gelles of the *New York Times*, "it's not unreasonable to expect that Mr. Miranda's unlikely hit will ultimately generate upward of $1 billion in sales." Merchandise—books, tee shirts, double CD sets, music streaming, books, tote bags, and other souvenirs, now being sold online and in a stand-alone store down the street from the Richard Rodgers Theatre, were expected to gross $15 million by the end of 2016.[27]

If the departure of the original New York cast brought the first phase of *Hamilton*'s history to a close, it created opportunities for a fresh crop of talented actors in New York, London, Chicago, and Los Angeles, and in touring companies. Many of the commenters who gathered to say goodbye to Miranda on July 9 may suspect that their digital connection to the star is more intimate and satisfying than actually witnessing a live performance, although they would like that too. "@Lin_Manuel you should Periscope again tonight so we can all sob together," @riseupramsay wrote. The #HamFam also expressed a sense of ownership and responsibility for ensuring the peaceful transition of power between the old and the new cast (many of whom had been understudies) that would allow their nation to endure.

Social media is a crucial place for twenty-first century community building but as we know, platforms like Facebook and Twitter are also spaces where grievances and conflict erupt, and during the 2016 election year, political conflict spiked. Hamilton's fan community is unusually capable of bridging partisan differences, as Renee Romano has pointed out in her essay in this volume, but this is partly because they don't permit political bickering. "There are Ten Group Commandments," moderator "George W. Frederick III" declared in a pinned post on the "*Hamilton* the Musical Fans" Facebook. The first two insist on civility, and the third commandment bans partisanship. "Posts on modern politics are gonna be erased," George III promises; "A ban's in place, so show restraint before an admin has to moderate / This is a public forum, so respect each other's views / So most disputes die with no misuse."[28] Experience suggests that this is a wise precaution; when Miranda and *Hamilton* cast members break the fourth wall in real life, the happy consensus that *Hamilton* speaks to everyone can dissolve. Ten days after Donald J. Trump's victory ended a brutal eighteen-month presidential campaign, the president-elect took to Twitter to chastise the new cast for having read a statement to Vice President-elect Mike Pence expressing their hope that the new administration would "uphold our American values" and "work on behalf of all of us."[29]

In other words, when Miranda and the cast leave the fictionalized past and speak to the political present, their own, deeply felt, identity politics—gay, of color, feminist—can not only raise hackles but also break the fantasy that the #HamFam is a peaceful and unified nation that exists to support Miranda's creative output. This fact, in turn, suggests that the apparent universal appeal of the show may depend, in part, on its light touch when it comes to early American racism, sexism, and nativism, and its emphasis on a rich republican past, overflowing with ideas and ideals that transcend human differences. It is notable, for example, that openly gay actors are prominent in the show, but that John Laurens, whose intense and romantic correspondence with Hamilton has prompted rumors of eighteenth-century same-sex love, is simply one of the tomcatting guys in *Hamilton*'s first act.

Similarly, three weeks after the Pence controversy, Miranda partnered with Prizeo to raffle off *Hamilton* tickets for those who donated as little as $10 to Planned Parenthood Federation of America, where his mother, Dr. Luz Townes-Miranda, serves on the board of the national political action division. Miranda's two previous Prizeo campaigns, for the Hispanic Federation and the Gilder Lehrman Institute for American History, had raised $2 million and drawn little public attention. Many comments on the Planned Parenthood post praised him for supporting women's reproductive health, and the

Hamilton raffle drew myriad hopeful fans. But other commenters expressed keen disappointment that Miranda would endorse abortion, and attacked him on *Hamilton*'s various fan Facebooks for "politicizing" the show by associating it with a feminist organization and reproductive choice, a right-wing lightning rod. Negative comments were repeatedly taken down, but those of us who were watching saw bitter fans, some bristling with racism, vow that they would never see the show now that it had become associated with abortion. Alexander Hamilton himself, some posted, might have been aborted had Planned Parenthood existed in the eighteenth century; in fact, cast members, they sneered, should not support an agency that would have happily aborted *them* if it had had the chance.[30]

Hamilton Nation

Regardless of whether audiences have learned history from *Hamilton*, and it seems that many have, does fandom actually translate a love for history into the liberal cultural politics to which Miranda himself is committed? Probably not, even though fans clearly see an alternative to their frustration with contemporary Washington gridlock in *Hamilton*'s depiction of a Constitution that survives despite its flaws; compromises between rivals Jefferson and Hamilton that benefit the new nation; Hamilton's endorsement of Jefferson's presidency despite their differences; and Jefferson's praise of Hamilton's achievements in the final moments of the show. For example, @BetseySHamilton, who uses a painting of Elizabeth Schuyler Hamilton as her profile picture, clearly views Hamilton's world as a useful platform for her liberal views, even though Hamilton would have more in common with contemporary conservatives. She keeps up a lively feminist political patter, blending retweets from Hillary Clinton with quotes from primary documents (many of which were originally tweeted by Yale historian Joanne Freeman, a consultant to the show); her #HamFam network; and Miranda's tweets, backstage shots, and videos.

Perhaps because of the strength of this fan community, and its ubiquity on social media, the *Hamilton* craze has not only survived the departure of all the original cast members, but thrived as lesser known actors populate the roles in multiple companies. In early October 2016, *Time* magazine proclaimed the birth of "Hamilton Nation."[31] Nations become real through the circulation of sacred texts that inspire emotion: Washington's Farewell Address or Miranda's Farewell Tweet; a #Ham4Ham video; Ron Chernow's original biography; or the score and libretto of *Hamilton* itself. Such nations are, as Benedict Anderson dubbed them prior to the Internet, "imagined communities" of simultaneous experience, expressed through a common language, history, set of cultural artifacts, and literature.[32]

Enabling people to imagine new communities is work that social media does exceptionally well, on a massive scale, and for free. But it offers the #HamFam something in return: an authentic and deeply felt connection to Miranda. It also offers the satisfaction of knowing that, although the show is comfortingly identical every night, the *Hamilton* phenomenon is driven by their creative energy, Miranda's endless capacity to broadcast new material, and a refreshed appreciation for America's past that is quite genuine. Questions, interests, and themes derived from the libretto have inspired a new affinity for traditional American national fetish objects like *The Federalist Papers*: when I checked in March 2017, several editions were nearly sold out on Amazon, and readers were giving it 4.5 (out of 5) stars – pretty good for 200 year-old political theory! But fans are as likely to bond over sacred texts that they fashion themselves: parodies and covers of *Hamilton* songs posted to YouTube, homemade memes, and mashups of cast member photos. Consciously performing their citizenship in a nation within the nation *Hamilton* celebrates, fans are linked by their love for Miranda, his love for them, and a new, if sometimes not entirely factually accurate, appreciation for the intricacies of the eighteenth-century world that the show has conjured for them.

Years from now, it may seem like a strange conceit to compare Lin-Manuel Miranda's 140-character departure from the role of Alexander Hamilton to George Washington's Farewell Address. The moment will also be hard to recapture, since understanding the history of any social media event relies on reproducing the pace and the timing of exchanges, thrilling and rich with meaning in the moment, but often puzzling and flat when narrated after the fact. Unlike the linear trajectory of a traditional archive, or even digital collections like email, the stories social media tells are notoriously nonlinear and frail; they become suddenly visible and, just as suddenly, are swallowed up and concealed by the next trending topic. Despite these difficulties, the #HamFam's social media channels are part of the show's history, and they are part of the discussion about history that the show provokes. They have much to tell us about the significance of *Hamilton*'s popularity, not as a narrative past with merits and absences so obvious to the historians in this volume, but as a place of cultural belonging and comfort at a moment when real politics, often played out on the same social media channels, could not have been more divisive. Social media filter bubbles may be a malevolent force in contemporary political culture, but *Hamilton* reminds us that those same bubbles are a powerful engine for community.

NOTES

1. @Lin_Manuel, tweet, 8:34, July 9, 2016. Last viewed September 22, 2016. Replies, and handles that follow, are all taken from the thread begun by Miranda.

2. Mark Binelli, "'Hamilton' Creator Lin Manuel-Miranda: The Rolling Stone Interview," *Rolling Stone*, June 1, 2016, http://www.rollingstone.com/music/features/hamilton-creator-lin-manuel-miranda-the-rolling-stone-interview-20160601, accessed May 13, 2017.

3. Alice Marwick and danah boyd, "To See and Be Seen: Celebrity Practice on Twitter," *Convergence* 17, no. 2 (2011): 139–158.

4. Alice E. Marwick and danah boyd, "I Tweet Honestly, I Tweet Passionately: Twitter Users, Context Collapse, and the Imagined Audience," *New Media and Society* 20 no. 10 (July 2010): 1–20; Miranda quoted in Hayden Wright, "Lin Manuel-Miranda Talks Trump, Oscars, and Social Media," *radio.com*, January 12, 2017, http://radio.com/2017/01/12/lin-manuel-miranda-trump-oscars-social-media/, accessed February 5, 2017.

5. Hamilton Memes and Things Facebook, Zachary Judkins, March 16, 2017, 9 P.M.; Hunter Lyons, March 16, 2017, 10:41 A.M.; Jasmine Wright, February 7, 2017.

6. Jay Rosen, "The People Formerly Known as the Audience," *Press Think: Ghost of Democracy in the Media Machine*, June 27, 2006, http://archive.press think.org/2006/06/27/ppl_frmr.html, accessed October 23, 2016.

7. Ted Devine, "5 Smart Marketing Lessons from 'Hamilton,'" *Inc.*, June 6, 2016, http://www.inc.com/ted-devine/5-marketing-lessons-from-hamilton .html, accessed March 24, 2017.

8. Mike Wallace, *Mickey Mouse History and Other Essays on American Memory* (Philadelphia: Temple University Press, 1996), 134.

9. J. Courtney Sullivan, "After the Broadway Show, a Trip to Hamilton's Grave," *New York Times*, March 5, 2016.

10. David Ng, "Average Cost of a Broadway Ticket Passes $100 for the First Time," *Los Angeles Times*, June 10, 2014, http://www.latimes.com/entertain ment/arts/la-et-cm-broadway-ticket-prices-20140610-story.html, accessed October 2 2016. Jesse Lawrence, "*Hamilton* Is Broadway's Most Expensive Show—Ever," *Daily Beast*, May 3, 2016, http://www.thedailybeast.com/articles/2016/ 05/03/hamilton-is-broadway-s-most-expensive-show-ever.html, accessed September 10, 2016.

11. Marc Stein, Facebook post, December 6, 2016.

12. Claire Bond Potter, "Thou Shalt Commit: The Internet, New Media, and the Future of Women's History," *Journal of Women's History* 25, no. 4 (Winter 2013): 353.

13. @bathtublegacy to @PresFDR, Twitter, April 25, 2017.

14. Jeremy Adelman, "History a la MOOC," *Perspectives on History* (March 2013), https://www.historians.org/publications-and-directories/perspectives-on -history/march-2013/history-a-la-mooc, accessed October 1, 2016; Anya Kamenetz, *DIY U: Edupunks, Edupreneurs, and the Coming Transformation of Higher Education* (White River Junction, VT: Chelsea Green, 2010), ix.

15. Wikipedia: s.v. statistics, https://en.wikipedia.org/wiki/Wikipedia: Statistics, accessed March 25, 2017.

16. Cox and Combes (Brad Neely), "George Washington," *Creased Comics*, YouTube, March 13, 2009, https://www.youtube.com/watch?v=l7iVsdRbhnc, accessed November 24, 2016. "Drunk History: Harriet Tubman Leads an Army of Bad Bitches," YouTube, September 23, 2015, https://www.youtube.com/ watch?v=VpTf1GFjCd8, accessed February 3, 2017.

17. Andrew Hartman, *A War for the Soul of America: A History of the Culture Wars* (Chicago: University of Chicago Press, 2015), 263–284; Christopher

Clark, Nancy Hewitt, Roy Rosenzweig, Nelson Lichtenstein, Joshua Brown, and David Jaffee, *Who Built America? Working People and the Nation's History*, 2 vols., 3rd ed. (New York: Bedford/St. Martin's Press, 2008) (1st ed. 1990 and 1992);. 2004 Annual Report of the American Social History Project/Center for Media and Learning, https://ashp.cuny.edu/sites/default/files/ar_2004.pdf, accessed December 12, 2016.

18. "The Kids' Guide to the Internet," produced by Frank Kilpatrick for Diamond Entertainment Corporation, https://www.youtube.com/watch?v=A 81IwlDeV6c, accessed October 4, 2016.

19. Tim Grove, "New Media and the Challenges for Public History," *Perspectives on History* (May 2009), https://www.historians.org/publications-and -directories/perspectives-on-history/may-2009/intersections-history-and-new -media/new-media-and-the-challenges-for-public-history, accessed September 24, 2016.

20. Rebecca Mead, "All About the Hamiltons," *The New Yorker*, February 9, 2015.

21. Katherine Brooks, "11 Things Every *Hamilton* Fan Wants You to Know," *Huffington Post*, January 31, 2017, http://www.huffingtonpost.com/entry/ham ilton-musical-fans_us_56c34d45e4b0c3c55052a5cd, accessed April 5, 2017.

22. Pew Research Center, "Social Media Usage: 2005–2015," October 8, 2015, http://www.pewinternet.org/2015/10/08/social-networking-usage-2005–20 15/, accessed August 4 2016. Amanda Lehart, "Teens, Social Media, and Technology Overview, 2015," *Pew Research Center: Internetand Technology*, April 9, 2015, http://www.pewinternet.org/2015/04/09/teens-social-media-technology -2015/, accessed August 4, 2016.

23. Crystal Bell, "Here Is How 'Hamilton' Is Radically Revolutionizing Fandom," *MTV News*, December 4, 2015, http://www.mtv.com/news/2680776/ hamilton-musical-revolutionizing-fandom/, accessed October 21, 2016; "#Ham 4Ham: Three Kings as Schuyler Sisters," YouTube, October 24, 2015, https:// www.youtube.com/watch?v=BuBaCpAzSK8, accessed September 12, 2016.

24. Lin-Manuel Miranda Vine, posted by TechGirlASmilz, YouTube, March 24, 2016, https://www.youtube.com/watch?v=TP9iNa8Aqeg, accessed August 12, 2016.

25. David Blight, *Race and Reunion: The Civil War in American Memory* (Cambridge, MA: Belknap Press of Harvard University Press, 2001); Drew Gilpin Faust, "'We Should Grow Too Fond of It: Why We Love the Civil War," *Civil War History* 50, no. 4 (2004): 373, 380–383; Tony Horwitz, *Confederates in the Attic: Dispatches from the Unfinished Civil War* (New York: Vintage, 1999); Wallace, *Mickey Mouse History*, 54, 165.

26. Laren Stover, "Another Variation on the Selfie: Get Ready for the Elfie," *New York Times*, August 21, 2017.

27. Michael Paulson and David Gelles, "'Hamilton' Inc.: The Path to a Billion-Dollar Broadway Show," *New York Times*, June 8, 2016.

28. George W. Frederick III, February 18, 2016, "Hamilton the Musical Fans" Public Group, https://www.facebook.com/groups/153617865021296/, accessed March 3, 2017.

29. Christopher Mele and Patrick Healy, "'Hamilton Had Some Unscripted Lines for Pence. Trump Wasn't Happy," *New York Times*, November 19, 2016; Eric Bradner, "Pence: 'I Wasn't Offended' by Message of 'Hamilton' Cast," *CNN Politics*, November 20, 2016, http://www.cnn.com/2016/11/20/politics/mike-pence-hamilton-message-trump/, accessed November 22, 2016.

30. "Lin-Manuel Miranda Teams with Prizeo for 'Hamilton' Experience to Benefit Planned Parenthood," *Hollywood Reporter*, December 6, 2016, http://www.hollywoodreporter.com/news/lin-manuel-miranda-teams-prizeo-hamilton-experience-benefit-planned-parenthood-953222?utm_source=facebook&utm_medium=post&utm_term=hamilton-december16&utm_content=healthfb, accessed December 15, 2016. Lin Manuel-Miranda Facebook page, December 7, 5:01 P.M., https://www.facebook.com/Lin-Manuel-Miranda-156195014444203/?hc_ref=SEARCH&fref=nf, accessed December 15, 2016. Prizeo Facebook post, December 7, 2016, 5:18 P.M., https://www.facebook.com/PrizeoUK/?hc_ref=SEARCH, accessed December 13, 2016.

31. Eliza Berman, "Hamilton Nation," *Time*, October 10, 2016.

32. Benedict Anderson, *Imagined Communities: Reflections on the Origin and Spread of Nationalism* (New York: Verso, 1991), 5–6.

Appendix

"Hamilton: A Musical Inquiry"
Course Syllabus

It's our duty, imagining each other.

> —Alan Garganus, *Oldest Living Confederate Widow*
> *Tells All* (1989)

Course Description

In 2015, the American playwright/composer Lin-Manuel Miranda premiered his new musical *Hamilton* at the Public Theater in New York (it has since moved to Broadway). This course brings *Hamilton* to Fieldston. There are three core components. The first is the play, which we hope to see. The second is Ron Chernow's 2004 biography of Hamilton, on which the musical is based. And the third is soundtrack of *Hamilton*. In addition to these core sources, the curriculum will include selections from Hamilton's voluminous writings, among them *The Federalist Papers*, along with other primary sources, such as writings by rivals like Thomas Jefferson and James Madison, as well as Hamilton's mentor, George Washington.

There are three major themes for the course. The first is to filter an age—the last quarter of the eighteenth century—through a single figure, one who happened to be an immigrant, a soldier, an intellectual, and a politician. The second is to explore the artistry of *Hamilton*—to evaluate the series of choices writers/composers/singers/ actors and other figures make in the process of creating a collective portrait. Finally, the course will trace the way history is made and understood by people who are not professional historians—which is the way most people experience history.

Course Textbooks

Hamilton, by Ron Chernow (New York: Penguin, 2004)
Hamilton: Writings (New York: Library of America, 2001)
Other course reading assignments (e.g. writings by George
    Washington and Thomas Jefferson) will be available in pdf
    format on Google Classroom.

Grading Criteria

Two exams: 20% each
Essay #1 and Essay #3: 20% each
Essay #2: 10%
Class participation/engagement: 10%

Color legend: Online reading assignments are in blue (links on
Google Classroom site); test dates and essay due dates are in red;
song titles are in green. Print readings (Chernow and Hamilton's
writings) are in orange.

Class Schedule

Week One (September 8–9)
Day 1: From *Hamilton* and *Grease* and back (by way of
    Ashanti and Ja Rule)
        Homework (hereafter HW): Chernow (henceforth
            RC), Prologue; *Vulture* interview with musical
            director Alex Lacamoire; Lin-Manual Miranda clip
            of performance at the White House, 2009
Day 2: Alexander Hamilton's America(s)
        HW: Ron Chernow, *Alexander Hamilton*, Chapter 1
            (henceforth RC Chapter #, e.g. RC 1)

Week Two (September 12–16)
Day 1: Discuss Alexander Hamilton's origins
        HW: RC 2; AH Stevens letter (*Writings*, p. 3)
Day 2: Discuss Hamilton's adolescence; Stevens letter;
    "Hurricane"
        HW: RC 3

Day 3: Discuss Hamilton at Princeton and Columbia;
"Aaron Burr, Sir"; "My Shot"
   HW: "Vindication of Measure of Congress" excerpt
      (*Writings*, pp. 30–34)
Day 4: Discuss Hamilton as revolutionary pamphleteer;
"Vindication" excerpt; "The Farmer Refuted"; "The Story
of Tonight"
   HW: RC 4

Week Three (September 19–23)
Day 1: Discuss Hamilton in the Continental Army; "Right
Hand Man"
   HW: RC 5
Day 2: Discuss Battles of Saratoga, Brandywine, and
Germantown; Charles Lee and the Conway Cabal; "Stay
Alive"; "The Ten Duel Commandments"; "Meet Me
Inside"
   HW: RC, pp. 107–117, 126–137; excerpt of AH letter to
      Henry Laurens (*Writings*, pp. 60–61); excerpt of
      letter to Eliza Schuyler (pp. 67–69)
Day 3: Discuss Hamilton's courtship and marriage; "A
Winter's Ball"; "The Schuyler Sisters"; "The Story of
Tonight" (reprise)
   HW: RC, pp. 137–149; AH to Gouverneur Morris on
      NYS Constitution (*Writings*, pp. 46–47); to John Jay
      on enlisting slaves as soldiers (pp. 56–58); to Eliza on
      Benedict Arnold and John Andre (pp. 89–92)
Day 4: Discuss Hamilton's relationship with Angelica
Schuyler; "Helpless"; "Satisfied"
   HW: RC, pp. 149–166

Week Four (September 26–30)
Day 1: Discussion of Hamilton the emerging policy wonk
   HW: RC, pp. 158–166; AH to Philip Schuyler and
      James McHenry (*Writings*, pp. 93–97)

Day 2: Discussion of AH's break with George Washington
    HW: RC 9; "History Has Its Eyes on You"
Day 3: Discuss the Battle of Yorktown and the end of the
    Revolution; "Guns and Ships"; "Yorktown"
    HW: prep for exam
Day 4: Exam on AH and the American Revolution
    HW: "General Washington Coddles a Protégé" (pdf on
    Google Classroom); AH letters to GW (*Writings*, pp.
    121–125) and GW to AH (also pdf on Google
    Classroom)

Week Five for C Band (October 3–7)
Day 1: No class (Rosh Hashanah)
Day 2: No class (Rosh Hashanah)
Day 3: Discussion of the Newburgh Conspiracy
    ("Washington Coddles," etc.)
    HW: RC, pp. 187–197; RC 11; letters to Philip and
    Angelica Hamilton (*Writings*, pp. 735, 810)
Day 4: No class (standardized testing)
    HW: RC 12

Week Five for D Band (October 3–7)
Day 1: No class (Rosh Hashanah)
Day 2: Discussion of the Newburgh Conspiracy
    ("Washington Coddles," etc.)
    HW: RC 187–197
Day 3: Discuss postwar AH and relationship with Aaron
    Burr; "Take a Break"; "Dear Theodosia"
    HW: RC 11 and 12; Letters to Philip and Angelica
    Hamilton (*Writings*, pp. 735, 810)
Day 4: No class (standardized testing)

Week Six for C Band (October 10–14)
Day 1: No class (Columbus Day)

Day 2: No class (College Visiting Day)

Day 3: Discuss AH family life; "That Would Be Enough";
"Take a Break"; "Dear Theodosia"
HW: RC 13

Day 4: Discussion of postwar AH and relationship with
Aaron Burr; "Wait for It"
HW: Work on Essay #1 assignment

Week Six for D Band (October 10–14)

Day 1: No class (Columbus Day)

Day 2: No class (Yom Kippur)

Day 3: Postwar AH and relationship with Aaron Burr; "Wait
for It"
HW: RC 13

Day 4: Discussion of Publius/*Federalist Papers*; "Non-Stop"
HW: Work on Essay #1 assignment

Week Seven (October 17–21)

Day 1: Essay #1 (on song from the cast album) due.
Discussion of Constitutional Convention.
HW for the week: *Federalist Papers* #1, 7, 17, 22, 33, 35,
70, 85 and "Speech on Ratifying Convention"
(*Writings*, pp. 171–484ff, 496–501. Begin the
following: Essay #2 question (500 words): What is
AH's vision of the United States?

Day 2 C Band: Discussion of Publius/*Federalist Papers*;
"Non-Stop"

Day 2 D Band: No class (standardized testing)
HW: Work on essay

Day 3: Review/discuss early GW administration; AH letters
to GW on taking presidency/presidential etiquette (in
class; *Writings*, pp. 511–513; 515–517)

Day 4: Overview of Thomas Jefferson; TJ letters to John Jay,
Edward Carrington, and James Madison (pdfs; in class);
"What'd I Miss?"

HW: RC 15. Note: *Hamilton* documentary on PBS tonight at 9 P.M.

Week Eight (October 24–28)
Day 1: Essay #2 due at 8:30 A.M. No class (half day)
    HW: RC 16
Day 2: Essay debrief
    HW: None (college applications)
Days 3 and 4: No class (Boston trip)
    HW: None (college applications)

Week Nine (October 31–November 4)
Day 1: Discuss Hamilton memo to George Beckwith (*Writings*, pp. 523–525, in class) and letters to Light Horse Harry Lee (p. 530) and Edward Carrington (pp. 736–739)
    HW: *Vox* article on "Cabinet Battle #1"
Day 2: Discuss "Cabinet Battle #1"
    HW: RC 18
Day 3: Discuss Hamilton's financial vision/banking in American history (Hamilton/Jefferson documents; in class)
    HW: RC 362–370, 409–418
Day 4: Discuss Hamilton's affair with Maria Reynolds; "Say No to This"
    HW: RC, pp. 529–545 (begin with "the author of this malice"; read excerpt from Reynolds pamphlet (*Writings*, last paragraph of p. 894 through first paragraph on p. 900)

Week Ten (November 7–11)
Day 1: Hamilton on the Reynolds affair; "We Know"; "The Reynolds Pamphlet"; "Burn"
    HW: RC 23

Day 2: The Deal for DC; "The Room Where It Happens"
  (and Cab Calloway, "Jumpin' Jive")
    HW: AH to Lafayette (*Writings*, pp. 521–522); AH
      memo on the French Revolution (pp. 833–836),
      Jefferson letter to Phillip Mazzei (pdf); AH letter to
      GW on fight with TJ (*Writings*, pp. 789–792); TJ's
      side of the story in his letter to GW (pdf)
Day 3, C Band: Discuss the Presidential Election of 2016
Day 3, D Band: No class (Modified Awareness Day [school
  symposium on summer reading])
Day 4: No class (College Visiting Day)

Week Eleven (November 14–19)
Day 1: Discussion of divisions over the French Revolution;
  "Cabinet Battle #2"; "Washington on Your Side"
    HW: RC 26
Day 2: Follow-up on the French Revolution; discuss the
  Whiskey Rebellion
    HW: RC 28; Washington, "Farewell Address" (pdf)
Day 3: Discussion of GW's departure; "One Last Time"
    HW: RC 29
Day 4: Discussion of John Adams; "I Know Him"
    HW: RC 31

Week Twelve (November 21–25)
Day 1: Discussion of the Quasi War; "What Comes Next?"
    HW: RC 32; excerpts from Madison, "The Virginia
      Resolution" and Jefferson, "The Kentucky
      Resolutions" (pdf)
Day 2: Discussion of Alien and Sedition Acts and the VA/KY
  Resolutions
Days 3 and 4: No class (Thanksgiving)
    HW: RC 35; AH "Memorandum on Strengthening the
      Government" and letter to Josiah; Ogden Hoffman
      (*Writings*, pp. 915–921)

Week Thirteen (November 28–December 2)

Day 1: Discussion of Hamilton, unraveling

> HW: RC 36; AH letters to Charles Pinckney and
> Martha Washington on the death of GW (*Writings*,
> pp. 922–923)

Day 2, C Band: No class (Fieldston Awareness Day—
symposium on racial justice)

Day 2, D Band: Discussion of Adams pamphlet; "The
Adams Administration" (C band to discuss 12/2)

Day 3: "Alexander Hamilton's New York" field trip

> HW: RC 37; AH letters to John Jay and Theodore
> Sedgwick on Adams (*Writings*, pp. 923–926) and
> confidential section of AH letter John Rutledge
> regarding Aaron Burr (pp. 974–976)

Day 4: Discussion of the election of 1800; excerpt from
Jefferson inaugural (discuss in class); "The Election of
1800

> HW: Study for exam

Week 14 (December 5–9)

Day 1: "Hamilton the Federalist" exam

> HW: RC 37; AH letters to John Jay and Theodore
> Sedgwick on Adams (*Writings*, pp. 923–926) and
> confidential section of AH letter John Rutledge
> regarding Aaron Burr (pp. 974–976)

Day 2, C Band: A conversation with Hamilton production
designer David Korins

Day 2, D Band: to be determined

> HW: RC 38; excerpt from AH letter to Gouverneur
> Morris (*Writings*, p. 986) letter to Benjamin Rush on
> death of Philip Hamilton (p. 987), and excerpt from
> AH letter to Rufus King on the state of the nation
> (p. 993)

Day 3: Discussion of Hamilton at bay; "Blow Us All Away";
"Ten Duel Commandments Reprise"; "Stay Alive

Reprise"; "It's Quiet Uptown"
    HW: RC, pp. 672–694 (end of Ch. 40 and all of 41)
Day 4: No class (post-Conference day)

Week 15 (December 12–16)
Day 1: Discussion of circumstances of Burr–Hamilton Duel;
    "Your Obedient Servant"
      HW: RC 42; AH letter to Liza on his death and
          "Statement Regarding the Duel with Burr" (*Writings*,
          pp. 1019–1022)
Day 2: Discussion of the death of Alexander Hamilton; "Best
    of Wives and Best of Women"; "The World Was Wide
    Enough"
      HW: RC 43
Day 3: Discussion of Hamilton's legacy; "Who Lives, Who
    Dies, Who Tells Your Story"
Day 4: Open/catch-up date

Weeks 17–18 (December 19-January 1): Winter Break

Week 19: (January 2–6): Workshops on Hamilton assessment essay

January 13, 2017: "Who Was Alexander Hamilton?" essay due

Essay Assignments

Essay #1: Choose a song (any song) on the *Hamilton* Broadway cast
album. Analyze in terms of orchestration, lyrics, and singing. Then
explain how the three work to illustrate what you understand to be
the larger point of the song.

Essay #2: You have been asked to read eight of Hamilton's *Federalist*
essays, and a speech he gave in support of ratification (see syllabus
for details). *What is Hamilton's vision of the United States?* In answering this question, you might want to consider what kinds of problems he's reacting to, and what criticism he's responding to, as a
means of considering what kind of nation he wants. Use the Chernow biography for context.

Essay #3: Now that we have surveyed the life of this remarkable man, you are tasked with a deceptively simple question: *Who was Alexander Hamilton?* Was he, for example, an arch-capitalist? A cultural conservative? A committed statist? Something else entirely? Your THESIS, which is your answer to this question, should draw on the assigned Hamilton writings from this semester as well as Chernow. Your MOTIVE will be your stance toward your answer, i.e., how you *feel* about Hamilton, and what you consider his legacy.

Chronology

1516   The first sugar cane crop in the Americas is planted in Brazil.

1626   The first eleven enslaved souls disembark in Manhattan.

1729   Alexander Hamilton's mother, Rachel, is born to Mary and John Faucett on the island of Nevis, a colony of Great Britain.

1740   Mary Faucett is granted a legal separation from John Faucett.
          • Hercules Mulligan is born in Ireland.

1743   Thomas Jefferson is born at Shadwell, in the Colony of Virginia.

1745   John Faucett dies, leaving his estate to Rachel, who marries sugar planter John Lavien on the island of St. Croix

1746   Rachel gives birth to Peter Lavien, who will be Alexander's half-brother.
          • Hercules Mulligan arrives in New York.

1748   John Lavien buys a half share in another small sugar plantation, enlarging his debt and squandering Rachel's inheritance.

1750   Rachel Faucett abandons John, her home, and her son. Charged with adultery, she is jailed for several months at Fort Christiansvaern. Upon her release, Rachel emigrates to St. Kitts.

1751–1754? Rachel Lavien meets James Hamilton; they establish a household on Nevis.

1752 James Madison is born near Port Conway, Virginia.

1754 John Laurens is born in Charleston, South Carolina.

1755–1757? Alexander Hamilton is born to Rachel Lavien and James Hamilton on Nevis.

1756 Aaron Burr Jr. is born in Newark, New Jersey.
  • Angelica Schuyler is born in Albany, New York.

1757 Elizabeth "Betsey" Schuyler is born in Albany, New York.
  • The Marquis de Lafayette is born in the Auvergne, France.
  • Aaron Burr's father dies.

1758 Aaron Burr's mother dies, leaving him and his sister orphans.
  • Margaret "Peggy" Schuyler is born in Albany, New York.

1759 A divorce granted to John Lavien permits him to marry again. Rachel is prohibited from remarrying, rendering Alexander and his brother James Jr. permanently illegitimate.

1765 James Hamilton abandons his family and emigrates to Christiansted, St. Croix. Rachel and her sons return to Nevis.
  • The British Parliament passes the Stamp Act.
  • Hercules Mulligan joins the Sons of Liberty.

1768 At the age of forty-seven Rachel succumbs to fever, and dies; Alexander, while taken ill, recovers.
  • Alexander and James are placed under legal guardianship of a cousin, merchant Peter Lytton.

1769 Peter Lytton commits suicide; Alexander Hamilton
      takes a clerkship with merchants Kortright and
      Cruger.
      • Aaron Burr is admitted to the College of New
        Jersey (now Princeton) at the age of thirteen.

1770 British troops fire on American Patriots in a
      confrontation thereafter known as the Boston
      Massacre. Crispus Attucks, a Black sailor and perhaps
      still legally enslaved, becomes the first American to be
      killed by a foreign enemy in defense of democracy.

1772 Alexander Hamilton meets Presbyterian minister
      Hugh Knox, ordained by College of New Jersey
      president Aaron Burr Sr., on St. Croix.
      • The Great Hurricane of 1772 makes landfall on
        St. Croix, causing widespread destruction.
        Alexander Hamilton writes a letter to his father
        detailing the tragedy. This letter is later published
        by the *Royal Danish American Gazette*. As a result,
        benefactors raise money to further Hamilton's
        schooling in the North American colonies.
      • Aaron Burr graduates from Princeton at age
        sixteen.

1772–1773? Alexander Hamilton arrives in Elizabethtown, New
      Jersey, where he enrolls at the Elizabethtown
      Academy, probably with the help of Hercules
      Mulligan.

1773 Alexander Hamilton meets influential New Jersey
      lawyers William Livingston and Elias Boudinot,
      securing access to New Jersey colonial society.
      • Alexander Hamilton enrolls at King's College.
      • Boston Patriots protest the tax on tea by dressing
        as Native Americans and throwing British imports
        of the product into the harbor, an event later
        known as Boston Tea Party. Alexander Hamilton

writes "Defense and Destruction of the Tea,"
published in the *New-York Journal*.
- Sally Hemings is born to Betty Hemings, an
  enslaved woman on the Wayles plantation in
  Virginia; her father was English planter John
  Wayles, Thomas Jefferson's future father-in-law.
- Abolitionist William Hamilton, later rumored to
  have been Alexander Hamilton's illegitimate son,
  is born.

1774   Alexander Hamilton is admitted to King's College
       (later renamed Columbia)

England responds to the Boston Tea Party with the
Coercive or "Intolerable" Acts.
- Representatives of all thirteen North American
  colonies assemble in Philadelphia as the
  Continental Congress.
- New York Patriots repeat the Tea Party in New
  York Harbor.
- Alexander Hamilton publishes a pamphlet "A Full
  Vindication of the Measures of the Congress."

1775   British and Continental troops clash at the Battle of
       Lexington.
- Alexander Hamilton publishes "The Farmer
  Refuted."
- Alexander Hamilton joins a cadre of King's
  College volunteers enlisting in a Patriot military
  company named Hearts of Oak.
- George Washington is named commander in chief
  of the Continental Army.

1776   Hamilton publishes "The Monitor."
- Abigail Adams writes to her husband, John,
  advising him to "Remember the Ladies" as he
  helps to build a new nation.
- Thomas Paine publishes "Common Sense."

- Hamilton raises a New York artillery company and is appointed a captain.
- The Continental Congress declares its independence from English rule in a document drafted by Thomas Jefferson.
- Defeating Washington's army at the Battle of Brooklyn, British troops occupy New York City.

1777   Alexander Hamilton is promoted to the rank of lieutenant colonel and becomes an aide-de-camp to George Washington, acquiring the nickname "Ham" or "Hammie" from other members of Washington's staff.

- John Laurens and Hamilton meet, taking an instant liking to each other, and forming a loving attachment.
- The Marquis de Lafayette arrives in the new American nation and joins Washington's staff. He leads Continental troops for the first time at the Battle of Brandywine in eastern Pennsylvania.
- Angelica Schuyler elopes with English-born merchant John Church.

1778   At the Battle of Monmouth, Major General Charles Lee falters; General Washington arrives on the New Jersey battlefield, rallies the troops, and prevents a rout. Numerous soldiers die of heat stroke.

- John Laurens proposes to his father Henry that the forty enslaved souls he stood to inherit be freed and enlisted as a brigade. His plan was turned down numerous times over the next four years by the government of South Carolina.
- The English Army turns south, capturing Savannah, Georgia.

- A Continental Army victory at Saratoga, New York, helps Benjamin Franklin negotiate an alliance with France.

1779   A fleet commanded by the Comte de Rochambeau sets sail from France in support of the American Revolution.

1780   Alexander Hamilton meets Angelica and Elizabeth Schuyler; he and Elizabeth (who Alexander will call "Betsey") receive permission to marry from her father, Philip.

- John Laurens is captured by the English during the Battle of Charleston and freed on parole.

1781   The Continental Congress ratifies the Articles of Confederation.

- General Cornwallis surrenders at Yorktown, Virginia, to troops commanded by the Marquis de Lafayette; Alexander Hamilton leads a critical charge on British troops with bayonets only.
- The Marquis de Lafayette returns to France and becomes embroiled in the French Revolution as a constitutional monarchist.
- John Laurens is sent to France with Thomas Paine as a special envoy.

1782   Philip Hamilton is born: Elizabeth and Alexander Hamilton will ultimately have eight children, including another son named Philip.

- Hamilton completes his legal studies, becomes a citizen of New York State, and takes a position as tax collector for the State of New York. He is appointed to the Congress of the Confederation, then resigns, setting up a law practice in Albany.
- John Laurens dies in one of the final battles of the Revolution, on the Combahee River in South Carolina.

1783   Unpaid Continental soldiers riot at Newburgh,
       New York.
       • November 25th is declared Evacuation Day, to
         mark an end to the seven-year occupation of
         New York City by the English.
       • Alexander, Eliza, and Philip Hamilton move to
         Wall Street in Lower Manhattan.
       • Angelica and John Church leave for Europe.

1784   The Bank of New York is founded: Alexander
       Hamilton is voted in as a director.
       • Alexander Hamilton helps to create, and becomes
         an inaugural member of, the New York Board of
         Regents.
       • Thomas Jefferson is appointed U.S. ambassador
         to France.

1785   The dollar becomes the official currency of the
       United States.
       • The Continental Navy in disbanded.
       • John Jay founds the New York Manumission
         Society; Alexander Hamilton and Hercules
         Mulligan are founding members.

1786   Alexander Hamilton passes the New York Bar.
       • James Hamilton dies on St. Thomas.
       • The New York Legislature names Alexander
         Hamilton and five other commissioners to the
         Annapolis Convention, where Hamilton
         reconnects with James Madison.

1787   A Constitutional Convention is convened in
       Philadelphia to amend the Articles of Confederation,
       which are eventually abandoned. The new proposed
       Constitution creates a centralized federal government
       that fails to abolish slavery or admit women to full
       citizenship.

- Defense of the proposed U.S. Constitution commences in a series of eighty-five pseudonymous essays (later known as *The Federalist Papers*) written by Alexander Hamilton, James Madison, and John Jay.
- Fourteen-year-old Sally Hemings, a slave, accompanies Thomas Jefferson's daughter to Paris, where she becomes sexually intimate with her owner. Hemings successfully bargains with Jefferson that he will free any children born from the union.

1788   George Washington is elected the first president of the United States, and John Adams becomes vice president.

- *The Federalist Papers* are published in two volumes.
- The Constitution of the United States is ratified.
- George III of Great Britain suffers the first of the many mental collapses that will lead to removing him from power.

1789   Jefferson and Sally Hemings return from France and proceed to Philadelphia, where Jefferson accepts George Washington's invitation to become secretary of state.

- Hamilton becomes the first secretary of the treasury.
- George Washington creates the first executive council to the president of the United States, eventually known as a cabinet.
- With the fall of the Bastille, the French Revolution begins.
- The American Constitution is successfully ratified by the thirteen states.
- David Ramsay publishes the first history of the American Revolution.

1790 Alexander Hamilton issues the First Report on the Public Credit, proposing that the new government assume state war debts.

- Congress approves the Residence Act, designating Philadelphia as the new nation's temporary capital with a promise to relocate it to present-day Washington, DC, in 1800.
- James Madison reverses his support for the Assumption Act, by which the federal government assumes state debts, ending his alliance with Alexander Hamilton. However, the act passes.
- Hamilton persuades Congress to commission a fleet of single-masted vessels as the nation's first Coast Guard.

1791 Congress ratifies the first ten amendments to the Constitution, now known as the Bill of Rights.

- Alexander Hamilton is admitted to the American Philosophical Society, the nation's oldest learned society, founded in 1743 by Benjamin Franklin and associates in Philadelphia.
- Alexander Hamilton creates the Customs Service.
- Alexander Hamilton f musters wide support for chartering the First Bank of the United States and drafts a Report on the Establishment of a Mint.
- Alexander Hamilton commences an affair with Maria Reynolds.
- Thomas Paine publishes *The Rights of Man*.

1792 Congress establishes the U.S. Mint.

- Speculation and the expansion of credit trigger the nation's first economic crisis, the Financial Panic of 1792.
- Increasing divisiveness results in the rise of political parties: Federalists, who are identified with Hamilton's pro-government policies, and

Democratic-Republicans, identified with Thomas
Jefferson and James Madison's opposition to
centralization.

• Opposed by Alexander Hamilton, Aaron Burr
  tries—and fails—to become governor of
  New York.

• George Washington is elected to his second term
  as president.

• Alexander Hamilton's relations with Jefferson
  continue to sour over Hamilton's admiration for
  British law and governance.

• James Monroe and his allies confront Hamilton
  over financial irregularities, and learn of blackmail
  payments made to Maria Reynolds's husband,
  James.

• French revolutionaries topple the monarchy and
  declare the first Republic.

1793 Louis XVI of France and his wife, Queen Marie
      Antoinette, are executed.

• France declares war against England, Holland,
  and Spain.

• Maria Reynolds is granted a divorce from
  James Reynolds.

• Alexander Hamilton survives yellow fever.

• Thomas Jefferson resigns from the State
  Department.

1794 A congressional investigating committee exonerates
      Alexander Hamilton from accusations of financial
      impropriety.

• Hamilton assists in suppressing the Whiskey
  Rebellion, a Pennsylvania tax revolt.

• Hamilton makes his final report to Congress:
  Report on a Plan for the Further Support of
  Public Credit.

1795 Alexander Hamilton resigns as secretary of the treasury. Subsequently, he defends his honor in two duels.

1796 Alexander Hamilton successfully argues *Hylton v. United States*; the Supreme Court upholds the power of the federal government to tax, legislation he had helped to pass. It was also the first time the Supreme Court ruled on the constitutionality of an act of Congress.

- Hamilton drafts Washington's Farewell Address, subsequently published in Claypoole's *American Daily Advertiser*.
- John Adams is elected the second president of the United States; Thomas Jefferson becomes his vice president.

1797 Journalist James Callender publishes a series of pamphlets under the title "The History of The United States for the Year 1796," publicizing Alexander Hamilton's affair with Mrs. Reynolds and reviving rumors that Hamilton used his position as secretary of the treasury for personal enrichment. In response, Hamilton writes *Observations on Certain Documents Contained in No. V & VI of "The History of The United States for the Year 1796" In Which the Charge of Speculation Against Alexander Hamilton, Late Secretary of the Treasury, Is Fully Refuted. Written by Himself,* otherwise known as "The Reynolds Pamphlet."

- Angelica and John Church return from Europe and take up residence in New York.

1798 Congress authorizes an army; Alexander Hamilton accepts an appointment as inspector general.

- Alexander Hamilton drafts broad outlines for the entire military apparatus, including its

foundational support services: hospitals,
administrative affairs, and military academies.
- Hamilton resumes his association with the New
York Manumission Society.

1799 Alexander Hamilton becomes one of six sponsors to
approach the Common Council of New York for a
charter to establish a private water company.
- Aaron Burr receives his own charter for a private
water company, the Manhattan Company. John
Church, Hamilton's brother-in-law, accuses
Burr of malfeasance and the two fight a duel:
both men fire and miss.
- Napoleon Bonaparte seizes control of France.
- The New York Legislature passes an Act for the
Gradual Abolition of Slavery.
- George Washington dies at his Mount Vernon
home.

1800 In the Election of 1800, the two-party system is born
amid escalating rancor. James Callender publishes a
pamphlet exposing Thomas Jefferson's relationship
with Sally Hemings. In the "Letter from Alexander
Hamilton, Concerning the Public Conduct and
Character of John Adams, Esq." Hamilton triggers a
split among Federalists that results in the defeat of
President John Adams, allowing Democratic-
Republicans Jefferson and Burr to emerge in a tie
for the presidency.
- Mason Locke "Parson" Weems publishes the first
biography of George Washington.

1801 A deadlocked presidential election goes to the
House of Representatives, as the Constitution directs.
Alexander Hamilton throws his support to Thomas
Jefferson who becomes the third president of the
United States in the thirty-sixth round of voting.
Burr becomes vice president.

- Philip Hamilton, defending his father's honor, dies in a duel in Weehawken, New Jersey.

1802 A new edition of *The Federalist Papers* is printed.
- Thomas Jefferson excoriates Federalists for presuming that "man cannot be trusted with his own government."
- The Grange is completed in upper Manhattan; this will be the only home Alexander Hamilton ever owns.

1803 An epidemic of yellow fever causes the Hamilton family to move upstate temporarily.

1804 Alexander Hamilton declares that "the real disease" in the American Republic is "DEMOCRACY."
- Aaron Burr runs for governor of New York State and loses, blaming Hamilton for opposing his candidacy. After a correspondence, Burr challenges Hamilton to a duel, and fatally wounds Hamilton on July 11. Hamilton is transported to Manhattan, where he dies. He is buried at Trinity Church.
- Elizabeth Hamilton struggles to satisfy Hamilton's financial debts; The Grange is sold, and later reclaimed on her behalf by her husband's friends.

1805 In *Martin v. Commonwealth of Massachusetts*, the state Supreme Court affirms coverture by arguing that a woman's political citizenship could not be separate from her husband's.

1806 Elizabeth Hamilton founds the New York Orphan Asylum Society.

1808 James Madison is elected president. He is reelected in 1812.

1811 Congress allows the charter for Hamilton's creation, the First Bank of the United States, to lapse.

1826   Thomas Jefferson dies at home in Monticello, Virginia.
- John Adams dies at home in Quincy, Massachusetts.

1827   Slavery finally ends in New York.

1834   Aaron Burr dies in a boarding house in Port Richmond, Staten Island.
- The Marquis de Lafayette dies in Paris.

1836   James Madison dies at home in Orange, Virginia.

1840–1841   John Church Hamilton, Alexander and Elizabeth's fourth son, publishes a two-volume biography of his father.

1848   The Married Women's Property Act ends coverture.

1854   Elizabeth Hamilton dies and is buried next to Alexander at Trinity Church.

1860   The United States adopts a uniform currency.

1861   Hamilton's appearance on a "Greenback Note" marks his first appearance on U.S. currency.

1866   The first modern musical, *The Black Crook*, opens at Niblo's Garden in Manhattan.

1921   *Shuffle Along*, the first Broadway hit to feature African American performers and music by Eubie Blake, opens in a desegregated theater.

1929   Alexander Hamilton's portrait is adopted for the ten-dollar bill.

1969   The musical *1776* debuts, putting the American Revolution on Broadway.

1991   The first hip-hop musical *So! What Happens Now?* opens at P.S. 122.

1996   *Bring in 'da Noise, Bring in 'da Funk* debuts at the Public Theater, and becomes the first hip-hop musical to move to Broadway.

1997   In an article in the *Wall Street Journal*, David Brooks
        and William Kristol praise Alexander Hamilton as a
        model conservative, reviving interest in his political
        legacy.

2001   Publication of Joseph Ellis's *Founding Brothers* and
        David McCullough's *John Adams* launches a new
        wave of "Founders Chic," a term coined by journalist
        Evan Thomas in 1999.

2004   Biographer Ron Chernow publishes *Alexander
        Hamilton*.
        • The New-York Historical Society mounts a major
          exhibit on the life of Alexander Hamilton.

2006   PBS debuts a television documentary about
        Alexander Hamilton.

2006   Economists Robert Rubin and Robert Altman found
        "The Hamilton Project" to revive "traditional
        American values of upward mobility."

2008   Lin-Manuel Miranda's hip-hop musical, *In the
        Heights*, moves to Broadway, winning four Tony
        awards.

2009   Lin-Manuel Miranda presents "The Hamilton
        Mixtape" at the White House to an audience that
        includes President Barack Obama and First Lady
        Michele Obama.
        • Miranda opens a Twitter account.

2015   Comedy Central debuts its web series *Drunk History*.
        • *Hamilton: An American Musical* debuts Off-
          Broadway at the Public Theater, and then moves
          to Broadway. It garners the most Tony
          nominations for any show in history (sixteen),
          winning eleven.
        • Treasury Secretary Jack Lew announces that
          Alexander Hamilton will be removed from the

ten-dollar bill, a decision that is reversed following
an uproar among by *Hamilton* fans and a 2016
visit to Lew by Lin-Manuel Miranda.

- President Barack Obama sees *Hamilton* in New
  York, and invites the cast to the White House for
  a special performance.

2016   Lin-Manuel Miranda hosts *Saturday Night Live* and is
       named one of *Time* magazine's 100 most influential
       people of the year.

- *Hamilton* becomes the first Broadway show to
  exceed $1,000 a ticket for some seats.
- The cast of *Hamilton* performs fundraisers for
  the Democratic National Committee and for
  Hillary Clinton.
- Newly elected President Donald J. Trump
  rebukes the cast of *Hamilton* in a series of tweets
  after they express their concerns about the policies
  of the new administration to Vice President-elect
  Mike Pence following a performance.
- *Hamilton's America* premieres on PBS's *Great
  Performances.*

2017   *Hamilton's* touring companies launch in San
       Francisco, Chicago, and London, England.

- North Carolina Senator Richard Burr, a distant
  relative of Aaron Burr, chairs a Senate Committee
  investigating the Trump campaign's possible
  collusion with Russia during the 2016 election.

Acknowledgments

Books require many hands to get them over the finish line, and collections even more. Claire would like to thank Renee for having this idea in the first place, and insisting that she listen to the cast album of *Hamilton*. Renee would like to thank Claire for being willing to explore doing a book on *Hamilton* before she had even had the chance to see the show or listen to the album. We would both like to thank our authors, who were engaged and cheerful, and willing to carve time out of their busy schedules to join us in this project. Our editor, Leslie Mitchner, has read each chapter with care and provided valuable feedback, support, and encouragement every step of the way. She and her staff at Rutgers University Press have done a superlative job of getting this book to its audience—in record time.

Renee would like to thank everyone who has been willing to listen to her talk about *Hamilton* as a subject of historical inquiry for the past year, especially her colleagues in the History Department and the Comparative American Studies Program at Oberlin College, as well as her students, who have never before been so eager to read faculty work-in-progress as they have been in this case. Special thanks to Caela Brodigan for finding time in her busy senior year to read and offer feedback on my essay, and to Wendy Kozol for her usual astute comments on my work. Thanks as well to dear friends and longtime reading group members Karen Dunn-Haley, Ariela Gross, Leslie Harris, Wendy Wall, and Alice Yang who workshopped the proposal for this book in June 2016 and offered valuable advice on how to move forward with the project.

Most of all, Renee thanks her family and especially her theater-obsessed daughter, Sabine, who shares her mom's enthusiasm for *Hamilton*, even if she prefers more experimental theatrical productions that typically revolve around far darker themes than Lin-Manuel Miranda's work. It was Sabine's passion for *In the Heights* that turned me into a Lin-Manuel Miranda fan, and she has been an excellent sounding board for many of the ideas in this volume. As for Sean and Owen, the men in my life, they even occasionally proved willing to "take a break" from talking about fantasy football to converse about theater—and in the case of fifteen-year-old Owen, to sing along with the *Hamilton* soundtrack. Sean, thank you for being willing to spend an exorbitant amount to take me to *Hamilton* (and for not telling me how much those tickets actually cost).

Claire continues to be astonished by the creativity of colleagues across The New School, as well as the university's commitment to innovative and creative scholarship. Provost Tim Marshall, Executive Dean Mary Watson, and School of Undergraduate Studies Dean Melissa Friedling provided funds for the purchase of illustrations, a ticket to *Hamilton* (that's true!), and research assistance. Their support for the Digital Humanities Initiative, where my thinking about social media and the Internet have matured, has been invaluable. History colleagues Julia Foulkes, Laura Auricchio, Eli Zaretsky, Jeremy Varon, Federico Finchelstein, Julia Ott, Natalia Mehlman Petrzela, and Aaron Jakes have helped to make The New School the perfect place for my career reboot. *Public Seminar* coeditor Jeffrey Goldfarb has become my new local friend and collaborator who "gets it" about why a general audience matters and will talk endlessly about the future of digital scholarship. My research assistant of three years, Christopher-Howard Woods, a man of unfailing good cheer and willingness to pitch in on matters great and small, made it possible to fit this project into an already overstuffed schedule. My newest assistant, Preston Charles, did the research for, and is a coauthor of, the timeline.

Nancy Barnes, after three decades living in more homes than we can count, can I say that you are the best of women, the best of writers, and the best of readers?

Finally, we thank each other. What else can you say about a friendship that has spanned two decades, three institutions, a book series, and two edited collections except—it seems to be working! What's next, you ask?

Just you wait.

Renee Romano
Oberlin, OH

Claire Bond Potter
New York, NY

Notes on Contributors

Joseph M. Adelman is an assistant professor of history at Framingham State University in Massachusetts. A historian of media, communication, and politics in the Atlantic world, he is currently working on a book about the circulation of political news during the American Revolution and the history of the U.S. Post Office.

Catherine Allgor is the president of the Massachusetts Historical Society in Boston, Massachusetts. She is the author of several books about women and politics in the founding era, including *A Perfect Union: Dolley Madison and the Creation of the American Nation*.

Jim Cullen is a history teacher at the Ethical Culture Fieldston School in New York City. He is the author of numerous books, among them *The American Dream: A Short History of an Idea That Shaped a Nation* and *Sensing the Past: Hollywood Stars and Historical Visions*.

Joanne B. Freeman is a professor of history and American Studies at Yale University, specializing in the politics and political culture of Revolutionary and early national America. An elected fellow of the Society of American Historians and an advisor to the National Park Service, she is the editor of *The Essential Hamilton* and *Hamilton: Writings*; and the author of *Affairs of Honor: National Politics in the New Republic*, which won the Best Book award from the Society for Historians of the Early American Republic. She is currently completing a study of physical violence in the U.S. Congress.

LESLIE M. HARRIS is a professor of history at Northwestern University. She is the author of *In the Shadow of Slavery: African Americans in New York City, 1626–1863*; and coeditor with Ira Berlin of *Slavery in New York*, which accompanied the groundbreaking 2005–2007 New-York Historical Society exhibition of the same name.

BRIAN EUGENIO HERRERA is an assistant professor of theater in the Lewis Center for the Arts at Princeton University. He is the author of *The Latina/o Theatre Commons 2013 National Convening: A Narrative Report* and *Latin Numbers: Playing Latino in Twentieth-Century U.S. Popular Performance*, which was awarded the George Jean Nathan Prize for Dramatic Criticism and received an Honorable Mention for the John W. Frick Book Award from the American Theatre and Drama Society.

PATRICIA HERRERA is an associate professor in the Department of Theatre and Dance at the University of Richmond, focusing on U.S. Latinx visual art, performance, and museum exhibitions. She is also an artist, performer, and educator who uses theater to promote social justice. She is the author of *Nuyorican Feminist Performance: From the Nuyorican Poets Cafe to Hip Hop Theater*.

WILLIAM HOGELAND is the author of three narrative histories of the founding period, *The Whiskey Rebellion*, *Declaration*, and *Autumn of the Black Snake*, as well as the expository books *Founding Finance* and *Inventing American History*. His essays have appeared in the *Boston Review*, the *New York Times*, the *Atlantic*, the *Oxford American*, and *Best American Music Writing*. He blogs at williamhogeland.com.

LYRA D. MONTEIRO is an assistant professor of history and teaches in the Graduate Program in American Studies at Rutgers University—Newark. She has published on issues in cultural heritage and archaeological ethics and is the codirector of the Museum On Site, a public humanities organization.

MICHAEL O'MALLEY is a professor of history at George Mason University. He is the author of *Keeping Watch: A History of American Time* and *Face Value: The Entwined Histories of Race and Money in America*.

JEFFREY L. PASLEY is a professor of history and the associate director of the Kinder Institute on Constitutional Democracy at the University of Missouri. His most recent book is *The First Presidential Contest: The Election of 1796 and the Beginnings of American Democracy*, a finalist for the 2014 George Washington Book Prize.

CLAIRE BOND POTTER is a professor of history at The New School. She is the author of *War on Crime: Bandits, G-Men, and the Politics of Mass Culture* and coeditor of the collection *Doing Recent History: On Privacy, Copyright, Video Games, Institutional Review Boards, Activist Scholarship, and History that Talks Back*. She is the executive editor of *Public Seminar*. Her essays have appeared in the *Chronicle of Higher Education*, *Dissent*, the *Washington Post*, *Inside Higher Education*, *berfrois*, and *Jacobin*.

RENEE C. ROMANO is the Robert S. Danforth Professor of History and Professor of Comparative American Studies and Africana Studies at Oberlin College. She is the author of *Race Mixing: Black–White Marriage in Postwar America* and *Racial Reckoning: Prosecuting America's Civil Rights Murders*, as well as coeditor of the collections *The Civil Rights Movement in American Memory* and *Doing Recent History: On Privacy, Copyright, Video Games, Institutional Review Boards, Activist Scholarship, and History That Talks Back*.

ANDREW M. SCHOCKET is a professor of history and American Culture Studies at Bowling Green State University in Ohio. He is the author of *Fighting Over the Founders: How We Remember the*

American Revolution and Founding Corporate Power in Early National Philadelphia. His writing has also appeared in the *Washington Post*, the *San Francisco Chronicle, History News Network*, and *Salon*.

DAVID WALDSTREICHER is Distinguished Professor of History at CUNY Graduate Center, and the author of *Slavery's Constitution: From Revolution to Ratification*; *Runaway America: Benjamin Franklin, Slavery, and the American Revolution*; and *In the Midst of Perpetual Fetes: The Making of American Nationalism, 1776–1820*. As an editor, his books include *John Quincy Adams and the Politics of Slavery: Selections from the Diary*; *A Companion to John Adams and John Quincy Adams*; *A Companion to Benjamin Franklin*; and *Beyond the Founders*.

ELIZABETH L. WOLLMAN is associate professor of music at Baruch College, CUNY, and a member of the doctoral faculty in the Theater Department at CUNY Graduate Center. She is the author of *The Theater Will Rock: A History of the Rock Musical, From "Hair" to "Hedwig"*; *Hard Times: The Adult Musical in 1970s New York City*; and the forthcoming *The Critical Companion to the American Stage Musical*.

Index